To: Harvey & Margaret Doorenbos

Blessings

Wendell Karsen

August 2017

CHRISTIANITY UNDER THE MICROSCOPE

IS CHRISTIANITY STILL WORTH BELIEVING IN A POSTMODERN WORLD?

An Interactive Study Book

Wendell P. Karsen

AMAZON CREATESPACE

AMAZON CREATESPACE

ISBN number: 13: 978-1537360096

ISBN number: 10: 1537360094

Table of Contents

Preface

"The gospel is God's power to save all who believe ... For the gospel reveals how God puts people right with himself: it is through faith from beginning to end." Romans 1:16-17

"You must ... continue on a firm and sure foundation, and must not allow yourselves to be shaken from the hope you gained when you heard the gospel." Colossians 1:23

"Let us rid ourselves of everything that gets in the way, and of the sin which holds on to us so tightly, and let us run with determination the race that lies before us. Let us keep our eyes fixed on Jesus, on whom our faith depends from beginning to end." Hebrews 12:1-2

These statements from the Bible are the foundation for what I most firmly believe about the Christian faith. Over my many years of ministry, I've been asked hundreds of questions about that faith. Many of them have been asked by Christian young people who wanted to have a clearer idea about their faith, its relationship to other faiths and its relevance for their daily lives. Most of them, however, have been asked by non-Christians to challenge, to probe, to sincerely attempt to find the truth, or perhaps to take the first faltering steps towards a personal faith.

I quickly found out that the old textbook answers expressed in traditional theological jargon didn't seem to communicate with most people, and particularly with young people. They wanted 'new wine' for the new skins of the 21st century. I also found out in a hurry that it doesn't pay to avoid the tough questions by talking around them, or to paper over the very real sins and weaknesses of Christians and churches by offering lame excuses for them.

If Christians have anything to say to today's honest inquirers, we must try our best to grapple with their tough questions, all the while acknowledging that we ourselves are still disciples 'on the way' who also have our human struggles with doubt, temptation and all the rest. We must 'talk their language' in such a way that Biblical teaching is 'translated' into language and symbols that avoid the kind of communication blocks that turn people in the Postmodern era off. We must also be honest enough to acknowledge truth wherever we find it and be open enough to learn a few things about our faith and life from those who may not share our perceptions and convictions. If people, and particularly young people, know that we are committed to making a sincere effort to listen to them, they will be more disposed to listen to us as well.

This book is an attempt to put these ideas into practice. It will have its shortcomings and contain ideas that some sector or other of the Christian community might find it difficult to agree with. How could it be otherwise when it deals with questions to which there are no easy black and white 'answers'? At these points, I trust that readers will see my attempt as being merely one among other possible interpretations or positions, and that they will use it as a means of fostering dialogue and further exploration. It is obviously impossible and undesirable in a book of this nature to explain all possible positions on any given question.

My deepest hope is that non-Christian readers will be helped to better understand the case for the Christian faith and perhaps want to take the first step towards making that faith their own. It is also my hope that Christian readers will interact with it in a way that will shed some light on their doubts, help them come to a fuller understanding of what the Christian faith is all about and enable them to develop deeper convictions about their faith as it applies to life today.

I dedicate this book to my loving, patient and supportive wife and best friend, Renske.

Wendell Karsen, Penney Farms, Florida, 2017

Introduction

Looking Through the Microscope

Things aren't always what they appear to be on the surface. Take water, for example. Put a drop of it on a piece of glass and what do you see? Nothing much. But put it under an ordinary microscope and a whole different moving, squirming world comes into view! What appeared as nothing much to your naked eye turns out to be a whole lot under the magnified 'eye' of the microscope. Put that same drop of water under an electron microscope, and what appears will be even more astounding!

A chemical analysis of that little drop of H_2O will reveal that it's made up of two invisible gases that are highly combustible, but that can be combined to form a visible liquid that can put *out* fire! Add the temperature factor and that same drop of liquid will either turn into a breathtaking sight of solid frozen crystals under our microscope, or boil into a vapor that will completely disappear! Wouldn't it be a pity if somebody missed all this because they weren't willing to take the time or make the effort to look at a drop of water under a microscope or because, when they had a chance to do so, they closed their eyes and declared that there was nothing more to water than that which meets the naked eye?

Some people treat the Christian faith that way. They only take a quick look at it at the surface level and quickly reject out of hand what they *think* it is without even taking the time and trouble to honestly find out what it *really* is. And some, when offered the opportunity by a friend or a teacher to take a deeper look at it through a microscope, as it were, close their eyes and loudly proclaim that they'll have nothing to do with it since it appears worthless to their 'naked eye.'

Like water, the Christian faith will never reveal its treasures to those who are only prepared to look at it on the surface. But to those who are ready to take a deep, serious, reflective look in order to satisfy the requirements of honesty and fairness in their search for truth, it will reveal a great deal. What I've attempted to do in this book is just that -- to take a long, hard, honest look at what Christians claim their faith is all about. In so doing, I deliberately tackle the hardest questions that people ask about the Christian faith. To do less would be dishonest. If Christians have anything to hide, it's not worth believing in their faith.

As we explore the answers to these questions, you will at times be tempted to take the easy way out and take your 'eye' off the 'microscope.' You may even be tempted to shut your eyes altogether, even though you know that isn't fair ... like the person who said, "My mind is made up. Don't confuse me with the facts." Try to keep your mind and heart open as you work your way through this book so that if there's any truth in it, you won't miss it when you see it. If you develop an 'eye of faith' while doing so, I hope you may find yourself discovering something far more significant than the wondrous properties of H_2O - the even more wondrous properties of the "water of life." (See John 4:13; 7:37-39) And if you've already made that discovery, I hope this book will help you to broaden and deepen your understanding of your faith.

Chapter One

IS RELIGION STILL RELEVANT?

Looking Through the Microscope |

The Assignment

When Dr. Cummings made the assignment, a groan went up from the class. Three hundred words on the topic "Is Religion Outdated?" They knew there were no easy answers to *that* one. *Whate*ver they wrote, they'd have to do a little research and a lot of thinking first. Oh well, they'd better get started since Dr. Cummings had made clear that they only had a week to complete the assignment.

A week later, after the papers were handed in, Dr. Cummings sat at his desk in his office reading them over. He was quite pleased with them. There were a few, of course, that had been done in haste without much thought having been given to them, and they weren't really worth reading. But the majority showed that most students had seriously struggled with the question.

A number of different viewpoints were given. Some reflected a deep religious faith, while others reflected an equally deep distrust of all religion. Some were based on well-thought-out and well-documented arguments, while others revealed a basic lack of knowledge in this area and some gross misconceptions and distorted ideas.

One student wrote,

> I think all religion is sheer superstition. People believed in religion in ancient times because they didn't understand the forces that affected their lives that were beyond their control. They invented all sorts of gods, spirits and taboos to explain what they didn't understand and to gain some kind of control over those forces by either pacifying the 'bad' gods or bribing the 'good' gods. Now, through modern science, we know that these forces aren't controlled by gods or spirits, but by scientific laws. The more we understand about these laws, the more control we ourselves gain over the processes and phenomena that affect our lives. For example, we now know that disease is caused by a bacterial invasion or a mal-functioning cell - not by the displeasure of some 'god.'

A second student wrote,

> I think religion is more relevant today than ever before. The more scientific discoveries people make, the more complex they discover the cosmos to be. For the first time, scientists are beginning to realize that there are limits to science. A new humility is growing wherein many scientists are convinced that there's much more to reality and life than can be measured or understood by the scientific method alone. They talk about a power behind the cosmos or a designer who's not a part of what he's designed. They see that if humans only have material significance, then, in light of what we now know about the size and complexity of the cosmos, we cease to be significant at all. Religion gives modern people faith, purpose and meaning.

A third student wrote,

> Religion is a psychological crutch needed by weak people.

Marx was right when he wrote that religion is the "opiate of the people." Religion paralyzes people with fear and inhibits their ability to do something about their own situation. For example, why try to pacify some fake flood 'god' to keep a river from overflowing? Why not get out there and build a dyke to prevent a flood yourself? Religion reduces people to helpless puppets who can't stand on their own two feet without the help of some 'god.' Freud was right when he taught that religion gives people an inferiority complex. The main aim of religious leaders is to play on the guilt feelings and superstitions of others so that they can keep them under their control. Only in modern times has it become possible to free ourselves from this ancient curse called religion once and for all!

Dr. Cummings had to smile at the grand vehemence with which this student had attacked his subject. He picked up a fourth paper.

I've found a great source of strength in my relationship with God to cope with the very real problems of life that all people face. I've also found a liberating force of forgiveness and joy. People who say that guilt is only a self-induced delusion are being dishonest with themselves. Human guilt can't be swept under the rug that easily. Neither can true freedom and joy be acquired that easily. People need help to correct what's wrong with them and to be enabled to become all that they were originally intended to be - unselfish, humble, loving, liberated, joyful beings. Psychiatrists, philosophers and moralists can help us gain insight into ourselves and our situation, but only God can provide the power to help us become what we know we ought to be and can be.

Next Dr. Cummings picked up a paper with grease stains all over it. Sam's writing was as messy as his paper and hard to read, but his ideas were quite sharp.

Religions are a dime a dozen. There are so many different religious teachers and sects all claiming to have the truth that it would take somebody a lifetime to sort them all out! Why bother? If they're all correct, then none of them is correct. If any of them is correct, then why are there so many others that claim it's incorrect? The best thing to do as far as religion is concerned is to stay out of the argument and enjoy some peace. If there really is a 'God,' I don't think he would be mixed up with all the hodgepodge that passes for religion. Religion only confuses people, and often makes a profit at their expense. More wars have been fought over religion than over anything else. Religion causes more problems than it solves. It would be better if everybody would keep their beliefs to themselves and peacefully go about their own business.

It was time for lunch, but Dr. Cummings decided to read one more paper.

There once were two poor men. One was rather lazy and indifferent, while the other was industrious and conscientious. One day a rumor reached the village that a large golden nugget had been buried in a nearby field by pirates long ago. The two men hurried off to see if they could find the nugget. However, when they reached the field, they discovered that it was swampy and full of rocks, trees, and junk. The one man gave up in disgust without ever seriously trying, but the other man searched and searched until he finally found the nugget! When he returned to the village, he was no longer poor, and the other man wished that he hadn't given up so quickly. The moral: the path to truth is not an easy one, but those who make the effort will be well rewarded. Just because there's a lot of rocks, trees and junk in the field of religion doesn't mean there isn't any gold."

What Do *You* Think?

1. Which one of these six points of view do you agree with the most and why?

2. Which one of these six points of view do you disagree with the most and why?

3. Which one of these six points of view are you most uncertain about and why?

4. Suppose you had been one of Dr. Cumming's students. How would you have written your essay? Outline the key points you would have made.

Bringing Things Into Focus |

True or False?

Which of these ideas do you think are true, which are false, and why?

- The majority of people in the world believe in some kind of religion.

- In a highly developed country like the United States, belief in organized religion is declining, but a commitment to 'spirituality' is not.

- In an atheistic country like China today, religious belief is steadily increasing.

- Many so-called 'religious wars' have actually been fought more over political, social and economic issues than over purely religious beliefs.

- The trend among an increasing number of scientists today is more towards religious faith than away from it.

- The founders of the world's great religions completely contradict one another in their teachings.

- The teachings of a religious leader, like Jesus Christ for example, have been completely outdated by developments in modern times.

- All religious teaching is based on mythology and superstition and not on historical or scientific fact.

- There's more to reality than can be measured by the scientific method alone. Therefore, there's room for valid religious belief that's beyond scientific measurement.

- There've been a number of movements to stamp out or discredit religion, but they've failed in large measure because human beings seem to be 'incurably religious.'

- A number of famous 19th century rationalist thinkers like Marx and Comte believed that religion would have completely died out by now.

- Most of the world's major religions are slowly dying out.

Gaining a Perspective |

The Rebellion against Religion

Before the year 1700, very few people in the world were without some religious belief or other. Then a rebellion against religion arose in the West during an era known as 'The Enlightenment.' Eminent thinkers in the fields of philosophy, history and science led an assault on religious faith that eventually spread around the world. Reinforced by startling scientific discoveries, the development of the scientific method and the advent of the industrial revolution, men like the English historian David Hume (1711-1776), the French philosophers Jean Rousseau (1712-1778), Francois

Voltaire (1694-1778) and Auguste Comte (1798-1857), the German philosophers Immanuel Kant (1724-1804), Georg Hegel (1770-1831), Karl Marx (1818-1883) and Friedrich Nietzsche (1884-1900) and the English naturalists Charles Darwin (1809-1882) and T. H. Huxley (1825-1895), either repudiated religion altogether, or distorted it beyond recognition.

Their ideas carried over into the 20th century and were further developed by people, among others, like the Austrian psychologist Sigmund Freud (1856-1939), the English philosopher Bertrand Russell (1872-1970), the Russian and Chinese Marxist theorists V. I. Lenin (1870-1924) and Mao Tse-tung (1893-1976), the American educator John Dewey (1859-1952), the American astrophysicist Karl Sagan (1934-1996) and what today are known as the 'new atheists' – Americans Sam Harris (1967-) and Christopher Hitchens (1949-2011) and Englishman Richard Dawkins (1941-).

Through the teachings of these people and others, a number of basic ideas were developed that still heavily influence many people's ideas about, and attitudes toward, life and reality today – including religion.

- Higher forms of life continually develop out of lower forms in a natural and automatic evolutionary process. (During the 20th century, this biological concept was applied to all aspects of reality – including the history of religion).

- In this fierce evolutionary competition, whatever is most fit survives through a process of natural selection, which guarantees a continuous process of evolutionary progress and development. (Again, this biological theory was universally applied to all aspects of human experience, with religion being relegated to humanity's 'primitive' past).

- Human history is a history of class struggle centering round economic or materialistic interests. All 'higher' aspects of life, such as religion, philosophy, art, etc. are merely inventions of people's minds to hide and promote their economic interests. Humanity, like the rest of the universe, can be explained in purely materialistic terms.

- The so-called 'higher' aspects of people's lives are actually nothing more than the lower, murky psychological products of a subconscious mind based on the unfulfilled urges of childhood. They are like psychological crutches invented for reasons of comfort and security.

- There are no such things as absolutes, laws, norms, standards or universal truths. All is relative. The test for anything is not whether it is true or false, good or bad, but whether it works - whether it's practical.

- Nothing can be known or is genuine unless it can be based on generally observable facts; that is, that it can be measured scientifically using the scientific method of the natural sciences.

- The cosmos is 'closed' in the sense that it is not subject to the whims of some external power interfering with natural processes. The only realities are those that can be empirically measured

- Modern people have outgrown the 'superstition' of religion and are capable of, and evolving towards, unlimited progress that will eventually lead to a utopian existence on earth.

What Do *You* Think?

1. Why do you think so many thinking people rebelled against religion during the last two centuries?

2. Which of their ideas do you agree with and why?

3. Which of their ideas don't you agree with and why?

4. Which of their ideas aren't you sure about and why?

<u>**Drawing Conclusions**</u> |

Science or Scientism?

Religion in general, and Christianity in particular, had been around a long time before these thinkers came on the world scene. Much of religious history had been inspiring and commendable, but some of it had become distorted both in theory and in practice. Some in the Christian Church, for example, had, on more than a few occasions, wandered from the original teachings of Christ and at times completely contradicted his way of life with their un-Christian practices. Others had developed interpretations of the Bible that conflicted with new scientific discoveries and had persecuted those who dared to stand by their scientific data.

In this situation, some Christians periodically struggled hard to reform the Church, and often succeeded in doing so. But others completely gave up on the Church and on all religion and launched an attack on it in the name of science and free inquiry. The problem was that in attacking a *distortion* of the original teaching and practice of Jesus and other religious figures, they became antagonistic towards *all* Christian thought and *all* religious ideas. They assumed that since *some* of what they understood as 'religious' teaching and practice was false, it followed that *all* of it must be false. Therefore, they 'threw the baby out with the bathwater,' so to speak, and in so doing created an even greater anti-religious distortion that has plagued us ever since.

It's interesting to see how people who insisted on objectivity, learning the truth from facts, drawing logical conclusions on the basis of scientific observation, and the like, abandoned most of that and let their emotions get the better of them when it came to the subject of religion. Although they prided themselves on being 'objective' and 'scientific,' they become very subjective and biased about matters of faith, except for *their* faith which could be called 'scientism.' This, of course, was and is a gross denial of the very scientific principles upon which they based their attack. It's hard to see, for example, how Sigmund Freud could have postulated his whole psycho-analytic theory on the subjective reports of his patients' dreams and accepted the same as scientific data, but ruled out people's reports of their religious experiences as so much subjective drivel. Or that he could have denied that some realities like love, faith and hope are beyond the scope of scientific measurement. People who ridiculed those who were 'religious' as superstitious and stupid tended to look at things on the surface rather than looking at things *beneath* the surface since much of reality isn't always as simple as it appears to the untrained eye. They all but ignored the fact that there's more to the cosmos than 'meets the eye.'

Another reason why these thinkers attacked religion is that they let success go to their heads. As one revolutionary scientific discovery after another was made, the temptation to resist taking great unscientific and illogical leaps to wrong generalizations and conclusions was too great. They became like children who think that because today they can add 1 + 1 and get 2, tomorrow they will become the masters of calculus. Unproven theories were uncritically accepted as 'scientific laws.' Theories postulated in a specific area (like biological evolution) were applied universally to all areas of knowledge with abandon. The whole universe became centered on humans and their inevitable achievements and possibilities. They wrongly concluded that because they could, through the scientific method, know *some* things and control *some* things, they eventually would be able to know *all* things and control *all* things.

Since there was *some* truth in what they had to say, it was difficult for them to keep from going on to claim that their ideas were the *whole* truth. The logical contradictions are not hard to see.

- No amount of empirical inquiry could verify any one of their major ideas beyond reasonable doubt.

- The universal application of their ideas to all aspects of reality was unwarranted by the narrow data upon which they were based.

- Relativism and Positivism were purely non-scientifically verifiable *ideas* and therefore disproved themselves.

- Against much evidence to the contrary, their ideas reduced humans to accidental collections of atoms, and denied the reality of intuitive knowledge such as love, justice, beauty, and the like.

If the presuppositions, methods and conclusions of such thinkers were on such shaky ground, why should anybody think their conclusions about religion were right? Obviously, a great number of people haven't. Millions of people around the world today testify that religion, rather than *impeding* life and growth, is the *basis* of it. To them, their religious experience is as real and as valid as the law of gravity. The number of such people is growing in the world, not diminishing. An exhaustive global study published in 2015 in *Demographic Research* by Hackett, Stonawski, and others, estimates that the religiously unaffiliated (self-identifying atheists and agnostics, as well as those who say their religion is "nothing in particular") who made up 16.4 percent of the world's population in 2010 will *decline* to 13.2 percent by 2050. Even among people in the increasingly secularized Western democracies who have rejected organized religion, a majority acknowledge the value of the spiritual dimension of life.

A number of thinkers in every field of knowledge have come forward to effectively challenge the false assumptions of the 'children of the Enlightenment.' First-rate thinkers like the English apologist C.S. Lewis, the American philosopher Elton Trueblood, the Chinese writer Lin Yu Tang, the English economist E.F. Schumacher, the American theologian Reinhold Neibuhr, the German physician Albert Schweitzer, the Danish philosopher Soren Kierkegaard, the German theologians Karl Barth and Emil Brunner, the English journalist Malcom Muggeridge, the American apologist Ravi Zacharias and a host of others have effectively argued the case for the relevancy of religion for modern people and the bankruptcy of these kinds of anti-religious positions based on pseudo-scientific theories.

An increasing number of scientists and philosophers, whether they're committed to religious beliefs or not, are calling all of these ideas into question today as well. A new wave of humility has swept over thinking people. Two disastrous world wars, a recognition that science has its limits, a new sense of wonder at the complexities in nature that modern science has revealed, an uneasiness about the mammoth problems that the human race is now encountering and a new appreciation for the value and meaning of the unseen realities have all combined to swing the pendulum back towards seeing religion as the context that gives value, significance, meaning and purpose to people's lives and to the cosmos. Many are seeing anew that the way to experience the totality of reality is not to close oneself off to *either* the empirical *or* the intuitive, but to embrace them both as two aspects of the one truth.

Is religion still relevant? The answer to that question that's being heard more and more among thinking people in our day is, "It certainly is."

What Do *You* Think?

1. What's the one thing about these conclusions you most strongly agree with and why?

2. Is there anything about these conclusions you strongly disagree with? Explain.

3. Do you feel religion is outdated/somewhat relevant/very relevant as far as the needs of modern people are concerned? Why?

4. What part has religion played in your life up to this point - an important part/a part/no part? Explain.

Chapter Two

IS THERE REALLY ANYBODY THERE?

> "No one can please God without faith, for whoever comes to God must have faith that God exists and rewards those who seek him."   Hebrews 11:6

Looking Through the Microscope |

Oh God!

Some years ago, a controversial film entitled "Oh God!" made the rounds of American theaters. Some devoutly religious people were highly offended by what they saw as a cheap spoof of religious ideas. Others thought it was a rather powerful statement about God and the struggle for faith on the part of those caught up in a modern, materialistic, secular way of life. To those who only looked at the film on the surface, it was nothing more than a good comedy that produced a lot of laughs. But to those who looked deeper, it raised a number of disturbing questions about the false ideas some people have about God, and made a number of profound points about the nature of true religious faith.

In the film, John Denver plays a young married man with two young children who works as a friendly produce manager in a supermarket. He's a typical modern young American - married, making a steady income, owning a house and car of his own, and generally enjoying life. Raised in a 'Christian' society, he and his wife aren't atheists or anti-religious, but they aren't exactly enthusiastic believers either. They're more or less neutral as far as

God is concerned - not denying he exists, but living as though he isn't around. They don't bother him, and they don't expect him to bother them. But that's where they're wrong!

As the plot unfolds, Jerry gets a note in the mail one day asking him to come to a meeting on the top floor of a downtown skyscraper. The note is signed 'God.' He laughs and shows it to his wife, convinced that it's the work of his practical-joke-playing friend Artie. He decides to humor Artie and the next day shows up at the appointed place and time only to find a bare room with a lone chair and an intercom on a stand in the middle of it. He laughs and is about to leave when a voice over the intercom suddenly invites him to sit down. Thinking Artie's disguised voice is coming over the intercom; he decides to humor him and does so. Even when the voice announces that it's 'God' speaking and that he wants Jerry to deliver a message from him to the people on earth, he still refuses to believe it's not Artie's joke. When the voice tells him to take the elevator down to the lobby and check out how many floors the building has, however, he's not so sure. The elevator panel shows only 17 floors, but his meeting had been on the 27th!

That night, he tells his wife about this strange experience, but feels too embarrassed to admit that he's a little puzzled by it. His puzzlement turns to astonishment the next day when, as he's blissfully driving along in his car listening to the radio, the music is suddenly interrupted by the voice of 'God!' Jerry is so startled that he almost hits a telephone pole! 'God' again tells him that he wants him to deliver a message to the earth's people - that when he made the place, it had been beautiful and all had been peaceful. Now everybody was destroying it and each other. He wanted to warn them to stop before it was too late.

Jerry's reaction is understandable. How could this possibly really be 'God?' And if it were, why pick on him!? He was only a lowly, unknown produce manager in a supermarket. He wasn't even what you would call religious. And what would people say if he suddenly were to announce that 'God' had spoken to him and asked him to deliver a message to humankind? They'd think he was crazy! So he pleads with the 'voice' to leave him alone and get somebody else to deliver his message - if he really was something more than a freak radio transmission and if he really had a message.

That night, Jerry is too embarrassed to tell his wife about the car incident. He's torn between wondering if he's cracking up or whether there might actually be something to this 'God' business after all. The next morning, his doubts are resolved. He's taking a shower when 'the voice' speaks to him again. He peeks out of the shower and sees a little old man with glasses in tennis shoes and a baseball cap standing there. In a very funny scene, the old man (George Burns) claims to be 'God!' At the look of incredulity on Jerry's face he says, "What did you expect?" When Jerry embarrassedly covers himself up with a towel, he says, "What are you embarrassed about? I made you, didn't I?"

Still breathless and unbelieving, Jerry and 'God' go for a ride together in his car. When Jerry asks for some sign to prove that he's really 'God,' 'God' makes it rain - inside the car! With water leaking out onto the street, a motorcycle policeman pulls Jerry over and demands to know what's going on. Jerry turns to 'God' for an explanation, but he's disappeared! Jerry is now finally convinced that the old man really is 'God' and that he should become his messenger. The catch is that only Jerry can see him! He has to try and convince everybody that he really has talked with 'God' and that he has a message from him, without being able to prove it! The results are predictable. His wife and children think he's crazy. Some newspapers and TV shows get hold of the story and turn him into a freak celebrity. Religious officials call him a false prophet. His 'Christian' boss fires him because of all the adverse publicity. Following 'God's instructions, Ronnie denounces a 'Christian' evangelist as a fraud who then takes him to court for defamation of character.

Throughout it all, however, 'God' keeps paying him visits. In some very funny exchanges, 'God' gives him advice, encourages him when he wants to quit, and becomes his closest friend. In the end, 'God' makes an appearance on his behalf in a courtroom and he's acquitted. But when all evidence that 'God' was there disappears, those who saw him (like the lawyers and the judge) refuse to admit that they had seen him - except for his wife who becomes a believer! 'God' appears to Jerry once more to encourage him to keep spreading his message. He tells him that he now is strong enough to be on his own but that they'll "keep in touch." 'God' slowly walks across a field and out of sight, and the film ends.

What Do *You* Think?

1. What do you think is the main 'message' of this film?

2. Do you think Jerry was foolish to do what he did? Why or why not?

3. As far as *your* ideas about God are concerned, who do you most identify with in this film - Jerry, his wife (at first), the religious officials, Jerry's boss, the policeman who couldn't "see God," the judge who refused to acknowledge that he had 'seen God,' none of these? Why?

4. Do you think God has ever made himself known in such a direct way to anybody in the past? Explain.

5. Read John 11:43-48, 53 and John 20:24-29 in the Bible. What do these incidents say in relation to this film?

Bringing Things Into Focus |

Take Your Pick

Here's a list of belief systems in our world today.

- **Pantheism** - the belief that everything is God and God is everything.

- **Polytheism** - the belief that there are many different gods that should all be worshipped.

- **Theism** - the belief that there is a God or gods.

- **Agnosticism** - the belief that one can't know for sure whether there's a God or not.

- **Monotheism** - the belief that there's only one true God.

- **Animism** - the belief that plants, inanimate objects and natural phenomena can be identified with the soul of God and worshipped.

- **Atheism** - the belief that God doesn't exist and that all of reality can be explained in purely material terms.

- **Deism** - the belief that God created the cosmos, but then left it to run on its own on the basis of natural laws.

- **Dualism** - the belief that there are two equal spiritual powers struggling for supremacy - one good and the other evil.

What Do *You* Think?

1. Which one of the belief systems listed above is nearest to your own? Explain.

2. Which one of the belief systems listed above is farthest from your own? Explain.

3. How many of the belief systems listed above do you know something about? Explain.

4. Rank the belief systems above in the order in which, in your opinion, they are most believable, and explain your choices.

5. Do you think Atheists have a stronger case in our modern age than they did before? Why or why not?

6. Do you think a person can practice 'spirituality' without believing in God? Why or why not?

<u>Gaining a Perspective |</u>

Pro and Con

Here are 14 reasons people often give for either believing or disbelieving in God. What would your choice be for each reason? Explain.

PRO	CON
1. People through the ages have testified to experiencing the reality of God in their lives.	Marx and his followers taught that 'God' is a superstitious myth.
2. A cosmos with God as planner, creator and sustainer makes much more sense than a cosmos of chance going nowhere in particular.	A cosmos of chance makes more sense because it means humans are free to make their own decisions rather than merely being the puppet of some 'god.'
3. The complexity and wonder of creation uncovered by modern science increasingly supports belief in God.	Belief in 'God' merely fulfils a personal psychological need.
4. Nobody can prove that God doesn't exist.	Nobody can prove that God *does* exist.
5. A majority of people believe in God.	The majority isn't always right.
6. The Bible says that God is real.	You can't see, hear, smell, taste or touch 'God.' He's a scientifically unverifiable, invisible unreality.

7. The Bible was inspired by God and is his Word of Truth.

The Bible was written by men recording their own fantasies.

8. God answers prayer.

People who pray often don't get what they ask for.

9. God has done and continues to do miracles.

Most so-called 'miracles' are fake. Scientists will eventually be able to give an explanation for every seemingly miraculous event.

10. God forgives sin and gives eternal life.

People who don't believe in 'God' live lives that are just as good as people who do. What lies beyond the grave is a mystery to us all.

11. God gives us strength and hope

'God' is for weaklings. Those who don't believe there's a 'God' are strong enough to take care of themselves.

12. Those who believe in God know where they've come from, who they are, why they're here and where they're going.

The only thing that has meaning is that I exist *now*. As far as the past and the future are concerned, all else is empty speculation.

13. God stands for and is bringing about what's good. Without him there would be no final difference between good and evil and no hope.

If 'God' is so good and powerful, why does he allow the righteous to suffer and the wicked to prosper?

14. Those I love and trust believe in God.

You've been brain washed.

Drawing Conclusions |

Somebody Really *Is* There!

In Chapter One, we've pointed out that the vast majority of the people of the world are followers of some kind of a religion. Since religion has to do with an attempt to know God and live life as he intended it to be lived, this means that the vast majority of human beings believe that 'Somebody' really *is* there. Certainly this fact alone would cause a thinking person to think twice before dismissing out of hand the idea of there being a God. It's true that the majority isn't always right, but it's also true that when a minority disagrees with the majority, the burden of proof rests much more heavily on the shoulders of the minority than it does on those of the majority.

Notice that in the 'Take Your Pick' section above, *every* point of view about God is described as a 'belief' - even the atheistic point of view that there's no God! This is important for us to understand because somehow the idea has been spread around that people who believe in God do so on the basis of their fanciful imaginations, or their subjective feelings, or their sub-conscious whims, while those who don't believe in God base their ideas on scientific research, objective evidence and self-evident logic. Believers are said to depend on faith, while disbelievers are said to depend on fact.

Nothing could be further from the truth. *Both* belief in God *and* non-belief in God are unproveable *beliefs*. For example, the writers of the Bible never try to *prove* the existence of God; they *assume* the existence of God based on their experience and on their interpretation of reality. Likewise, an atheist can't *prove* that God doesn't exist, but *assumes* that he doesn't exist on the basis of *his or her* experience and interpretation of reality. If this is so, then the key question becomes, which experience and interpretation of reality is more credible? Which more closely matches what we can know about reality today? Which is most likely to be true?

Any honest analysis of the facts will show that it takes much more faith to be an atheist today, or even an agnostic, than it does to be a theist. Any scientist who is fair will acknowledge that the *old* view of science (that everything in the cosmos operates on the basis of observable, provable laws; that it's only a matter of time before all facts will be knowable and all events will be predictable; and that only what can be proved by the scientific method based on the assumption that natural phenomena are strictly explained by reference to natural laws or material processes can be termed real) is being discarded. A new view (in which scientific 'laws' are seen as theories to be disproved; in which science itself is seen as being based on the assumptions of an observer rather than on 'provable facts;' and in which there is room for non-scientific explanations of some aspects of reality) has taken its place. This change in viewpoint has mainly been brought about through Mayer's Second Law of Thermodynamics, Einstein's Theory of Relativity and Heisenberg's Uncertainty Principle.

In yet another example, scientists now acknowledge that the various laws and constants of nature appear to be so precisely calibrated and fine tuned in order to allow for life in our universe that even those scientists who are committed to a material explanation for all things have abandoned their insistence that this all came about by chance.

In his December 25, 2014 article in *The Wall Street Journal*, Eric Metaxas convincingly points this out.

> Today there are more than 200 known parameters necessary for a planet to support life - every single one of which must be perfectly met, or the whole thing falls apart. Without a massive planet like Jupiter nearby, whose gravity will draw away asteroids, a thousand times as many would hit Earth's surface. The odds against life in the universe are simply astonishing...Can *every one* of those parameters have been perfectly established by accident? At what point is it fair to admit that science suggests that we cannot be the result of random forces? Doesn't the assumption that an intelligence created these perfect conditions require far less faith than believing that a life-sustaining Earth just happened to beat the inconceivable odds to come into being?
>
> There's more. The fine-tuning necessary for life to exist on a planet is nothing compared with the fine-tuning required for the universe to exist at all. For example, astrophysicists

now know that the values of the four fundamental forces - gravity, the electromagnetic force, and the 'strong' and 'weak' nuclear forces - were determined less than one millionth of a second after the 'big bang.' Alter any one value and the universe could not exist. For instance, if the ratio between the nuclear strong force and the electromagnetic force had been off by the tiniest fraction of the tiniest fraction – by even one part in 100,000,000,000,000,000 – then no stars could have ever formed at all. Feel free to gulp. Multiply that single parameter by all the other necessary conditions and the odds against the universe existing are so heart-stoppingly astronomical that the notion that it all "just happened" defies common sense. It would be like tossing a coin and having it come up heads 10 quintillion times in a row. Really?

In the old view, the universe was 'closed.' There was no room for God in reality and atheists had a fairly easy time believing in their theory. But in the new view, the momentum in all fields of knowledge, in light of recent developments and insights, is in the direction of acknowledging not only the *possibility* but the *probability* of the presence and work in the cosmos of a presence, or power, or intelligence, or some being we can call 'God.' For example, Francis Collins, director of the National Institutes of Health and former director of the US National Human Genome Research Institute, in his book *The Language of God*, recounts how he moved from atheism to theism after encountering the incredible complexity of the gene structure in human beings. The list of prominent contemporary Christian scientists in Wikipedia's "Christians in Science and Technology" who subscribe to the new view is impressive. Seventeen who made significant contributions to science, but who have died since 2001, are listed first. They are followed by a list of 25 current scientists who have made major contributions in biological and biomedical sciences, five who have done so in chemistry, 35 who have done so in physics and astronomy, six who have done so in engineering and 11 who have done so in general. Eleven of them have won Nobel prizes and six have won the Templeton prize!

On the basis of what we've briefly outlined as the new humility of scientific inquiry alone, we would have to conclude that honest atheists today must have a difficult time believing there is no God because they believe what's much less likely to be true according to the best scientific evidence available. Add to this the evidence from other areas, and an insistence on non-belief in God becomes a biased stubbornness in not recognizing the truth when one sees it.

For example, if there were no God, there would be no difference between right and wrong, good and evil, criminals and law-abiding citizens. All values and acts would be relative, and nobody would be answerable to anybody for anything. Even though some people might hold this as an interesting theory, they would not act on the basis of it. If somebody was going to murder their child, they would try to prevent it, and if they couldn't, they would label such an act as evil. But how would they know that? How do *we* know that? We know it because our heart (or conscience) tells us. We all know that good cannot possibly be the same as evil, and vice versa. And the reason why we are so sure of that is because 'Someone' has made us that way and has made our universe that way. In other words, 'Someone' has created a place in which there is moral order and in which we are all ultimately answerable to that 'Someone' and responsible for our deeds.

Or take the question of order and beauty. Atheists tell us that everything began by chance and that chaos evolved into what we today know as order - by chance. (They can't explain where the first cell or the first spark of energy came from, of course.) But is that a reasonable theory in light of our experience and observations? Hardly. Nowhere in the cosmos do we find chaos producing order at random, so that the orderly and beautiful arise out of mere chance. Instead, we find order on an incredible scale.

If we think about the Big Bang and the flow of matter in all directions, one would think the universe would be in chaos. No matter how long it would take, the idea that most matter would be organized in an incredible way would be unthinkable. However, the opposite is the case. For example the Moon orbits around the earth in a perfect fashion. Not one, but millions of systems are like this. The earth circles the Sun, and again there are millions of examples like it.

Our stars circle the center of our galaxy in a predefined path. Again billions of stars do this! When we look at the matter that is organized (has found fixed orbit) versus that which is not, almost 90% of matter is organized. These billions of objects have fixed trajectories and stable paths. Consider that there is not just *one* galaxy but *billions* of them, all of similar shape, like or spiral, which have stars.

According to John Carl Villanueva writing in Universe Today, what can at present be observed of the known universe through the Hubble Telescope is estimated to span roughly 93 billion light years. In 2016, a German supercomputer ran a simulation and estimated that around 500 billion galaxies exist within range of observation. (A more conservative estimate places the number at around 300 billion). Since the number of stars in each galaxy can run up to 400 billion, then the total number of stars may very well be over 100 sextillion (1.2×10^{23}) On average, each star can weigh about 10^{35} grams. Thus, the total mass would be about 10^{58} grams (1.0×10^{48} metric tons). Since each gram of matter is known to have about 10^{24} protons, or about the same number of hydrogen atoms (since one hydrogen atom has only one proton), then the total number of hydrogen atoms in that exist in the observable universe would be roughly one-hundred thousand quadrillion vigintillion (10^{82}). This estimate only accounts for the *observable* universe (some 10% of the estimated whole) which reaches 46 billion light years in any direction, and is based on where the expansion of space has taken the most distant objects observed.

The observable matter of the universe is also spread isotropically; meaning that no direction of observation seems different from any other and each region of the sky has roughly the same content. The universe is also bathed in a wave of highly isotropic microwave radiation that corresponds to a thermal equilibrium of roughly 2.725 kelvin (just above Absolute Zero). All evidence points to the fact that physical laws act uniformly throughout the universe and should, therefore, produce no observable irregularities in the large scale structure. You begin to get the picture.

The incredible complexity of God's creation on a micro scale also boggles the mind:

- in the hatching of eggs ...

  - the eggs of the potato bug hatch in 7 days
  - those of the canary in 14 days
  - those of the barnyard hen in 21 days
  - those of ducks and geese in 28 days
  - those of the mallard in 35 days
  - those of the parrot and the ostrich in 42 days.

  (Notice, they're all divisible by 7, the number of days in a week!)

- and in the makeup of various animals ...

  - An elephant's four legs all bend forward in the same direction. No other quadruped is so made. This animal has a huge body, too large to lift on two legs. With four fulcrums, it can easily rise from the ground.
  - A horse rises from the ground on its two front legs first. A cow rises from the ground with its two hind legs first.

- and in the arrangement of sections and segments in fruit

  - Each watermelon has an even number of stripes on the rind.
  - Each orange has an even number of segments.
  - Every bunch of bananas has on its lowest row an even number of bananas, and each row decreases by one, so that one row has an even number and the next row an odd number.

- and in the arrangement of sections and segments in grains

  - Each ear of corn has an even number of rows.
  - All grains are found in even numbers on the stalks.

- and in the arrangement of the rhythm of the seas ...

  - The waves of the sea roll in on shore twenty-six to the minute in all kinds of weather.

- and in the blossoming of flowers at certain specified times during the day ...

- Linnaeus, the great botanist, once said that if he had a conservatory containing the right kind of soil, moisture and temperature, he could tell the time of day or night by the flowers that were open and those that were closed!

• And that's only the beginning of the story:

- By this time tomorrow, your heart will have beaten 100,000 times...
- There are 100,000 miles of white matter fibers in your brain...
- There are about 200 different types of cells in your body...
- Within these cells there are about 20 different types of cells in all, each cell functioning like an independent town.

To believe that the human eye, a field of wild flowers, or a bird in flight are products of sheer chance stretches the imagination to its wildest limits and flies in the face of all evidence to the contrary. For anyone to believe such and then accuse a religious person of being naive for believing that the cosmos is a creation of a God of order is to twist things completely around.

Looking at it from another angle, without God, the whole of life becomes meaningless and purposeless. Suppose we take God completely out of the picture for a moment. What would we have left? A world that began by chance, is run by chance and is heading into the future willy-nilly like a cork in a rushing stream with no direction or purpose; a world where humans are mere collections of atoms, accidentally present, but without knowing why they came about, what they are here for or where they are going; a world where society is a moral and ethical jungle in which might makes right, the end justifies the means and it is every man for himself. No wonder that in the face of modern developments people who believe in these ideas develop philosophies of despair!

Now let's put God back into the picture. What do we have then? A world that was created according to plan, that is run by an orderly process and that is headed towards a meaningful goal; humans as responsible created beings, charged with discovering, developing and managing creation, and having an ever fuller life ahead; society as a global family whose members are responsible to God and for each other, are to relate lovingly and unselfishly to one another and are called to live according to a given moral order. No wonder the Christian Gospel, for example, is called the 'Good News!'

However, if belief in God is so self-evident today, why do some people still refuse to believe that he exists? For three reasons:

- They still base their belief in atheism on the old scientific view rather than on the new one.

- They have a distorted view of what the real God is like and reject that distortion rather than the 'real thing.'

- They intellectually understand the evidence for the existence of God, but emotionally reject it. In the end, faith in God is more a matter of the will than of the intellect. As the old proverb says, "You can lead a horse to water, but you can't make him drink." (For example, the Pharisees never disputed the fact that Jesus raised Lazarus from the dead, but they made plans to kill him anyway!)

In addition, some people, don't want to admit that their lives are not all they should be or could be; that they need forgiveness and healing - and so they profess atheism to avoid having to face up to their personal need. Others want total independence (which, of course, is an impossibility anyway), and think that the best way to keep an interfering God out of their lives is to deny that he exists. In these, and similar cases, it is a matter of the will overcoming the mind and driving a person to adopt a belief that contradicts the evidence.

Is there really anybody there? If there is, the next question is, what is he like and how can we get to know him? It's this question that the great religions of the world attempt to answer.

<u>What Do *You* Think?</u>

1. I agree with/disagree with/am not sure about the conclusions of this chapter because ......

2. When I think about God, I ......

3. One question I have about God is ......

4. As far as believing in God is concerned, I need to ......

Chapter Three

WHICH PATH LEADS HOME?

> "Paul said: 'That which you (Athenians) worship…is what I proclaim to you. God, who made the world and everything in it, is Lord of heaven and earth…it is he himself who gives life and breath and everything else to everyone.'" Acts 17:23-25

Looking Through the Microscope |

The 'Spiritual Food' Restaurant

The neon sign on the restaurant blinked on and off - 'Spiritual Food'...'Spiritual Food'...'Spiritual Food.' It was a different kind of restaurant than anybody had ever seen before. It was called the 'Restaurant of Religions.' Being spiritually hungry and honestly searching for truth, a group of college students decided to go in and see what the restaurant had to offer.

They sat down at a table and a waiter brought over a menu. The menu offered a great variety of spiritual dishes - something for everybody (or *almost* everybody). One student took a quick look, got up and left the restaurant mumbling, "Nothin' for nobody!" He was very hungry, but not hungry enough to eat *this* kind of food. He'd try to satisfy his hunger elsewhere - at the 'Thrills Cafeteria' or the 'Million Dollar Floating Restaurant' or the 'Diploma Dining Room' at the University.

The others, however, continued to study the menu carefully. It would be difficult to choose, not only because there were so many different kinds of spiritual dishes to choose from, but because some of the dishes were described in terms they couldn't understand, while others were known to them only vaguely through the word of friends who had tried them or through what they'd read about them in a spiritual gourmet book.

The restaurant offered a number of options. One plan allowed you to pay a fixed price and choose anything you liked. You could choose every dish on the whole menu if you wanted to - if you could eat it all! One guy decided to try this, but the others wondered whether eating so much and eating so many different types of things together might not make you spiritually ill. How could you eat the sour pickle 'dish of many gods' while drinking the milk of 'one true God,' for example? It was enough to turn your stomach.

Another less expensive plan allowed you to choose a sampling of each type of main dish, without having to eat the whole dish and all the trimmings that went with it. This appealed to several of the students who prided themselves on being open-minded. They felt there must be *something* good in every dish. Otherwise, why would the restaurant bother to offer all these dishes since nobody would buy them if that weren't true? Besides, they felt the best way to find out the truth about spiritual food was to try at least a little of everything. They liked this plan better than the first plan because even though every spiritual dish would have some truth mixed in it, it would also have some error mixed in it as well. The trick was to pick out of your sampling what you felt to be the truth (or what suited your spiritual taste), and leave the rest.

A third kind of offering on the menu was what might be called a 'set lunch.' There were several kinds of these at different prices. The menu claimed they were all balanced and spiritually nutritious meals. One in particular was advertized as being all that a person needed to fully experience life now and forever. The menu claimed that if you ordered that lunch, you would never need to order another one. It was, of course, quite expensive.

Some of the set lunch descriptions said that all of the other food on the menu was pure rubbish. One, however, claimed that the restaurant had included what was genuine spiritual food from all the other dishes, added its own unique ingredients according to the chef's secret recipe, and produced a meal that was pure truth and 100% spiritually nourishing. To buy a set lunch, of course, meant that you could not dabble in any of the other dishes. The management was very strict about that. If you chose it, you were choosing *only* it. A number of students chose one of the set lunches.

One girl was very hungry, but also very frugal. She carefully looked through the entire menu to find the cheapest dish available. When she found it, she knew that it wouldn't be very satisfying, but she ordered it anyway. She was simply not willing to pay the price of a more costly meal that could truly satisfy her spiritual needs. She wanted to save her time, her money and her energy to spend on what she thought were more worthwhile things than religion. Her friends warned her that she would be damaging her spiritual health and that the other things she was concerned about were of little value compared to the life-giving nourishment she could get in this restaurant, but they couldn't convince her.

While all this had been going on, a number of people had gathered around the students' table to try to influence their decisions concerning what was available on the menu. One recommended this dish as being the best tasting one of the lot. Another recommended that dish as costing the least in terms of what you had to give up in order to get it. A third said he'd tried them all and had found them all to be delicious. A fourth whispered in tones that the manager couldn't overhear that he too had tried them all and that they had all been lousy. He advised them to leave and find another restaurant! The set lunch people were the most insistent. They were so keen on getting the remaining students who hadn't yet ordered to order the set lunch that they'd recommended that two of them got into a heated argument over it.

One student got up and left in disgust, declaring that the whole thing was so confusing he didn't feel anybody could ever really find out the truth and satisfy his spiritual hunger no matter what he would eat. But the others stayed, made their choices and ate their food. They knew that to let the confusion of others cause them to give up on their search for truth would mean to go through life perpetually hungry and perpetually searching. And that would be far worse than working through a little confusion now.

Some weren't satisfied with what they'd eaten and ordered other dishes. Others were fairly satisfied, but knew that there must be still more life-fulfilling food to be had than what they'd sampled so far. Still others were ecstatic over the food they'd eaten - particularly the ones who had chosen the set lunch with the chef's secret recipe. While the rest of the students pored over the menu again, undecided, or sampled this or that, these students felt fully refreshed and ready to leave the 'Restaurant of Religions' to go about their work and play with a new vitality, joy and purpose. They urged their classmates to try the same lunch, bid them farewell and went out the door.

What Do *You* Think?

1. Look back over the various decisions made and options available in the 'Restaurant of Religions.' Which decision would you have made, or which option would you have chosen?

2. Is this your actual view of religion in real life? Explain.

3. In your opinion, which world religion is the most inclusive religion and why?

4. In your opinion, which of the following is correct? Explain your choice.

   a. All religions have some truth.

   b. Only one religion is true, while the rest are false.

   c. Most religions have some truth, but only one religion is all true.

5. In your opinion, which of the following is correct?

   a.   Religion is the most important part of life.

   b.   Religion is a very important part of life.

    c.   Religion is not a very important part of life. (If this last sentence read "of *my* life," would that change anything? Explain).

6. Do you think people ought to try and influence other people about religion? Why or why not?

7. Which religion is represented in the story as a set lunch with the chef's secret recipe? Do you think it's better than the other religions? Why or why not?

Bringing Things Into Focus |

The World's Religions

There are 12 major religions in the world (which are subdivided into a total of 270 large religious groups, and many smaller ones) that every thinking person should know at least something about. (There are, of course, many other minor sects, cults and religious groups, along with various kinds of local religious practices called 'folk religion,' which are beyond the scope of this book to describe in detail.)

- **Judaism** teaches there is one true, righteous, all-powerful God called Yahweh who has given us a moral law to live by, whom we can know and worship and who has promised to send a Messiah (a Savior) who will restore the fortunes of his people in the future. Judaism has three main branches: Orthodox, Reform and Liberal. The most important section of its holy book, *The Hebrew Bible*, is called *The Torah*. Approximate number of adherents: 14.5 million.

- **Zoroastrians** believe there is one good, but limited God who is involved in a cosmic struggle against equally powerful Evil Forces. This God calls on us to be involved with him in the fight against those Evil Forces. Its sacred writings are called *The Avesta*. Approximate number of adherents: 2.7 million.

- **Islam** calls on people to submit to the one divine World-Potentate called Allah by observing the 'Five Pillars' of the faith: the Faith statement that "Allah is God and Mohammad is his prophet," Prayer (five times daily), Charity, Fasting (especially during Ramadan) and the Hajj (a pilgrimage to Mecca). Allah rules the world according to his personal whim so that people's lives are determined by 'kismet' (fate). Those who are faithful now will enjoy a lavish existence in Paradise in the future. Islam's two main branches are Sunni and Shiite. Its sacred book is called *The Koran.* Approximate number of adherents: 1.57 billion.

- **Hinduism** uses the word 'Brahman' to describe the various gods who represent the many forces at work in life and the universe. The goal of life is to escape material existence and enter a state of eternal bliss called 'Nirvana.' This journey takes a long time since people live a series of lives by means of a process called 'reincarnation' during which they try to build up enough 'Karma' (spiritual credit) through religious rites and good acts to reach the state of Nirvana. Hinduism has six major schools of thought: Samkhya, Yoga, Nyaya, Vaisheshika, Mimamsa and Vedanta. Its main scriptures are called *The Vedas, The Brahmanas, The Upanishads* and *The Epics.* Approximate number of adherents: 950 million.

- **Christianity** teaches that there is one true, all-powerful, righteous God who created the cosmos good, came in the person of his Son to save the world from evil and will one day see his plan for the renewal of his creation fully completed. People can be saved and renewed through faith in God's Son (the God-man Jesus Christ who gave his life to redeem the world and who rose from death to demonstrate his divinity). They'll begin to experience the fullness of life as God intended it now and fully do so in the life to come as they commit themselves to God's way of living as taught and demonstrated by Jesus Christ. Christianity has three main branches: Roman Catholic, Orthodox and Protestant. Its sacred book is called *The Bible*. Approximate number of adherents: 2.039 billion.

- **Shinto** emphasizes Nature-Worship, Emperor-Worship and Purity of Body. Thousands of gods (in trees, gems, etc) called 'Kami' are worshipped. The Emperor is also thought to be a god. This faith has neither a definite set of beliefs about God nor a defined code of morality. Shinto has scores of sects under two main branches: Sect Shinto and New Religions Shinto. Its holy books are called *The Records of Ancient Matters* and *The Chronicles of Japan*. Approximate number of adherents: 2.7 million.

- **Taoism** teaches that if people follow the right 'way' (the Tao) they will live a perfect, contented life. The path to this way is to think and meditate, live simply and peaceably, be helpful and humble, do exercises and perform magical rites. The Tao is eternal, impersonal and mystical. The goal is to fit in with the universe through inactivity or non-striving and to keep the Yin and the Yang (forms of male and female energy) in balance within oneself and within nature. Its sacred book is called *The Canon of Reason and Virtue*. Approximate number of adherents: 2.7 million.

- **Jainism** emphasizes living an ascetic, humble, inoffensive and non-vindictive life. Its followers are rigidly forbidden to take life at any level and are vegetarians. It teaches that the body and the material are vile, while the soul and the spiritual are pure. The goal is to suppress the body and its desires in order to liberate the soul to enter 'Nirvana' (a state of non-material bliss) through a process of reincarnation (re-birth) and a system of 'Karma' (spiritual credit for good living). Its sacred writings are called *Agamas* (precepts). Approximate number of adherents: 4.3 million.

- **Confucianism** could be termed a philosophy, but it has enough religious elements woven through it to be classified as a religion as well. It might be called the religion of social propriety. According to Confucius, the way to a good life can be found by conducting the five basic relationships between people honestly, fairly and respectfully. These are relationships between ruler and subject, father and son, husband and wife, older sibling and younger sibling, and elder friends and junior friends. People are inherently good and can do this if they really want to. Filial piety is demonstrated by venerating one's ancestors. There is an impersonal supreme being which should be recognized, but who does not interfere in the daily affairs of life. The veneration of the founder, offering of sacrifices and temple rituals all lend a religious flavor to this system of thought. Its sacred writings are called the *Lun Yu*. Approximate number of adherents: 6.3 million.

- **Sikhism** has some things in common with both Hinduism and Islam, but significantly differs from them as well. Like Islam, it emphasizes that there is only one true God, but holds that he has made himself known through all of the Hindu gods, for example. The world is vain, transitory and passing away. The goal is to save oneself by being absorbed into God through repeating his name and living a life of faith, love and devotion throughout the process of reincarnation. The reward for the faithful is life in a lavish paradise in the future.

  Sikhism has no idols or sacrifices as a part of worship. Adherents must dress according to the law of the 'Five Ks' - Kesh (uncut hair), Kangha (a wooden brush for the hair), Kara (a metal bracelet), Kachera (a type of undergarment) and Kirpan (a dagger). The Five Ks are not just symbols, but articles of faith that collectively form the external identity and the Khalsa devotee's commitment to the Sikh way of life. The sacred book of this faith is *The Granth*. Approximate number of adherents: 23.8 million.

- **Buddhism** is concerned with helping humans escape suffering and reaching 'Nirvana.' The way to achieve this is to follow 'the middle way' and reach a state of 'not wanting,' since desire is what causes suffering. The way to achieve 'not wanting' is to believe the 'Four Noble Truths' - The Truth of Suffering (Kutai), The Truth of the Cause of Suffering (Jutai), The Truth of the Cessation of Suffering (Mettai), The Truth of the Path to the Cessation of Suffering (Dotai).

  To walk this 'Eightfold Path' is to have Right Views and to practice Right Thoughts, Right Speech, Right Conduct, Right Livelihood, Right Effort, Right Mindfulness and Right Meditation. The goal is to escape the process of 'Reincarnation' and reach 'Nirvana' through the building up of good 'Karma.' Adherents of the Mahayana School believe some monks become saintly saviors (Bodhisattvas) after they die and can help others on their spiritual journey.

  Buddhism has two major schools: Theravada and Mahayana. The sacred scriptures of this religion are called the *Tripitaka* ('Three Baskets'). Approximate number of adherents: 500 million.

- The **Bahá'í Faith** emphasizes the spiritual unity of all humankind. There are three core principles underlying Bahá'í teaching: the unity of God (there is only one God who is the source of all creation); the unity of religion (all major religions have the same spiritual source and come from the same God); and the unity of humanity (all humans have been created equal, and all races and cultures are worthy of appreciation and acceptance). Adherents are to learn to know and love God through prayer, reflection and service to humanity. The elaborate Baha'i international headquarters are located in Israel. The sacred scriptures of this religion include the writings of the Báb, Bahá'u'lláh, `Abdu'l-Bahá, Shoghi Effendi and the Universal House of Justice. Approximate number of adherents: 7.4 million.

<u>What Do *You* Think?</u>

1. Which religion do you know the most about, and why?

2. Which religion do you know the least about, and why?

3. For each religion listed, what aspect of that religion most impresses you the most, and why?

4. For each religion listed, what aspect of that religion most bothers you the most, and why?

<u>Gaining a Perspective</u> |

The 'House' of Comparative Religion

When it comes to religion, people have many different points of view about religion in general and about other religions in particular. We might illustrate this by comparing these views to different rooms in a house.

- **The Basement** (a place of darkness). Our religion is totally right and all other religions are totally wrong. Those who practice them are in the dark. E.g. **Conservative Muslims and Christians.**

- **The Nursery** (a room where the innocent play). Religion was needed by primitive people to cope with the unknown, but now that we have advanced into the scientific age, we humans can explain and manage our own destiny. Worthy values can be conserved, but metaphysical theology must be left behind. E.g. **Secular humanists.**

- **The Library** (a room for intellectual stimulation). All come and leave as equals. All will be enriched. Nobody has a corner on the truth. E.g., The Parliament of Religions, the Comparative Religion School.

- **The Dining Room** (a room with a whole smorgasbord of goodies to choose from). All in common recognize/worship a Person/Power beyond/behind the universe which fills the craving of the human heart. All should have the freedom to work out their own details. All religious roads lead to 'God.' One road is not necessarily 'better' than another. E.g. Vivekananda.

- **The Kitchen** (a room where ingredients are blended into a 'dish'). All religions have value. We must break through religious peculiarities to the common essence that can unify us all in a new universal faith. We can do this through a process of syncretism that levels all faiths down to a common denominator. E.g. Bahai, Unification Church, Theosophical Society.

- **The Workshop** (a room where incomplete projects can be finished). Other faiths have some truth and some right practices, but they're incomplete. They also have some beliefs and practices that need to be discarded. E.g. Emil Brunner.

- **The Attic** (a place filled with tempting junk). All 'religion' is the final stronghold where humanity seeks to fashion its own security and avoid dependence on a gracious God. Systems, rituals, structures, rubrics, false 'images' of God and distortions of God, all, in reality, substitute for and shut out God in the name of seeking God through a process that might be described as groping in the dark from the bottom up. Faith only becomes truly such as it humbly submits to the revelation of God through a process that might be described as light from the top down. E.g. Karl Barth, Dietrich Bonheoffer, Leslie Newbigin.

- **The Guest Room** (a room for strangers who become friends and eventually, perhaps, even 'family.') All people are children of God who've been touched in some way by grace and truth through their own religion(s) whether they recognize it or not. As such, they can be called 'anonymous believers' and should be treated as such, not as strangers. E.g. Karl Rahner.

What Do *You* Think?

1. Which one of the above viewpoints do you most agree with, and why?

2. Which one of the above viewpoints do you most disagree with, and why?

3. Which one of the above viewpoints do you think would be the most popular in our culture today, and why?

4. Are you personally acquainted with people who believe in no religion or a different religion than you do? Describe how you relate to these people.

Drawing Conclusions |

How Can We Tell If a Religion Is True?

Perhaps you're feeling right now like the student who took one look at the Menu in the Restaurant of Religions, decided that it was all too complicated and contradictory for him and impatiently gave up trying to work his way through bewilderment and skepticism to understanding and faith. That's the way a good many people react to religion when they don't want to take the time or make the effort to pursue the truth until they find it. They conclude that since they can't cut through all the 'red tape' in a hurry and find quick and easy answers, the search is not worth the bother. Other people might find something valid in religion, but not them. There might be something to faith after all, but they can't see it and they aren't going to hang around trying to find it.

As countless people can testify, this attitude is a delusion that leads to a dead end. For spiritual hunger in people is as strong as physical hunger. If somebody gives up trying to find satisfaction for his or her spiritual hunger, s/he will try to satisfy it from some other source - which, of course, is impossible. As a famous Christian named Augustine once said, "You have made us for yourself and our hearts are restless until they rest in you, O Lord." (*Confessions, Book I, Chap. 1*). He should have known since he had no time or use for religion at all when he was young. But he, like so many others, found out that just because somebody walks out of the Restaurant of Religions doesn't mean that his or her search for spiritual fulfillment ends. It goes on and on throughout a person's lifetime right up until that person is lying on her or his death bed - an inner emptiness that cries out to be filled; a wondering about why I am here and where I am going; a no-answer 'answer' to the tough questions of life; an inexplicable inability to be all that a person knows s/he could be or should be. No, even though there are so many dishes on the Menu, it's worth staying in the Restaurant to try and find the religion that will satisfy one's spiritual hunger if one hasn't found it already.

It's obvious that not all aspects of every religion can be right. For example, there's no resemblance whatsoever between the Allah of the Muslims and the nature gods of the Shintoists. Nor can one possibly reconcile the Hindu, Jain, Sikh and Buddhist ideas of salvation by Karma (earning it through good living) with the Christian idea of salvation by grace alone (receiving it as a free gift from God). Therefore, some aspects of at least some religions must be false.

The temptation is to think that if this is so, then none of the religions is worth believing. This doesn't follow. There are some aspects of every religion that may be true and that are therefore worth believing. The point is to find out which - to learn how to separate the sheep from the goats, so to speak.

There's also the possibility that one religion may be completely right! Wouldn't it be exciting if we could actually discover that this was the case!? This doesn't mean that all aspects of all other religions would then have proved to be false, since the one true religion could agree with and include and develop whatever was true in any of the other religions. Truth is truth no matter where it might be found. The second century Christian teacher Justin Martyr once said, "Whatsoever things have been rightly said by all men are the property of us Christians." (2 *Apology*, 13:4) Or, as it says in the Christian Bible, "Put all things to the test: keep what is good." 1 Thessalonians 5:21

For example, all of the major religions encourage people to be virtuous, not evil. Whatever in other religions truly helps people towards this end would be embraced by the one true religion. All religions believe something about some kind of a higher power. Whatever views about a higher power that are true would be a part of the teaching about God of the one true religion as well. In this sense, the one true religion would be the correction of what was not true in the other religions, the fulfiller of what *was* true in those religions and the developer of whatever truth was beyond the present scope of those religions.

The key question, of course, is this: *is* there such a religion? And if there is, how can somebody know for sure which one it is? It's obvious that there's no final answer to this question, no ultimate proof of the truth of any religion. As the English proverb has it, "The proof of the pudding is in the eating." That is, only as a person commits himself or herself to a certain religious belief, meets the living God through that commitment, and experiences new life as a result, can that person *know* intuitively *for sure* that s/he has found the truth. And even then, at times, s/he will have doubts. Nevertheless, there are ways in which we can measure the religions to determine which is most probably true, so that when we make such a commitment, it will be on the basis of a reasoned step and not merely some wild subjective leap in the dark hoping we might strike it lucky. What are the ways in which we can measure the world's religions?

1. Is the religion historically verifiable?

When Hindus themselves, for example, teach that their scriptures are collections of mythologies whose purpose is to serve as a vehicle through which people might come into contact with the great divine spirit, or Brahman, we know that we are not dealing with historical data that is verifiable using accepted methods of historical criticism. This means that such a religion demands a highly subjective leap of faith on our part to believe it is true.

2. Is the religion anti-scientific?

We've seen that the scientific method cannot be called upon to verify all aspects of reality. In this sense, *no* religion can be scientifically measured in full. Yet there are some aspects of each religion that can be tested in this way to ascertain whether it is more likely or less likely true. For example, it is a well-established fact that Taoists practice alchemy, magic and the like. During the Boxer Rebellion of 1900 in China, some Taoists believed their bodies would be immune to foreigner's bullets. Sadly, their dead bodies were a conclusive scientific proof that that belief was false.

3. Does the religion make sense?

Again, not all aspects of a religion will necessarily seem sensible or logical to human beings. After all, "God's thoughts are higher than our thoughts and his ways beyond our understanding." Isaiah 55:8 Yet there are some aspects of any religion that can be tested by reason, logic and common sense. For example, Sikhism arose in 1400 A.D. as a conscious attempt to harmonize the two most powerful rival religions in India. On the one hand, it emphasizes the stern anti-idolatrous monotheism of Islam, but on the other hand, it also teaches the vague mystic pantheism of Hinduism, with its notorious tendency towards polytheistic idolatry. Is this not a logical contradiction that defies the accepted norms of reason and common sense?

4. **Does the religion call people to the highest and the best in all respects?**

Every religion does this to some extent, but should not a true religion do so in *every* case? For example, Jainism has some praiseworthy aspects to it, but as far as women and the family are concerned, it has nothing but words of total condemnation. How can a religion that holds a position like that be all true?

5. **Does the religion provide the means for helping people be and do what it asks them to be and do?**

Most people would agree that much of Buddhist ethical teaching is most commendable. However, the problem is that people are simply called to follow the 'eight-fold path' without being given the spiritual power and resources necessary to do so. History teaches us that the human problem is not so much that people don't know what's right and good, but that they somehow can't find the spiritual strength to consistently *do* what's right and good. A religion that can't help people solve this problem doesn't contain all that an effective, true religion must contain.

6. **Is the religion universally applicable?**

That is, can any person of any race, culture, nation, sex, social class, economic status and age practice it? When we look at Shinto, for example, we would have to answer this question with a "no."

Shinto is so tied to Japanese culture and nationalism that it would be almost impossible for a non-Japanese to meaningfully practice it. How can a religion that is tailored for a particular people in a particular place be a candidate for the one true religion? It obviously can't.

7.   Did the founder of the religion practice what he preached?

If he didn't, why should we assume that what he taught is true and workable for others? For example, Mohammed, the founder of Islam, taught charity towards enemies, but took revenge against the Jews in Medina. He limited the number of wives Muslims could have to four, but removed the limit for himself by decreeing a special dispensation. Equally embarrassing questions hang over the character and the spiritual qualifications of the founders of several other religions as well.

8.   Does the religion forthrightly come to grips with the totality of reality?

In other words, does it have a sense of balance? The adherents of most faiths err in one way or another by taking a part and making it the whole; by pushing one aspect of reality to an extreme that results in the negation of another aspect. For example, secularists reject the intuitive as a mirage while mystics reject the empirical as an illusion. Confucian humanists insist that people are free to act, while deterministic Hindus see people as pawns in the hand of fate. Islam and the Pre-Literary Society religions view the Creator as so transcendent that he can't have a personal relationship with those he has created, while Hindus and Shintoists see the divine as so immanent that there's no distinction between creator and creation. Confucianists stress that as far as we know, this life is all there is and we should therefore concentrate on it, while Jains consider this life to be worthless and something we should try to escape from at the earliest opportunity.

9. **Does the religion have the concept of *grace* as its basis and at its core?**

Does the religion subject its adherents to the impossible rigor of having to *earn* their salvation in one way or another by placating the malevolent god/s or spirits and supplicating the benevolent god/s or spirits by what they do and/or offer? Or does it view salvation as a totally unearned *gift* of God to which humans have no claim and which they cannot merit so that the motivation for living a 'good life' comes as an act of *gratitude* for a salvation already received?

We return to our original question. Is there one true religion that's the correction of what's not true in other religions, the fulfillment of what *is* true in those religions and the development of whatever spiritual truth lies beyond the scope of those religions? In other words, is there any one of the world's major living religions that can pass *all* of these tests? *Is* there actually a religious path that truly leads home? Christians claim there is, and we shall see why they make such a claim in the next chapter.

What Do *You* Think?

1. I agree with/disagree with/am not sure about the conclusions of this chapter because ...

2. The religion that seems to me to offer the most to people is the _____ religion because ......

3. I agree/do not agree that spiritual hunger in people is as strong as physical hunger because ......

4. In my personal religious search, I have made good/some/little progress. Explain.

Chapter Four

WHAT'S SO UNIQUE ABOUT CHRISTIANITY?

> "Jesus is the one of whom the scripture says, 'The stone that you the builders despised turned out to be the most important of all.' Salvation is to be found through him alone; in all the world there is no one else whom God has given who can save us."
>
> Acts 4:11-12

Looking Through the Microscope |

From Pagan to Christian

From Pagan to Christian is a book written in 1959 by Lin Yu Tang, one of China's most famous writers, linguists and inventors of the twentieth century. Before his death in 1976, he had written some 26 books, published the most authoritative Chinese-English dictionary and invented the Chinese typewriter. He wrote a number of famous novels about Chinese life, but a number of his other titles suggest that he was a very scholarly man with an in-depth understanding of ancient and modern religious, philosophical and scientific thought in China and elsewhere. He, more than any other Chinese writer, succeeded in interpreting

Chinese thought, belief, culture and customs to the West.

Lin Yu Tang's father was a Christian minister in a small town in Fujian Province. He grew up in a Christian home and went to a Christian school in Xiamen, China. He later attended the then famous St John's College in Shanghai and went on to enter seminary in preparation for the Christian ministry. From this point on, people might think they know where this story is headed and what its outcome will be. They might think that he remained an ardent Christian, went on to become a Christian minister (along with all the other things he accomplished) and wrote books trying to persuade Chinese students to become Christians. But the opposite was the case!

The more he studied what he *thought* was 'Christianity,' the more disillusioned he grew with it until he dropped out of seminary and gave it up altogether. From that point on, he began a long journey through one religious, philosophical, or rational system after another, trying to find the truth in order to satisfy his intellectual honesty and his spiritual hunger. *From Pagan to Christian* is an account of that long and interesting journey that took almost half a century. In the end, as the title suggests, he came full circle and once again embraced the Christian faith, but this time with a new enthusiasm and depth of understanding born of long years of searching, comparing and testing.

In a chapter entitled "The Grand Detour Begins," Lin tells how he left Shanghai as a young Westernized intellectual to search for his Chinese roots in Peking (today's Beijing) where he took a post as a teacher at Tsing Hua University. He was furious at discovering how much of the richness of Chinese thought and life he had missed by being raised in the confines of the kind of Christian environment that had had a rather narrow view of life and a lack of appreciation for the wealth of Chinese wisdom and culture.

As he moved on in his career and in his search, he turned to one system of thought after another. He began in what he describes as "The Mansion of Confucius," soaking in the great ideas of social conduct and "the way of the mean" of the great master and of his later disciples, Tse-sze and Mencius. But he concludes, "One could be terribly tired of Reason; a properly rational society in which man always acted according to reason could be very boring to a grownup, just as a mansion, well scrubbed and well dusted and well ordered by a staff of efficient servants could be to a normal child. Man has feelings, and sometimes not unreasonable dreams. Therefore, Romanticism had to follow Rationalism." (pp. 105-106)

And so he immersed himself in the romanticism of Lao-tse, the founder of Taoism, and, most enthusiastically of Chuang-tse, one of Taoism's greatest thinkers. He describes this part of his quest in a chapter entitled "The Peak of Mount Tao." He was quite happy with what he found, but it wasn't enough, particularly in light of the degradation to which the lofty ideals of these philosophers had later been corrupted by popular religion. "The history of Taoism is a curious thing. Never was there greater degeneracy than from the height of Lao-tse's wisdom to the occultism, the magic, and the frightful spirits and demons of 'popular' Taoism." (p. 147)

From there it was on to the "Dissolving Mist of Buddhism." The investigation of Buddhism was no simple matter. Arriving in China around the time of the birth of Christ, Buddhist thought eventually evolved into some ten sects, eight of them belonging to what is known as the Mahayana school and two to the Hinayana school. Lin paid particular attention to the Shan sect's line of thought and looked at Zen Buddhism as well. After all was said and done, however, he came to this conclusion:

> If religion means that we must run away from this present, sentient life and 'escape' from it as fast as possible, like a rat abandoning a sinking ship, I am against it. One ought to, I think, with Chinese common sense, come to live with the world and make terms with it, bravely, in the sense of the acceptance of the grace of living ... And I feel strongly that so long as religion, *any* religion, clings to an otherworldliness, this tendency to deny and escape from this sentient life which God has given us so abundantly, we will, by doing so, by just so much prevent religion, *any* religion, from being in touch with the modern man's consciousness. We shall be in a true sense ungrateful children of God ... (p. 176)

Moving away from religion, he turned his mind to reason. Perhaps rationalism was the answer to the questions of origin, existence and behavior. Here too, however, he became more critical than accepting.

> In the realm of material knowledge or of scientific knowledge of facts, the tools of reasoning by the categories of time, space, motion and causation are supreme and unquestionable, whereas in the realm of significances and moral values - in religion and love and human relationships - this method is curiously unadapted to the purpose and in fact wholly irrelevant ... For religion ... is a gift of intuitive understanding by a man's whole consciousness, a total response to the universe by his moral nature...The war of the scientific temper and the religious temper is due to...the subjugation of the realm of moral knowledge to the methods suitable to the exploration of the realm of nature. (pp.177-178)

What about materialism? Would the views of Darwinians, Marxists and the anti-supernaturalists hold water? Again, his answer was "No."

> The general conflict of modern thought with religion stems from a materialistic interpretation of the universe, an interpretation that the entire universe can be explained mechanically by physical-chemical laws, without residue...Especially in the last few decades, spirit and matter have moved closer, largely through the new vistas opened up by science. And, strangely enough, the rapprochement is due to matter yielding ground to spirit rather than spirit yielding ground to matter. (pp. 197, 206)

Lin's journey had now been completed. New depth and insight had been gained along the way. What was the result? The last chapter is entitled, "The Majesty of Light." It begins,

> Blow out the candles! The sun is up!...The world of Jesus is the world of sunlight by comparison with that of all the sages

and philosophers and the schoolmen of any country...Jesus' teachings have that immediacy and clarity and simplicity which puts to shame all other efforts of men's minds to know God or to inquire after God...the world of Jesus contains both that power, and something else - the absolute clarity of light, without the self-limitation of Confucius, the intellectual analysis of Buddha, or the mysticism of Chuang-tse. Where others reasoned, Jesus taught, and where others taught, Jesus commanded ... Jesus communicated the feeling of the immediate knowledge and love of God, and further, immediately and without qualification, equated that love of God with obeying His commandment...Jesus' teachings are such that they cannot be affected by any changes in fashions of thought or in economic or physical concepts. (pp. 223, 225, 228)

What accounts for this dramatic return to the Christian faith after such a long excursus? Was it because Lin found no truth anywhere else? His entire book is a denial of that. It was simply that, as he said, compared to any other religious or secular ideas he encountered, the Christian faith was like the sun compared to candles. He finally 'saw the light,' and in the process met the living God.

(Note: this honest, witty and stimulating account is still available on Amazon.com for those who might be interested in reading this book for themselves).

What Do *You* Think?

1. What do you find most interesting in this account about Lin Yu Tang?

2. If you could ask Lin one question about his experience or his ideas, what would it be?

3. What do you think of his final conclusion?

4. Where would you describe yourself as being in your own quest for truth?

Bringing Things into Focus |

What's the Difference?

In your opinion, which of the four choices under each question is the correct one?

1. **What's the essential difference between the Christian faith and Buddhism?**

   a. Buddhism teaches the material world is evil, life is suffering and the goal is to escape our present existence, while the Christian faith teaches God created the world good, life can be renewed and the goal is to live fully and gratefully now and in the life to come.

   b. The emphasis in Buddhism is on inner spiritual renewal through divine power, while the emphasis in the Christian faith is on high ethical and moral standards.

   c. Buddhists don't believe in heaven and hell, but Christians do.

   d. Buddhism might be described as a religion of social activism, while Christianity might be described as a religion of self-gratification.

2. **What's the essential difference between the Christian faith and Islam?**

   a. Christians don't believe in drinking alcoholic beverages, while Muslims do.

   b. Christians believe God came in Jesus to make himself known and to save his world, while Muslims believe Jesus was merely a great prophet and teacher.

    c. Christians believe there's one true God, period, while Muslims believe the one true God has revealed himself in three persons.

    d. The Christian faith doesn't hold women in very high esteem, while Islam could be said to be a woman-emancipating faith.

3. **What's the essential difference between the Christian faith and Judaism?**

    a. Christians think people should worship on Saturday, while Jews believe they should worship on Sunday.

    b. Christians only accept the Old Testament as a revelation from God, while Jews accept the entire Bible as God's Word.

    c. Christians believe Jesus was God's promised Messiah (Savior), while Jews believe the Messiah has not yet come.

    d. Christians believe salvation comes through carefully obeying the law of God, while Jews believe salvation is an unearned free gift of God's grace.

4. **What's the essential difference between the Christian faith and Hinduism?**

    a. Hindus believe there's only one true God, while Christians believe one Great Spirit manifests itself through many gods.

    b. Hindus believe people live one life and then pass into the world to come, while Christians believe people pass through many lives in different forms before they finally pass into the realm of heavenly bliss.

    c. Hindus believe all people are created in God's image and are equally valuable, while Christians believe there are different grades of people (depending on what they did in their former life), and that people can't change from one grade to another until their next life (depending on what they do in this life).

    d. Hindus believe the way to salvation and heavenly bliss is to amass as much spiritual credit as possible through living a good life and doing good deeds, while Christians believe the way to salvation and eternal life is by accepting by faith the free gift of salvation and new life made possible by God's son who gave his life as a sacrifice on their behalf.

5. **What's the essential difference between the Christian faith and Shinto?**

    a. Christians believe that as the Creator, God is distinguishable from his creation, while Shintoists believe that nature itself consists of thousands of gods.

    b. Christians believe their message is aimed at a particular people in a particular place, while Shintoists believe their message is universally applicable and available to all.

    c. Christians believe their sacred scriptures do not necessarily reflect historical events, while Shintoists believe their sacred scriptures do reflect such events.

    d. Christianity does not have a specific historical person as its founder, while Shinto does.

6. **What's the essential difference between the Christian faith and the Sikh faith?**

    a. Sikhs believe the one true God has revealed himself and

is personally knowable, while Christians believe God is an inscrutable, mysterious, mystical being who has manifested himself in many different forms.

b. Sikhs believe the world and life are basically good and can be enjoyed, while Christians believe the world and life are basically evil and need to be escaped.

c. Sikhs believe men can cut their hair, while Christians believe they can't and must wear turbans over their uncut hair as a sign of their faith.

d. Sikhs believe people are helpless, submissive creatures who simply accept their fate, while Christians believe people can be freed for creative living and action and can often make a difference in the way things turn out.

7. **What's the essential difference between the Christian faith and Zoroastrianism?**

a. Zoroastrians believe Evil Forces and a good God are locked in an equal power struggle, while Christians believe God is supreme, has already ensured the defeat of evil and is in the process of completing that defeat.

b. Zoroaster taught that he who takes up the sword shall die by the sword, while Christ advocated spreading the Christian faith by armed conquest.

c. Zoroastrians place great emphasis on the importance of inner faith, while Christians place great emphasis on the importance of ritual ceremonies.

d. Zoroastrianism can be said to be a missionary religion, while Christianity can be said to be a complacent religion.

8. **What's the essential difference between the Christian faith and Jainism?**

   a. Women are elevated in Jainism, while in Christianity they are utterly condemned.

   b. The Jains are vegetarians, while Christians believe that both plants and animals can be eaten.

   c. Christians are forbidden to take life at any level, while Jains would think nothing of killing a mosquito, for example.

   d. Christians believe people should suppress their vile bodies in order to liberate their pure souls, while Jains believe the body is a gift of God that should be cherished, cared for and enjoyed.

9. **What's the essential difference between the Christian faith and Taoism?**

   a. Christians practice magic, witchcraft, alchemy and the like, while Taoists don't.

   b. Taoists teach God is an impersonal, mystical, inactive, indescribable being, while Christians teach the opposite.

   c. Taoists are activists, while Christians are conformists.

   d. Christians believe in immortality, heaven and hell, but Taoists don't.

10. **What's the essential difference between the Christian faith and Confucianism?**

   a. Confucianists believe people as they are, are capable of right conduct based on right knowledge while Christians believe people need an inner conversion from selfishness to self-giving love through the power of God in order to be and do what they know they should be and do.

b. Christians concentrate on preserving what is, while Confucianists concentrate on improving what is.

c. Confucianists believe people will be held responsible for their conduct in a future judgment, while Christians say nothing about this subject.

d. The foundational principle of Confucianism is self-giving love, while the foundational principle of Christianity is personal propriety.

11. **What's the essential difference between the Christian faith and the Baha'i faith?**

a. Adherents of Baha'i believe there's only one true faith in one true God, while Christians believe all religions lead to God.

b. Christians believe God is one, while adherents of Baha'i believe there's one God who has expressed himself in three persons.

c. Adherents of Baha'i believe God revealed himself through the founders of the various faiths, while Christians believe God uniquely revealed himself through the person of Jesus Christ alone.

d. Christians believe God is transcendent and inaccessible, while adherents of Baha'i believe people can have a personal relationship with a personal God who is accessible to them.

What Do *You* Think?

1. Which of the above religions do you think has the most in common with the Christian faith, and why?

2. Which of the above religions do you think has the least in common with the Christian faith, and why?

3. In light of the above, what would you say to a person who believes that "all religions lead to God?"

4. Do you think Christians are intolerant when they insist their faith is the one true path to the one true God? Why or why not?

Gaining a Perspective |

Christian Claims

Following is a list of quotations from the Bible that Christians believe show there is something unique about the Christian faith.

- Jesus' disciple John wrote, "No one has ever seen God. The only Son (Jesus Christ), who is the same as God and is at the Father's side, he has made him known." John 1:18

- Jesus said, "...those who drink the water that I will give them will never be thirsty again. The water that I will give them will become in them a spring which will provide them with life-giving water and give them eternal life." John 4:14

- Jesus said, "...those who hear my words and believe in him who sent me have eternal life. They will not be judged, but have already passed from death to life." John 5:24

- Jesus said, "I am the bread of life. Those who come to me will

never be hungry; those who believe in me will never be thirsty."
John 6: 35

- Jesus said, "I am the light of the world. Whoever follows me will have the light of life and will never walk in darkness." John 8:12

- Jesus said, "I am the gate. Those who come in by me will be saved; they will come in and go out and find pasture...I have come in order that you might have life - life in all its fullness...I am the good shepherd who is willing to die for the sheep." John 10:9-11

- "Jesus said, "I am the resurrection and the life. Those who believe in me will live, even though they die; and those who live and believe in me will never die." John 11:25-26

- Jesus said, "I am the way, the truth, and the life; no one goes to the Father except by me...Whoever has seen me has seen the Father...I am in the Father, and the Father is in me." John 14:6,10

- Jesus said, "I am the vine, you are the branches. Whoever remains in me, and I in him, will bear much fruit; for you can do nothing without me." John 15:5

- Jesus said to his disciples, "The world will make you suffer. But be brave! I have defeated the world!" John 16:33

- Jesus' disciple John wrote, "God has given us eternal life, and this life has its source in his Son. Whoever has the Son has this life; whoever does not have the Son of God does not have life." 1 John 5:11-12

- Jesus' apostle Paul wrote, "God was making all human beings his friends through Christ. God did not keep an account of their sins, and he has given us the message which tells how he makes them his friends." 2 Corinthians 5:18-19

- Jesus' disciple Peter said, "Salvation is to be found through (Jesus) alone; in all the world there is no one else whom God has given who can save us.'" Acts 4:12

What Do *You* Think?

1. Do you believe these statements are true or false? Why or why not?

2. Which six of these statements do you think most strongly support the Christian claim that the Christian faith is unique? Explain your choices.

3. Some people believe that all religions are equally valid and are simply different paths to the same God. Do these statements support or deny that idea? Explain.

4. On the basis of these statements, do you think Jesus was a liar, a lunatic, a legend or the Lord he claimed to be? Explain.

Drawing Conclusions |

Does the Christian Faith Truly Lead Home?

At the end of chapter three, we said Christians believe the Christian faith is the one true faith, is the correction of what's not true in other religions, is the fulfillment of what *is* true in those religions and is the development of whatever spiritual truth lies beyond the scope of those religions. If true, this would be very good news indeed! Our search for truth would be rewarded and our spiritual hunger would be satisfied. But *is* it true? Is the Christian faith truly the path that leads home? Christians believe it is, but on what do they base that belief?

Christians base that belief on their conviction that the Christian faith passes *all nine* tests that can be used to show which of the religions is most probably true, while no other religion can do so.

1. The Christian faith is historically verifiable.

Seventy-five years ago, few would have dared say that too loudly. By then, the Bible had come under large-scale attack by skeptical historians. It was charged, for example, that Abraham could never have existed, since the civilization he was described as having been a part of was unknown as early as 2,000 B.C. It was said that Moses could not have written one word of the first five books of the Bible, since writing had not yet been invented by 1400 B.C. It was alleged that many of the geographical facts, names of government officials, and other data mentioned in the Bible were in error since they didn't tally with known historical data. And there was more.

However, through the modern sciences of archaeology, paleontology, philology, anthropology, geography and historiography, these wrong-headed, ill-informed and biased judgments have been reversed. The historical data of the Christian scriptures has been shown today to be as fully accurate as that of any other ancient historical source (and in some cases even more so). For example, the historical evidence that Jesus Christ actually lived is even stronger than the evidence that the Roman Emperor, Julius Caesar, ever existed.

Compared to all the other religions of the world, the Christian faith is not unique because it advocates a major philosophical idea (although it has some brilliant ones) or a great ethical principle (although it has some outstanding ones like the Ten Commandments and the Golden Rule) or even because it tells a compelling story (since other faiths have fascinating mythologies). It is that the Christian story actually happened in history! The gifted writer Dorothy Sayers once said, "Jesus is the only God with a date in history," and the great mythologist C. S. Lewis once remarked, "In the Christian faith, myth became fact." Donald Williams, an editor of *Touchstone* Magazine puts it this way: "Nobody knows when Krishna appeared as an avatar of Vishnu, but Jesus was born when Quirinius was governor of Syria, and he was crucified under Pontius Pilate. Christianity has its legends, but the life of Jesus is not one of them. Like the Exodus from Egypt which preceded it, it was history and it changed history." (*Touchstone* May/June 2015, p. 6)

2. The Christian faith is not anti-scientific.

As far as the scientific method can legitimately be used to test certain aspects of the claims of a religion, the Christian faith is found to be authentic. It is true that the Bible is filled with events that are popularly termed 'miraculous,' but nowhere does Jesus Christ teach, practice, or condone anti-scientific superstition. It's also true that the Bible contains outdated scientific views and physical data that, from our 21st century perspective, we would term erroneous, but nowhere do the Bible writers teach those views or present that data as religious truth to be believed for all time. Their outdated understanding of the universe at the time they wrote is simply the context within which the timeless truths of the Christian faith are presented. The context has changed, but the truths have not.

3. The Christian faith makes sense.

Lin Yu Tang returned to the Christian faith because he began to concentrate on what Jesus said more than on what others said about Jesus. What he found most convincing was that all that Jesus said rang so true to life. Jesus authoritatively and unhesitantly faced up to the hard questions and the real problems of real life. He didn't spin idealistic theories or dwell on speculation. His teaching had a compelling logic and timeless relevance that convinced a thinking person like Lin that, as a Christian, he could be both intellectually honest and sincerely devout - even in the atomic age.

4. The Christian faith calls people to the highest and the best in all respects.

If there's anything that even many non-religious people agree on, it is that Jesus calls for the best as far as the dignity of persons, the sanctity of relationships, the meaning of life, the call to service and sacrifice, and a lot more is concerned. Who could point out any teaching or practice of Jesus that brought or could bring harm to people? Whether it is the dignity of women, the wrongness of prejudice, the call to peaceful relationships based on self-giving love, forgiveness and acceptance, the development of inner virtue, and the like, Jesus is always found to be on the right side of the issue, and calling on others to be on that side as well.

5. The Christian faith provides the means for helping people be and do what it asks them to be and do.

Some religions have rather lofty ethical and moral teaching. Their chief problem, however, is that they ask us to do the impossible. That is, without a fundamental change of nature, we too often simply can't seem to do what we know we should do. The great philosopher, Immanuel Kant, made one of his most serious errors when he coined the phrase, "I ought, therefore I can." Our own experience teaches us that this isn't a true assumption.

The Christian God is one who also knows that this isn't a true assumption, and he's done something about it. He's come in the person of Jesus to give people forgiveness and new life - a life in which his Spirit brings about a change in our nature so that we can more and more do the 'ought' that he calls us to do. In this view, to be a Christian doesn't mean to be a moral weakling, but a saved realist, while to be a non-Christian doesn't mean to be a moral giant, but a lost idealist.

6. The Christian faith is universally applicable.

Why did the Christian faith spread so rapidly in the ancient world in such a short time? Why is it today a faith that can truly be called a *world* religion? Simply because people of every race, culture, sex, age, nation, occupation, social position, or economic situation can say, "That's the faith for me." Jesus Christ challenges, forgives, calls and saves *whoever* comes to him. *All* people can be his friends, his brothers/sisters, his disciples, his witnesses and God's children. The Christian fellowship is world-embracing and all-inclusive. Its aim is to bring people together - to reconcile them with God and with one another.

7. The founder of the Christian faith practiced what he preached.

Some people may disagree with some of Jesus' ideas, but they can never call him a hypocrite. He preached simplicity, and he lived it. He preached service, and he gave it. He preached love and compassion, and he demonstrated it. He preached sacrifice, and he did not flinch when the time came to offer it. He knew that if he said what he believed, it would lead to his certain death, but he said it anyway. Some people have become his followers simply because for them, he was the only person in history who completely "put his money where his mouth was." If Jesus was anything, he was completely, 100% genuine.

8. The Christian faith comes to grips with the totality of reality.

The Christian faith has a sense of *balance*. It doesn't take a part of the truth and make it the whole truth by pushing one aspect of reality to an extreme that results in the negation of another aspect. For example, it takes into account the reality of both the intuitive and the empirical. It recognizes that people are free to act and therefore responsible, but also acknowledges the sovereignty of a God that is actively involved in bringing about his purposes in history and in the world. It teaches that the Creator is transcendent but that he can have a personal relationship with those he has created. At the same time, it acknowledges that although in Jesus Christ the divine became immanent, there's a definite distinction between the Creator and his creation. It stresses that this life is valuable and that we should invest in living it to the full, but that the life to come will be an even more fulfilling experience

9. The Christian faith has the concept of *grace* as its basis and at its core?

There are a number of significant words that could be used to sum up the Christian faith: 'love', 'joy', 'peace',' hope' and 'forgiveness' to name a few. But the key word that sets the Christian faith apart from any other faith is the word 'grace.' Other religions focus on what people must *do* to either influence their benevolent god(s) to grant them forgiveness, healing, good fortune, wealth, etc. or to ward off their malevolent god(s) to keep them from harming them through illness, bad luck, death and the like. With the Christian faith, it's the other way around. The Christian good news is that before a person has done *anything*, God has already acted in Christ to do *everything* that is necessary for forgiveness, for renewal, for salvation. "God has shown us how much he loves us," writes the Apostle Paul. "It was while we were still sinners that Christ died for us! By his blood we are now put right with God." Romans 5:8 In other words, there's nothing one can do to *deserve* one's salvation with all the benefits that it brings. Nor can people bribe God to forgive them and in some way to *buy* their salvation. It's his free *gift* of grace that can only be *accepted*.

Even after a person has accepted this gift by faith and has become a follower of Jesus Christ, even then the motivation for living a Christian life is not to influence God to be merciful, to forgive, to love, to bless, but to express heartfelt gratitude for all that God has given and continues to freely give to his people. This is why Paul in his letter to the Romans, after explaining why people need to be saved and how they can be saved, spends the last third of that letter encouraging Christians to live a life that is pleasing to God, that is meaningful to them and that is helpful to others as an *offering of thanksgiving* to this God of grace. (See Romans 12-16)

The Christian faith is centered in a person.

By now it's become evident that what's most special about the Christian faith isn't a set of religious dogmas, or an ethical system, or a social service rationale, but a person - Jesus Christ. This is why this faith is called the *CHRIST*ian faith. It all stands or falls with him. In most other religions, people attempt to somehow find God, or a system of truth, or an ethical formula - and to save themselves in the process, which is why they've lost the way. The Christian faith is the reverse - God coming in search of us in the person of Jesus.

Through him, God lets us know what he's like, calls us to become what he originally intended us to be, and does what realistically needed to be done for us and in us to make this possible. The image Jesus left with the world is the cross. His atoning death on the cross stands unique among all other world religions. Many of them have gods, but only one has a God who cared enough to become a human being and die for his creation.

But was Jesus of Nazareth really who he claimed to be and did he really do what he claimed he had come to do? (If you need to recall what those claims were, read over the above list of statements once again.) He could have simply been a **legend**, invented by his followers. But we've seen that reliable historical evidence says otherwise.

He could have been a **lunatic** suffering from grand delusions. But does a lunatic teach the way he did and act the way he did? Hardly! And would brilliant thinkers like Lin Yu Tang, and the thousands of others like him who have become Jesus' followers down through the centuries, be taken in by the ravings of a lunatic? Again, hardly!

He could have been history's greatest **liar**, knowing all along that he really wasn't who he said he was and that he really couldn't save and renew *himself*, let alone the world. But does he sound and act like a liar? And do liars usually lie themselves right onto a cross? Once more, hardly! And if he actually *was* a liar, even only about some things, why would *anybody* want to call him a great moral teacher and the world's number one example of genuine sincerity? You can't have it both ways. Either he spoke the whole truth that must be believed in its entirety, or he was a total fake and should be repudiated as such.

Christians believe that the obvious conclusion is that he must have been who he said he was - the **Lord**; and he must have done what he said he had come to do - bring forgiveness and new life to the world. *He* is what is special about Christianity. *He* is the one who calls both religious and non-religious people to the true and fulfilling faith and life that he came to make possible - a life of fellowship with God and of harmony with others through a relationship with him.

What Do *You* Think?

1. Do you agree that the Christian faith passes all nine of the above tests? Why or why not?

2. Which claim do you find most compelling, and why?

3. Which claim do you find least compelling, and why?

4. Which claims do you feel you need more information about, and why?

How Can Christians Relate to People of Other Faiths?

As we've said, Christianity's claim to having all the truth or light doesn't mean other Faiths have no truth or light. Christians have an obligation to search for and affirm that truth and light. They should also realize that the Christian Faith is as bewildering in terms of doctrines, interpretations, schools, sects, movements and historical ambiguity to people of other Faiths as their Faith is to them.

Like other Faiths, the Christian Faith also has tensions and tentative 'answers' in dealing with difficult issues like suffering, evil, Hell and the like. Some aspects of other Faiths may be based on superstitions, mythology, cultural influences, and the like, but Christians too need to deal with popular superstitions, mythology and cultural influences that have at times distorted the teaching and practice of their own Faith. Christians also need to acknowledge that some teaching and practices of other Faiths can at times enrich and/or correct distortions in the Christian Faith.

Christians don't have a right to share their Faith unless they have first made a serious effort to learn about and understand another person's Faith. Any 'sharing in the dark' will be unproductive and even an affront to a person of another Faith. It will be a sharing that will not be directed to that person's felt needs, will fail to utilize his/her spiritual and cultural context, and will not be based on a relationship of understanding and respect.

Reasons Why Christians Can Affirm the Truth/Light/Revelation that Adherents of Other Faiths Have Received and Responded to.

Christians understand that God has not left himself without a witness. Every one of his children has received and is responsible for some light at some level. (See John 1:4; Acts 14:17; 17:23-28; Romans 1:18-23; Hebrews 1:1). God's will is that every one of his children should realize the fullness of life that he intended when he created him or her. (See 1 Timothy 2:1-6; 4:10; Titus 2:11-14; Hebrews 2:9; 2 Peter 3:9). God grieves over every child of his who refuses his gifts of grace, even over children like Saddam Hussein Osama Bin Laden. (See Psalm 78:40-41; 81:11-12; 116:15; Hosea 11:1-9; Luke 13:34ff; 19:41ff).

God's power to create and sustain the cosmos is awesome, but his most awesome and mysterious power is his capacity, as the Parent of every human being (and particularly of those who spurn his grace and are intent on pursuing a course of self-destruction) to suffer. From the failure of his first daughter and son (Eve and Adam) until today, his shoulders have been broad enough to bear all the grief, sorrows, waywardness and rebellion of his children. His love has never wavered, and he continues to stand on the road with his arms outstretched calling all his daughters and sons (whether rebels on the 'outside' or on the 'inside') 'home.' (See Luke 15:18-24, 29-32) The cross, the ultimate concentration of his suffering on behalf of all of his children, is at the same time totally mysterious and totally wonderful. The depth and breadth of his suffering demonstrate the breadth and depth of his all-embracing love. (See Romans 5:6-11).

God's children have seen and responded to God's light/truth/revelation at different levels. The crucial factor is whether they've been open to God *at that level* and continue to be open for further light when they see it. Paul's argument for the Jew/Gentile situation of the first century is directly applicable to the

Christian/non-Christian situation in our time. (See Romans 2:14-29 and read 'gospel' for 'law,' 'Hindu' for 'Gentile,' 'Christian' for 'Jew,' 'baptism' for 'circumcision' and 'live out' for 'obey.') Romans 1:18-32, and other passages like it, don't describe non-Christians indiscriminately, but are speaking only of those non-Christians (unlike those described in chapter 2) who are closing themselves to the level of light they have with the resultant evil effects on their lives. There's a difference between a Gandhi and a Mao Tse-tung!

All of God's children are held accountable to positively respond to, and live according to, the level of light they've received. They'll experience the blessings of life in that light or the self-judgments and consequences of living in the dark, depending on their choices. (See Romans 1:3-9; 2:25-29; Luke 12:47-48) This same principle holds true *within* the visible Christian community as well as outside of it. Christians are also described as not totally walking in the light. (See Titus 1:10-16, for example). For this reason, the imperative mood is a major mood in the New Testament urging Christians on to spiritual growth and development. (See Philippians 2:12-16, for example).

The Dynamic Character of 'Faith.'

Like people of other faiths, Christians are also in the process of opening or closing their lives to the light in the dynamic flux of life in their relationship to God, and taking responsibility for the same. As with those at a different level of light, the question is whether the dominant flow of a person's life, at the level of light s/he has, is moving towards God or away from him, opening to him or closing to him. There are those whose faith flow at their level of light is dominated by openness mixed with a little closedness, and vice versa. However, things are never static, but dynamic. At times the little closedness in a 'believer' and the little openness in an 'unbeliever' (at whatever level of light they happen to be) waxes or wanes depending on the response to the ups and downs of life. For example, the distraught father's response to Jesus: "Lord, I believe. Help my unbelief!" Mark. 9:24. Or the hesitation of an atheist: "All religion is superstition, but then again, I wonder." At times, the littleness of belief in an 'unbeliever' or of unbelief in the 'believer' gains momentum to the point of completely reversing the flow. The small openness overcomes the closedness and the person opens up to the light at his/her level and blossoms accordingly, or vice versa.

Faith is never a static entity in the Bible. The paradox of faith is that as soon as somebody thinks s/he has it 'in the bag,' s/he discovers that s/he is on the way to reversing the flow in his or her life in the direction of unbelief! (See Luke 18:9-14). This dynamic quality of faith as a lived-out experience of struggle with unbelief is reflected in Paul's statement in Romans 7:14-25. A close study of the lives of the apostles demonstrates that in the heat of life, even after the events of Pentecost, even *they* experienced the waxing and waning of belief (openness) and unbelief (closedness). (See Acts 15:36-41 and Galatians 2:11-14, for example).

Why a person succumbs to unbelief or closedness or heading towards the dark, is shrouded in the mysterious irrationality of evil that even the wisdom of *God* can't penetrate. (God must still be scratching his head over *why* Adam and Eve did what they did when they had every reason not to). Why a person responds to the Light, however, is very clear. God has illuminated the path ahead so that a person can see that it leads towards the realization of the potential for the full life for which s/he yearns and for which s/he has been created. (See John 10:10). So the point is not whether a person has 'heard' all there is to know about the Christian faith in order to qualify for the Kingdom of God, but whether at the level of light that person has received, his or her 'faith flow' is moving in the right direction.

We might use the illustration of a mountain to clarify this picture of God's children being acceptable to him if their faith flow is moving in the right direction at the level of light they have. At the tip of the mountain is God in all his blazing Light. At the bottom of the mountain is total darkness. There are paths (religions or faiths) leading from the bottom part way up the mountain - away from the darkness and towards the Light. Some of these paths go higher than others do. The higher a path goes, the more light there is. All paths, except one narrow, tortuous one, eventually end at paths going *around* the mountain. The only way from these circuitous paths to the top is via the narrow one. The Christian mission is to help people on the other paths find the way around to and up the narrow path.

Some people won't even begin the climb towards the light from the bottom, but resolutely turn their backs on *any* path and prefer to remain in darkness. (See John 3:19-20). Others start up, but eventually turn around and head back with the same result. Some, however, keep climbing as far as they can during their lifetime, always desiring to face the Light they have and to find more. (See John 3:21). Some make their way to and begin up the narrow way. Still others are born at the entrance to the narrow way. Many go up it, but some head downwards towards the dark or wander off on one of the other paths. (See Matthew 7:13-14). Those who head towards the Light become increasingly aware of the fact that their progress towards the top has only been made possible by the *Source* of the Light that illumines the path and that (in Christ) comes down to meet them along the way to make it possible for them to continue their journey towards the top. (See Ephesians 2:4-10).

What Blocks God's Light from Getting through to All People.

What keeps God's full light from fully getting through to all he wants to save so that they might experience the fullness of life he intended - namely to *all* his children?

- **His self-limiting love.** To *force* his light and love upon those who prefer darkness would be to destroy them as persons. God is willing to risk losing his children by giving them the freedom to walk away from him because he knows that a coerced relationship is no relationship. (See Mark 10:17-23).

- **The Forces of Evil.** God is involved in a very real struggle with the F.O.E. whose aim is to perpetuate darkness. (See John 1:5). Although God will be the ultimate victor, there are times when, and places where, he can't act without destroying the basis on which his Kingdom is being built in this age - freedom and faith. (See Mark 6:5-6). At times the F.O.E. intensify and erupt in society and in individuals (e.g., the Holocaust, illness, death), and the struggle waxes and wanes. The major power God has in overcoming the F.O.E. is the power of loving suffering (as concentrated in the cross) which he himself supremely underwent in Christ (See Matthew 27:46) and which he continues to undergo when his children go astray, suffer calamities or reject him.

- **The strategy of the Kingdom**. It's not always obvious to the 'troops' in the front lines, who are caught in the realities of the struggle of life, that there's an overall coherent strategy for the winning of the war against the F.O.E., (or on a more positive note, a strategy for the establishment of the Kingdom of God and the renewal of all creation). What's called for is faith in the Commander whose general strategy is not always specifically apparent to all people in their particular situation. (See Isaiah 55:8-9).

  Why God, for example, decided that the best strategy for spreading his light to the human race would be primarily through the Jews rather than through some other people like the Chinese is not immediately apparent, especially to the Chinese! However, God sees the 'big picture,' and we don't. The main point here is that he doesn't hold the Chinese, for example, responsible for responding to more light than they had/have at any particular moment in history. That is, he doesn't hold them responsible for knowing, and acting on the basis of, a general strategy that they wouldn't have had more than a vague clue about.

- **The frailty of those he depends on to carry out his mission in the world**. (See Galatians 2:11-12). God decided to carry out most of his mission of bringing wholeness to the whole of his creation through the followers of Jesus; that is, through people who believe, but who are still 'on the way' as far as their spiritual development is concerned. As a result, the history of the Church is a mixture of advances and retreats.

  The good news that Christians can share with the adherents of other faiths (including 'faiths' like atheism, secularism) is that although they've received and responded to some light, there's always more light that leads in the direction of the fullness of life that Jesus Christ offers to all. Christians share this good news not as superiors, but in great humility. They recognize that Christ has revealed the light of God most fully, but that there's more to be known about God than even Christians have yet been exposed to. (See Revelation 21:1-4, 22-27; 1 Corinthians 13:12). Nor have Christians fully apprehended the light that they've received (and, in fact, have too often distorted it). (See Acts 15:36-41; 1 Corinthians 14:23; 1:1-13; 15:12).

What Christians Can Offer People of Other Faiths.

The basic light Christians have to offer is the Good News that God-in-Christ set the whole human race free *from* the power of evil, suffering, death, fear, guilt, darkness and meaninglessness *for* a life that is whole, full, free and meaningful, and that has a hopeful and purposeful future. (See Romans 8:1-11). Jesus' death and resurrection accomplished that. He was, and is, God's YES to all of humanity. (See 2 Corinthians 1:19-20). Jesus' sacrifice set all people free from the curse of the 'first Adam's' act and the power of evil. Because of this, every person is again free to make Adam's decision of whether to receive God's gracious free gift and remain free, in the light, redeemed, a friend of God, saved, *or* whether to rebel and choose darkness and all its consequences all over again. The only sin that will condemn a person is the sin of unbelief - an irrational refusal of God's grace that results in 'death,' self-condemnation and destruction. (See John 3:18-21). In this sense, the 'Second Adam' (Christ) gives the 'sons and daughters of Adam' a second chance. (See Romans 5:15-19). The acceptance of God's gift in the present doesn't *effect* a person's salvation, but merely *affirms, appropriates* and *makes experiential* what's already been accomplished once and for all by Christ in the past. (See Ephesians 2:4-10). This inclusive redemption through Christ is the one and only basis on which people, responding on any level to the amount of light they had or have at that level (whether they're specifically aware of the Christ event or not), are accepted by God. (See Acts 4:12).

<u>What Do *You* Think?</u>

1. Do you think Christians should try to persuade people of other faiths to become Christians? Why or why not?

2. Do you agree that God will accept people according to the level of the light that they are exposed to? Why or why not?

3. Do you agree that God's light is sometimes blocked from getting through to people? Explain.

4. Do you agree with the principle that the more light a person is exposed to, the more responsibility that person has to respond to it? Explain.

Chapter Five

WHO CAN ANSWER THESE QUESTIONS?

> "'My thoughts,' says the Lord, 'are not like yours, and my ways are different from yours. As high as the heavens are above the earth, so high are my ways and thoughts above yours.'"   Isaiah 55:8-9

Looking Through the Microscope |

Focus On Religion

Host: "Good evening ladies and gentlemen. Welcome to another telecast of the 'Focus on Religion' series. During the past few months we've had a series of programs aimed at airing the pros and cons of religious belief in general and belief in Christianity in particular. Tonight we're going to concentrate on the reasons why some people have particular difficulty in believing in the Christian faith. With me in the studio are five distinguished guests: Mr. Daniel Bishop from the Universal Atheists Society; Ms. Sophie Campbell from the American Agnostics Association, Mr. John Kay from the Movement to Stamp out Superstition, Mr. Peter Daniels from the Secular Humanist Organization and Ms. Josephine Douglas from the Coalition to Ban Religion from Public Schools. Panelists, welcome to 'Focus on Religion.'"

All: "Thank you ... thank you very much."

Host: "During the past few weeks, we've been interviewing a number of distinguished Christian theologians, Church leaders, and Christians from all walks of life. We've asked them to explain what they conceive the Christian faith to be and to give reasons why they believe it to be true. Out of fairness to this topic, we've invited you here tonight to express your opinions on the subject and to present, as it were, 'the other side of the coin.' You're well known for *not* believing in the Christian faith. Can you tell our viewers some of the reasons why you find it difficult to believe in the Christian God, for example? Mr. Bishop, perhaps you could start it off."

Mr. Bishop: "Sure. Let me say immediately that I believe every person is entitled to his or her own opinion and that I respect that right. I admire many people who are ardent Christians and feel that they sometimes state their case for religious faith quite well. However, I simply can't agree with many of their conclusions and feel they often give evasive and shaky answers to the most difficult questions people ask them about 'God.'

"For example, if, as they say, there's a 'God' who's eternal, righteous and all-powerful and who created the whole of the cosmos good, then how did evil get started and why did he ever permit it? Don't you think it strange that a good 'God' who had control over everything would allow something to arise that would foul up what he'd made and thwart the plans he had for it? I find that it makes more sense to believe in no 'God' at all than to believe in a so-called 'God' who would be that foolish or that weak."

Host: "Ms. Campbell?"

Ms. Campbell: "Many people in my Association are also disturbed about this problem of evil that Mr. Bishop raises. However, we're not so much concerned about where evil comes from, but why 'God,' if there is a 'God,' doesn't put a stop to it. I mean, here you have a 'God' who's supposed to be all-knowing, all-wise, all-powerful and perfectly good. As such, he's said to hate evil and to punish those who do it. But why doesn't he just put a stop to it altogether? Why doesn't he simply do what needs to be done to change people or compel people so that they will live in unselfish harmony and peace together? I very much hope there is a 'God'...I think we certainly need one! But this question bothers me very much."

Host: "Mr. Kay?"

Mr. Kay: "I would like to follow that one step further. That this so-called all-powerful, just 'God' doesn't immediately put a stop to evil is a serious problem. But an even more serious one is why such a 'God' allows *good* people to suffer! I mean, pain and suffering and injustice might make some 'sense' if it only fell on the heads of those who caused it by doing wrong. However, much of the time it falls on the heads of perfectly innocent people who don't in any way deserve it. And not only that, the very people who cause innocent people these problems are often the ones who seem to prosper most! How could a just 'God,' for example, allow a man to enjoy a life of ease and luxury that's been made possible by underpaying his workers, or robbing others of their possessions, or paying bribes to high officials, and the like? A 'God' like that just wouldn't be worth believing in. And belief in a 'God' like that is, in my opinion, a superstition that needs to be wiped out."

Host: "Mr. Daniels?"

Mr. Daniels: "My question is this: what about people who've never had an opportunity to hear what Christian's describe as 'the way of salvation?' Perhaps they're even people who believe in some kind of a 'god' in another religion and are living decent moral and ethical lives - lives that sometimes put

Christians to shame. Is 'God' going to knock these innocent people over the head just because they don't exactly believe what Christians think they ought to believe?"

Host: "Mrs. Douglas?"

Mrs. Douglas: "What most bothers me about Christianity is what it teaches about salvation. It puzzles me why this 'God' should have waited untold years until he made himself known to Abraham, then 2,000 more years until he sent a 'savior,' then 2,000 more years before people in all nations had a chance to hear about him, and who knows how many more years before he will complete what Christians call his plan to save whoever he's going to save. Why such a long drawn out, round-about process that in the end won't even save all of the people but only some of the people anyway? And how could one man's death possibly have 'paid for' all the sins that have ever been committed by everybody? Why doesn't 'God' just declare a general amnesty and be done with it instead of playing out this long, traumatic historical drama?

"These questions make it impossible for me to accept Christianity, although there's much that's good about it. And questions like these are one of the reasons why our Coalition is against the teaching of Christianity or any other religion in the schools. It only fills young people's minds with misleading data and confuses them."

Host: "Thank you for being so frank. Are there any other questions that you would like to raise?"

Ms. Campbell: "Yes. I've had quite an interest in Christianity and have done a lot of reading in the Bible. Much of what I've read has been uplifting and helpful, but some of it has been confusing and contradictory. Take 'God,' for example. In the Old Testament he's described as being a distant, holy, powerful tyrant who orders people to kill their children and wage holy wars on their neighbors - wars whose objective is to wipe out those neighbors, right down to the last man, woman and child.

"In the New Testament he's described as being a present, loving, merciful Father who doesn't want any to perish, but all to have eternal life. Christians say that this is one and the same 'God' How can this be?"

Mrs. Douglas: "I have another question that's always bothered me about the Christian idea of 'God.' If, as Christians claim, 'God' knows everything that's going to happen in the future, then everything is determined ahead of time and life and history lose all meaning. What will be, will be, so why bother, and who can be held responsible?

If on the other hand, 'God' *doesn't* know what's going to happen in the future, how can he be in control, be working things out according to his plan, be all-knowing, all-powerful and all-wise? I don't see how Christians can escape this dilemma."

Mr. Kay: "Christians say they believe in *one* God. And yet the Bible talks about a 'Father God, a 'Jesus God' and a 'Holy Spirit God.' To say, as they do, that each of these 'gods' is a separate person in his own right, but that at the same time they all join together to make up one God is to my mind a sheer logical contradiction. You can't have it both ways.

At least the Muslims are consistent on this point in their insistence that there's only one God and that Jesus was one of his greatest prophets, but not divine."

Mr. Bishop: "When the first Russian Cosmonaut, Yuri Gagarin, first circled the globe, he said he didn't see 'God' or bump into 'Heaven.' For a long time, Christians have taught that 'God' lives in 'Heaven' and that 'Heaven' is 'up there' in space above the earth. In an age of scientific illumination and space travel, we now know that these ideas are, and always have been, sheer fantasy."

Mr. Daniels: "Speaking about 'Heaven,' what about 'Hell'? Christians think everybody who doesn't believe the way they do will be sent there. If 'God' is loving, merciful and good, how could he possibly send people to a place like 'Hell' where they will be in torment forever? That sounds more like a cosmic sadist wreaking vengeance on people than a loving 'God' to me!"

Host: "A big thank you to our panelists on today's program. On the next program in this series, we'll be inviting eminent Christian scholars to try to answer the number of very thorny questions that you've raised. Unfortunately, that's all the time we have for today. I want to thank each one of you again for your stimulating contributions."

Mrs. Douglas: "It was our pleasure."

Host: "Tune in to 'Focus on Religion' again next week when another panel of distinguished guests will make their appearance in our continuing look at the meaning and relevance of religion for the 21st century."

What Do *You* Think?

1. In your opinion, which one of the eleven objections raised by the panelists do you feel is the most difficult to answer, and why?

2. In your opinion, which objection is the easiest to answer, and why?

3. Do you think the subject of religion should be taught in public schools? Why or why not?

4. Are there any additional objections or doubts about the Christian faith that you have, or have heard others express?

Bringing Things Into Focus |

Can You Answer These Questions?

How do you suppose the Christian guest panelists who were invited to the next telecast of 'Focus on Religion' would have answered the eleven questions raised by the previous week's panel?

1. Why did God allow evil to begin?

2. Why does God allow evil to continue?

3. Why does God allow good people to suffer and evil people to prosper?

4. Is God going to punish innocent people who have never heard the Christian message of salvation?

5. Why did God use such a long and complicated method to bring salvation to the world?

6. Is it possible for the death of a single person like Jesus to pay the penalty for the sins of the whole world?

7. Is the fearsome God of the Old Testament the same as the loving God of the New Testament?

8. If God knows the future, doesn't that determine things ahead of time and make history and life meaningless?

9. Who is *really* God – the Father, Jesus, the Holy Spirit, or all three?

10. Hasn't modern science and space exploration proved that there's no such place as 'heaven' or no such person as 'God' 'up there?'

11. How could a good and loving God send people to suffer eternal punishment in a place like 'Hell'?

What Do *You* Think?

1. Which of these questions bothers you the most, and why?

2. Have you been satisfied with the answers to these questions that Christians have given you before? Why or why not?

3. Have you ever had people ask you any of these questions before? If so, which ones and how did you answer them?

4. In your opinion, do you think the remark "We can't understand some of these things now, but when we get to Heaven it will all be clear" is a satisfactory answer to these difficult questions? Explain.

Gaining a Perspective |

Match Them Up

Which of the following statements from the Bible help to answer which of the 'Bringing Things into Focus' questions above, and why?

1. "Now the message that we have heard from his Son and announce is this: God is light, and there is no darkness at all in him." 1 John 1:5

2. "Where could I go to escape from you? Where could I get away from your presence? If I went up to heaven, you would be there; if I lay down in the world of the dead, you would be there. If I flew away beyond the east or lived in the farthest place in the west, you would be there to lead me; you would be there to help me." Psalm 139:7-10

3. "Go then, to all peoples everywhere and make them my disciples: baptize them in the name of the Father, the Son, and the Holy Spirit, and teach them to obey everything I have commanded you. And I will be with you always, to the end of the age." Matthew 28:19-20

4. "Remember what happened long ago; acknowledge that I alone am God and that there is no one else like me." Isaiah 46:9

5. "The LORD says,'...."I alone know the plans I have for you, plans to bring you prosperity and not disaster, plans to bring about the future you hope for." Jeremiah 29:10-11

6. "The Gentiles do not have the Law; but whenever they do by instinct what the Law commands, they are their own law, even though they do not have the Law. Their conduct shows that what the Law commands is written in their hearts. Their consciences also show that this is true, since their thoughts sometimes accuse them and sometimes defend them. And so, according to the Good News I preach, this is how it will be on that Day when God through Jesus Christ will judge the secret thoughts of all." Romans 2:14-16

7. "When Israel was a child, I loved him and called him out of Egypt as my son." Hosea 11:1

8. "For God loved the world so much that he gave his only Son, so that everyone who believes in him may not die but have eternal life." John 3:16

9. "And Christ himself is the means by which our sins are forgiven, and not our sins only, but also the sins of everyone." 1 John 2:2

10. "God's anger is revealed from heaven against all the sin and evil

of the people whose evil ways prevent the truth from being known. God punishes them, because what can be known about God is plain to them, for God himself made it plain. Ever since God created the world, his invisible qualities, both his eternal power and his divine nature, have been clearly seen; they are perceived in the things that God has made. So those people have no excuse at all!" Romans 1:18-20

11. "But you have a hard and stubborn heart, and so you are making your own punishment even greater on the Day when God's anger and righteous judgments will be revealed. For God will reward each of us according to what we have done. Some people keep on doing good, and seek glory, honor, and immortal life; to them God will give eternal life.

    Other people are selfish and reject what is right, in order to follow what is wrong; on them God will pour out his anger and fury. There will be suffering and pain for all those who do what is evil, for the Jews first and also for the Gentiles. But God will give glory, honor, and peace to all who do what is good, to the Jews first and also to the Gentiles. For God judges everyone by the same standard." Romans 2:5-11

12. "But when the right time finally came, God sent his own Son. He came as the son of a human mother and lived under the Jewish Law, to redeem those who were under the Law, so that we might become God's children." Galatians 4:4-5

13. "The Lord is not slow to do what he has promised, as some think. Instead, he is patient with you, because he does not want anyone to be destroyed, but wants all to turn away from their sins." 2 Peter 3:9

14. "God is our shelter and strength, always ready to help in times of trouble. So we will not be afraid, even if the earth is shaken and mountains fall into the ocean depths." Psalm 46:1-2

What Do *You* Think?

1. In your opinion, which statement gives the strongest answer to the question it pertains to, and why?

2. In your opinion, which statement gives the weakest answer to the question it pertains to, and why?

3. Can you think of other statements from the Bible can you think of that would also help to answer these questions?

4. Have you ever tried Goggling these questions on the Internet? Have you found any information that has proved helpful in answering them?

Drawing Conclusions |

Are There Any Answers to These Difficult Questions?

The questions raised by the TV panelists are questions that bother many other people as well. Many feel that if they could get these questions answered, the Christian faith would be a lot more attractive to them. *Are* there any answers to these most difficult questions? Let's explore that a bit.

1. Why did a good, all-powerful, eternal God ever permit evil to begin and foul up his good creation and his good plans?

To be frank, there's no clear, direct answer to this question in the Bible. However, to be fair, the questioner has no clear, direct answer to the problem of the origin of evil either. Ask our TV panelist from the Atheists Society how and why evil got started in the universe and the most he will be able to come up with is a theory. The question then becomes, whose theory is more credible?

The Christian theory is deduced from what God has revealed about himself. God isn't some kind of master computer who's created a robot cosmos to follow a pre-programmed mechanical script. Rather, he's a freedom loving God who brought a dynamic cosmos into being that had (has) the element of the *possibility* of disobedience, defiance and revolt built into it. Of what interest would a robot cosmos be to a loving, personal God? He didn't want a universe where his creatures would be *forced* to obey him, but one in which they could freely *choose* to obey him and thus would have the capacity to *love* him and to have a *real relationship* with him. The only way such a God could bring such a universe into being was to create a situation where his creatures had the possibility of *not* obeying him or loving him. This was risky, but at the same time, freedom of choice guaranteed the possibility of true love, obedience and a dynamic personal relationship between God and his created beings.

God isn't a passive God who, having programmed his master plan at the beginning, now just sits back with his arms folded and watches his plan play out. He's an active God who, having taken the risk of introducing freedom into creation, is right now working to redeem, renew, thwart and overcome whoever or whatever has, is and will try to destroy his good creation and his good plans. And he's doing so at great cost to himself. Why anybody would have wanted to take advantage of the *possibility* of revolting against God when they had everything they could have hoped for as God's creatures is an inexplicable mystery. Who can 'explain' pride, lust for power, selfishness and all the rest of what we mean by 'sin?' It's totally irrational. But somewhere, somehow for some irrational reason, some creature *did* take that irrational step, and evil was born. And with that step, the revolt against God and goodness was begun. Fortunately, God, through Christ, has created a way to overcome it - *again* involving risk and freedom and great cost to himself.

2. Why doesn't such a good, all-powerful, loving God simply put a stop to all evil once and for all and be done with it?

The implication of this question is that if God is unwilling, he's immoral and if he's unable, he can't really be God.

Many people have difficulty believing in God because they're troubled by this question. Unfortunately, since the Enlightenment, our 'modern' and now 'postmodern' and 'scientific' culture has tended to focus on the physical realm and ignore the spiritual realm. In the process, many have not only questioned the existence of God, but also the reality of the presence of the F.O.E. – the Forces of Evil. Christians not only believe in the existence of a powerful God, but also in the existence of powerful evil forces that are at work in the cosmos. They *don't* believe in dualism - the idea that there are two equally powerful forces that are locked in mortal combat in the spiritual world without our knowing which force will triumph in the end. They *do* believe that God is locked in a real struggle with a very powerful force that cannot be underestimated, but that in the end, his triumph over evil is assured. Meanwhile, the struggle goes on.

This cosmic struggle could be compared to the great struggle between the Allies and the Axis powers in World War II. In June of 1944, the Allied Supreme Commander, Dwight Eisenhower, issued an order for the commencement of the giant invasion of Europe that came to be known as 'D Day.' He agonized over giving that order, knowing that in doing so, he was sending thousands of good men to their deaths and contributing to the deaths of further thousands of innocent civilians who would be caught in the middle of the resultant holocaust. Nevertheless, in the cause of the right, this decision was the lesser of two evils and had to be made.

Once the landings and the follow-up were successful, the outcome of the war in Europe wasn't in doubt. It would only be a matter of time before the Allies would be victorious and 'VE Day' would bring the final defeat of the Axis powers and the liberation of Europe. Meanwhile, however, due to the 'Battle of the Bulge,' the desperate struggle would go on for almost another year, and millions more good people would be killed or suffer grievous injuries or be displaced or languish in concentration camps waiting for liberation.

So it is with God's struggle against evil. Like General Eisenhower, God painfully sends his 'troops' out to battle the forces of evil in a variety of ways, knowing that they, and millions of other innocent people, will suffer pain, loss, and even death in the struggle. But as in WWII, this sacrifice is necessary if, in the end, the war against these powerful forces is going to be won. Since 'D Day' (the death and resurrection of Jesus Christ), the final outcome has never been in doubt. 'VE Day' (the return of Christ and the end of this age) is as sure to come as the sun is to rise in the morning.

Meanwhile, however, the battle rages on. Every death in combat is even more painful for God than the deaths of his soldiers or innocent civilians were for General Eisenhower. The writer of Psalm 116 spells it out. "How painful it is to the LORD when one of his people dies!" Psalm 116:15 And the shortest verse in the Bible says it all. When Jesus arrived at the tomb of his friend Lazarus, John says, "Jesus wept." John 11:35 Of course, unlike Eisenhower, God has the power to stop the war at any moment. However, to do so would mean the equivalent of dropping a super atomic bomb that would destroy everybody and everything on the planet and defeat the aims of the war - to defeat the enemy in such a way that there will be something and someone left to redeem. (For example, an all out nuclear war today would not only defeat an enemy, but also destroy the 'victor.') So, out of his mercy and grace, God chooses to patiently slog it out with the great enemy in order to liberate, rather than destroy, as many people as he can. In the end, Christians believe he will be victorious. The enemy will be destroyed once and for all.

Evil seems to especially flare up here and there in history from time to time, precipitating a fierce battle between the F.O.E. and God and his forces, but the strategy of the F.O.E. often backfires and more people are 'redeemed' by God *through* the desperation and chaos of a battle than would have been the case without the battle. For example, the 1967-76 Cultural Revolution in China *appeared* to have wiped out the Christian Church (and *all* religious belief for that matter) throughout the entire country, but today the Christian Church in China is the fastest growing church in the world! In this sense God 'recycles' history's blackest moments to further his own good ends.

In the end, God's decisive intervention in the world through Jesus Christ teaches us something about God's methods of intervention.

- He came incognito.

- He intervened to bring wholeness and holiness where faith was present, but was blocked from doing so where it was absent.

- He confronted the F.O.E. and forced a retreat.

- He released the ultimate power of vicarious suffering that fatally wounded the F.O.E. (The 'power' of weakness overcame the 'weakness' of power)

Today, he continues to intervene in the same way throughout his created order.

3. Why does a good, loving, all-powerful God allow good people to suffer and evil people to prosper?

Or to put it another way, if there is a God, why do bad things happen to good people and good things happen to bad people?

First of all, the Bible makes it very clear that suffering, disease, and death are caused by the forces of evil, not by God. God is *against* all evil and its result - suffering. He didn't include either of these in his original creation, and neither will be present when he completes the renewal of his creation in the future. (See Revelation 21:1-5a) He underlined this truth in the person of Jesus who never harmed anybody, but who was devoted to helping, comforting and healing those who were hurting.

God wants to intervene for good in *all* lives, but he's often blocked from doing so by unbelief and shallow faith. He can't intervene against people's will or force people to love him, because to coerce free human beings against their will is to destroy them as persons. Instead he offers himself in love and waits with open arms for a response. Where people welcome his intervention, he brings healing, wholeness, renewal and the strength and courage to persevere through the trials and tribulations that his 'soldiers' must endure while they are engaged with him in 'the war' against the forces of evil.

The Bible also makes it very clear that God understands people's suffering, is with them in it and will see them through it as they are open to his grace and strength. To understand that, we only have to look at the unimaginable suffering that God-in-Christ went through when he died a horrible death to bring the possibility of forgiveness and new life even to those who were crucifying him! That's why the Apostle's Creed includes the phrase "He descended into Hell." In other words, God-in-Christ suffered Hell for our sakes. God is *more* grieved about suffering than we are. He *knows* what suffering is all about from personal experience, and he's shown that it can be borne and transformed into a power that even brings good out of evil. He promises those who suffer strong help in time of trouble, and millions have testified that this is not an empty promise. (See 1 Corinthians 10:13; James 1:1-4, 12-13).

A third certainty is that, in the long run, those who suffer will prevail over those who cause suffering. A good student of history can see that this is usually the case even in this life, and a good student of theology knows that God has promised that it will be 100% the case in the life to come. "The last shall be first." Mark 10:31 Some people, like Joseph, see this truth verified in their own lifetime. (See Genesis 37-50). Others, like Stephen, die believing they'll see it verified in the life to come. (See Acts 6:8-7:50)

We can see the truth of this maxim as it has worked itself out over the last century in modern history - the triumph of the Allies over the Axis powers in WWII; the triumph of Gandhi over British colonialism in India; the triumph of Martin Luther King's civil rights movement over the Ku Klux Klan in America; the triumph of Nelson Mandela's African National Congress over the Afrikaans Apartheid Government in South Africa; the triumph of People Power over the Marcos regime in the Philippine Islands; the triumph of democratic forces over totalitarian communist regimes in the USSR, Eastern Europe and China, etc.

Finally, none of us is totally innocent, even those who are being renewed by God's grace. We are all in some way and to some degree involved in creating suffering for ourselves and for others. This isn't to say that a person's suffering can be traced back to his or her own evil act(s) in every case. Evil and suffering pervade the whole of the cosmos, which means we're all stuck in a kind of general evil morass in which it's often difficult to clearly connect cause and effect. Fortunately, God is at work straightening out this morass and extricating those who put their faith in him from it or strengthening them to endure it.

Christians believe that "…in all things God works for good with those who love him, those whom he has called according to his purpose." Romans 8:28 God 'recycles' the bad, the ugly, the pain and the suffering endured by his people and transforms it into something good - the strengthening of faith (See James 1:1-4), the inner peace "…which is far beyond human understanding" (See Philippians 4:7), the ability to comfort others who are going through similar trials (See 2 Corinthians 1:3-5), the 'power' that is generated by suffering to overcome evil forces (See Ephesians 6:10-13), the assurance of hope for the future (See 1 Peter 5:8-10) and more.

This can be compared to the making of a tapestry. If you look at the back of a tapestry, it looks like a hopeless mass of tangled threads, but if you turn it over, you can see that a master craftsperson has been at work turning something that seems ugly and in chaos into something that is beautiful and ordered. The F.O.E. only has the power to wound, but not to ultimately destroy since a believer's personhood is rooted in God and that person-in-God will be sustained and retained - even through death. In the end, as we've seen, Christians believe the enemy will be destroyed once and for all; there will be no more crying, disease, suffering, oppression, exploitation and death, and the cosmos will be restored and renewed.

However, until God's offer of salvation expires, evil will continue to be present. And where evil is present, suffering will also inevitably be present. Anything different would again mean reducing God to a divine computer and us to moral robots. For freedom demands the existence of the possibility to choose wrongly, and to suffer as a result.

4. Is God going to punish innocent people who have never heard the Christian message of salvation?

That some people will end up in Hell is taught throughout the New Testament. *Who* exactly will be in Hell is in God's hands - a God, by the way, that is loving, compassionate and the most *fair* being in the totality of reality. The Bible doesn't spell out exactly what will happen to people who have never heard the Christian message, but there are two clues that there will be different strokes for different folks.

Jesus' parable about the master of the house going on a journey and placing the chief servant over his household is one. He returns to find the servant mistreating the other servants and mismanaging the household. That servant is severely punished, but the servants under him (who were at his mercy) receive a lighter punishment. "Much is required from the person to whom much is given; much more is required from the person to whom much more is given." (See Luke 12:42-48)

The other passage is in Romans 2 where Paul declares that whenever "the Gentiles do by instinct what the Law (of God) commands, they are their own law....Their conduct shows that what the Law commands is written in their hearts. Their consciences also show this is true, since their thoughts sometimes accuse them and sometimes defend them. And so, according to the Good News I preach, this is how it will be on that Day when God through Jesus Christ will judge the secret thoughts of all." Romans 2:14-16

We don't know how all of this will work out, but we do know that God (unlike us) will do what is *right* and *fair* in every case.

5. Why did God use such a long and complicated method to bring salvation to the world?

The answer to this question might be summed up with the phrase, "Rome wasn't built in a day." People aren't very easy beings to save! One reading of the Bible or any book on human history will convince you of that. The story of the human race has mainly been one of resisting, thwarting and rebelling against God's efforts to bring peace, order, harmony and renewal to people's lives. It's a marvel that God's patience and love have been so long-suffering and so deep. Most of us would've given up with Adam and Eve!

But God had a lot invested in his creation, and he had a vision of what it could become. He's never given up on that vision and has vowed that he'll continue to work in his creation to see that vision realized some day. To do that, God has had to take people where they were, and to work with them as they were - a long, slow process.

He began with one man, Abraham, and then used a nation, Israel, to make his presence and purpose known. He himself came into this world in the person of Jesus Christ, and on this foundation he built an international fellowship and witnessing body - the Christian Church. His message has now almost reached every tongue, tribe and nation. And when it does, then perhaps he'll complete the final act in the long history of salvation. Nobody has ever known when God would make his next move, but he's always made his moves when the time was right. As Paul writes, "But when the *right time* finally came, God sent his own Son." Galatians 4:4 People have always wanted to hurry God's process up, but if it was to be done by faith and light rather than by fiat and superstition, God knew he would need all of the time that it has taken and is taking.

6. Is it possible for a single person like Jesus to pay the penalty for the sins of the whole world?

And what about his method? Can the death of one man, Jesus, possibly be the means by which the debt for the entire world's wrongs was fully paid? Suppose your son throws a rock through one of the windows in your house but has no money to pay for it. Who *will* pay for it? You will, of course! Perhaps your son was sorry he did it and you forgave him. That would still not pay for the window. Because your son is your son, and because you love him, you'll be called on to do what your son can't do for himself - pay for the window.

God is our father. We've broken his 'windows' (laws). Even though we're sorry and he forgives us, we have nothing to pay him with. He decides to pay for them himself because he loves us. He does it by coming in the person of his Son and dying the death we were supposed to die for breaking his 'windows.' In doing so, his Son (the God-Man) has earned enough 'money' to 'pay' for all the 'windows' that have ever been broken. And besides that, he'll help us overcome our 'window breaking' ways in the future. The Good News is as simple and as profound as that.

7. Is the fearful God of the Old Testament the same as the loving God of the New Testament?

Yes and no. Any fair reading of the Old Testament will show that there's a lot of love, mercy, kindness, grace, etc. in the God of the Hebrews, while a similar reading of the New Testament will show that there is a good bit of wrath, holiness, judgment and justice in the God of the Christians - and all with good reason. For example, nobody would want a God who would simply smile and benevolently overlook the horrible deeds of somebody like Hitler, Stalin, Pol Pot, Mao Tse-tung and the leaders of ISIS! Therefore, we can't simply say that the Old Testament and the New Testament paint two different pictures of God.

And yet there are profound differences. What accounts for them? For one thing, the early Hebrews reported God to be what they *perceived* him to be in their own ancient rough and tumble context. Like a record with mildew and scratches on it, for example, the true God's 'voice' comes through on the Old Testament 'record.' However, that voice is at times distorted by ancient cultural and cultic misperceptions so that in the end, some of what is attributed to God doesn't really describe the true God. For example, the prophet Amos says that as part of his judgment on Israel, God will "command the sea monster to bite them." Amos 9:3 We now know, of course, that this is a reference to the ancient belief that the sea was inhabited by a great monster that was regarded as being under God's control.

Another thing that accounts for these differences is that in revealing himself to the ancients, God had to begin where they *were*, not where he wished them to be. For example, he couldn't begin with a lofty concept like 'love your enemies' when they were fighting a war of survival in a 'tooth and claw' era. The Israelites were in a cultural and spiritual kindergarten as it were. Through a process that we might call 'progressive revelation,' God, through his priests, judges, kings and prophets, and finally through his Son, led them on through spiritual primary school, then through high school and finally through university as far as their understanding of him and what he wanted of them were concerned. This is why God's revelation through Jesus Christ is like the bright light of the sun when compared, for example, to the candles of the Old Testament Judges. Therefore, the rule of thumb should be, when there's any clear discrepancy between an Old Testament and a New Testament description of God, the New Testament description must be taken as the latest and most accurate word we have on the subject.

However, in a sense, even after Jesus, we will never have a 100% accurate picture of God since he is infinite and we are finite. Through events and revelations in the past, and particularly through Jesus, he has, as it were, 'translated' himself into terms that we finites can understand. We are like small children who find it impossible to grasp abstract concepts until the teacher explains them by using concrete illustrations. Then children get some idea as to what their teacher is talking about. We now know all we need to know about God, but we certainly still don't know all there is to know about God. This should help us to better understand how difficult it was for God to make himself as fully and clearly known to the Old Testament ancients as he was able to do some 2,000 years later to the New Testament Christians.

8. Does God know all that's going to happen in the future? And if he does, doesn't that mean that everything is already determined and that history and life are therefore meaningless?

The Bible writers make it clear that God does know the future, but at the same time, they also make it clear that history and life have meaning. How can these both be true at the same time? They can be if we don't insist on worshipping a three dimensional God; that is, if we don't limit God to a partial understanding of reality that is determined by our ideas of time, space and motion.

The God of the Bible is, so to speak, a 'ninth dimensional God.' That is, although he can operate within the dimensions known to us, he is far beyond those dimensions in a reality that is far greater than our wildest science fiction dreams. For most of us, as the well-known Christian writer J.B. Phillips has pointed out, our God is "too small." When we think of God, we need to think big!

Suppose, for example, that 'time' for God is not in a lineal straight line sequence as we know it (past, present, future), but is circular! That is, imagine God as an all-seeing eye in the middle of a circle. All events from eternity to eternity (if we can even speak that way) would be included on the circular line, and the all-seeing eye would see them *all at the same time*. In other words, to God all things would be one great big PRESENT, and everything would be happening at once. It would not then be a matter of God playing out a computerized tape of events planned 'back then' but played out in a lineal time sequence called 'history' now. Rather it would be a matter of God being actively involved in all things at once as they were happening.

Fiction, you say? Perhaps so. But whatever concept we might use, let's never imagine that just because it *seems* to us as though God's knowledge of the future and a history that has true value are an irreconcilable contradiction, there is in fact no such a contradiction. Rather, we're dealing here with what's known as a paradox - two things that *seem* to be contradictory but that in fact are not. And the reason why they're not is because we're trying to grasp a 'ninth dimensional God' with a three dimensional mind.

9. Who is really God - the Father, Jesus, the Holy Spirit, or all three?

The most fundamental truth that God has revealed about himself is that there is only *one* true God - and he is it! How then, can we speak of Jesus as being 'God' and of the Holy Spirit as being 'God' as well? We can't if we see them as two different 'Gods,' distinct from the one true God.

Some people have tried to solve this problem by saying there's only *one* God, but that he consists of three 'persons' - Father, Son and Holy Spirit. These three persons are distinct divine persons in their own right who blend into one God in a mysterious way that is beyond our comprehension. The problem with this view is that God then ceases to be a person to whom we can relate. If he has a split personality as it were, how can we relate to that?

Perhaps it will help our understanding to look at it this way.

- God the Father = God as distinct from his creation

- God the Son   = God in contact with his creation

- God the Holy Spirit = God in action in his creation

All are the same God, but God making himself known or acting in these three ways.

When he was on earth, Jesus made it very clear that he was God taking on the form of a human being. He was the unique God-Man - "God with us" as Matthew puts it. Matthew 1:23 And yet, he also made it very clear that he himself was not the totality of God. There was more to God than 'the Son' alone. Even while God was 'with us' in Jesus, in some sense he still remained distinct from us. How could Jesus get this difficult idea across to us? He did so by referring to the 'otherness' of God as 'the Father' while at the same time saying that he and the Father were 'one.' (See John 10: 30)

We might think of God as being like a diamond. A diamond is only one stone, but as you turn it in the sun, you see that it has different facets. 'The Father' facet of the divine diamond stresses God as being separate from and greater than that which he has made. 'The Son' (or Jesus) facet stresses God in contact with that which he has made. (It's interesting to note, for example, that God always comes into contact with his created order *through* his 'Son.' "*Through* him (The Word)," writes John, "God made all things." John 1:3 The 'Holy Spirit' facet of the divine diamond stresses the reality of God's presence and power in that which he has made. This power is not separate from either the Father or the Son, but is the *means* by which the Father-Son (God in Christ) acts to work out God's will in his creation.

This concept of the Trinity can be compared to the roles of an actor in an ancient Roman play. One actor often played several different roles by holding different masks in front of his face at different points in the play. In other words, though it was *one* actor, he assumed several different 'persons.' So it is with the one God who has revealed himself in three 'persons' (from the Latin 'persona' originally meaning 'mask' or 'false face,' such as those of wood or clay worn by actors in Roman theaters.)

Some people are troubled when the Bible talks about Jesus as "going to the Father," or as "sitting at the right hand of God," or depicts the Holy Spirit as "coming down like a dove," or as having personal characteristics. We must remember that this is the kind of picture language that a 'ninth dimensional God' uses to somehow try to translate the complexity of his being into terms that will allow his 'third dimensional children' to get some idea of what he's like.

We're not to take these pictures or symbols as a literal reality, but to look for the meaning *behind* them. For example, the seat at the right hand of the Roman Emperor was reserved for a person of honor and power. This is the *idea* that is meant to be conveyed in the New Testament by the picture of Jesus seated in heaven at the right hand of God, *not* two literal thrones with God and the God-Man (Jesus) sitting on them as separate persons. The Father, the Son and the Holy Spirit are three ways of talking about the *one* God, depending on which facet of the divine diamond you are concentrating on at the moment.

10. Is there a real place called 'Heaven' where God lives and where his people will live?

Yes, but not the kind that many people think there is. The problem here again is three dimensional small thinkers like Yuri Gagarin. Unfortunately, the Christian Church has also at times had too many thinkers like that - thinkers who based their ideas about

Heaven more on the literal ancient, and scientifically outdated *context* in which the Bible writers set their ideas on this subject, than on the ideas themselves.

According to the Bible, God is a spirit who is unlimited by our three dimensions of time, space and motion. He is, as we've said, a 'ninth dimensional God.' To be in Heaven means to be in the presence of God. Wherever God is, then, Heaven also is. The reality of God and Heaven is an unseen reality that is far beyond what we as finite human beings can conceive, particularly if we try to do so in three dimensional concepts. This is why the Bible writers, for example, always strain for words when writing about this subject, and why they always use symbolic language when trying to describe God or Heaven. A symbol is not the reality, but merely *points* to the reality. Symbols can only give us some idea of literally indescribable subjects.

When seen in this way, to talk of God or Heaven as being 'up' there or even 'out' there is to use three dimensional language to describe something (or some*body*) that is 'ninth dimensional.' Of *course* Yuri Gagarin didn't 'see' God or bump into Heaven in his orbit around the earth. And the reason why he didn't do so was because his 'god' was too small! He didn't realize that on his entire journey he was *surrounded* by God and was but an infinitesimal speck in what God knows as the totality of reality.

When we think of God and Heaven we need to think BIG! Heaven isn't merely some glorious extension of earthly reality - it's a whole *new* reality - *in touch with* earthly reality, but far beyond it in scope and dimension. So there is a real Heaven where God lives and his people will live, but live in a way that's beyond human language to literally describe.

Christians have different viewpoints on what a transition from this life to the next will be like and what their identity in Heaven will be like. Some early Christians were influenced by Greek ideas about the afterlife and there are many Christians today who subscribe to those same ideas. When a Greek died, his or her skull was fractured to let what they perceived to be the noble soul escape from an inferior body and go on to the next life. Likewise, many Christians today believe that at death the body remains in the grave but the soul goes to Heaven to "be with the Lord." However, the main theme of the Bible on this subject is that both body and soul are precious and can't be separated, even at death. The New Testament doesn't focus on the immortality of a soul that resides in Heaven in some kind of an ethereal intermediate state, but on the resurrection of a person as a psycho-somatic whole who enters Heaven when the dead are raised to life upon the return of Jesus Christ at the end of history as we know it. To use an illustration, death can be compared to a mother rocking her baby to sleep. The child goes to sleep because it feels secure in its mother's arms. Once asleep, the child doesn't know the difference between sleeping for an hour, a day, a year or a thousand years. All it knows is that when it awakens in the morning, the sun is out and a glorious new day has begun. So it will be for the Christian who dies secure in the arms of God.

What will the new resurrected person be like? All the New Testament writers can do when trying to describe this 'ninth dimensional' reality in third dimensional terms is to use metaphorical language. Paul writes that "flesh and blood cannot inherit the Kingdom of God," and that resurrected Christians will therefore have a new "spiritual body." (See 1 Corinthians 15:42-44, 50) This will be a real, completely renewed body for a real person that will have continuity with the person that lived on earth. Paul compares it to a seed that's dropped into the ground which then grows into a plant that looks nothing like the original seed. But there's continuity. The seed produces a *particular* plant and that plant's identity is tied to that *particular* seed. In other words, you can't plant beans and get tomatoes. (See 1 Corinthians 15:35-38, 51-53) In the same way, Christians believe that a Christian will not lose his or her identity, but will live as a new person in a new marvelous realm that will afford him or her endless opportunities for creativity, development, invention, growth, exploration and enjoyment in the company of God-in Christ and fellow Christians of all times and from all places.

Jesus' appearances to his followers after his resurrection serve as an example. In one sense he was the same old Jesus who ate with them, talked with them and taught them. In another sense, however, he was different. He appeared and disappeared and locked doors were no obstacle for him. So at the same time, there was continuity and discontinuity. So it will be for resurrected Christians. Paul writes, "Just as we wear the likeness of the man (Adam) made of earth, so we will wear the likeness of the Man from heaven (Jesus, the second Adam)." 1 Corinthians 15:49

11. How could a good and loving God send people to suffer eternal punishment in a place like Hell?

Jesus often spoke of judgment and Hell. For example, "Do not be afraid of those who kill the body but cannot kill the soul; rather be afraid of God, who can destroy both body and soul in hell." Matthew 10:28 On the one hand, he talked about God's judgment on those who refuse his grace, turn down his Kingdom, live for themselves and perpetrate evil. (See John 3:18-21) On the other hand, he described God as a loving Father who is grieved over the disobedience of his children and who has come in Jesus to pay an enormous price to save them. In him God has made it possible for all to be in his Kingdom. (See John 3:14-17).

The examples that Jesus used to describe existence in Hell are word pictures that communicate *ideas*. When he talked about flames, gnashing of teeth, tormenting thirst, etc., he was not describing a literal furnace or some kind of an eternal torture rack. He was describing a state of existence in which people will undergo unimaginable suffering of their own making. People in Hell will regret that they made wrong choices and committed evil deeds, and be utterly depressed. They will live in gloom and darkness and will feel that way within themselves. There will be no music, light and gladness. They will feel isolated and be terribly lonely. They will be stuck living with people who are all selfishly taken up with their own wants and not at all concerned about anybody else's needs. They will be stripped of all the perks, prestige and comforts that they traded their lives for while on earth. They will continue to struggle with sorrow, disease, evil and the 'second death' (existing apart from God).

This existence, like life in the future Kingdom ('Heaven'), will be in a different dimension from the dimension of space, time and motion that we now know. Therefore, the best way Jesus could describe either Hell or Heaven was to use examples from the world that we know. These examples give us some *idea* about what existence in Hell or life in Heaven will be like in the future.

The argument that people usually make against Hell is syllogistic. A. If God is love and loves all people, and B., if Hell and eternal punishment are the opposite of love, then C., there can be no Hell. This premise may sound logical, but that's not what the New Testament teaches. Rather, it teaches that God perfectly balances love and justice, redemption and judgment, Heaven and Hell.

There's general agreement that 'tough love,' a love that doesn't enable destructive behavior, that holds children accountable for their behavior and that enforces consequences for bad behavior, is the best way to parent children. Some people mistakenly think a loving God can't be the 'tough love parent' described in the Bible, but should be more like a doting grandfather in the sky who, in the end, doesn't hold us, his children, accountable or enforce consequences and therefore actually *enables* destructive behavior.

Christians believe that the Good News that Jesus and the apostles preached and taught was a two-sided coin. It was an *an*nunciation of salvation, redemption, forgiveness and hope, but it was also a *de*nunciation of evil, unbelief, self-righteousness and judgment. It wasn't, to use Dietrich Bonheoffer's phrase, a 'cheap grace' kind of news, namely that in the end you can have it both ways. One statement from Jesus will suffice: "Those who believe in the Son are not judged; but those who do not believe have already been judged, because they have not believed in God's only Son." John 3:18.

The problem isn't from *God's* end. Peter writes, "He is patient with you, because he does not want *anyone* to be destroyed, but wants *all* to turn away from their sins." 2 Peter 3:9 John writes, "For God loved the *world* so much that he gave his only Son, so that *everyone* who believes in him may not die but have eternal life." John 3:16 The problem is from *our* end.

People can spit in God's face and say, "I don't need your grace, forgiveness and eternal life. I'm happy with who I am, where I am and where I'm going." Again, to quote Jesus: "This is how the judgment works: the light has come into the world, but people love the darkness rather than the light, because their deeds are evil. Those who do evil things hate the light and will not come to the light, because they do not want their evil deeds to be shown up." John 3:19-20 In Romans 8, Paul gives a whole list of what can't separate people from the love of God in Christ, but notice that his list doesn't include the *self!* People can refuse God's love, set their course and persist in what could be called self-condemnation.

Amazingly and irrationally, many people want *out* instead of *in!* They walk away and even run away from their loving, gracious Father. He longs for their return, but unlike the son in the story in Luke 15:11- 32, they never come back. In fact, they want nothing to do with God or with the way of the Kingdom. And by saying to God in word or by the way they live, "I don't give a damn!" they damn *themselves.*

In a sense, by separating themselves from God and his way of life, they've begun to move towards the lifestyle of Hell while still in this life. Unless there's a reversal, by the time they arrive at death, they want nothing to do with God, with eternal life or with the coming Kingdom. They would feel out of place there. They've concentrated on themselves and their comforts, perks and prestige and have committed evil for so long that they can't give them up or stop doing what they've been doing, no matter what the price. They've sought to justify themselves as 'okay' for so long that they're past even seeing what needs forgiving and cleansing in their lives. They'll 'go down in flames' before they'll admit to the need for, or accept grace and mercy from, anybody.

A person like Stalin, for example, when faced with Hell, would nevertheless most likely grit his teeth and go on opposing and cursing God ad-infinitum. In other words, he would be 'hell bent' on going to and staying in Hell. C. S. Lewis in his book *The Great Divorce* portrays such people as visiting Heaven, experiencing it as Hell for them, and wanting to get back to Hell as fast as they could. As Lewis puts it in his book *The Problem of Pain*, "The doors of Hell are locked on the *inside*. We are rebels." (p. 127)

Is God pained by this? Of *course* he is. Over and over again, the writers of the Bible make it clear that God longs for his children to 'come home.' For example, the prophet Ezekiel writes, "'Do you think I enjoy seeing evil people die?' asks the Sovereign LORD. 'No, I would rather see them repent and live.'" Ezekiel 18:23 He, just like any human father, is grieved over the destructive behavior of an adult child over whom he has no control. But, like an earthly parent, he took the risk of bringing us, even Stalin, into the world and then giving us the freedom to make decisions - decisions that have consequences for good or ill. Like any earthly father, he won't, and can't, *compel* repentance, faith and obedience. He loves and hopes to be loved, but he can't *compel* our love.

Christians also believe that if there's no Hell, then the whole of what could be termed the moral universe collapses. If in the end, there'll be no difference between what happens to Moses and what happens to Hitler, then what sense does it make to even differentiate between good and evil? Why should there be police, courts and prisons if the verdict in every case should be "Case dismissed?" If we humans insist on justice, consequences and judgment (sometimes in the form of life imprisonment or even execution), why do we insist that God cannot, indeed *should* not, do the same? Why when it comes to God do we deny what in our gut we know is right, just and fair on the earthly human plane, but object to it on the divine heavenly plane?

Will this existence of suffering for those in Hell go on forever? Will there be some who will 'see the light' at last and have a change of heart? After suffering for their wrongs and their rejection, will they be given another chance by God to enter the Kingdom after all? This is a question that the writers of the New Testament don't address. One would hope that in the end, even the Hitlers of this world would repent and enter the Kingdom. But the reactions of people like the Pharisees suggest otherwise. The more they saw and heard of the Kingdom, the harder their hearts became.

People like our panelists, and even some Christian teachers, object to the idea that the consequences of going to Hell are everlasting. They reason that A., since God's love always has a redemptive purpose and B., since eternal punishment in Hell would contradict that purpose, then C., there can be no such punishment and the whole human race will in the end be redeemed.

However, after World War II, the Allies executed Nazi and Japanese war criminals, for example, which meant those people had no chance to ever redeem themselves in this life. Justice was seen to be justly carried out.

Even if life sentences *had* been handed out for the murder of each individual, how many life sentences would the German dictator, Adolf Hitler, have accrued? And if Jesus and C. S. Lewis are right, after serving them all, he would still have been as defiant and as deviant as ever. As Lewis succinctly puts it in *The Problem of Pain*, "In the long run the answer to all those who object to the doctrine of Hell is itself a question: 'What are you asking God to do?' To wipe out their past sins and, at all costs, to give them a fresh start, smoothing every difficulty and offering every miraculous help? But he has done so, on Calvary. To forgive them? They will not be forgiven. To leave them alone? Alas, I am afraid that is what he does." (p. 128)

What Do *You* Think?

1. Which of these eleven questions do you feel have been answered in a way that you've found helpful, and why?

2. Which question(s) do you feel has/have not been answered satisfactorily, and why?

3. Which of these eleven questions do you feel you want more information about? What kind of information?

4. Are there other questions you have about the Christian faith that haven't been dealt with here? If so, what are they?

5. Do you agree with the conclusions as spelled out in this chapter? Why or why not?

Chapter Six

WHERE DID THESE IDEAS COME FROM?

"Jesus said, 'Everything written about me in the Law of Moses, the writings of the prophets, and the Psalms had to come true.'   Luke 24:44

"Jesus said, 'Heaven and earth will pass away, but my words will never pass away.'"   Matthew 24:35

Looking Through the Microscope |

Revelations

He sat bolt upright in bed. This was the third time he'd had this same dream - a vision in which a voice told him to pull up his roots in Haran and move to the land of Canaan where he would have many descendents and be the father of a great nation. He got up and went about his daily business, but he couldn't shake off that dream. It was as though an inner force was compelling him to do what the voice had commanded! He thought about what his old father had often told him: dreams were sometimes the way the power beyond made known his wishes. He also remembered the other things his father had told him - fascinating stories about how the world had begun, how things had gone wrong, the tradition of a great flood, and all the rest. He suddenly made up his mind. He would follow his dream.

****

An eighty year old man stood in the middle of a desert in Midian, shepherd's crook in hand. With nothing much better to do, he was day-dreaming about his childhood. He could still picture his father and his mother, and even his grandparents in Egypt, in his mind's eye. He thought about the stories they'd told him about long ago and far away - stories of his ancestors; people like Abraham who had listened to the power beyond and moved to Canaan; people like Isaac, Jacob, Joseph and all the rest to whom the power beyond had made himself known. He knew every story by heart - passed on from one generation to another - as did his children. Should he so much as miss a jot or a title in the telling of them, his children would be swift to correct him! ... It had been a long time since anybody had heard from the power beyond.

He was startled out of his musings by a nearby bush that suddenly burst into flames! Curious, he went over to investigate and was even more startled when he heard a voice telling him to take off his shoes and listen! He was completely jarred out of his senses when the voice of the power beyond instructed him to go to Egypt and set his people free from slavery there. He argued. He wished the power beyond would leave him alone! Why did he have to appear *now* and to *this* particular shepherd when he hadn't gotten in touch with anybody for so long? In the end, he put on his shoes and went to Egypt. What a story he would have to tell to *his* children and grandchildren!

****

He sat in his tent and worked long hours into the night by oil lamp. On many of these nights, Joshua would come to keep him company. He would urge him to get some rest when it got too late…and to help him remember. Writing was hard work and took a long time. First the soft clay tablets had to be prepared. Then, after the marks had been made on them, they had to be baked so they would harden. There was so much to remember. It would only be possible to write down the bare details of the most important events, along with a few words about the *meaning* of those events. This was particularly important because in later years, somebody might be tempted to say that the miraculous crossing of the Sea of Reeds had been sheer luck or that that the Hebrew's astounding victory over the Egyptians had been due to brilliant strategy. He knew better!

He wanted to make sure that everybody else would be crystal clear about what Yahweh had done for Israel for as long as people were alive to read the story. Of course, a lot would still need to be passed on by word of mouth, as had been the case for many years. But at least there would be some kind of a more permanent record of the essential facts to make sure that people's memories didn't fail them.

****

The king hummed the familiar tune as he let his eyes run over the words of a Psalm that was so neatly printed on the scroll. "The Lord is my shepherd, I have everything I need." "What a beautiful picture of our relationship to God," he thought. He wished that *he* had been endowed with the talent that his ancestor David had. Here was a whole song book filled with magnificent poems about God and man, about nature and about the nation...and so much more. He could picture David as a lad sitting under a tree in the pasture, deep in thought, humming to himself, and suddenly getting the inspiration to write one of the poems that he now held in his hands. "Only a person in close touch with God and moved by his Spirit could possibly write poetry like that," he thought.

****

The prophet was angry! The situation in the country was going from bad to worse. Crime was common in the streets. Dishonesty was widespread. The rich were unmercifully exploiting the poor and living in unbridled luxury. Materialism was rampant. The king was scheming with heathen allies to try and defend the country through what the prophet knew would be useless alliances. And all the while the people had been carrying on elaborate rites in their seemingly pious worship and making hypocritical noises about obeying God's commands. His indignation was like a fire in his bones. Dangerous or not, he *had* to speak! God was *compelling* him to speak! He stood in the square and shouted: "Thus says the Lord!" One of his assistants wrote down his words.

****

They followed him from all over Palestine. Some said he was the Messiah, others that he had a demon. But the common people heard him gladly. A growing number of disciples knew that nobody had ever before spoken like this man was speaking, and that nobody had taught with the kind of authority he was teaching with. He claimed to have been sent from God and that he had the power to forgive sins!

Once he preached a moving sermon on a mountain side. One of his followers took notes. On another occasion, he healed a blind man. A different disciple recorded that event. He told many parables, and his followers wrote down as many of them as they could remember. He died, rose again from the dead and explained what it all meant. Breathlessly, his disciples passed it all on. And after he left the earth, a medical doctor went around interviewing his mother, his brothers, his disciples and every other eye witness he could find, and set down an orderly account of his life and teaching.

Then, in Book Two, he recorded what had happened during the early days of the spread of the movement - much of which the doctor himself was involved in - all the while feeling as though God himself were standing over his shoulder, helping him to sift through his data and include only that which would most clearly help people understand the significance of what had happened.

****

He couldn't remember exactly how many letters he'd written, but it had been many. He'd been the leading spirit behind the spread of the movement, and its leading scholar as well. The churches had depended on him to give advice about solving their problems and to give encouragement to live as Christ's true disciples in the world. They had eagerly awaited his letters like messages from God.

Once, he had made a great effort to write a long treatise explaining the whole of the Christian faith and had sent it to the

Christians at Rome. He'd prayed and struggled much as he wrote it. He wanted it to reflect the whole truth about God's action to save the world through Jesus Christ. When it was finished, and he had read it over, he knew that God had answered his prayers and rewarded his struggles. He had clearly felt his presence and guidance, and the long treatise reflected it.

* *

The Council had come to a conclusion. The delegates were happy. They'd prayed for God's Spirit to help them determine which books should be on the final list of books to be included in the Christian Bible. They felt that he'd answered those prayers. The task had actually not been all that difficult. All the included books had been accepted by all of the churches for many years as authentic records of God's acts throughout history, and of the right interpretation of those acts. The Old Testament books had been accepted as such by the Jews for centuries, while the New Testament books had been written by disciples of Jesus or their close associates. The ideas in all the books faithfully reflected all that God had been telling his people through the centuries. They had now simply officially recognized what for a long time had already been an accepted fact.

They knew that these writings would be important in the years to come to keep people's ideas about God clear, and to be a means by which he might continue to speak to them in their new situations. What he had said to Abraham, Moses, David, Amos, Luke, Paul and many others in dreams, burning bushes, pastures, crises and reflections in the past would always be relevant for everyone's present. But above all, they knew that these writings would be the means by which people could once again 'meet' God, and in meeting him, know the Way, hear the Truth and experience a new Life. God's revelation had been centered on his Son, and through the guidance of his Spirit, God had now completed that revelation.

What Do *You* Think?

1. Suppose you were God, and nobody knew anything about you. How would you go about making yourself known (revealing yourself) to people?

2. In your opinion, do the above vignettes about Abraham, Moses, Hezekiah, Jeremiah, Luke, Paul and the Council of Carthage (397 A.D.) accurately describe the way God actually did go about revealing himself? Explain.

3. In our postmodern world, many people believe that whatever might be true must be discovered through research and reason, not revealed by an outside source. Do you agree with this idea? Why or why not?

4. Do you think the Christian Bible contains an accurate record of God's mighty acts in history and an accurate interpretation of those acts? Why or why not?

Bringing Things Into Focus |

True or False?

Which of these ideas do you think are true, which are false, and why?

- Ideas (such as some things are good while others are bad; people should get married and live in families; self-giving love is a noble ideal and the like) came from a source beyond the human race.

- People have always been capable of finding out the truth about things without any help from the 'outside.'

- There are some truths, principles and values that are universally true and eternally valid.

- Christian ideas about God, Jesus Christ, salvation and all the rest are products of people's wishful thinking and imagination.

- God actually revealed himself to the human race and is the source of all good and true ideas.

- The way in which the Bible describes God making himself known to the human race through the ages makes sense.

- The writers of the Bible invented mythical events and wrote down their own subjective interpretations of those events.

- The biblical records are historically accurate in all they intend to teach.

- The living God comes to people today and reveals himself to them through the events and ideas recorded in the Bible.

- The Bible is an inspiring book to read.

What Do *You* Think?

1. What book of the Bible most interests you, and why?

2. What book of the Bible least interests you, and why?

3. Do you think God was involved in the process of some 40 writers writing the 66 books of the Bible over a period of some 1500 years? If so, how? If not, why not?

4. In your opinion, is there any difference between the Bible and the sacred writings of other faiths? Why or why not?

<u>Gaining a Perspective |</u>

The Bible Speaks for Itself

Here are some statements from the Bible that tell us about the way the Bible came into being and/or what the people mentioned in the Bible thought about its content.

- **2 Timothy 3:16**: "All Scripture is inspired by God and is useful for teaching the truth, rebuking error, correcting faults, and giving instruction for right living."

- **2 Peter 1:21**: "For no prophetic message ever came just from the human will, but people were under the control of the Holy Spirit as they spoke the message that came from God."

- **Jeremiah 1:4-9**: "The LORD said to me, 'I chose you before I gave you life, and before you were born I selected you to be a prophet to the nations.' I answered, 'Sovereign LORD, I don't know how to speak; I am too young.' But the LORD said to me, 'Do not say that you are too young, but go to the people I send you to, and tell them everything I command you to say. Do not be afraid of them, for I will be with you to protect you. I, the LORD, have spoken!' Then the LORD reached out, touched my lips, and said to me, 'Listen, I am giving you the words you must speak.'"

- **Isaiah 6:8**: "Then I heard the Lord say, 'Whom shall I send? Who will be our messenger?' I answered, 'I will go! Send me!'"

- **Exodus 24:3-4**: "Moses went and told the people all the LORD's commands and all the ordinances, and all the people answered together, 'We will do everything that the LORD has said.' Moses wrote down all the LORD's commands."

- **Joshua 24:24-26**: "The people said to Joshua, 'We will serve the LORD our God and obey him.' On that day Joshua made a covenant for the people, and there at Shechem he reaffirmed for them decrees and laws. And Joshua recorded these things in the Book of the Law of God."

- **Galatians 1:11-12**: "Let me tell you, my friends that the gospel I preach is not of human origin. I did not receive it from any human being, nor did anyone teach it to me. It was Jesus Christ himself who revealed it to me."

- **1 Thessalonians 2:13**: "And there is another reason why we always give thanks to God. When we brought you God's message, you heard it and accepted it, not as a message from human beings but as God's message, which indeed it is."

- **Amos 7:14-15**: "Amos answered, 'I am not the kind of prophet who prophesies for pay. I am a herdsman, and I take care of fig trees. But the LORD took me from my work as a shepherd and ordered me to come and prophesy to his people Israel."

- **Ezekiel 2:1-4**: "Then I heard a voice saying, 'Mortal man, stand up. I want to talk to you.' While the voice was speaking, God's spirit entered me and raised me to my feet, and I heard the voice continue, 'Mortal man, I am sending you to the people of Israel. They have rebelled and turned against me and are still rebels, just as their ancestors were. They are stubborn and do not respect me, so I am sending you to tell them what I, the Sovereign LORD, am saying to them. Whether those rebels listen to you or not, they will know that a prophet has been among them.'"

- **2 Peter 3:15-16**: "Look on our Lord's patience as the opportunity he is giving you to be saved, just as our dear friend Paul wrote to you, using the wisdom that God gave him. This is what he says in all his letters when he writes on the subject. There are some difficult things in his letters which ignorant and unstable people explain falsely, as they do with other passages of the Scriptures. So they bring on their own destruction."

- **Matthew 5:18**: "Remember that as long as heaven and earth last, not the least point nor the smallest detail of the Law will be done away with—not until the end of all things."

- **2 Kings 20:20**: "Everything else that King Hezekiah did, his brave deeds, and an account of how he built a reservoir and dug a tunnel to bring water into the city, are all recorded in *The History of the Kings of Judah.*"

- **John 17:17**: "Dedicate them (Jesus' disciples) to yourself by means of the truth; your word is truth."

- **1 Kings 14:19**: "Everything else that King Jeroboam did, the wars he fought and how he ruled, are all recorded in *The History of the Kings of Israel.*"

- **John 16:13-14**: "Jesus said (to his disciples), 'When the Spirit comes, who reveals the truth about God, he will lead you into all the truth ... he will take what I say and tell it to you.'"

What Do *You* Think?

1. Some people say that "the law is what we make it." In light of our human experience, do you think we humans can set our own standards about what to believe and how to live? Why or why not?

2. What different methods do the above statements reveal that God used to deliver his message to the world?

3. People throughout history have claimed to have had special 'visions' or "God told me to do this" messages in their heads that in the end have proven to be false and have sometimes done great harm to people. How do the revelations communicated to the ancient writers and editors of the Bible compare with these?

4. In your opinion, which three of the above biblical statements make the strongest case for the writings in the Bible to be considered as a revelation from God? Why?

Drawing Conclusions |

The Word of the Lord

Everybody believes it's wrong to steal, to kill somebody or to lie. All people believe that we should be kind to children, respectful to parents and loyal to friends. Who wouldn't support just punishment for those who break the law and heartfelt thanks to those who serve the community? And nobody would say that drugs were good for you, or that unemployment was an ideal, or that prostitution was a desirable profession.

Where did all these ideas come from? "From my parents," you might answer. And where did they get *their* ideas? "From *their* parents," might be your reply. We could fill up the rest of this chapter going all the way back to zero. But how did these ideas, or all of the other ideas that people know in their hearts to be right, ever get started? Did somebody suddenly decide in 1839 that murder was a bad idea and announce it to the world? Was stealing once a good idea, but then people eventually changed their minds? Has lying only recently gone out of style? Was there a time when people were all unkind to children, disrespectful to old people and disloyal to friends?

Why punish those who break the law? Whose law are they breaking anyway? Who gave whom the power to decide what the law was, and when did they give it? Did somebody way back when wake up one morning, yawn, stretch, and suddenly have the bright idea that it's wrong to commit adultery pop into her head? Or did some great thinker long ago, after a lifetime of deliberation, finally conclude that the best way for society to function was for males and females to enter into some kind of a marriage agreement, have children and live in families? Or has the idea that it's right to tell the truth, along with the whole of humanity's moral and ethical understanding of things, slowly evolved over thousands of years so that it's a comparatively recent product of the moral development of the human race?

Are there really laws that people always have been, are and will be required to obey? Or are what we call 'laws' simply the personal decisions of some powerful people who force their way of thinking on society as history moves along? Are there such things as morals? And who decides what's moral or immoral? Are ethics the invention of some starry eyed philosophers sitting in ivory towers? Are they simply trying to make life difficult for the rest of us who have to slog it out in the streets? If not, who *does* decide what's ethical and what's unethical?

Are all these questions decided by simply seeing what works and what doesn't work? If so, how do we agree on what works and what doesn't work? Are there no 'right' answers to all these questions? Is right and wrong decided by each individual within his or her own circumstances at the time? Or are there certain basic things that everybody should always do no matter what?

Do we decide that something is good because it feels good at the time? In other words, if something 'feels' good to us, should we go ahead and do it? Is there one standard against which any individual or any society can measure its behavior at any time under any circumstances? Or to put it another way, is there a given when it comes to ethics and morals and human behavior?

The ancient Hebrews answered all of these questions by saying that *they themselves* didn't have any answers to them. They made it clear through their writings (in what we call the Old Testament of the Bible) that the moral and ethical code they followed had not been invented by them. Neither had it grown out of their long experience as a people through some trial and error method. They also totally disagreed with the idea that people could do what was right in their own eyes as long as it seemed good or loving to them at the time. They had no patience with people who said something was okay to do or not to do depending on how a person felt.

To the Hebrews, the answers to all of these questions came from the 'outside.' They came from a great authority who revealed those answers to them. They came from Almighty God himself. He *gave* them a Law. He *presented* them with ethical and moral standards. He *expected* them to share those laws and standards with all nations. They were to apply to all peoples in all places at all times under all circumstances. They could not be argued with. They were right all of the time, not only part of the time. They were to be obeyed whether somebody felt like it or not. They were the *word of the Lord.* People could not decide to keep these laws or not to keep them on the basis of their own wisdom, ideas or experience. They were given in the perfect wisdom of an almighty, just, righteous, loving and merciful God. As their Heavenly Father, he knew exactly what his earthly children needed to live life fully.

Other ancient civilizations, of course, also developed legal, moral and ethical systems. Parts of them have survived to this day, and some parts overlapped the Hebrew Law. This happened because the human race had a common beginning. People were originally made in the image of God. They had the ability to lovingly relate to him, to their environment and to each other. Because of this, their descendents inherited some sense of good and bad and right and wrong, which are reflected in these systems. However, the Hebrews believed that very early on, the human race became corrupt and lost much of its sense of moral oughtness and rightness (See Genesis 3-9). As a result, human beings lost their way and wandered around in the dark trying to find and do the right. Some were more successful than others.

The Hebrews also believed that for this reason God broke into the affairs of the human race and came to its rescue. He did this by once again revealing his pattern for living life fully. The result was startling. No other legal code or moral system developed by any other ancient civilization equaled the clarity, the powerful simplicity and the moral uprightness of the Hebrew Law. No other system was based on the idea of self-giving love alone. For this reason, the Hebrews believed then (and Christians believe today) that spirituality, morality and ethics have been, are and always will be a divine '*given.* ' They were and are convinced that this given serves as a standard for the human race. It shows us what to believe and how to behave for all time.

However, the greatest difference between the Hebrew Law and other ancient codes lay in the area of motivation. For the most part, people obeyed other civilization's codes for three reasons. The first was to avoid being punished for doing wrong. The second was to please angry gods who were all too ready to harm them. The third was to bribe friendly gods who might be persuaded to help them.

The God of the Hebrews certainly made it clear that he was righteous and just and that there would be consequences for those who broke his laws. However, his warnings came out of his loving concern for their welfare. He knew that people would harm themselves and others if they broke his laws. But if they kept them, "everything will go well with you and your descendants forever." Deuteronomy 5:29 They were never to keep his laws simply to escape punishment. They were to keep them in order to live good, productive and enjoyable lives.

The God of the Hebrews was a just God, but he was also a merciful and a loving God. He didn't hope people would step out of line so he could have an opportunity to zap them. People weren't to keep his laws in order to persuade him not to harm them. In fact, if his people did break his laws, but repented, he would forgive them and heal them (See Psalm 103:1-2).

Neither were people to obey him in order to win his favor. *He had already shown them his favor* when they were a ragged group of powerless slaves in Egypt. They had done *nothing* to earn his attention or his favor. He had freed them from slavery because of his own love and mercy. He had rescued them from the Egyptians in order to faithfully keep his promises to their ancestors (See Deuteronomy 7:7-11; 11:1-13). There was nothing the Hebrews could ever do to be worthy of his grace and his mercy. They were a *free gift*. He wasn't like other so-called gods who had to be bribed to get their attention. He was not a god whose favors had to be earned by keeping rules or by carrying out rituals.

These ideas, along with many others about God, human behavior and the like have been around since anybody can remember. They're built into what we know as reality - either present by some freak, accidental, inexplicable chance, or introduced by somebody from the 'outside.' Which do you think is more credible?

Let's take people's ideas about God for example. There are those who teach that religious ideas developed through an evolutionary process. According to them, pre-literary peoples first thought that the forces of nature they couldn't understand, or the events in their lives that were beyond their control, or what would happen in the future, were all in the control of divine forces. They worshipped those forces in primitive ways, developing rites to either limit the power of the forces that could harm them or to win the favor of the forces that could help them. Eventually, they began to give names to these forces - calling them 'gods,' constructing images of them, and the like. Then their thoughts rose higher as they began to understand more about themselves and the universe, until they conceived of only one God as the creator and sustainer of the cosmos. Upon the rise of modern science, however, they moved into a 'post-religion' period. The idea of 'God' was no longer needed to explain what could now be explained by modern science concerning both the nature of the cosmos and of human life.

There are a number of problems with this view. First, nobody can adequately explain why pre-literary peoples should have independently thought up the idea that things were in the control of *divine* forces. Second, why do the 'advanced' and the 'primitive' views still exist side by side, even in some of the most scientifically advanced countries of the world (like animistic Shinto worship in Japan or polytheistic Hinduism among highly educated Indians)? Third, and most serious, this view doesn't honestly reflect reality. While people have made impressive technological and material progress, can the same be said for their moral and spiritual development? Do we not, for example, insult the 'primitives' when we say that people who can produce a Hitler's Germany or a Stalin's Russia or a Mao's China or an Idi Imin's Uganda or a South Africa's apartheid system, or an ISIS Caliphate are their moral superiors? Isn't the Bible right when it insists that it's been the other way around? God made people as morally and spiritually healthy beings, but rather than remaining that way, people chose to foul things up and disrupt their relationship with the true God. As a result, they've been in a moral and spiritual fog ever since as they grope and search for their own solutions to the problems of life and their own answers to the questions of life. (See Romans 1:18-32 and 2 Timothy 3:1-5).

An honest review of history and a true picture of reality reveals that whatever correct moral and ethical principles people have had, or whatever true ideas about God people have believed, have come to them not from within, but from without. Christians believe that

God came from 'the outside,' as it were, to cut through the moral and spiritual fog in which humanity was lost and to shine as a "light in the darkness." People would never have been able to find God by searching for him, so God had to come in search of *them*. He did so by acting in history to save his people, and by explaining the meaning of those acts to them. He also explained to them the implications of their salvation for their own lives and for the life of the world as a whole. He moved people who were in close touch with him to record these acts, explanations and implications in their own styles in a permanent record we call the Bible, so that people would not again go wandering off into the fog searching for new false gods made in their own image. This process went on for some two millennia (from Abraham to Paul), and involved over 40 people in the writing process alone, a process in which people became ever clearer about who God was and what he wanted them to be.

Of course, nobody can ever 'prove' that the Bible actually contains a true revelation of God about the human condition and about life. Only those who have met the living God through reading its pages or through hearing its message from others can know that it truly does. However, there are a number of things that point in this direction and can be of great help to those who are honestly open-minded and really want to know - especially as they compare it with the books of other religions that claim to contain the truth about God as well.

1. **More people have testified to God's truly revealing himself to them through the Bible than have done so for the writings of any other religion.**

Numbers don't prove anything, but they do mean something. According to Guinness World Records, the Bible is the best-selling book of all time with over five billion copies sold and distributed. Surely the impact this book has had on so many must at least point in the direction of its authenticity. Add to this the fact that the Bible continues to be bought and read by more people than any other book year after year, and that it has now been translated into almost all of the world's known languages and dialects, and again, you get the picture of a powerful book that has a powerful attraction for a great number of people.

2. The Bible has by far passed the most exhaustive tests ever applied to any written source.

During the last two hundred years, the Bible has undergone a series of attacks that for their vigor, intensity, and attention to microscopic detail, have been unparalleled in the known history of literature. Archaeologists, paleontologists, philologists, anthropologists, geologists, historiographers, theologians and the like, have all subjected it to intensive scrutiny, especially as to its historical accuracy. At first it looked like it might be as scientifically discredited as other religious sources have been. However, in the last 75 years, in the light of hundreds of new discoveries, it has shown that it can stand up to whatever honest tests people might want to apply to it.

Dr. W.F. Albright, recognized as one of the world's leading archaeologists, once stated, "There can be no doubt that archaeology has confirmed the substantial historicity of the Old Testament tradition." (W.F. Albright, *Archaeology and the Religion of Israel*, p.176) Nelson Glueck, famed Jewish archaeologist, once wrote, "It may be stated categorically that no archaeological discovery has ever controverted a biblical reference." (Nelson Glueck, *Rivers in the Desert*, p.31) In fact, it was Dr. Glueck who first broke with the trend of assuming that the Bible was in error until proven right by archaeological discovery on any disputed point. Once he and others assumed the reverse, they made rapid progress in solving many of what had been archaeological puzzles. In the same way, Dr. F.F. Bruce, in his famous book *Are the New Testament Documents Reliable?*, confirmed the historical accuracy of the data in the New Testament as well.

Subsequent archaeological discoveries have been made that further underscore these claims.

- In 1920, archaeologists discovered a hexagonal clay prism that records Assyrian King Sennacherib's military campaigns, including his campaign against Judah's King Hezekiah whom he claimed to have "imprisoned within his own royal city (Jerusalem) like a caged bird." The prism also records Sennacherib's miraculous defeat as recorded in 2 Kings 19:35-36.

- In 1947, Bedouin shepherds accidently discovered The Dead Sea Scrolls in caves at Qumran on the northwestern shores of the Dead Sea. The leather, papyrus and copper scrolls proved to be Hebrew manuscripts that push the date of the complete Hebrew Bible back to hundreds of years B.C.

- In 1961, archaeologists uncovered a stone bearing a dedicatory inscription to Tiberius Caesar from the Roman Prefect of Judea, "Pontius Pilate." The stone was discovered among the ruins of Caesarea, the Roman capital of Palestine during the time of Jesus. (The names of Gallio, proconsul of Achaea, and Lysanias, tetrarch of Abilene, both mentioned in the book of Luke, have likewise been similarly confirmed).

- In 1986, an archaeologist named Barkay discovered several amulets containing etched inscriptions bearing a shortened version of the priestly blessing in Numbers 6:24-26. Barkay dated the inscription, based on the archaeological context and style of script, to the late seventh or early sixth centuries B.C., 400 years older than the Dead Sea Scrolls!

- In 1990, the burial grounds of Caiaphas, the Jewish high priest, and his family were uncovered in Jerusalem.

- In 1993, Israeli Archaeologist Avraham Biran uncovered the Tel Dan Stele - a 9th century B.C. stone containing an inscription bearing the words "The house of David," a testimony to the biblical King David and the dynasty that he established in Israel in the 10th century B.C.

- In 2007, Israeli archaeologists discovered the tomb of Herod the Great whom Caesar and the Roman Senate called the "King of the Jews." Herod was in power when Jesus was born.

- In 2008, archaeologists unearthed a 3000 year old piece of pottery dating back to the Kingdom of David and with the oldest Hebrew text yet confirmed. The pot shard was found above the hillside where David was said to have fought Goliath.

- In 2009, archaeologists discovered ancient Egyptian coins bearing the name and portrait of the biblical Joseph.

- In 2010, a team of Israeli archaeologists discovered a wall nearly 35 feet tall and 230 feet long in Israel from the period of King Solomon and the First Temple confirming the Bible text in 1 Kings 3:1.

- In 2012, Israeli archaeologists confirmed the authenticity of a Bethlehem seal dating back to 700 B.C. excavated outside of Jerusalem's old city. The inscribed Hebrew script bears the name of "Bethlehem" which is the first time the town of Bethlehem (the town where Samuel anointed David to be king over Israel and where Jesus was born ten centuries later) is mentioned in any ancient artifact apart from biblical manuscripts.

- In 2013, among the Byzantine ruins at the foothills of Judaea, Israeli archaeologists uncovered the ruins of what they believed to be a palace of King David dating back to the tenth century B.C.

- In 2014, archaeologists unearthed an enormous 18th century B.C. structure that isolates and protects the Gihon Spring and is believed to be the Jebusite fortress described in the Book of Samuel that King David later conquered.

- In 2015, a rare ancient seal was excavated at the Temple Mount in Jerusalem dating back to the time of the Jebusites and King David. The seal belonged to a high ranking person from the First Temple era.

Further, the existence of at least 70 biblical characters, including kings, servants, scribes, and courtiers have been confirmed over the last two centuries of research. In the last two decades many more people have been added to this list through the discovery of seals, seal impressions, ostraca and monumental inscriptions. A number of recent archaeological finds coincide with events recorded in the Gospel according to John. Archaeologists have unearthed the five porticoes of the pool of Bethesda by the Sheep Gate (John 5:2), the pool of Siloam (9:1-7), Jacob's well at Sychar (4:5), the 'Pavement' (Gabbatha) where Pilate tried Jesus (19:13), and Solomon's porch in the Temple precincts (10:22-23)

There are, of course, other scholars, like Bart Ehrman (Professor of Religious Studies at the University of North Carolina at Chapel Hill), Marcus Borg (the late Professor of Religion and Culture at Oregon State University and a leading fellow of The Jesus Seminar), and others who have sought to discredit the historicity of the biblical record through numerous publications and video courses. However, since Ehrman, for example, is a professed atheist, one has to wonder how he, and others like him, can come to unbiased conclusions about these matters.

3. The Bible has been more accurately preserved through time than any other ancient book.

One of the well known phenomena of history is the exhaustive effort of the Jews to preserve the books of the Old Testament in a way that no other manuscripts have ever been preserved. They kept tabs on every letter, syllable, word and paragraph. Whoever counted the letters, syllables and words of Plato, Aristotle, Cicero or Confucius?! The 800 Hebrew Dead Sea Scrolls dating as far back as 150 B.C. confirmed the astonishing fact that later texts hardly varied from these ancient texts! In 2016, experts using a computer imaging program virtually unwrapped a charred ancient scroll and recovered a 2000-year-old fragment of the Old Testament that was identical to the authoritative Masoretic text of the Hebrew Bible!

As for the New Testament, more than 26,000 manuscripts (complete and incomplete) have survived from antiquity, with hundreds more possibly waiting to be found. No other work from classical antiquity has such a wealth of material available to cross check its accuracy. For example, only 100 copies of Sophocles' writings exist, and the earliest of these manuscripts dates 1400 years after his death! By contrast, the New Testament is confirmed by more than 6,000 Greek manuscripts dating from the second, third and fourth centuries after they were written.

4. The Bible shows a consistency and continuity that are remarkable.

Consider that this book was written by some 40 different authors, with a variety of personalities and backgrounds, living under widely different conditions, writing in every imaginable literary style and doing all of this over a period of some 1400 years! How could the Bible help but be a hopelessly confused hodgepodge containing major contradictions (a great weakness that is found in other religious writings)? And yet, one can read the 1300 pages of this library of 66 books and find an amazing unity of theme and outlook. What could possibly account for this other than the one true God being the ultimate source of its content and controlling the process by which it came into being?

5. Jesus Christ, who demonstrated that he was a reliable authority in every respect, personally verified the truth of the entire Old Testament.

- **Matthew 4:4, 7, 10**: "The scripture says, 'Human beings cannot live on bread alone, but need every word that God speaks...The scripture also says, 'Do not put the Lord your God to the test…The scripture says, 'Worship the Lord your God and serve only him!'"

- **Matthew 5:17-19:** "Do not think that I have come to abolish the Law or the Prophets; I have not come to abolish them but to fulfill them. For truly I tell you, until heaven and earth disappear, not the smallest letter, not the least stroke of a pen, will by any means disappear from the Law until everything is accomplished. Therefore anyone who sets aside one of the least of these commands and teaches others accordingly will be called least in the kingdom of heaven, but whoever practices and teaches these commands will be called great in the kingdom of heaven."

- **Matthew 19:4-5**: "Haven't you read (the scripture) that at the beginning the Creator made them male and female, and said, 'For this reason a man will leave his father and mother and be united to his wife, and the two will become one flesh?'"

- **Matthew 22:29**: "How wrong you are! It is because you don't know the Scriptures or God's power."

- **Matthew 26:31**: "This very night all of you will run away and leave me, for the scripture says, 'God will kill the shepherd, and the sheep of the flock will be scattered.'"

- **Mark 9:12-13**: "Elijah is indeed coming first in order to get everything ready. Yet why do the Scriptures say that the Son of Man will suffer much and be rejected? I tell you, however, that Elijah has already come and that people treated him just as they pleased, as the Scriptures say about him."

- **Mark 12:28-31**: "A teacher of the Law…came to him with a question: 'Which commandment is the most important of all?' Jesus replied, 'The most important one is this: 'Listen, Israel! The Lord our God is the only Lord. Love the Lord your God with all your heart, with all your soul, with all your mind, and with all your strength.' The second most important commandment is this: 'Love your neighbor as you love yourself.' There is no other commandment more important than these two.'"

- **Mark 14:21**: "The Son of Man will die as the Scriptures say he will; but how terrible for that man who will betray the Son of Man! It would have been better for that man if he had never been born!"

- **John 10:34**: "It is written in your own Law that God said, 'You are gods.' We know that what the scripture says is true forever."

- **John 13:18**: "I am not talking about all of you; I know those I have chosen. But the scripture must come true that says, 'The man who shared my food turned against me.'"

- **John 17:12**: "While I was with them, I kept them safe by the power of your name, the name you gave me. I protected them, and not one of them was lost, except the man who was bound to be lost - so that the scripture might come true."

- **Luke 4: 16-21**: "Then Jesus went to Nazareth, where he had been brought up, and on the Sabbath he went as usual to the synagogue. He stood up to read the Scriptures and was handed the book of the prophet Isaiah. He unrolled the scroll and found the place where it is written,

> 'The Spirit of the Lord is upon me,
> because he has chosen me to bring good news to the poor.
> He has sent me to proclaim liberty to the captives
> and recovery of sight to the blind,
> to set free the oppressed
> and announce that the time has come
> when the Lord will save his people.'

Jesus rolled up the scroll, gave it back to the attendant, and sat down. All the people in the synagogue had their eyes fixed on him, as he said to them, 'This passage of scripture has come true today, as you heard it being read.'"

6. The Bible doesn't suffer from the limitations of other religious writings. On the contrary, it has a very high view of God, creation, human beings, salvation, the new life and the like.

The Bible isn't prudish, but deals with sex, sin and the facts of life realistically. It is not ascetic, but knows that human appetites are real and God-given. It's not fanatical, but asks us to do the *opposite* of the strange, the weird, the fantastic, the foolhardy or the ridiculous. It's not highly mystical, but has a balanced approach to engaging with both mind and heart in spiritual communion with God. The great bulk of its content emphasizes the holy, the true, the good and the beautiful. The Bible describes God as possessing all of the qualities we would hope he would have. He's not a fickle, immoral all-powerful despot, but a loving heavenly Father who forgives us and gives us new life at great cost to himself.

There are a number of other things that point to the authenticity of the Bible:

- The historical fulfillment of the prophecies made in it.

- Its unique treatment of themes like creation, love and suffering.

- The scope of its content that covers the whole story of the cosmos from the beginning to the end (which is portrayed as a new beginning).

All of this is by and large in some way or other in stark contrast to the texts and scriptures of other faiths. But pointers can't *prove* anything. No matter how good the evidence might be, only the person whose mind and heart are open to meeting the living God through its pages will, in the end, be convinced that God has really made himself known in this way. Only the person who is truly open to seeking the truth will find that all of the ideas that are worth knowing and believing in the areas of faith and life have ultimately come from God through the experiences and explanations recorded in this book.

<u>What Do *You* Think?</u>

1. I agree with/disagree with/am not sure about the conclusions of this chapter because ......

2. I think Christianity is the product of humanity's search for God/God's search for humanity because ......

3. Of the six cases presented for the authenticity of the Bible, I think #_____ is the most persuasive because ......

4. Of the six cases presented for the authenticity of the Bible, I think
5. #_____ is the least persuasive because ......

Chapter Seven

DO SCIENCE AND CHRISTIANITY CONFLICT?

> "In the beginning, God created the universe."
>
> Genesis 1:1
>
> "It is by faith that we understand that the universe was created by God's word, so that what can be seen was made out of what cannot be seen."   Hebrews 11:9

Looking Through the Microscope |

The Debate

The two debate teams walked onto the platform, and the buzzing conversation in the packed hall quieted down. The moderator welcomed the participants, introduced the judges, explained the rules and announced the resolution to be debated.

Resolved:
That There Is a Conflict
Between Modern Science and the Christian Faith

The moderator invited the first speaker for the affirmative side to give his team's opening statement, and the debate was on. The speaker walked to the microphone. "This resolution has been well stated. It's become increasingly clear that the advance of modern science over the past 275 years has meant the retreat of religion.

Before the 18th century, people needed religion to explain what they couldn't understand about the universe or about the forces that controlled events. Since that time, one scientific discovery after another has provided the answers to their questions, the explanations for what puzzled them, and the solutions to the problems they experienced. One only has to look at the advances made in the area of medicine alone, for example, to clearly see this. Although such answers, explanations and solutions are not yet complete, it's only a matter of time before they will be, since the fundamental breakthroughs pointing to the possibility of such completion have already been made.

"Due to these advances, 21st century humans have been liberated from superstition. People now know *they* are in charge of their own destiny. They no longer need 'god' or religion to provide the answers, explanations and solutions to what was before mysterious. Modern people, through modern science, have grown up. They no longer need the old 'pacifier' of religion that they needed in their days of infancy and insecurity. We shouldn't look at this as a loss of something valuable, but as the gain of a new sense of freedom, dignity and responsibility for the human race.

"Unfortunately, some people haven't yet, as it were, grown up. For example, they acknowledge the advances of science and enjoy the benefits, but at the same time they want to hang on to their old religious 'security blanket.' Although it's a logical contradiction, they endorse science with their left hand and religion with their right hand and somehow try to reconcile the two. Since science and Christianity are diametrically opposed to one another, this is an untenable position. Scientists deal with objective facts based on careful clinical observation, while Christians are lost in their own subjectivity and can spin any wild theory they want about 'god,' reality, or whatever, with no possibility of ever proving or disproving their fanciful ideas.

"To demonstrate the absurdity of religious belief, it's only necessary to take a look at the Bible, for example. Its pages are filled with superstitious beliefs and myths which are either beyond scientific verification or have actually been disproved by scientific investigation. For example, who in their right mind would ever seriously believe that a man named Jonah was swallowed by a whale for three days, and that he lived to tell the tale? Or who would ever step forward with a scientifically acceptable explanation for Joshua's making the sun stand still to enable the Israelites to fight on in abnormal daylight? Or who would not agree that science has proved that the claim that God created the universe in six days is a completely false claim?

"And then there are the miracles. Why are they called 'miracles'? Because they defy all the well-known laws of science, that's why. How can we possibly accept these fanciful accounts of turning water into wine, feeding some 10, 000 people with two fish and five pieces of bread, etc, etc, when these feats are scientific impossibilities? No, we can't have it both ways. Either we need to call Christianity by its true name - anti-scientific superstition - and give it up, or we must give science up. The two are mutually contradictory."

The moderator now invited the first speaker from the opposing team to state her case. She cleared her throat and stepped up to the microphone.

"The foundations of modern science can be traced back to Christian beliefs. Christians have always been nature affirming people. They believe that God created the world good, and that therefore nature, and all the processes and principles that maintain it, can be affirmed, enjoyed and utilized for good. They also believe that God created human beings as unique beings and gave them a unique task - to explore, discover, develop and responsibly manage the whole of creation. Therefore, Christians haven't been afraid of nature, or tried to escape from the material world. Instead, they've been fascinated by it and have eagerly plunged into the task of understanding it and utilizing it for the good of all.

"Christians have seen no tension, let alone contradiction, between what they've called the 'two books' - the book of nature (seeing God through his creation) and the book of revelation (having a more direct encounter with him through some event or experience or the revealed truth contained in the Bible). Truth is one. Whatever is discovered to be true in the 'book of nature' by scientific means can't and won't be contradicted by whatever is discovered to be true through God's revelation, and vice versa. Even though at times it may have *seemed* as though there was a contradiction, time and patience have revealed that what appeared to be a contradiction was only an *apparent* contradiction that was caused by our limited knowledge or limited faith at that moment. This has proved to be true time and time again, particularly during the last 100 years.

"The point is to see that these two 'books' can *at the same time* reveal truth about a given subject, but often from different perspectives - one scientific (to use the word in its presently understood narrow sense) and the other from a faith-based perspective. These perspectives do not *contradict* one another, but *complement* one another, since they are talking about the same truth, but from different angles. What I mean is that modern scientists are chiefly concerned with discovering the 'how' or the mechanics of something, not with explaining the 'why' or the meaning of something. Christians are also interested in the 'how' of something, but are chiefly concerned with discovering the 'why' or the meaning of something. Both scientists and Christians are concerned with *what* happened or happens, but scientists concentrate on *analyzing* what happened or happens, while Christians concentrate on *interpreting* what happened or happens. Scientists mainly depend on empirical knowledge (what can be physically measured) for their conclusions, while Christians mainly depend on intuitive knowledge (what can be known by immediate insight) for their conclusions.

"For example, a scientist can describe a sunset by giving you all the mathematical data and physical formulas needed to explain how it happens, but does that describe the whole of it? I hope not! Although he knows nothing about all of this data, an unlettered fisherman's exclamation of awe and wonder at the beauty of a sunset reflected on the water is also a true description of the sunset, but from a different perspective and at a different level. Nobody would say that these two descriptions *contradict* each other. On the contrary, they *complement* one another and *together* get closer to the whole truth about the sunset than either one of them could do separately. So it is with modern science and Christianity. They both speak of the *one* truth, but from different perspectives. This is why many of the greatest scientists in the past, and many of those in the present, were and are devout Christians who see no contradiction whatsoever between their profession and their faith. Rather, they're excited by being in the enviable position of seeing the whole truth about things in a way that many of the rest of us can't do without their help.

"How then has this false idea that science and Christianity contradict one another come about? It's come about because some Christians have wrongly used their faith to formulate an unscientific view of the 'how' of things, and because some scientists have wrongly used their scientific method to formulate an unscientific view of the 'why' of things. People have failed to recognize that on the one hand, the Bible doesn't claim to be a science textbook, while on the other hand, a scientist can't apply the scientific method to spiritual realities. For example, did the Bible writers intend to give us a scientific explanation of the nature of the cosmos as we now know it? Of course not. Or can a scientist analyze what we call 'love' in a test tube? Again, of course not. It's only when Christians pontificate on scientific matters using the criteria of faith, or scientists pontificate on matters of faith using the criteria of the scientific method that an *apparent* contradiction between Christianity and science appears. But it's only *apparent* and not real.

"As for the charge that the Bible's pages are filled with superstitious beliefs and myths which are either beyond scientific verification or have actually been disproved by scientific investigation, quite the contrary is true. It's the people who don't read or understand the Bible correctly that are the problem. Take the case of Jonah, for example. The Biblical record states that there was an actual historical figure named Jonah who did prophesy in Israel during the reign of King Jeroboam II (786 -746 B.C.). However, in observing the literary style of the book that bears his name and in doing proper historical research, it's quite clear that he couldn't have written the book. For example, the book is written in the third person and there's no record of any such visit to Nineveh or any such mass conversion in Assyrian records, which is unusual seeing that the king played such a prominent part in it.

"The book was most likely written in post-exilic times by an author who used the name of a known historical person as his main character - a practice commonly used at the time. Like Jesus often did, the writer used the medium of a parable to get his message across to the proud and isolationist-minded Jews - that Israel was to be God's messenger to the Gentiles, his 'missionary' to the world. The saga of a three-day ride in the belly of a great fish or the sudden mass conversion of the entire city of Nineveh is therefore simply part of the 'tale.' Jesus refers to Jonah's saga in the New Testament, but that doesn't mean he thought it literally happened. For example, if a person today were to say, "As Charlie Brown would say, 'Good Grief!'" would that mean that Charles Schultz's famous cartoon character was an actual literal historical person? Of course not.

"Take the case of the sun standing still for Joshua, for another example. It's certainly possible that God *could* have caused the earth to stop rotating and the sun and moon to consequently appear to stop in the sky for a whole day at Joshua's command so that Israel could win a victory, but hardly probable. For one thing, God usually works *through* the laws of nature he has set up to achieve his purposes, not contrary to them. For another, the scientific consequences of such a phenomenon would have been staggering. But more importantly, the context and the type of literature involved in the account of this event actually lead to the conclusion that such a phenomenon did *not* literally occur.

"In order to understand this account better, it should be compared with one in Judges 5 which records a song celebrating Israel's victory over the Canaanite King Jabin under Israelite Judges Deborah and Barak. The song actually says the stars fought from the sky against Jabin's general Sisera on behalf of Israel! Obviously, no one would take this as a statement of literal scientific fact because of the context in which the statement is made and the poetic nature of the song. The same can be said for the statement in Joshua 10 upon close examination of the text. The writer quotes the phrase about the sun and the moon standing still from the (now lost) Book of Jashar - and the phrase is in poetic form! It appears that the author lifted this phrase out of a hymn celebrating Israel's victory over the coalition of kings that was similar to Deborah and Barak's hymn celebrating Israel's victory over Jabin and Sisera. Neither of these references was meant to be taken as literal statements of scientific fact.

"In my opinion, if those disparaging seemingly 'unscientific' events in the Bible would do their literary and historical homework, they would find most of their objections more than adequately met.

"In sum then, rather than seeing science and Christianity as contradictory enemies, we should see them as complementary friends. Both are needed to understand all of the wonders of reality, but each in its own way. If we depend only on science for our understanding of reality, we'll end up with a materialistic-technological, and therefore warped, view. If we depend only on faith for our understanding of reality, we'll end up with a mystical-magical, and therefore equally warped, view. God meant for us to use *both* of our 'eyes' to see the totality of his reality, not just one or the other."

The debate continued, with each side having an opportunity for rebuttal and summation in turn. After the final argument, the teams waited nervously for the judges' decision. It would be difficult to decide, since the decision had to be based on the types of arguments used and the skills of the debaters, not on whether, in the judges' opinions, the arguments were right or wrong. After the announcement of the winner and the subsequent applause, the students filed noisily out of the hall, with everyone agreeing that it had been a spirited and interesting debate.

What Do *You* Think?

1. Which speaker did you most agree with, and why?

2. Did you agree with all/most/some/none of what the first speaker had to say? Explain.

3. Did you agree with all/most/some/none of what the second speaker had to say? Explain.

4. What do you think of Albert Einstein's statement that, "Science without religion is lame. Religion without science is blind."?

5. When *you* think of the relationship between modern science and the Christian faith, what is the one thing that most bothers you?

<u>Bringing Things Into Focus |</u>

True or False?

Which of the following statements are true, which are false, and why?

1. The Bible teaches that God created the heavens and the earth in six 24 hour days.

2. The concept of the evolution of all things (including humans) through natural selection is as yet an unproven scientific theory, not a law.

3. Modern science and the Christian faith are more contradictory than complimentary.

4. The "Big Bang" theory of the origin of the cosmos contradicts the account of creation in Genesis 1.

5. An honest non-Christian scientist would have to say that as a scientist, he could not answer the question as to whether or not there was a God who created matter and out of that matter created the cosmos.

6. The writer of Genesis 1 had a very different concept of the origin and development of the cosmos than we have today.

7. The writer(s) of Genesis 1 and 2 are not so much dealing with *how* God brought the earth and life into being, but *that* he did so.

8. What distinguishes human beings from the animals is the fact that God created humans with a soul.

9. Scientists say the earth is 4.5 billion years old and that the first humans appeared some 200,000 years ago, while it can be

deduced from the Bible that the earth and humans are only 6,000 years old.

10. Being created in the image of God means that humans are relational, responsible and God's representatives on earth.

Gaining a Perspective |

Science and the Scriptures

Here's a list of controversial statements from the Bible.

- "In six days I, the Lord, made the earth, the sky, the sea, and everything in them." Exodus 20:11.

- "God ... took out one of the man's ribs ... He formed a woman out of the rib and brought her to him." Genesis 2:21-22.

- "All the outlets of the vast body of water beneath the earth burst open, all the floodgates of the sky were opened, and rain fell on the earth for forty days and forty nights ... the water ... went on rising until it was 23 feet above the tops of the mountains. Every living being on the earth died ..." Genesis 7:11, 20-21.

- "Joshua spoke to the Lord. In the presence of the Israelites he said, 'Sun, stand still over Gibeon; Moon, stop over Aijalon Valley.' The sun stood still and the moon did not move until the nation had conquered its enemies." Joshua 10:12-13.

- "Roar, sea, and every creature in you; sing, earth, and all who live on you! Clap your hands, you rivers; you hills sing together with joy before the Lord." Psalm 98:7-8.

- "God sends earthquakes and shakes the ground: he rocks the pillars that support the earth ... God hung the stars in the sky ...

He crushed his enemies who helped Rahab, the sea monster, oppose him." Job 9:6, 9, 13.

- "But God is my King from long ago; he brings salvation on the earth. It was you who split open the sea by your power; you broke the heads of the monster in the waters. It was you who crushed the heads of Leviathan and gave it as food to the creatures of the desert." Psalm 74:12-14 "Can you catch Leviathan with a fish-hook? ... Flames blaze from his mouth, and streams of sparks fly out. Smoke comes pouring out of his nose." Job 41:1, 19-20.

- "At the Lord's command a large fish swallowed Jonah and he was inside the fish for three days and three nights." Jonah 1:17.

- "And so, in honor of the name of Jesus all beings in heaven, on earth, and in the world below will fall on their knees." Philippians 2:10.

- "He showed me Jerusalem, the Holy City coming down out of heaven ... The city shone like a precious stone ... It had a great, high wall with twelve gates." Revelation 21:10-12.

What Do *You* Think?

1. Do you think these quotations from the Bible are scientific statements? Why or why not?

2. Which quotation do you find the easiest to accept, and why?

3. Which quotation do you find it the most difficult to accept, and why?

4. Do you think the writers of the Bible had a dated or a modern view of the physical world? Explain

Drawing Conclusions |

Conflicting or Complementary?

The best way to demonstrate that there is no conflict between modern science and the Christian faith is to concentrate on a few concrete cases that have seemed to some people to prove that there is such a conflict.

1. The first case has to do with the origin of the cosmos.

There've been a number of scientific theories to explain the origin of the cosmos, the latest of these being the 'Big Bang' theory. According to this theory, around 13.8 billion years ago there was a tremendous cosmic explosion that originated from an infinitesimal compressed entity and extreme heat that expanded at an enormous speed resulting in the formation of the universe in which our earth finds itself (a universe that is still expanding at a rapid rate). (Interestingly enough, even this theory has lately been questioned due to new data coming from space probes.)

Christians also have a theory: in the beginning, God created matter, and out of that matter he created the universe (See Hebrews 11:3 and Genesis 1:1). Notice that the Christian theory doesn't conflict with the various scientific theories put forward. No one has yet come up with much of an explanation as to how *matter* originated, but if and when they would, and if it were correct, Christians would congratulate scientists for having discovered *the process that God used*! And if, in fact, our universe *was* formed by a huge explosion once matter was present, Christians believe they know WHO *caused* that explosion.

Conversely, if the question were put to an honest non-Christian scientist as to whether God created matter and out of that matter created the cosmos, s/he would simply have to say that as a scientist, s/he couldn't answer the question. It's a question that has to do with a matter that's beyond the scope of the scientific method to either prove or disprove. It's a theory to be believed or disbelieved. (Although at present it would appear that the case for believing it is much stronger than the case for disbelieving it. See Chapter Two.) A problem only arises when this question is asked of a *dis*honest scientist, namely one who's a believer in 'scientism.' 'Scientism' is the 'faith' that by mechanistic definition rules out any possibility of there being a God. It *believes* in the theory that everything started by sheer chance and that natural phenomena are explained strictly by reference to natural laws or material processes, without any scientific foundation for those beliefs whatsoever. In this case, there's no problem of a conflict between science and the Christian faith, but a problem of dealing with a 'scientist' who claims to be a prophet. Christians don't mind that this person *believes* in a different theory about the origin of the universe. That's his or her right. But Christians do mind his or her falsely cloaking his or her theory in the robes of 'scientific objectivity.'

2. **The second case has to do with the way in which our earth, and the creatures living on it, developed.**

The most popularly accepted modern scientific theory has been that the earth and life developed over a long period of time through an evolutionary process. It should be remembered that this is still very much an unproven *theory* that has recently come under increased criticism by some scientists themselves. Be that as it may, at the present time, it still seems to be one possible credible explanation for the development of the natural world.

This theory has troubled a number of Christians because they've seen it as a direct contradiction of the accounts of creation as outlined in Genesis 1-2 in the Bible. For example, some Christians believe the Bible teaches that God created the world in six literal 24 hour days. Others believe the Genesis 'days' might have been longer periods of time, but that the order in which Genesis says things were created must be correct. Still others have favored other interpretations. Although they may have different interpretations of the data, most of these Christians have agreed on two things: they believe the Genesis account is a scientifically accurate account of the creation of the world, and they are determined to discredit the evolutionary theory as a dangerous contradiction of that account.

Could the world have suddenly been created in six days, or periods, or whatever, and in the order and the way it's described in Genesis? These are all possibilities, but in light of the present findings of science, none of them are as probable as the present evolutionary theory (although that theory may certainly be laid to rest, like a lot of other theories have been, by new discoveries and observations in the future). However, whatever the theory might turn out to be, if the theory is correct, it will not be in conflict with the Christian faith, or with the Genesis accounts. Those accounts are not *scientific* descriptions of *how* God brought things into being, but *theological* statements of the *meaning* of God's creative work, *whatever* act or process he may have used. If we want an explanation of the mechanics of the development of our world, we had best consult our science books and not the Bible.

The conflict over the Genesis accounts has not basically been the fault of some anti-religious scientific attack, but of misguided Christians who have insisted on using the Bible as a science text book and have thereby created an *apparent* contradiction between the Bible and modern science. This quarrel has been made worse, of course, by some scientists who *are* anti-religious. As we've said, these scientists try to eliminate the possibility of God being involved in the creation process altogether (whether that be through the process of 'natural selection,' or whatever) in the name of science, by dishonestly using unscientific criteria.

How do we know that Genesis 1-2 is not a scientific account of creation? For one thing, an insistence on seeing it as such means that a Christian must struggle to explain a number of items in these chapters that contradict firmly established scientific data. For example, how can vegetation appear on day 3, and the sun appear on day 4, when the sun is vital to the process of photosynthesis which makes plant life possible? But this kind of negative reason is not a good reason upon which to base our view, since it would then appear that the only reason we are adopting it is to escape present (and perhaps temporary) difficulties in reconciling these accounts with modern scientific data. There are much better positive reasons for believing that these accounts are not scientific statements. We can see what these are by asking three basic questions.

--What were the Bible writers *intending* to say?--

Were they more interested in conveying ideas about theology, or about biology, zoology, physics and chemistry? A careful study of these creation accounts will show that they were mainly concerned about *theology*, with the rest being incidental to their main themes. Some of these theological themes are:

- 1:1-2 - God is the sovereign Creator of all.

- 1:3-4 - Time, as well as life and things, belongs to God.

- 1:3-5, 14-19 - God creates light and dispels darkness.

- 1:6-8 - God brings order out of chaos.

- 1:4, 10, 12, etc - God's creation is orderly, dependable and good.

- 1:26-27 - God created men and women in his own image.

--What literary device did the author of Genesis 1 employ?--

If Genesis 1 was intended as a serious scientific account, one would expect the writer to have expressed it in a prose framework, not a poetic framework. However, a careful study of the Hebrew text reveals that chapter 1 is written in the style of a grand hymn of praise, the construction of which is the work a poetic genius. Looking at the chapter in this way will demonstrate this clearly.

Introduction (Genesis 1:1-2)

Day 1: Light (1:3-5)   **Day 4: Luminaries (1:14-19)**

Day 2: "Sky" & Water (1:6-10) Day 5: Birds & Fish (1:20-23)

Day 3: Plants (1:11-13)   Day 6: Animals &Humans (1:24-31)

Day 7: Conclusion (Rest) (2:1-4a)

Notice that what was created on days 4-6 matches what was created on days 1-3! This is no accident. It's a deliberate literary device to convey timeless truths about God, his relationship to his world and to us in a non-literal way within the context of the ancient cosmology of that day.

--What was the scientific context within which the author of Genesis 1 was writing?--

A little detective work through the pages of the Old Testament, and even through the New Testament (since by the time of the birth of Christ, people's ideas about cosmology hadn't changed much) reveals a picture of the author's concept of the universe that looks like this.

THE HEBREW CONCEPT OF THE UNIVERSE

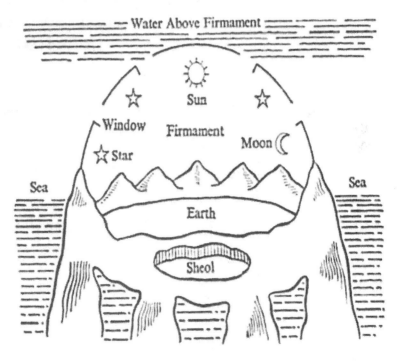

The ancient Hebrews believed that the earth was flat, standing on pillars in the water (that were sometimes bumped into by giant sea monsters causing earthquakes). The spooky world of the dead was a large cavern under the earth called 'Sheol.' The water surrounding the earth was kept from flooding the earth by a ring of mountains around the edges. The water above the earth was kept out by a dome called the 'sky,' but the dome had 'windows' in it that God could open or shut to let in the rain. The sun, moon and stars moved on fixed tracks within the dome, and God lived above the waters above the dome.

You may think this picture of the universe quite amusing, but it was actually quite profound for someone who was trying to figure out how everything fits together with his naked eye while lying on his back! Profound or not, all would agree that this concept of the physical universe has now been shown to be totally wrong from a scientific viewpoint. The question then naturally arises: how could somebody who had such a scientifically inaccurate picture of the universe have possibly written a scientifically accurate account of the development of the earth and life as we now know it? Obviously he couldn't have. Does this take anything away from the accuracy of his theological ideas or the way in which he interpreted what he saw and experienced? Not at all since he was supremely qualified to write about that, *whatever* his scientific views might have been. (And this is exactly why his timeless 'hymn' continues to speak powerfully to us today even though we have a very different view of things, scientifically speaking, than he did, and might have a still different view tomorrow). There is, therefore, no conflict between Genesis 1 and modern science.

3.   The third case has to do with the origin of human beings.

Again, an *apparent* contradiction has been raised in this area by some misguided Christians on the one hand and some misguided scientists on the other. These Christians got worried because they heard evolutionists say that human beings are descended from the animals. They thought this contradicted the Biblical record that humans are physically and spiritually distinct from the animals, and that God created people with a 'soul.' Some evolutionists didn't help matters by insisting that humans are merely the highest animal form, *and nothing more.* Again, those who held such a view were expressing an article of faith in the 'creed' of scientism, not a conclusion based on scientifically acceptable evidence. When, on the one hand, we take a careful look at what the Bible actually has to say on this matter and, on the other hand, consider the opinion of honest scientists, we will see once again that what *appears* to be a contradiction between the two is not, in fact, a contradiction at all.

Let's be clear from the start that the kind of literature we're dealing with in Genesis 2 (and indeed, all the way up to Genesis 11:27) is not a straightforward account of 'history' as we normally think of it today. It is more like what's known as 'saga' literature - accounts that may be built around a historical core of factual people or events (called 'pre-history'), but that are basically attempts to convey timeless truths using a story or parable approach.

For example, the Hebrew words 'man' and 'woman' mean 'from the ground' and 'from the man,' while the names 'Adam' and 'Eve' mean 'humankind' and 'mother of humanity.' Adam and Eve could have been persons who actually lived in ancient times. However, it also could well be that the story of Adam and Eve in a garden setting is a profound representative parable on the origin of the human race, the uniqueness of human beings, the origin of marriage and family, the peaceable relationship between all creatures (and between them and the environment) and the origin of sin rather than a factual historical record of the lives of two people. Whether the people in the early Genesis stories as recorded in Genesis 1:27-31 and 2:7-11:26 actually lived or not, we cannot say, but that doesn't matter since the writer(s) main interest is to tell stories that will convey truths about mankind and the meaning of life, sin, death and salvation. These stories are like Jesus' parables. His emphasis was not on whether the characters in his parables were actually real people, but on the timeless points that he was making by the telling of them.

But don't some of the New Testament writers refer to Adam and Eve as historical people? Not necessarily. For example, if a person today were to refer to 'Shylock's pound of flesh', or to say, "As Mackey Mouse would say' would that mean that Shakespeare's famous character in *The Merchant of Venice* or Walt Disney's famous character in his cartoons were actual, literal historical people? Of course not. Similarly, simply because Adam, Eve, Job, Jonah and others like them are mentioned in the New Testament doesn't prove or disprove that they actually lived in history as real people.

What then does the writer of Genesis 2 actually teach us about people through the Adam & Eve account? Does he make it clear that there's something very unique about us that's not true of the rest of the creatures that God brought into being? Emphatically yes! What makes people unique - that they're physically different from the animals? Not at all. People are described as having been made out of the same material that the animals were made of, with God using the same method for the creation of both. (Compare Genesis 2:7 and 2:19, for example). Are human beings unique because they have a 'soul' and the animals don't have one? Again the answer is "no." The same life-giving breath God breathed into human beings to make them come alive, is the same life-giving breath he breathed into the animals to make them come alive. (Compare Genesis 2:7 and 7:15, 21-22, for example). Also note that the Bible doesn't teach that humans are made up of several 'parts,' including one part called 'the soul.' Rather, they're described as being unified psycho-somatic beings whose spiritual nature permeates and is inseparable from the rest of their being.

If the physical makeup of human beings and the method in which they were created are not unique, then what does it matter as to the process God used to bring the human race into being? He could have used a long process of evolutionary development, or he could not have. That's a question for science to answer, as long as scientists are willing to leave open the question of whether *God* was behind and working through such a process or not - a truth that the writer(s) of Genesis 1-2 most strongly affirm(s).

What do the writer(s) of Genesis 1-2 then say *is* unique about humans? *That people are created in the image of God*! (See Genesis 1:27). But what does *that* mean? If we carefully study the record, we can see that it means three things.

- **God made *people*, not the animals, his *representatives* who** were charged with managing his creation and equipped for the task. (See Genesis 1:28 and 2:19-20). That's why nobody would ever dream of appointing a pig as the Governor of California!

- **God made *people*, not the animals, morally *responsible*** for their actions, and equipped them to make moral decisions. (See Genesis 2:16-17). That's why nobody would ever dream of taking a cow that had trampled their garden to court!

- **God made *people*, not the animals, able to freely and lovingly *relate*** to him and to one another, and equipped them with the ability to do so. (See Genesis 2:24-25 and 3:21). That's why nobody would ever dream of marrying a horse!

How and by what process people came to be this way (what we can call beings with a spiritual nature) is not clear, but the idea *that* God made us this way is very clear.

4. The fourth case has to do with Noah and the Flood.

Some Christians have insisted that the story of Noah and the great flood as recorded in Genesis 6-9 be taken as a literal event in all its detail. But to do so is to misread the evidence and invite a scientific rebuff. Like the stories of the creation and the Garden of Eden, the Flood account isn't intended to be a scientific and historical description of a series of events. It's obvious that the writer(s) use(s) hyperbole as a literary device that includes a cataclysmic event, a massive ark which holds representatives of "every living creature on Earth," a flood which flows over the tops of the highest mountains in the world and a period of 40 days, a symbolic number representing a period of testing and trial. (This number is mentioned 149 times in the Bible, the most noted of which are Moses' 40 days on Mount Sinai, Elijah's 40 day fast in the wilderness and Jesus' 40 day temptation in the desert). These clues strongly suggest that we are dealing with a theological story here, not with ancient journalism.

There are other clues that bear this out. One is the command given to Noah to separate "clean" animals from "unclean" animals, even though these categories would not be given to the Israelites until the time of Moses some 15 centuries later. Even a massive 450 foot long, 75 foot wide, and 45 foot high ark could hardly have contained two (and sometimes seven) pairs of every animal, bird, and insect on the entire earth, let alone all the necessary food, the means of keeping the boat clean and the cages needed to keep thousands of species from devouring one another.

Archaeologists have discovered evidence for three major floods in the ancient Mesopotamian region - one at Kish and another at Shruppak around 3500 B.C., and one at Ur around 2900 B.C. It could well be that one of these floods formed the basis for the core narrative in Genesis which was then elaborated upon. The known 'world' at that time was made up of the fairly small region of Mesopotamia. This region was believed by the Mesopotamians to be all that made up the entire earth which explains the "whole world" language the writer(s) used. This narrative, at first orally transmitted down through generations, appears to have formed the historical core around which a saga then developed. This core most likely also have contained some factual aspects about humans and animals being rescued from one of these floods in a boat.

The writer(s) of Genesis used this narrative as a framework through which to convey some very important timeless truths about God, people and the world. For example, God will hold humans accountable for their behavior; God is willing and able to save those who have faith in him; both God's warnings and promises can be depended upon. While the writer(s) of Genesis recount real events (such as the creation of the universe and the special place humans have in it, the Flood, the Tower of Babel, etc.), they record them in ways that focus on the purpose of the story rather than on a plain scientific or historical narration of facts as we understand them today. All ancient peoples (including the Israelites) wrote historical accounts, especially those concerning "primeval" events near the beginning of history, in this way. And they wrote these accounts not only through the lens of ancient literature, but also within the context of the ancient cosmology that we've already discussed. Seen in this way, the account of Noah and the Flood doesn't create a conflict between honest Christians and honest scientists.

In sum, through this account of Noah and the Flood, God chose to communicate his message through ordinary people by accommodating himself to their limited knowledge in order to draw them to him. In the end, this story communicates an inspired and powerful message about judgment and grace that has taught God's people throughout the ages about his hatred of sin and his love for his creation - a love that would eventually see the God of grace coming in the person of his son, Jesus Christ, to take the judgment for human sin upon himself and to bring forgiveness and salvation to the *entire* world as we know it today.

5. The fifth case has to do with the Exodus of the Hebrew people from slavery in Egypt.

At first glance, the Biblical record in Exodus 8-14 seems to present the ten plagues visited upon the Egyptians and the escape of the Israelites from Egypt as supernatural miracles. However, upon closer examination, it becomes apparent that these plagues were a series of events that could well have been caused by natural phenomena - changes in the Egyptian climate and an environmental disaster that happened hundreds of miles away.

Most archaeologists now think the plagues occurred over the course of a year or more at the city of Pi-Ramses on the Nile Delta (the capital of Egypt during the reign of Pharaoh Ramses II who ruled from 1279-1213 B.C.) Climatologists have discovered that there was a dramatic shift in the climate in that area towards the end of Ramses II's reign. The warm, wet weather that characterized the region gave way to an unusually dry period that would have had serious consequences and may well have triggered the first plague. The rising temperatures probably caused the fast flowing Nile river to turn into a slow moving and muddy watercourse. These conditions would have been perfect for the arrival of the first plague, which in the Bible is described as the Nile turning to 'blood.' This phenomenon was most likely the result of a toxic fresh water algae called Burgundy Blood algae that is known to have existed 3,000 years ago and that still causes similar effects today. It multiplies massively in slow-moving warm waters with high levels of nutrition. And as it dies, it stains the water red.

The spread of this algae most likely set in motion the events that led to the second, third and forth plagues - frogs, lice and flies. The maturation of tadpoles into frogs is caused by hormones that can speed up their development in times of stress. The toxic algae would have precipitated such a transformation and forced the frogs to leave the water. As the frogs died, mosquitoes, flies and other insects would have flourished without the predators necessary to keep their numbers under control. This could have led in turn to the fifth and sixth plagues - diseased livestock and boils. Insects often carry diseases like malaria, so the next step in the chain reaction would have been the outbreak of catastrophic epidemics among both animals and people.

Another major natural disaster that took place more than 400 miles away from Egypt is now also thought to be responsible for triggering the seventh, eighth and ninth plagues - hail, locusts and darkness. One of the biggest volcanic eruptions in human history occurred when Thera, a volcano on the island of Santorini, just north of Crete, exploded around 3,500 year ago, spewing billions of tons of volcanic ash into the atmosphere. Scientists believe the volcanic ash could have clashed with thunderstorms above Egypt to produce dramatic hail storms. The volcanic fallout from the ash would have caused higher precipitation and higher humidity which are exactly the conditions that would have produced hordes of locusts. The volcanic ash could also have blocked out the sunlight causing the plague of darkness. Scientists have found pumice, stone made from cooled volcanic lava, during excavations of Egyptian ruins despite there not being any volcanoes in Egypt. Analysis shows that the rock came from the Santorini volcano!

Archeologists also think that the last plague, the death of the first born sons of Egypt, could have been caused by a fungus that may have poisoned the grain supplies. Since the first born sons would have been fed with the best of the grain first, they would have been the first to have succumbed to the contaminated food.

Many people assume that when the Israelites escaped from

Egypt, they miraculously crossed the Red Sea with giant walls of water on both sides of the path through the sea. Upon closer examination of the Hebrew text, however, they actually crossed at the Sea of Reeds which was a shallow reedy area at the northern end of the Red Sea between Lake Timsa and the Bitter Lakes. The text says, "Moses held out his hand over the sea, and the LORD drove the sea back with a strong east wind. It blew all night and turned the sea into dry land. The water was divided, and the Israelites went through the sea on dry ground, with walls of water on both sides." Exodus 14:21

What's being described is a common natural occurrence called a typhoon in the East and a hurricane in the West. As the strong wind blew in a westerly direction, it blew the water out of the shallow Sea of Reeds. The Israelites then crossed the dried out marshy area throughout the night before the wind shifted and came back in the opposite direction just when the Egyptians were pursuing them through the reeds in their chariots. Their chariot wheels got stuck in the mud and the piled up water rushing back into the temporarily dried Sea of Reeds overwhelmed and drowned them. This is supported by the statement in Exodus 14:30, "On that day the LORD saved the people of Israel from the Egyptians, and the Israelites saw them lying dead on the seashore." That would've been on the *eastern* shore which confirms that the wind had dramatically reversed in that direction.

Many commentators estimate that on the basis of the information found in the book of Exodus, as many as 1.5-2.5 million people crossed the Sea of Reeds. But how could that many people have made the crossing in only one night? The answer is that they would not have done so in the way depicted in the epic 1960 movie *Exodus* – in a long fairly narrow column. The Israelites would have been strung out for four to five miles along the edge of the Sea of Reeds and would have crossed en masse along a wide front rather than in some long narrow column. The "walls of water on both sides would have referred to their position *between* Lake Timsa and the Bitter Lakes which would have prevented the Egyptians from doing an end run around either side of the Sea of Reeds to intercept them.

Is this kind of explanation simply an attempt to erase the

miraculous and 'supernatural' element in this account? Not at all. The point is that we should not see *super*natural miracles where there are none. The 'miracle' was not in the natural phenomena described in the account, but in the *timing* of the events. God didn't contradict the natural processes described, but *utilized* natural means to bring about his mighty act of rescuing his people.

These five cases demonstrate that patient, persistent and honest enquiry can once and for all lay to rest the myth that there's a conflict between science and Christianity. They don't conflict, but are complementary. "But," someone says, "doesn't the main problem between science and Christianity arise in the area of miracles? What about them?" We'll deal with that importation question in the next chapter.

What Do *You* Think?

1. Of the five cases discussed above (the origin of the earth, the development of the earth, the origin of human beings, the Flood and the Exodus account), which discussion has been the most helpful in giving you some new insights into the relationship between science and Christianity, and why?

2. Do you have any problem(s) with the conclusions drawn in this chapter? Explain.

3. If you were writing this book and could discuss a sixth case having to do with the supposed conflict between science and Christianity, what would it be and why would you want to discuss it?

4. After working through this chapter, do you think there's an actual contradiction between science and Christianity? Why or why not?

Chapter Eight

CAN WE STILL BELIEVE IN MIRACLES?

"In his disciples' presence, Jesus performed many other miracles which are not written down in this book. But these have been written in order that you may believe that Jesus is the Messiah, the Son of God, and that through your faith in him you may have life."
John 20:30-31

Looking Through the Microscope |

Miracles or Mirages?

A mother was talking to a neighbor while her little boy was playing with his ball nearby. Suddenly, the ball rolled out into the street. The little boy ran out into the street to retrieve it - right into the path of an on-coming car! The brakes screeched! The mother whirled around and screamed! Her little boy lay on the pavement, stunned by the impact. She ran out into the street and bent over the boy. He slowly sat up. He was not seriously hurt! The relieved mother burst into tears and cried, "It was a miracle that you weren't killed!"

****

The famed magician Houdini carefully got into the trunk. The lid was shut and padlocked. Padlocked chains were also wrapped around the trunk. The trunk was lowered into the river and sank from sight. The crowd on both shores held its breath. They knew the air in the trunk would only last a few minutes. They also knew that even if Houdini could manage to get the lid open, his chances of getting free of the trunk before drowning were seemingly impossible. Houdini had done unbelievable feats before, but this time …

The minutes ticked by. The crowd grew restless. A few looked at their watches and shook their heads sadly. Some said that Houdini had pulled off some amazing stunts in his career, but this time he'd bitten off more than he could chew. But suddenly a gasp of amazement arose from the crowd. Houdini had bobbed to the surface and was splashing his way ashore! He'd done the impossible! The crowd cheered wildly! The morning news headlines told the story: "HOUDINI MAKES MIRACULOUS ESCAPE FROM TRUNK!"

****

He was teaching in a crowded house. Some dirt began falling from the ceiling. Everybody looked up and watched in amazement as the tiles on the flat roof were removed one by one until a large hole appeared. The teacher stopped talking as all eyes were fixed on a man lying on a mat being lowered through the hole in the roof by means of some ropes! Some in the crowd recognized him immediately. He was the man in the village who'd been paralyzed for a long time and was unable to move or walk.

The teacher admired the persistence of the man's friends. They hadn't given up on getting their friend to him just because they couldn't get into the crowded house. The teacher looked at the man, and in a kindly voice told him to get up, roll up his mat and go in peace. A neighbor in the crowd began to chide the teacher for asking the man to do what was impossible since he was totally paralyzed, but the words stuck in his throat. For before his eyes, the man, with a look of wonder and determination on his face, slowly got up, bent over, rolled up his mat, and walked out of the crowded house! A great murmur arose from the crowd. In sheer amazement they said to one another, "Have you ever seen such a marvelous thing as this in your life?! We've truly witnessed a miracle today!"

****

People came from miles around to view the ceremony. Even some tourists were there with their cameras ready. The devotees were waiting, their white sarongs and shining bodies gleaming in the bright sun. The fire path had been carefully prepared. The coals were now white hot and thin wisps of smoke rose into the air. The devotees were mumbling chants and working themselves into a trance-like state. An elder nodded. The first devotee, without hesitation, began slowly walking across the long path of white hot coals … in his bare feet! The tourists eagerly snapped their pictures. They'd never seen such an amazing sight before. The devotee got to the end of the path. He showed no sense of pain, and the bottoms of his feet were completely unharmed! "I can only think of one word for it," said one of the tourists, "Miraculous!"

****

The woman was suffering from terminal cancer. The doctors had done all they could do. They had tried everything known to medical science to arrest the disease, but it was now useless to continue. The woman would certainly die and there was nothing more they could do to prevent it. They broke the news to the woman and her family as gently as they could and discharged her from the hospital so that she could spend her remaining time at home with her family.

But the woman did *not* die. Six months later, all traces of the 'incurable' cancer had disappeared! She had become a healthy woman. The doctors were completely baffled. As scientists, they didn't put much stock in miracles. But as one of them said, "If I didn't believe in miracles before, I sure do now!"

****

A neon light above the altar in a temple in Taiwan began to flicker strangely. Someone said it must be the influence of a spirit. Before long, a rumor spread around the town that a spirit with magical power was dwelling in the flickering neon tube. Hundreds of people rushed to the temple, convinced that this spiritual phenomenon was an omen that would bring good luck to whoever presented the proper fruit and wine offerings to this new 'god.'

The light eventually burned out and stopped flickering

altogether. Some people laughed and said the whole thing could be chalked up to an old defective bulb. But others hotly denied this and offered various 'proofs' that the spirit in the bulb had miraculous powers. One woman's arthritis had been healed. Another man had closed a big business deal. A student had gotten all A's in an examination. Some called this mere coincidence, but others called it miraculous.

****

The German army rolled through France, sweeping all before it. It moved relentlessly towards the coast as the British Expeditionary Force steadily gave ground. Finally, the British troops were surrounded with their backs against the sea, holed up in a French town called Dunkirk. The Germans, sure of victory, paused to re-group and consolidate their positions. They were convinced they could force the British to surrender without a major battle and the risk of major losses.

The British call went out. "Every last boat afloat must go to Dunkirk and help evacuate the army!" The boats came by the thousands - big ones, small ones, and those in-between. In a few days' time, braving the sea and German fire, this great armada ferried the bulk of the British forces safely home to England to fight another day. Some German generals later called what happened at Dunkirk a major German military blunder. However, the British Prime Minister, Winston Churchill, called it a miracle.

What Do *You* Think?

1. I think all/most/some/none of the above are descriptions of true miracles because ......

2. In my opinion, the incident that most closely resembles what I conceive a miracle to be is ____ because ......

3. In my opinion, the incident that most closely resembles what I conceive a miracle *not* to be is #____ because ......

4. I think miracles only happened long ago/miracles still happen today/ miracles have never happened because ......

Bringing Things Into Focus |

How Do You Define a 'Miracle'?

Look up the following words on the Internet and choose the definition for each word that most applies to the subject we're considering.

****

1. 'Miracle'   2. 'Superstition'   3. 'Wonder'

4. 'Supernatural'   5. 'Natural'   6. 'Marvel'   7. 'Magic'

8. 'Extraordinary'   9. 'Unique'   10. 'Weird'

****

Here are ten ways in which people often use words like 'miracle,' 'supernatural' and the like in their every day conversations.

- "He made a miraculous recovery!"

- "This insurance company is not liable for any damage caused by an 'act of God.'"

- "He prescribed one of the new miracle drugs."

- "The Bible is full of miracles."

- "It was a supernatural act."

- "Wonder of wonders…she fell in love with *me!*"

- "I know it seems extraordinary, but I believe there's a perfectly natural explanation for it."

- "It disappeared into thin air, like magic!"

- "I think it was an absolutely unique experience!"

- "All I can say about it is that it was completely weird."

What Do *You* Think?

1. Explain what you think is meant by each of the ten phrases listed above.

2. In your opinion, which phrases use the word 'miracle' (or its equivalent) correctly and which do not? Explain your choices.

3. In your opinion, which words in the above list best express what you consider to be an unusual event, and why?

4. Do you think genuine 'miracles' still happen? Why or why not?

Gaining a Perspective |

Tom, Dick and Gerry

Tom's dog looks at his empty water bowl and moans, "Empty! And I'm about to die of thirst!" He then picks up the bowl with his teeth, walks over to a water spigot, holds the bowl expectantly under the faucet and waits....with no result. Then it starts to rain, and then to pour, and pretty soon his water bowl is full of water. He trots back to his dog house with his bowl, laps up the water, climbs up on the roof, lies down on his back and thinks, "That's something I'll to have to think about for awhile."

****

Dick is up to his eyeballs in tall weeds looking for an errant golf ball. He calls to his partners, "I can't find it!" They holler back that he should just pick it up. He shouts back in an exasperated voice, "Waddya mean just pick it up?! How could *anybody* think they could find a golf ball in weeds like these? Why did you ever hit it out here in the first place?! It's impossible!" They holler back asking if he's looking. "OF COURSE I'm looking! I said I can't find it! If I *could* find it, I wouldn't still be out here looking, would I!?" He keeps looking and yells, "This is ridiculous! Nobody could find an

AIRCRAFT CARRIER out here if it….” He looks down and says weakly, “Wait a second…,” and disappears into the weeds. Then he pops up, triumphantly holds the ball high in the air and says, “I found it!! Miracles still happen!”

****

Tom and Gerry are playing fetch with Tom’s dog. Tom throws the ball into a field of high grass. The dog races into the field and disappears from sight. He then pops up, looks wildly around, but has lost his bearings. He re-appears determinedly running towards Tom *on top of the grass*! When he returns the ball to them, Tom says to Gerry, “When you’re afraid of snakes, you learn to walk on *top* of the grass.”

****

Tom walks up to Gerry and Dick and says, “What in tarnation are you two standing here for?” Dick answers, “We’re conducting an experiment.” Gerry chimes in, “We think that Dick might be a ‘rain-stopper,’ so we’re standing here hoping that it might rain so that we can find out once and for all.” She puts her hand out and says, “Oh, Oh! I think I felt a drop! It’s beginning to rain! This might be it!! This might be the big scientific moment!” It begins to rain harder. Gerry looks at a now rather dubious Dick and says, “Give it all you’ve got Dick! Make it quit raining!” It now begins to rain harder and Gerry tells Dick, “Hurry up! Say the magic words! Make it quit raining!” Dick is now tongue tied. Gerry screams, “HURRY UP! SAY THE WORDS! SAY THE WORDS! SAY THE WORDS!!” Dick, now in a panic, shouts, “GO AWAY TODAY. RAIN SOME OTHER WAY FAR AWAY SOME DAY!” The three of them are now standing in the pouring rain soaked to the skin. Gerry says, “Oh, you dumbbell!”

What Do *You* Think?

1. What would you say the first dialogue has to say about the subject of miracles? Explain.

2. What would you say the second dialogue has to say about the subject of miracles? Explain.

3. What would you say the third dialogue has to say about the subject of miracles? Explain.

4. What would you say the fourth dialogue has to say about the subject of miracles? Explain.

Drawing Conclusions |

A New Way of Looking at 'Miracles.'

We've seen in other chapters how some people believe that we live in a universe in which *all e*vents can be accounted for by natural, and therefore scientifically measurable, laws. To them, anything that's said to be 'supernatural,' or an act by a force from 'outside' that can override those laws, is merely the figment of somebody's superstitious imagination. Some events *do* seem inexplicable at present, but either they never actually happened, or, if they did, science will someday show that they were brought about by natural means. Add to this the popular understanding of the word 'miracle,' and it's not hard to see why so many people have difficulty with this subject. Miracles for most people are events that contradict or suspend the laws that normally govern things; are the work of a power from outside that intervenes in or interrupts the normal or natural course of events; are extremely rare; and usually happen under mysterious circumstances. To them, anything that happens that can't be readily explained is called a 'miracle.' Is this what you understand the term to mean?

Defining a Miracle

Christians are said to be people who believe in the supernatural and in miracles. But perhaps the time has come to discard these terms as being more misleading than they are helpful because of the popular misconceptions about them. What if we said that as far as a Christian understanding of the relationship of God to creation and to history is concerned, we don't need them? Would that surprise you? Let's explore that a bit.

Suppose we said that the whole of God's realm could be called the 'natural,' or the 'norm.' This realm, which we've called 'the ninth dimension' in other chapters, would *include* and give meaning to the third dimensional world of our present experience. However, it *would not be limited* to that world or to that experience!

For example, we might think that someone's rising from the dead might contradict all known physical laws about death. But simply because there are known *third dimensional laws* about death doesn't mean there can be no higher 'laws' about resurrection from the dead - laws that we, as of yet, are unaware of; laws that don't contradict the known third dimensional laws about death, but that supplement them or supersede them. There's certainly a lot in our experience that may *seem* unnatural, super-natural or miraculous to us, but that doesn't appear that way to God at all since the 'ninth dimension' includes natural realities that third dimensional creatures can't even dream of. We can see the truth of this point when we consider that even our *third* dimensional level contains a lot that we can't even dream of! Things that were considered as 'miraculous' 100 years ago, for example, are now accepted as common everyday occurrences of life. Who would consider surviving a flu epidemic today as anything out of the ordinary?

Things that were ridiculed as 'impossibilities' 100 years ago are now happening with such speed that we're all becoming hard to surprise anymore. For example, 73 percent of technically 'dead' people now live over 5 more years with other people's trans-planted hearts. Astronauts fly space ships to the moon and back. Babies are begun in test tubes. In all of this, it seems as though we've just barely begun to scratch the surface of what lies ahead. People now talk about the possibility that we might be near to experiencing what lies *beyond* what we now conceive of as third dimensional reality - a possibility that's increasingly taking into account the spiritual as well as the physical nature of things. For example, ideas like the 'time warp' are no longer merely the imaginings of science fiction writers, but are serious subjects of discussion by sober scientists. These same scientists are exploring ways in which psychology, philosophy, theology, and the physical sciences can blend together to enable humanity to break through to a deeper and more complete understanding of what is possible.

As a result of all this, we're moving into an era where thinking people are more and more saying that it's unthinking dogmatism to say that *anything* is an absolute impossibility, or that we should describe something as 'miraculous' simply because we can't understand at the moment how it could have happened, or that so far it's only happened once. Should this then not give people great pause who are tempted to doubt, for example, that Jesus could have turned water into wine, walked on water, raised the dead to life, multiplied bread and fish, and the like?

Do we not have here a person in touch with the 'ninth dimension' to whom the idea of a time warp and all of these other things were perfectly normal and natural, and therefore not miraculous or supernatural at all? Was this not a person who broke through the third dimensional barriers of his day as a sign that there was a whole lot more to God's 'natural' realm than people could have possibly imagined? Was he not a person who showed people that they should not mistakenly equate the 'natural' with only that which they, in their *very* limited capacity, could measure at any given moment in history using what they falsely understood *at that moment* to be laws that governed and determined *all* of reality?

Jesus' acts didn't *contradict* 'the laws of nature,' but *superseded people's partial understanding of them*. Their understanding was *too limited* - a point that we're finally beginning to appreciate in a new way today. To say, for example, that the *creator* of both water and grape juice could not produce wine from water is to betray small and biased thinking in light of the possibilities that even *we* now know exist for the unusual to be shown to be the usual and the 'impossible' to be shown to be the possible.

When American scientists were interpreting the data being sent back by the Saturn space probe, for example, to their great surprise, they discovered that one of the rings around Saturn twists back upon itself like a big pretzel, defying all known laws of physics. Nobody suggested that since this phenomenon had never been observed before, it was only an illusion, a photographic trick, or the like. They simply accepted the fact that such a fantastic phenomenon existed and set to work trying to figure it out.

Probably they will succeed, but it's possible that they might never succeed. Why should it be any more difficult for people to accept wine made from water, without being able, as of yet, to understand the process, than it is to accept a phenomenon like this?

The Power of the Mind over Matter

Another factor that reinforces the view that we should not so lightly apply the terms 'supernatural' and 'miracle' to anything that doesn't seem to fit our presently known third dimensional framework is the phenomenon of the power of the mind over matter. In recent years, much time has been devoted to the study of the human brain. Although neurologists have made great progress in brain science during the last 100 years, they all admit that we still know comparatively little about one of the greatest wonders of God's creation. In particular, they've been studying the power of the mind over matter. Doctors, for example, now know that the mind has a great deal of influence as far as illness and healing are concerned. According to a December 2016 *National Geographic* article by Erik Vance, "Whether it takes the form of a touch of the Holy Spirit at a Florida revival meeting or a dip in the water of the Ganges, the healing power of belief is all around us. Studies suggest that regular religious services may improve the immune system, decrease blood pressure, add years to our lives...The impact of religion might in a very literal sense be what Karl Marx defined as 'the opium of the people': It can tap into the ability to access our own store of beliefs and expectations, especially when we're surrounded by other believers who are doing the same...'There is a different way of thinking here (at the Chapel of Gracce in Altotting, Germany), said Thomas Zauner, a psychotherapist and deacon...'Prayer seems to actually work.'" (pp. 34, 55)

Then there's the phenomenon of the fire walkers that we spoke of at the beginning of this chapter, and others like them, or the cases of people doing 'super-human' feats when under great stress. It would seem that these phenomena defy the present known physical laws governing the body, and that there's a great deal of mental-spiritual power available to human beings that most people have barely begun to tap.

Doctors talk about 'the will to live.' Psychiatrists talk about the 'instinct for survival.' Moralists talk about 'the power of positive thinking.' The Bible talks about 'faith.' Jesus made clear to the people he healed that what he was really doing was setting them free to tap into a source of power within themselves that they never even knew existed - the power of unfettered mind over matter; the power to heal themselves! After many such healings, Jesus expressly said to the healed ones, "Your faith has made you well." (See Matthew 9:22; Mark 10:52; Luke 17:19) What he meant was, since they had believed in him strongly enough to enable him to free them to tap the power for wholeness that God had endowed them with in the first place, they had become well. Why then should we be so surprised at such healings and call them 'miracles' as though they defied the 'laws of nature?' What they did was to underline how little we really *know* about the 'laws of nature' - even today! But present research continues to point out the same truth - that the mind has powerful possibilities if only we knew how to utilize those possibilities more effectively. Jesus showed that he *did* know how to do that and that he *can* enable others to discover how to do that - through spiritual emancipation.

The Bondage of All Creation

This brings up another point - the bondage that all creation (including the people in it) presently finds itself under. The Bible makes it clear that in the beginning it was not so, and that in the end it will not be so. The picture in the beginning is of a creation without blemish. "God looked at everything he had made, and he was very pleased." (Or, in other translations, "God saw all that he had made, and behold, it was very good." Genesis 1:31 This was creation in its *normal* or *natural* state. We find a picture of a beautiful garden (paradise) in which there was no pain, suffering, death, pollution, or the like, and in which people lived in perfect harmony with themselves (no inner tensions), with one another, with the animals, with the environment, and with God.

Then things went seriously wrong. People managed to mess things up in terms of their inner life and in terms of their relationships with others, with the animals, with the environment and with God. Pain, suffering, sin, pollution, destruction, death, and all the rest, came into being and ruined what had been so perfect - not completely, but enough to make the earth almost unrecognizable from its original state. Instead of healthy, whole people going joyfully about their God-given tasks of unselfishly discovering and developing his creation, we now have unhealthy, warped people going relentlessly about their self-centered work of desecrating and destroying that creation. (One look at the record of our past with all of its wars and suffering is enough to confirm that, or one look at our performance in the present, with huge arms stockpiles on the one hand and huge masses of people starving on the other, is enough to underline that.) Fortunately, God is at work bringing things right again. But meanwhile, things are in an *unnatural* or *abnormal* state. They were not meant to be this way!

This is a very important point to see. For we've become so used to the way things *are*, that we think this way is natural or normal! But that's a big mistake. The way things *were* and the way things *will be* are the natural and the normal, but the way things *are* is the *un*natural and *ab*normal. Therefore, when a perfectly natural and normal person like Jesus does perfectly natural and normal things to restore people or things to their natural and normal state, we unnatural, abnormal people in our unnatural, abnormal situation think that Jesus and his mighty acts are strange or peculiar, and we term them 'supernatural acts' or 'miracles' because they seem so out of the ordinary and unnatural. But *we* are the ones who are unnatural and unable to see the light when it shines in our eyes. And light it is, for Jesus puts us in touch with the 'ninth dimension' and, like a breath of fresh air, lets us get a glimpse here and there of the way things used to be and the way they someday will be again. Disease, deformities, demons, disasters, death - none of these are natural or normal, but unnatural and abnormal. Jesus and his acts are not then 'supernatural,' but *signs* of the natural and normal that appear in a temporarily unnatural and abnormal world.

This is why the word 'sign' is so often used by the gospel writers to describe what appear to us as unusual acts on Jesus' part (what people usually call 'miracles'). Signs are *pointers* to the reality of the way things once were and to how they'll be again. They're not weird phenomena, but flashes of light from the normal reality of the Kingdom of God cutting through the darkness of the abnormal world in which we presently live and struggle.

Daily Miracles

Another myth about 'miracles,' or 'supernatural acts,' is that they're called such because they're so rare and mysterious. The only reason we think this way is because we've become so immune to the hundreds of 'miracles' going on within us and around us every day. For example, you cut your finger with a knife. After you get the blood stopped (a rather phenomenal process in itself!), you wash the wound, and put a band-aid on it. Then you hardly give it another thought. You simply take it for granted that a scab will eventually appear and drop off, and that your finger will be as good as new in no time at all. Have you ever stopped to study in a detailed way under an electron microscope all that's involved in healing that rather innocent looking cut on your finger?! It'll take your breath away! Why do we have to wait until somebody makes a remarkable recovery from cancer to start talking about 'miracles?' Does the fact that cut fingers simply occur more often than cancer rob the healing of those fingers of the classification of 'miracle'?

Have you ever considered your heart a 'miracle?' As we've seen, by this time tomorrow, your heart will have beaten more than 100,000 times! Have you ever considered your brain a 'miracle?' Have you ever studied one very closely? As we've said, if you were to stretch out the fibers in your brain that make up its white matter, they would stretch over 100,000 miles! Have you ever considered your body a miracle? Again, there are 70 *trillion* cells in your body, and every one of them is a miniature city with its own factories, defense system, waste management system, transportation system, and nutritional system. Would you say your eyes might qualify as a miracle? Or that a flower might? Or that a new-born baby might? Or that the forces that keep the planets from colliding might? Or ... or ... or?

How do you measure a 'miracle?' How can you get things very much more 'super' than they are within us and right around us every day of the week? How much more does God have to do to convince us that the whole of the way he set things up is one giant miracle, and that one more 'super' this or 'super' that is only like one more drop in a bottomless bucket? Why do we have such a hard time believing that God in Christ could heal the blind, cure the sick, make the lame walk and the deaf hear, and even raise the dead, when we see him doing similarly 'spectacular,' 'super' things around us or within us every day? Is it because he often does these things through doctors, or medicines, or research, or discoveries, or whatever, that we don't notice him because we're paying too much attention to the *instrument* rather than to the One *behind* the instrument? Again, when we see things in this perspective, we'll then see that what people usually mean by the terms 'miracle' and 'supernatural' does not really describe the Christian understanding of things. *All of life* is a miraculous work of God, a work that's not contradicted by science, but a work that's only *partially described* by science in halting three dimensional terms.

Insisting on Seeing 'Miracles' Where There Are None

Another reason why some people have problems with what they term 'anti-scientific miracles' is because some Christians insist on seeing 'miracles' where there are none. For example, there are Christians who think the collapse of Jericho's walls during Joshua's conquest of that city were the result of a direct supernatural act of God that caused the walls to fall when the Israelites gave a great shout upon the completion of their seventh march around the city.

However, when examining the ruins, Archaeologists agree that the most likely explanation for the collapse was the perfectly natural phenomenon of an earthquake. It was the *timing* of the earthquake that the Israelites recognized as a miracle. As in other instances that we have noted, God once again utilized *natural* means to bring about his purpose.

It's interesting to note, however, that the earthquake struck in such a way as to allow a portion of the city wall on the north side of the site to remain standing, while everywhere else the wall fell. The record states that the Canaanite prostitute, Rahab, who hid the two Israelite spies who came to reconnoiter the city, lived in a house that was built against the city wall. (Joshua 2:15). Before returning to the Israelite camp, the spies told Rahab to bring her family into that house at the time of the attack and they would be saved. The Bible records that, incredibly, Rahab's house *was* spared while the rest of the city wall fell. (Joshua 2:14-21; 6:22-23). This is exactly what archaeologists found. The city wall on the north side of the city had houses built against it and was still standing!

Incidentally, this account once again demonstrates that the Bible's historical data can be trusted. The writer of Joshua notes that at the time of the Israelite attack, Jericho was heavily fortified (Joshua 2:5,15). Archaeologists found piles of mud bricks at the base of the tell verifying the fact that the city was surrounded by a formidable wall. They also found an earthen embankment around the city that required the attackers to go "up the hill into the city" as described in Joshua 6:20. They further unearthed a 3-foot thick layer of ash with burned timbers and debris demonstrating that the Israelites did indeed "set fire to the city and burned it to the ground, along with everything in it." (Joshua 6:24). Surprisingly, many large jars full of charred grain were found in the destroyed buildings which was a rare find since, because of its value, grain was normally plundered from a conquered city. The large amount of grain at Jericho demonstrates that the harvest had just been taken in as stated in Joshua 2:6; 3:15; that the siege was short (Joshua 6:15) and that the Israelites didn't plunder the city (Joshua 6:18).

As we've seen, a number of extraordinary events recorded in the Bible are like this. Their *timing* is extraordinary, but their *manner* is not. As we said above, there *are* events recorded that are not yet able to be explained using limited third dimensional categories, but Christians do themselves and others a disservice when they insist on labeling as 'miraculous' (and therefore by implication, anti-natural) those that are.

Distinguishing Genuine Acts of God from Sheer Superstition

One last problem needs to be discussed: how can we distinguish genuine acts of God from sheer superstition? Most religions and cults claim that some power is working and acting in a special way through their particular religion or cult and try to 'prove' it by citing extraordinary phenomena. There are a number of tests that can be applied, although in the final analysis, absolute 'proof' or 'disproof,' as with anything else, isn't possible.

- **Is the act a type of magical "trick" that's performed merely to impress somebody?** If so, the true God doesn't act in that way. (For example, Jesus consistently *refused* to do 'tricks' for skeptics.)

- **Do the circumstances of the act portray God as the tool of human beings or as an independent actor?** If it's the former, the God of Christianity has had nothing to do with it, since God is always breaking in on things, doing the unexpected, causing people to react, and not vice versa. (Who would have expected God to come to earth in the form of a baby, for example?!)

- **Does the act reinforce a truthful message?** The God of the Bible, for example, does not simply act capriciously, but because he wants to underline a genuine message. The validity of an act can always be tested by the validity of the message that goes with it. (For example, when Jesus fed 10,000 people [counting women and children], he went on to explain how the act demonstrated the truth of his message that he was the Bread of Life). One can often see no rhyme or reason for many so-called miraculous acts in other religions.

- **Is the One doing the act beyond reproach and consistently good, righteous and loving?** If so, s/he can be trusted. (For example, if Jesus had moral faults, like those of the founders of some religions and cults, one could legitimately question whether his acts were genuine.)

- **Does the act have a discernible positive purpose, or is it merely some mysterious, aimless phenomenon?** (For example, Jesus' mighty works were called 'signs' because they had a two-fold purpose: to bring benefits to people, and to open people's eyes to the nature and reality of God.)

Christians believe the mighty acts of the God of the Bible pass these tests, while the acts of other 'gods' or 'isms' that lay claim to the 'miraculous' or the 'supernatural' don't do so.

The Christian faith doesn't teach that God's mighty acts are only confined to Christians. As we've seen, he has been and is now constantly at work in his whole creation, daily doing 'super' things, and he will ultimately bring his unnatural and abnormal creation back to the natural and normal state it was in when he created it. True, there's a lot of superstitious 'religion' in the world that shouts 'miracle' here and 'supernatural' there to try to prove its case. However, the ultimate superstition in our world today is a refusal by many 'moderns' to acknowledge the natural work of the true God, and instead to relegate it to the categories of 'miracle' and 'supernatural' and then dismiss it (and him) as being a superstitious contradiction of the canons of third dimensional science.

Why Were There More Miracles in Jesus' Day?

Someone might ask, "If genuine miracles do occur, why did more miracles occur during the ministry of Jesus and the apostles than occur today?" It seems as though there are critical times in the history of God's dealings with his people when he poured out his Spirit in a special way to confirm his presence and his work. One of these periods was during the time of the Exodus when Israel was formed into a nation. Another was during the time of Elijah and Elisha, the two great prophets who called Israel to repentance and renewal. The major outpouring was during the time of Jesus and the early church when God wanted to confirm that his Reign had broken into history in a new and decisive way.

The Old Testament prophets, Jesus himself and the New Testament writers all talk about another such outbreak that will occur at the end of history as we know it. A spate of mighty works will announce in a spectacular way the arrival of God's Reign in all of its fullness. Meanwhile, the periods in-between these outbreaks have continued and will continue to experience the on-going presence and work of God's Spirit, but not in such a dramatic way.

Why Were/Are Some Healed and Not Others?

Someone else might ask, "Why did Jesus heal some people and not others?" There were, of course, thousands of people in Jesus' day who were ill or disabled. They needed healing, but they didn't get it. In fact, on some occasions, Jesus only picked out one person from a *crowd* of ill and disabled people, and only healed that *one.*

For example, there was a pool near the Sheep Gate in Jerusalem to which disabled people and sick people used to go. These people believed that once in a great while an angel would swoop down and disturb the surface of the water. The first one into the pool after that happened would be healed. Jesus was there one day and took pity on a man who'd been sick for 38 years. He'd had no one to help him get into the pool. From what Jesus said to him, it's obvious that this was a case where the man's illness had been caused by his immoral life. Jesus reached out to him and healed him anyway, but he healed nobody else! (See John 5:1-18)

Why did he only heal *one* when there were so many other needy people around? And why, of *all* people, *this* one who had led an obviously sinful life?! Some may say that he knew who would have the faith to enable their healing. That may be true. But on other occasions it appears that large numbers of people were made well by simply touching his clothes without his even knowing who they were. (See Luke 4:34-36; Matthew 15:29-31)

The key answer appears to lie in the word 'sign.' In his Gospel, John always uses that word to describe Jesus' mighty works. Jesus did mighty deeds to meet people's pressing needs, but he always did them in such a way that they would communicate a *message* about the Kingdom. They were reminders that God's Reign had in fact come through him. It was not yet the time for wholesale healing. That lay in the future. Meanwhile, people would have these signs to help them believe that one day God's Reign would fully come. It would be a day when all Kingdom people would be healed and raised to eternal life. And these signs were the proof that it *was truly coming!* (See Revelation 21:3-4)

But why was *this* person healed and not *that* one? In the end, healing finally depended on God's mercy and not on how well people lived or on how much faith they had or didn't have. The same is true today. The case of the man at the pool demonstrates that his healing certainly had nothing to do with his *worthiness.* He did have faith. He acted on what Jesus told him to do even though it seemed impossible for him to do so. But he certainly could not have claimed to have been *worthy* of being healed.

Circumstances also played a part. In this case, Jesus healed the man without telling him who he was and then quietly slipped away. Even then, the event ended up causing a dangerous clash with the authorities. Suppose he had healed the man out in the open and stayed around long enough to heal the whole crowd. He might very well have never healed another person again! There were undoubtedly many ill and disabled people in Palestine in Jesus' day who were faithful believers in God. They were excellent candidates for healing, but they weren't healed. Perhaps they were simply not in the right place at the right time. If Jesus had seen them instead of others, he may well have healed *them.* His healings often seemed to be unplanned responses to people's needs. Besides, although he was the Son of God, both his energy as a human being and his physical presence were limited.

What about the Casting Out of Demons?

Another person might ask, "What's this thing of Jesus casting out demons all about?" What psychiatrists today call 'mental illness' was in Jesus' day known as demon possession. For example, the man among the tombs in his crazed state carried on a conversation with Jesus as though he were a mouthpiece for the evil powers that controlled him. (See Luke 8:26-39) Where does mental illness begin and being controlled by evil power end? This is still a difficult question to answer. In reacting to the first century idea that insane people were possessed by demons, people in the twenty-first century have gone to the opposite extreme. The sciences of medicine and psychiatry have tended to blame purely physical and mental factors for *all* human distress.

Recently, however, as we have seen, more and more doctors and psychiatrists have begun to recognize that the spiritual dimension plays a larger role in a person's physical and mental well-being than has been thought. People have begun to seriously think about how much a person's physical health is influenced by that person's inner (spiritual?) condition. They wonder where the line should be drawn between mental illness and spiritual stress. There's also a growing acceptance of the reality of evil power and its influence on human behavior.

On the one hand, Jesus cut through the superstition of his day on this subject. Unlike the popular notion, he taught that physical or mental illness could not always be blamed on the sins of individuals. (See John 9:1-3) On the other hand, he also pointed in the direction in which some physicians and psychiatrists are moving today. He recognized the reality of the power of evil. He stressed the links between a person's spiritual, physical and mental well-being. And he clearly saw the connection between all types of human distress and the presence of evil in the world.

Two things are clear from Jesus' encounters with people who were influenced by the power of evil. First, it is unnatural for a person to be mentally ill. God never intended that anyone should be less than whole. A second is that whatever is wrong with the world, and with the people in the world, can be traced to the influence of the power of evil, not to God.

Second, Jesus can free people to become whole persons again. However, this renewal isn't brought about by some *supernatural* act from without, but by his enabling a person to experience a 'natural' renewal from within. In setting these people free, Jesus tapped into a power within them that had always been present in God's natural realm, but that once sin entered into the human experience, had been hidden and had gone unused.

Wasn't a Resurrection from the Dead Impossible?

A final question that some people might ask is, "Healing is one thing and resurrection from the dead is another. Doesn't the idea of a resurrection from the dead blatantly contravene the most fundamental principles of nature?"

It would seem that in Jesus' raising of Lazarus from the dead, we have a *super*natural act of the first order. (See John 11:1-44) But was it? We can see where both at the beginning and at the end of the scriptures, death is an *unnatural* state that God never intended for his people. Instead, life is the natural state that he did intend (and intends) for them to enjoy. To reverse the death process would *seem* to be a miraculous act that contradicts all known laws of nature. (That is, all known *third dimensional* laws of nature). But what about the 'ninth dimension' (our imaginary term for God's Realm)? In Lazarus' resurrection, Jesus demonstrated that in the 'ninth dimension' the law of life supersedes the law of death. Death is *un*natural and can be overcome. Life is natural and triumphs.

So far, the realities of God's 'ninth dimension' have only broken through the limitations of our third dimensional, unnatural world in scattered, brief ways. When this has happened, it has pointed to the *greater* realities of God's natural Realm. The brightest of these 'flashes' was the resurrection of Jesus from the dead. This event showed that God isn't going to let things in our world continue as they are forever. Someday he's going to completely reassert the natural laws of his natural Realm.

The 'law' of death is only a temporary, unnatural thing that can be overcome by God's law of life. Therefore, the resurrection of Lazarus, for example, was not a miraculous *supernatural* act. It was instead a demonstration by Jesus of God's natural realities re-asserting themselves in the unnatural context in which we find ourselves.

<u>What Do *You* Think?</u>

1. I agree with/disagree with/am not sure about the conclusions of this chapter because ......

2. I agree/disagree/am not sure that Christians can discard terms like 'miracle,' 'supernatural,' etc, as they are popularly understood, when referring to God's actions in history because ......

3. I think/don't think/am not sure that all of reality can be understood in three dimensional terms because ......

4. Of the five tests offered for distinguishing genuine acts of God from sheer superstition, the one I find most helpful is _____ because ......

Chapter Nine

WHY CAN'T CHRISTIANS AGREE?

> "You are the people of God...Be tolerant with one another and forgive one another...And to all these qualities add love, which binds all things together in perfect unity. The peace that Christ gives is to guide you in the decisions you make; for it is to this peace that God has called you together in the one body."
>
> Colossians 3:12-15

Looking Through the Microscope |

The Coffee Can

The tourist had often heard about the many varieties of coffee available at The Coffee Can. He had looked forward to a visit to this place for a long time. He had sampled a few types of coffee in his own country, but he wanted something better, something that was more suited to his taste - something that was a bit stronger perhaps.

As he entered The Coffee Can, he was confronted by a mixture of aromas that took his breath away. Everywhere he looked, there was coffee...coffee...coffee. There were green cans, red cans and blue cans; square cans, round cans and flat cans; jars of Jamaican coffee, Brazilian coffee and Kenyan coffee - all kinds of containers holding every kind of coffee you could ever imagine.

Behind every counter stood a salesperson, all trying to sell their own brand of coffee; all holding out their hands to the tourist beckoning him to sit down and try a nice warm cup of *their* brand of coffee. Most of the salespeople knew each other, and their competition for sales was quite friendly. Some even cooperated quite closely together in organizations known as the National Coffee Council, the North American Coffee Sellers Association and the World Council of Coffee Growers. Coffee sellers who belonged to these organizations each had their organization's logo hung on the wall behind their counter.

At times they would run joint coffee sales, sponsor social events for the community, conduct cooperative campaigns to promote coffee drinking, and the like. However, some coffee sellers kept very much to themselves. They occupied counters in separate corners of The Coffee Can where they looked with suspicion at the other coffee sellers and sold brands labeled 'True Coffee,' 'Pure Coffee,' 'Orthodox Coffee' and 'Strict Coffee.'

One large corner of The Coffee Can was taken up by a coffee company called the WCRC Coffee Company. The WCRC brand was quite famous since it consisted of a blend of some of the best older brands of Protestant coffee. Another large corner was taken up by the Orthodox Coffee Company which specialized in more exotic brands like 'Incense Coffee' and 'Mystical Coffee.' The biggest coffee seller in the whole place, however, was a huge consortium known as The Roman Universal Coffee Exporters Company. This consortium was managed by an Italian firm and took up over half the floor space

The tourist thought to himself, "I could spend my whole day in this one place alone just sampling coffee!" He wasn't quite sure where he should begin, but he sat down on a stool in front of a counter with a large sign behind it reading 'Lutheran Coffee.' He thought he would only be there a moment and sample one cup of coffee, but he got the shock of his life when the clerk asked him, "Which brand of Lutheran coffee would you like to sample?" He exclaimed, "You mean there's more than one kind?!" He knew immediately that he had asked a stupid question, for it was only then that he noticed that the Lutheran counter was sub-divided into mini-counters with signs like 'Evangelical Lutheran Coffee,' 'Lutheran Church, Missouri Synod Coffee' and 'Wisconsin Synod Lutheran Coffee,' each offering their own brand of Lutheran coffee! He glanced at the other counters and noticed that the same thing was true of them. It began to dawn on him that there was no way in the world he would possibly be able to sample *all* of the coffees in The Coffee Can in one day. He'd have to limit himself to a sip here and a sip there.

He sampled one or two of the Lutheran coffees and asked one of their salespersons what was so special about Lutheran coffees compared to other coffees. "Well," said the salesperson, "you see, we sell the oldest brand of Protestant coffee available. Our company was founded in 1517 by the most famous Protestant coffee grower of them all - M.L. Brew. In his day, there weren't many brands of coffee available, especially in the West where the entire coffee trade was controlled by The Roman Universal Coffee Exporters Company. M.L. felt that the original coffee trees developed by the author of *The Coffee Grower's Bible* had been improperly cared for, and that the coffee then being produced was nowhere near the original in its purity, flavor and goodness. So he set up his own coffee company, experimented with the RUCE trees, and tried to develop a coffee that would once again taste like the original, as explained in *The Coffee Grower's Bible*. We think he succeeded quite well, although we've made a few alterations to improve the flavor even more. Some of our workers feel that we should only sell M.L.'s original brew, while others disagree on which alterations should be made and how to make them, which is why we offer different brands. But all Lutheran brands have a similar distinctive color and flavor."

The tourist moved on to the Baptist counter. Whereas the Lutheran coffees had been brown, the Baptist coffees were black. After sampling a few, he asked a Baptist salesperson the same question that he'd asked over at the Lutheran counter. "Our major distinction in coffee production is the way we water our coffee trees," he said. "You see, some coffee companies believe you should water coffee trees by merely sprinkling water on them. Others think the best way to do it is by pouring water on them. But we think the method that produces the best results is to dig a trench around a tree, fill it with water, and make sure the roots are immersed in it. We also feel strongly that you should only water and pick beans from the adult trees. Young trees aren't ready for immersion irrigation, and their beans don't make good coffee."

Thanking the Baptist salesperson, the tourist moved on to another counter labeled, 'Methodist Coffees.' He was beginning to feel a bit full, so he didn't sample as much there. This counter had a high-powered salesperson that began to explain the virtues of the Methodist line of coffees while the tourist still had his mouth full. "We used to belong to the Anglican Coffee Company." He waved his arm in the direction of the Anglican counter. "They used to belong to the Roman Universal Tea Exporters Company, but they had problems with the RUTE because one of their kings (they were all originally English) wanted to get married against the wishes of the RUTE's Board Chairman. So they set up their own English coffee company and began their own export business.

"At first things went fairly smoothly, but before long, some people felt that the Anglican Company was afflicted with the same problems that had plagued the RUTE - a corrupt management that affected the workers, depending too much on company tradition and not enough on the *Coffee Grower's Bible*, and so on. A man named J. W. Blend began to criticize the way the company was doing business and questioned the quality of its coffee. He developed a new type of 'Revival Coffee' and began to sell it to farmers and workers who had long been neglected by the Anglican Coffee Company. His product sold rapidly, and before long, small coffee drinking societies sprang up all over, singing the praises of 'Revival Coffee.' Eventually, an independent Methodist Coffee Company came into being, with J. W. as the first chairman of the Board. Frugal living, good singing, coffee sharing and a love for the *Coffee Grower's Bible* has characterized our company and given our coffee the unique Methodist flavor that it has."

The tourist thought it might be interesting to get the Anglican

Company's side of the story as well, but he knew he wouldn't be able to visit all of the counters in The Coffee Can. He did sample some of the WCRC Company brand, the Congregationalist Company brand, the UCC Company brand, the Reformed Company brand and others. The Reformed blend's salesperson claimed that her brand included beans from both young and old trees and that the same quality coffee could be obtained whether you watered the trees by sprinkling, pouring or immersion. He also passed The Evangelical Group of Tea Exporters counter and noticed that *The Tea Grower's Bible* was very prominently displayed.

By now the tourist had drunk so much coffee, that it was practically running out of his ears. But he decided he couldn't leave The Coffee Can without trying at least some of the coffees offered by the world's original coffee company - The Roman Universal Coffee Exporters Company. He had always assumed that this old and giant coffee company had only ever offered one brand of coffee, especially since it had been run for a long time by one Board of Directors with a powerful Chairman. But he noticed that the RUTE *also* had a large number of sub-counters selling several types of coffee in cans of all sizes, shapes and colors. There was the 'Maryknoll Social Justice' coffee, the 'Jesuit Spread the Light' coffee, the 'Franciscan Serve the Poor' coffee, the 'Dominican Guard the Faith' coffee,' the 'Augustinian Glory to God,' coffee, the 'Legion of Mary' coffee and many more.

"How amazing," thought the tourist as he walked out of The Coffee Can, "all these brands of coffee have been developed from one simple original coffee created by the author of the *Coffee Grower's Bible*. I wonder what *he* would have to say about all of this? Not everybody has the same tastes I suppose, but is this much variety really necessary? And what about the people that don't like coffee very much? Would the bewildering variety of coffees on offer in The Coffee Can be more confusing to them than helpful? I wonder if any of these current brands tastes exactly like the original. From all that I've heard, *that* was one terrific coffee!"

What Do *You* Think?

1. What's the point of The Coffee Can story?

2. Name two positive results of the formation of various Christian churches and denominations.

3. Name two negative results of the formation of various Christian churches and denominations.

4. Does the fact that the various 'companies' in The Coffee Can all sold *coffee* suggest anything?

Bringing Things Into Focus |

Agree or Disagree?

Which of the following statements do you agree with and which don't you agree with, and why?

• It was Jesus' intention that the Christian Church should be visibly united. (See John 17:20-23)

• If the Christian Church is visibly united, there can be no diversity of style, opinion, feeling, traditions etc. (See Ephesians 4:1-6, 15-16)

• The problem of disunity has plagued the Christian Church from its earliest days. (See I Corinthians 1:10-17)

• All Christians accept the basic beliefs outlined in the Apostles' and Nicene Creeds. (See 'Christian Creeds' on the Internet).

• Some Christians include more books in the Bible than other Christians.

- All Christians celebrate all of the Christian festivals, like Christmas and Easter, on the same dates.

- Some Christian churches may have different names, histories, identities and traditions, but their beliefs and practices are more or less identical.

- The Bible spells out exactly what Christians should believe on all issues, how they should worship God, how they should run the church and how they should live in the world. Therefore, if Christians seriously follow the Bible, there's no need to have any differences of opinion.

- Whatever their faults might be, the Christian churches have brought more peace and healing to the world than they have brought strife and discord.

- The Christian churches today are even more divided than they were 100 years ago.

What Do *You* Think?

1. Do you think most Christian churches are close to/fairly close to/not very close to/far away from the original idea of the church that Jesus intended? Why or why not?

2. Is the fact that there are a number of different Christian groups a problem for you? Why or why not?

3. In your opinion, what basic teachings of the Christian faith should all Christians agree on?

4. What are some of the positive things that the Christian churches have done for the world down through the church's history?

Gaining a Perspective |

Ecumenical Movements and Organizations

The World Council of Churches (WCC) was founded in 1948. The roots of the WCC can be traced to a an ecumenical Missionary Conference held in Edinburgh, Scotland in 1910 when representatives from a number of churches and mission organizations gathered to launch what would eventually become the WCC. This spawned the 'Faith and Order' movement whose goal was to work out a common understanding of Christian belief and organization, and the 'Life and Work' movement whose goal was to work out how Christians can express their faith in daily life and society. These movements, plus the 'International Missionary Council' eventually united to form the **(WCC)** in Amsterdam, Holland in 1948. 146 Church bodies were represented at that first Assembly. A number of Assemblies have been held since then, and the membership has grown to over 348 Church bodies from around the world. The WCC's on-going work is carried out by three program units: 'Faith and Witness,' 'Education and Renewal' and 'Justice and Service.' The organization's Headquarters are in Geneva, Switzerland.

The **National Council of the Churches of Christ in the USA (NCCCUSA)** was formed in 1950 and is comprised of 38 Christian communions. (There are 64 similar councils in countries around the world). The NCCCUSA's statement of faith reads as follows: "The National Council of Churches is a community of Christian communions, which, in response to the gospel as revealed in the Scriptures, confesses Jesus Christ, the incarnate Word of God, as Savior and Lord. These communions covenant with one another to manifest ever more fully the unity of the Church. Relying upon the transforming power of the Holy Spirit, the communions come together as the Council in common mission, serving in all creation to the glory of God."

The **Christian Conference of Asia (CCA)** was formed by 48 Asian Churches and Councils at its first Assembly in Kuala Lumpur, Malaysia in 1959. Since then, a number of additional Assemblies have been held, and the membership has grown to over 100 Christian churches and 17 Christian Councils from all over Asia. The goals of the organization are to help Asian Christians discover their identity and common destiny as Asian Christians, and to discover their unity and responsibility as Christians in that part of God's world. The CCA's work is carried out through three program clusters: 'Message and Communication' (confessing the Christian faith in Asia), 'Faith and Action' (assisting Asian Christians to contribute to the renewal of Church and society) and 'Justice and Service' (meeting the challenges of society with compassion, hope, care and action for development). The organization's Headquarters are in Thailand. There are six other similar regional councils or conferences in other regions of the world.

The **World Communion of Reformed Churches** (**WCRC**) is the largest association of Reformed churches in the world and the third largest Christian communion in the world, after the Roman Catholic Church and the Eastern Orthodox Churches. It has 229 member denominations in 108 countries which claim close to 80 million members. There are 22 similar organizations (referred to as 'Church Families') representing various worldwide Christian traditions (Anglican/Episcopal, Lutheran, Baptist, Methodist, Mennonite, Eastern Orthodox, etc.) around the world.

The **Church of South India (CSI)** came into being by a union of Anglican and Protestant churches in South India in 1947. It combined the South India United Church (union of the Congregationalists and the Presbyterians); the then 14 Anglican Dioceses of South India and one in Sri Lanka; and the South Indian District of the Methodist Church. With a membership of over four million, it is India's second largest Christian church after the Catholic Church in India. CSI is one of three united churches in the Anglican Communion, the others being the Church of North India and the Church of Pakistan. There are 27 other such national ecumenical churches in the world.

The Roman Catholic Church traces its roots back to the first century A.D. From 1963-1965, a conclave of Catholic Bishops met in four extended sessions in Rome, Italy to introduce major reforms into the Roman Catholic Church. Called by Pope John XXIII, the

Vatican II conclave brought together some 2,400 Bishops representing the more than 500 million Roman Catholic Christians around the world. This assembly brought about big changes in the official prayers, ceremonies and customs of the Church, making them more relevant to the faithful and allowing them to worship in their own languages.

The conclave also reviewed and made more practical the Roman Catholic Church's teaching about the world and its needs and how Catholic Christians are to be involved in meeting those needs. It also clarified the Church's expression of the Christian faith and how Christians are to live in their own society. It further stressed renewal in the church, an emphasis on the Scripture as the basis of the church's teaching and greater participation in the oversight of the church by the Bishops working together.

The **Lausanne Committee for World Evangelization (LCWE)**, more commonly known as the **Lausanne Movement**, is a global movement that mobilizes evangelical Christian leaders to collaborate for world evangelization. The stated vision is 'the whole church taking the whole gospel to the whole world.' The Lausanne Movement grew out of the 1974 International Congress on World Evangelization (ICOWE) and promotes active worldwide evangelism. The Lausanne Covenant provides the theological basis for collaborative work in the area of mission and evangelism. The Cape Town Commitment defines the movement's goals.

Since 1974, dozens of Lausanne-related conferences have been convened. Global gatherings include the Consultation on World Evangelization (Pattaya 1980), the Conference of Young Leaders (Singapore 1987), the International Congress for World Evangelization (Manila 1989), the Forum for World Evangelization (Thailand 2004) and the Younger Leaders' Gathering (Malaysia 2006). Lausanne has inspired many regional networks and issue-based conferences such as the Asia Lausanne Committee on Evangelism (ALCOE), Chinese Co-ordination Centre for World Evangelization (CCCOWE), a series of Nigerian congresses on world evangelization, and several international consultations on Jewish evangelism.

The Third Lausanne Congress on World Evangelization was held in Cape Town, South Africa in 2010. Some 4,000 leaders from 198 countries attended as participants and observers; thousands more took part in seminaries, universities, churches, and through mission agencies and radio networks globally, as part of the Cape Town GlobaLink.

What Do *You* Think?

1. Were you surprised to learn there are so many large communions of Christians around the world? Why or why not?

2. Which communion do you know the most about and which do you know the least about, and why?

3. Do you think Christians should aim at having one united worldwide Christian Church? Why or why not?

4. What do you think are some of the most important and some of the least important stumbling blocks that divide Christians?

Drawing Conclusions |

How the Christian Church Became Divided

Take a moment to Google 'Christian Denominations' in Wikipedia. Quite a bewildering variety, isn't there?! In one sense that's good. It demonstrates there's room in the Christian Church for all types of people worshipping the same God in a mosaic of patterns carrying on a variety of ministries. "Variety is the spice of life," and in that sense, the Christian Church is very much alive! When one thinks of every name on that site as representing a group of committed followers of Jesus Christ carrying on its Christian life and work in the way that seems best to it, the list takes on more of a human face and becomes a little less bewildering.

Yet in another sense, such a diversified list isn't so good, and many Christians, with sad hearts, would be the first to admit it. If all these groups would recognize each other as flowers on the same tree - each having its own beauty and contribution, each fervently following the same Christ and equally 'Christian,' each needed by the others to make up the wholeness of the one Christian body, each not interested in gaining or losing at the other's expense, each content to not duplicate or compete with the others - that would be one thing. But the honest truth is that this isn't the way things are - not yet anyway. That long list in Wikipedia represents too much un-Christian history that hasn't yet been put right; too much suspicion of people's motives and beliefs; too much pride in various man-made traditions; too much jealousy of the accomplishments of others; too much emphasis on particular peculiarities; too much wandering away from the original Christian faith and life; too much inflexibility about methods and approaches; too much self-righteousness about who has the 'real' truth - and too much more 'too much.'

Did Jesus Christ plan it that way? Of course he didn't. His vision was for a world-wide movement that would be open to all, but that would be united as one by the power of his Spirit. Did the early Church leaders plan it that way? Of course they didn't. Every time a dispute arose in one of the churches, they moved quickly to solve the problem and to heal the dispute. They constantly pleaded with the members of the fast-growing and diversifying church to learn how to accept one another's cultural, ethnic and other differences in living out the way of Christ through their worship, witness and work. They also taught flexibility about non-essentials in terms of customs, traditions, styles of worship, methods of work, etc. They deplored any jealousy, competition, self righteous pride, un-loving attitudes, and the like. Then how did things ever get to where they are today? Why is the Church divided into so many groups, each too often going its own way? The answer lies in a careful study of Church history.

Early Challenges

The first factor that caused division within the early church was heresy from within. The Church had to wrestle with this danger right from the beginning. Wherever the true gospel was proclaimed, there were those who distorted it by denying some crucial aspect of it or by taking *part* of the truth and claiming that it is was the *whole* truth. How much deviation is allowable in the name of flexibility before too much of the truth is lost? And how do you deal with those who insist on spreading false or semi-false views in the name of the truth? It's easy to see how over the 2000 year history of the Christian Church there would have been plenty of room for enough deeply felt disagreements to cause division.

Wrestling with false teachers and their distortions of the faith forced the church to more precisely define what it believed. The Church began to hold great Ecumenical Councils to try to work out a well-defined version of the Christian faith on which they could all agree. However, in some cases, that was easier said than done.

One difficulty Christians wrestled with was that on a number of issues, the Bible presents what *seem* like two contradictory concepts that need to be held in balance (or tension) to see the truth of the whole (like looking at one diamond that has many facets). This type of paradoxical truth does not easily lend itself to precise, systematic definitions and can be distorted by over emphasizing one concept at the expense of the other, or vice versa. A second difficulty Christians wrestled with was that the Bible gives us general principles for Christian living, but sometimes does not spell out exactly how they are to be applied in varying cultures and circumstances. A third difficulty Christians wrestled with was the question of what was absolutely essential to believe as a Christian and what may be left to individual conscience or custom.

Christians found themselves on various 'sides' of these issues, and the essential unity of the Church was only maintained with great difficulty, with some groups who found themselves too far from the center dropping out or being forced out.

The Church also very quickly encountered great pressure from without. Christians were severely ridiculed and persecuted by Jews,

Romans and others. Some Christians felt strongly that to be a Christian meant to be one openly and consistently without compromise of any sort, even in the face of death. Others felt that you weren't betraying Christ if you went through some external state ritual, like bowing to the emperor's image as to a 'god,' to save your life. You didn't believe he was a 'god' in your heart. You did believe that there was only one true God whom you worshipped and followed and whom you urged your family and friends to worship and follow - but in secret. Those who suffered for their public stance had a hard time accepting and loving those who didn't because, in their eyes, they had taken the easy way out. These were deep and wrenching issues to try and resolve, and Christians were not always able to do so without splitting into factions.

Christians also had to decide how to come to terms with the non-Christian culture around them. How far could Christians go in accepting Greek philosophy, for example, before their Christian beliefs would be compromised? How should they respond to the other religions around them - with implacable hostility; with attempts at trying to find something in common with them, or with what? And how different did their Christian lifestyle have to be from those around them? If they were regarded as too peculiar by their neighbors, wouldn't that develop into a barrier to their acceptance of the Christian faith that could never be broken down? The Bible laid down principles regarding these concerns, but not specifics, and it was in wrestling with the specifics that some Christians lost patience with or misunderstood other Christians, and parted ways.

Church and State

When Emperor Constantine (who ruled Rome from 306 to 337 AD.) proclaimed Christianity to be the official Roman state religion in the Edict of Milan in 313 A.D., some Christians saw this as a great opportunity, while others saw it as a great danger. (In retrospect, it turned out to be both!) There were sharp disagreements as to how much of a role the state should play in running the Church and how much of a role the Church should play in running the state. Again, the Bible provides the basics as far as answers to these questions are concerned, but not a blueprint. Centuries later, Christian groups called 'state churches' and others called 'free churches' would come into being as two different answers to these questions. Christians honestly disagreed over these issues, and it was too bad that their love for one another in some cases did not prove as strong as their convictions about these matters.

Other Issues

As the Church moved on in history, and crossed more and more cultural, racial, national and other boundaries, new questions and new challenges arose that taxed the best within Christian hearts - hearts that sometimes were not equal to the taxing - and the Church suffered further splits. These splits and divisions were caused by various factors: social, economic, liturgical, political, geographical, cultural, theological and personal. Here are some examples to illustrate what happened.

- The faith of the leader of a country often determined the faith of the people of that country. For example, King Henry VIII of England could not get the Roman Catholic Pope to annul his first marriage so he could be free to marry somebody else. He therefore withdrew his country from the Roman Catholic Church, formed a new church called the Church of England (or Anglican Church) and had himself appointed as its head! In that way he obtained his annulment from his 'own' Church. He then persecuted English Catholics who remained loyal to the Roman Church which resulted in the majority of his people becoming Anglicans instead of Roman Catholics.

- The ethnic background of Christians often determined the kind of church they would belong to. For example, the Reformed Church in America and the Presbyterian Church, USA have practically identical theology, church government and worship practices, but the Reformed were originally Dutch-speaking Christians who came to America from the Netherlands in 1628 and brought their Church with them, while the Presbyterians were English-speaking Christians from England and Scotland who came to America in the 1630s and did likewise. The Presbyterian Church is named after the common Presbyterian/Reformed system of government, while the Reformed Church is named after the common Reformed/Presbyterian system of theology. The two churches have close ties, but remain separate to this day.

- Economic practices sometimes caused problems for the Church. For example, the Roman Catholic Pope was raising money for the building of St. Peter's Cathedral in Rome during the 16th century. One of the methods used was to collect fees from people who wished the priest to assure them that their sins were forgiven. This is one practice among others that led to a revolt of a large number of Christians in what was called the Reformation. These people subsequently became known as Protestants because of the protest movement that led to the formation of several new denominations - the Lutherans following Martin Luther and the Reformed churches following John Calvin.

- Great social upheavals often affected the churches. For example, the Civil War in the United States in 1860-65 split the Presbyterian, Baptist and Methodist churches into 'North' and 'South.' The Baptist split has not been healed to this day.

- People of different cultural backgrounds spoke different languages, were more or less emotional in their approach to life, had different ways of relating, took different approaches to solving problems and lived different lifestyles. These differences resulted in the creation of various types of churches that suited these various kinds of people - from the Quakers to the Orthodox.

- Some churches were formed out of disagreements over the interpretation of the Bible on one or more issues. For example, Baptists believed that only adults should be baptized, and that they should be baptized by totally immersing them in water, while Presbyterians believed that infants belonging to Christian parents should be baptized, and that they could be baptized by merely sprinkling water on their heads.

- There were times in the past when people were forced to change their church depending on where they lived. For example, if they crossed from Protestant Sweden to Roman Catholic Poland in the 17th century, they would be under great pressure to change from Protestant to Roman Catholic, and vice versa.

- Unfortunately, some churches competed with one another for members, influence, and the like. For example, if one denomination built a church in a small town, another denomination that was very similar in belief and practice would build one of their own a short distance away out of a competitive and selfish spirit.

- Churches developed different styles of worship over the years. For example, some, like the Roman Catholic, Anglican, Orthodox and Lutheran churches, used regular set forms of liturgical prayers and readings, followed the Church Calendar and tended towards a more formal service of worship using symbols, colors, robes, incense, etc, while others, like the Baptist, Christian and Missionary Alliance and Independent Bible Churches, observed few rituals, did not follow the Church Calendar, emphasized more spontaneity and informality and used fewer symbols, colors and robes.

The picture of Christian disunity looks pretty grim, doesn't it? However, when we look back at all the pressures the Church has faced over the centuries; all the problems it has had to contend with; all the different types of people that have come into it; all the contexts and cultures in which it has taken root, and all the possibilities for the development of misunderstandings that it has had to deal with, the miracle of all time is that there is any Church left intact at all! But not only has the Church survived through its churches (unfortunate as their divisions might be), it has thrived in the sense that new groups of Christians and various Christian movements have sprung up through the centuries to revive it, renew it and pull it back towards what God wants it to be. And the most exciting development in this direction is occurring in our own time through what has become known as the Ecumenical Movement.

Efforts towards Unity

Rather than continuing to split into further branches on the one Christian tree, most Christians today are concentrating on working their way back from the branches to the 'trunk' of that tree, as it were. A new realization of the need for unity of faith, worship, life and mission in an increasingly fractured world and society is pulling Christians together again. New efforts are underway to increase understanding, agreement, cooperation, and even reunion. There is a long way to go, but significant progress has been made. With the exception of the Roman Catholic Church, the great majority of the world's Christian churches are cooperating through the World Council of Churches (with even the Roman Catholics present as observers) and regional councils and conferences. United national churches have emerged in Japan, India, China and some 25 other nations. The reforms of Vatican Council II have paved the way for increasingly fruitful talks and cooperation between the Roman Catholic Church and other churches. At present, there are many churches of different confessions in a number of countries holding unity negotiations.

The Christian Church is a worldwide family of churches containing almost a third of the human race. All Christians do not yet agree on everything, and they probably never will, but the Spirit of God is doing a new thing in the hearts of his people today. He is healing past hurts and helping Christians leave past history behind. He is moving Christians towards a new unity in their diversity that shows that their message of forgiveness, love and new life through Jesus Christ is genuine and a true hope for the future.

<u>What Do *You* Think?</u>

1. What's the one thing that most surprised you in this chapter, and why?

2. Of the nine reasons given for the development of disunity in the church, which one seems the most important to you, and why?

3. Of the seven Ecumenical Movements and Organizations listed above, which one do you think is most promising in the effort to bring about Christian unity, and why?

4. What's one concrete suggestion you could make as to how

5. Christian unity could be furthered in our day?

Chapter Ten

ARE CHRISTIANS HYPOCRITES?

> "It seems to be a fact of life that when I want to do what is right, I inevitably do what is wrong. I love to do God's will so far as my new nature is concerned; but there is something else deep within me, in my lower nature, that is at war with my mind and wins the fight and makes me a slave to the sin that is still within me. In my mind I want to be God's willing servant, but instead I find myself still enslaved to sin... Oh, what a terrible predicament I'm in! Who will free me from my slavery to this deadly lower nature? Thank God! It has been done by Jesus Christ our Lord. He has set me free." Romans 7:19-25

Looking Through the Microscope |

The Great Excuse

The old man sat on the edge of his bed in the retirement home. He'd been thinking and struggling for a long time, but today it had come to him in an especially strong way - the feeling that he'd been a stubborn fool for so long, using THE GREAT EXCUSE to keep God out of his life. Why hadn't God just let him alone? Why had he kept pursuing him like some 'hound of heaven'? Now suddenly he knew the answer. His eyes misted, his lip trembled, and he said a few silent, difficult words to God that he never in his 86 years thought he would ever say - even within the privacy of his own heart.

His mind made up, he stood up. It was as though a great weight had rolled off his shoulders. All these years he had struggled to ward off this moment with what he now knew had been the paper thin GREAT EXCUSE. He wanted to immediately run next door to her room to tell her, but after all these years it would be a very difficult thing to do. No, he would bide his time and let her know in some other way.

He smiled to himself as he picked up the Bible that she had always left "just lying around," hoping, he knew, that he would read it. Because of her, he'd come to know a lot of what was in that book, even though he'd never read much of it directly himself. But he'd listened when she had read it and discussed it with the children. He'd been a good husband and she loved him dearly and respected him greatly, but he knew that his silence during those discussions had always been painful for her.

And even more painful had been her asking the children to close their eyes while she prayed, knowing that he would bow his head, but keep his eyes open - a fact that didn't escape the peeping notice of the children! But to have closed his eyes would have been hypocritical, and if there was one thing he couldn't stand, it was hypocrisy. He might cause her pain, but he must be honest. How could he pretend to pray to a God in whom he didn't believe - or in whom he'd *said* he didn't believe anyway.

Actually, believing in God hadn't been his main problem. His main problem, and what had blocked every thought of his ever becoming a Christian, had been those HYPOCRITES! He'd met them in church on Sunday. Yes, he'd gone to church - for her sake, and for the sake of the children. He was a *family* man, and even though he'd wanted nothing to do with a church that had hypocrites in it, and had made it plain to anyone who asked that he wasn't a 'believer' and didn't want to join the church, he'd gone and sat through the services for the sake of family togetherness.

There had been a lot of good and sincere people in that church, he'd had to admit - his wife being one of the best of them. She had her faults, but he had a deep love and great respect for her. It was the others who'd bothered him, who'd made him furious inside. They'd been so dishonest - sitting there praying and singing like 'saints;' promising to lead upright Christian lives; serving as ushers and members of the choir - when all along he knew that they had cheated in their businesses, or had cheated on their tax returns or had cheated on their wives, or had been mean to their children, or had drunk too much, or had cursed when they thought nobody was listening, or....

He'd had his faults too, of course, but he hadn't done things like *that*. And when he had done something that he'd been ashamed of, at least he'd been honest about it and had made it right instead of hiding behind a false pretense of religious piety. No, he'd been absolutely certain that he didn't want to join a church that had people like that in it or have anything to do with the religion that produced them! And throughout his long life, *that*, he now knew, had been his GREAT EXCUSE. He had used it as a defense against God. And now he'd finally come to see it for what it really was.

Why had he only concentrated on the few bad apples in the barrel? Why had he so blindly ignored what God was doing in and through the lives of the great majority of the Christians in that church - and particularly in and through the life of the one who had shared life so intimately and happily with him all these years? She had personified all that Jesus Christ claimed he could do with a person right before his eyes! And yet, he'd ignored it. Why? Because he'd *wanted t*o ignore it. He'd *wanted* to hang on to his GREAT EXCUSE to keep God out of his life!

Why had he been so afraid of God? He chuckled to himself. Now that he'd made peace with God, he'd found out that God wasn't anybody to be afraid of at all. He hadn't come into his life as some angry power who was upset with him for having so stubbornly held out against him for so long, or as a judge ordering him to obey the law, or else! No, he'd turned out to be a forgiving Friend; a loving Father who had welcomed him home with joy as a long lost son; an Encourager who wanted to help him overcome his weaknesses. He chuckled again as the thought crossed his mind that the Father would even be willing to forgive and welcome home those hypocrites he'd always been so self-righteously indignant about!

While he was thinking about all of this, it suddenly occurred to him how he would let her know what had happened. Two days later, he went with her to the weekly worship service that was held in a little chapel in their retirement home as he'd always done. Here again, he'd steadfastly held his ground in the past. Everybody had known that John just came along to keep his wife company, not because he believed. He'd never closed his eyes during the prayers, and he'd *never* sung any hymn whose words expressed anything personal about faith in God. He'd been honestly and doggedly consistent, and nobody had known this better than she had. They'd had many discussions about this - she gently encouraging him, he steadfastly refusing, and always using the GREAT EXCUSE as his reason. There was one hymn in particular that she knew he'd always refused to sing - Psalm 57, and today it was on the order of service as the opening hymn.

The pianist played the introduction and the old people began to sing with quavery voices, but in a way that reflected a deep and steady faith mellowed by the years. "I call to God, the Most High, to God, who supplies my every need ... I have complete confidence, O God; I will sing and praise you! ... Your constant love reaches the heavens; your faithfulness touches the skies."

At first she didn't notice, but when she did, her mouth dropped open and she stopped singing. He turned towards her, still singing, and smiled. Tears welled up in her eyes. He took her hand and squeezed it. Together they finished singing the hymn the best they could between their tears of joy ... joy that after 86 years, THE GREAT EXCUSE had finally been laid aside!

What Do *You* Think?

1. Do you think there are more hypocritical Christians than genuine ones? Why or why not?

2. What do you think John would have done differently if he'd had his life to live over again?

3. Do you think John made the right decision? Why or why not?

4. What other excuses do people make to keep God at arm's length?

Bringing Things Into Focus |

Faith and Works

Here are 12 statements that reflect what Christians for the most part have believed and done and the Biblical basis for their faith and actions.

- Christians laid the foundation for the eventual abolition of the practice of slavery. (See Ephesians 6:5-9; Philemon 15-16; Galatians 3:26-29; 1 Corinthians 12:12-13.)

- Christians have opposed racial and ethnic prejudice. (See Acts 10:34-35)

- Christians have insisted on recognizing the equal value and dignity of women. (See Galatians 3:26-29)

- Christians have highly valued children and the family as a sharing-caring unit. (See Ephesians 6:1-4)

- Christians have placed great emphasis on ministering to the needs of the poor, the sick, the disabled and the deprived. (See Matthew 25:34-40)

- Christians have opposed social injustice, oppression and exploitation. (See Amos 5:10-15)

- Christians have been involved in fighting the pollution and destruction of the environment. (See Genesis 1:27-28; 2:15)

- Christians have been committed to working for what is ultimately best for their country. (See Romans 13:1-7)

- Christians have been active in bringing about prison reforms and rehabilitation programs. (See Hebrews 13:3; Romans 12:17-21)

- Christians have been committed to just and harmonious relationships between employer and employee. (See Ephesians 6:5-9; Galatians 3:28)

- Christians strive for honesty, integrity, responsibility, virtue and the like in their personal lives and relationships. (See Galatians 5:19-26)

- Christians are motivated to live upright lives out of gratitude for God's love and care, not to *earn* that love and care or other kinds of rewards. (See Ephesians 2:8-10; Romans 12:1-2)

What Do *You* Think?

1. Look back over these statements and identify any that are contradicted by a Christian that you know personally.

2. On the basis of your experience, are there any more such statements that should be added to the list? If so, what are they and why should they be added?

3. In your opinion, are Christians making a greater contribution to the common good than non-Christians? Why or why not?

4. Would you say, on the basis of what you know about Christians, that these statements describe all Christians none of the time/some Christians some of the time/most Christians some of the time/most Christians most of the time/all Christians all of the time? Explain.

Gaining a Perspective |

Picture Talk

Here are twelve illustrations drawn by Annie Vallotton for the *Today's English Version* of the Bible depicting how Christians are to live according to their faith and the struggles that they face in trying to do so. In your opinion, what message does each illustration portray? (You can check the accuracy of your interpretation by looking up the Bible references listed.)

1.　Galatians 6:2

2.　1 Corinthians 10:17

3.　Matthew 18:3

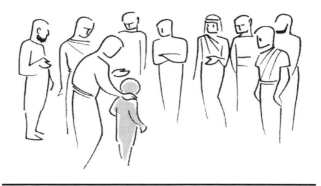

4. 1 Corinthians 9:24

5. Luke 10:33

6. 1 Corinthians 9:24

7. Luke 12:22

_____

8. Romans 15:1

_____

9. Philemon 17

10. James 5:14-15

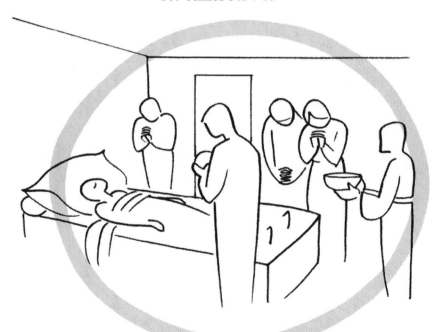

11.   1 Peter 5:14

12.   2 Thessalonians 3:15

What Do *You* Think?

1. In your opinion, which drawing best illustrates what a Christian ought to be, and why?

2. Which drawing best illustrates what a Christian ought not to be, and why?

3. Which drawing can you most picture yourself being in, and why?

4. What kind of illustration might you draw to illustrate Jesus' challenge to "do unto others what you would have them do unto you?" Luke 6:31

Drawing Conclusions |

Practicing What They Preach?

"Why don't Christians practice what they preach?" That's a fair question to ask, but it implies more than it should and is often asked by people who don't have a very good understanding of what the Christian faith is and how it works. It implies more than it should because it could be taken to mean that *no* Christians practice *anything* of what they preach. Now even the most severe critics of Christianity wouldn't state their case so baldly unless they were totally dishonest and closed to the evidence all around them to the contrary. The history of the Christian Church is filled with accounts of the lives of Christians that disprove that idea, and any honest observation of a single Christian congregation will disprove that idea. The *least* one would have to fairly conclude would be that *some* Christians practice *some* of what they preach. A more accurate assessment, however, would probably be that *most* Christians practice *some* of what they preach and that *many* Christians practice *most* of what they preach.

Humility

Christians are very reluctant to defend themselves against the charge that they don't practice what they preach. For example, it would be impossible to find a true Christian who would claim that s/he practiced all of what Christ preached, for two reasons.

First, to do so would be to deny the very thing s/he was claiming! One of the chief Christian virtues is humility. If a Christian were to make such a proud boast, s/he would be disqualifying herself or himself in the making of it. In fact, the closer Christians come to actually living out the lifestyle of Jesus, the more they'll sincerely deny that they're doing so, since the closer people draw to Christ, the more painfully aware they become of what's sill un-Christ-like in their lives. A person who claims to be practicing all of what Christ preached reveals that s/he has missed the heart of what it means to be a Christian at all.

Second, to do so would be a denial of what Christians believe the Bible teaches and what they've experienced. Nowhere does it teach that 'the saints' (a word that refers to all Christians, not just a few of the best ones) will fully become 'saints' in this life (in the sense of the word in which it is popularly thought of, i.e. one who is holy, perfect and pure). Rather, it teaches that people who open their lives to God and become followers of Jesus embark on a life-long battle to overcome their old selves (or 'natures') and to evolve into new Christ-like persons. This means they will *want* to practice all they 'preach,' but that sometimes they will fail to do so. True Christians will be the first to sadly plead guilty to the charge that they don't always practice what they preach. Fortunately, in God's mercy, they can experience daily forgiveness and renewal, which enables them to continue the struggle and to make progress in winning it.

Some people who self-righteously ask, "Why don't Christians practice what they preach?" don't really understand how the Christian faith works. They often have a black and white view of it. That is, they think that becoming a Christian is like crossing a river. The person who becomes a Christian today will become a 'saint' tomorrow. The reason why people get this distorted view is because they only read a *part* of what the Bible teaches about salvation and mistake it for the *whole* of what it actually does teach about this subject.

Salvation Past, Present and Future

When you look closely at *all* the Bible does teach about salvation, you discover what at first appear to be contradictions. In some places the Bible talks about people as *having been* saved/changed/renewed in the past (See 2 Corinthians 5:17); in other places it talks about people as *being* saved/changed/renewed in the present (See 1 Corinthians 1:18); and in still other places it says that people *shall be* saved/changed/ renewed in the future. (See Romans 5:9-10) Which is right, or can they all be right at the same time?

They can! The one describes what Christ did for people through his death and resurrection in the *past*. He died for everybody and paid the penalty for their sin. Because of this, God has accepted people on a new basis and *considers* them as being new persons, even before they've actually become so. In *theory* they're proclaimed and accepted as changed persons; in *fact*, that change has just begun. That actuality, that process of people being changed into what they've already been declared by God to be, is what the Bible describes as the *present* process of 'being saved.' It's a process in which God is at work through his Spirit in people's lives helping them win the struggle over their old nature.

Jesus describes this beautifully when he likens a person's becoming a Christian to the birth of a baby. (See John 3:1-8) Once a baby has been born, it can never be 'unborn.' Once people have truly committed themselves to becoming followers of Jesus, they can truly claim the name Christian. But notice that a baby is born a baby, not an adult! In the same way, when people become Christians, they become 'baby' Christians, not 'adult' Christians. A human baby can't do much for itself when it's first born. It needs someone to feed it, clothe it, change its diapers, teach it to walk, to talk - and all the rest. The baby learns by trial and error - sometimes painfully! It *gradually* 'grows up' and becomes an independent, mature adult. (Of course, there are *some* people who never quite seem to make it!)

So it is with Christians. When they're spiritually 'born,' they need lots of nurture, support, guidance and all the rest (which is why regular prayer, Bible reading, meditation, participation in the life of a church family, involvement in service and witness opportunities, and so on, are so vitally important). They gradually 'grow up' and spiritually mature. (Notice this has nothing to do with a person's age or physical size. Some Christian young people can be more spiritually 'mature' than older individuals who've been weak Christians all their lives).

The point is that *every* Christian is moving through this life-long spiritual growth process, and that not even the 'best' Christian will live to see it fully completed as s/he struggles to live a Christ-like life in an 'alien' environment. (See Paul's acknowledgement of this in his own experience in Philippians 3:12-14). However, the Bible makes clear that this maturing process will definitely be brought to a successful conclusion in the *future* - in the life to come. (See Philippians 1:6) That's why, even though Christians sadly acknowledge that they don't always practice what they preach, they don't give up in despair. They're people of hope! They know that God will not give up on them and that they therefore need not give up on themselves. They know that they're slowly winning the struggle, that someday the struggle will be over and that they will, by God's grace, have won the battle!

Yes, to those who would level the charge that Christians don't always practice what they preach, we'll have to reply, "You're right. We're guilty. Please forgive us and pray for us. We're trying. We're gaining. But there's a lot in us and about us that we'd like to be rid of that causes you pain and detracts from what our Lord wants to see in his people and in his church. Keep pointing out to us what that is so that we can work on correcting it and overcoming it. We need you. But better yet, despite our discrepancies, come and join us in the struggle. It's worth it. Criticism of our weaknesses will do nothing to meet your spiritual needs or to fulfill your life as a person. Come join us in the struggle - and know what the joy and hope of overcoming is all about!"

"Blessed Are the Merciful"

Some critics who level the hypocrisy charge at Christians are rather unmerciful. They treat all Christians as though they're exactly the same and demand equal perfection from all. Not all Christians start from the same line, as it were. The critic should not only consider how far a Christian still has to go in terms of being all that s/he is supposed to be, but also how far s/he has come from what s/he was before!

For example, here's a man who's become an alcoholic. He's let his drinking take over his life to the point where he's lost his job, his family, his self respect - everything. He wanders around the seedy section of the city in a drunken stupor most of the time, begging for money to buy another drink and living on scraps out of garbage cans. One night he wanders into a Christian rescue mission. He hears the Good News of forgiveness and salvation through Jesus Christ. He knows that he's a wretch and that he's beyond saving himself. He commits himself to becoming a follower of Christ even though he hardly understands what that means. He then begins the long process of 'drying out' with many slips and failures. He overcomes his alcohol problem, gets a simple job and begins rebuilding his life. He's still a long way from what one might call a 'saint,' but his heart is in the right place and he's making progress. He doesn't yet practice all of what Christians preach, but what a distance he's come!

Forgeries

Critics are also unfair when they discover a few 'forgeries' that are 'Christian' in name but not in practice, and proceed to label *all* Christians as fakes. Put yourself in the shoes of the average pastor. Somebody begins attending worship services. The pastor calls on her at her home. The woman says she wants to become a Christian, be baptized and join the church. The pastor invites her to an instruction class. The woman faithfully attends and joins the church. Everything seems fine.

Meanwhile, however, unknown to the pastor and the people of that church, the woman cheats in her business, cheats on her husband, neglects her aged parents, and the like. How was the pastor supposed to know that? Did s/he have a special spiritual periscope by which s/he could see into the woman's heart and mind? Of course not. Why did she want to join the church? Perhaps to gain a false respectability as a 'religious' person; perhaps out of some guilt over her secret evils (in which case there might still be some hope for her), and so on.

If and when the pastor should find out that the woman was a fake, s/he would take steps to confront her with her double life and encourage her to confess and change. If she refused, the pastor would have no choice but to sadly recommend that the church drop her from the membership. Meanwhile, however, the damage would've been done. The critics who knew about the woman's double standard would have seized on her as a case in point to 'prove' what hypocrites Christians are.

Then there are, of course, the serious scandals that have rocked the church right from the beginning. One only has to read through Paul's two letters to the Church at Corinth to get some idea as to the list of problems that church was struggling with. There are many other warnings in the New Testament about false teachers, false prophets and fake 'Christians' that plagued the early Church. These problems and failures didn't disappear. One only has to read church history to discover that people who claimed to follow Christ have too often let him and the Church down with their unchristian behavior and false teaching. In our own day, Christians have been appalled by the major scandals involving prominent television evangelists or by the repulsive behavior of priests sexually molesting young boys who were placed in their care. Christians are distraught when these things happen and they earnestly pray for honest confession, repentance and forgiveness for the damage done to innocent people and inflicted on the Christian community, and the tarnishing of the Church's witness in the world.

As we've seen, those who ask, "Why don't Christians practice what they preach?" raise a legitimate complaint. But shouldn't the critics also have to answer a few questions? For example, "Was Jesus a hypocrite?" Isn't it fair to say that even most of the critics would agree that he wasn't; but that, on the contrary, he was the most honest and genuine person that ever lived? "Then why don't you stop avoiding him with the excuse that his followers aren't genuine? If he *is* genuine, he deserves to be followed no matter what those who say they follow him do or don't do. Doesn't your criticism of the shortcomings of his followers miss the point and evade the issue? He asks you not to look at others (See Matthew 7:1-5), but to look at *him* and follow *him*. Why then don't you respond?" Finding answers to these questions is much more crucial to a person's life than finding an answer to the question posed by this chapter. For in the end, the ultimate question that every person must answer is this: How do *you* measure up to what God intended *you* to be?

What Do *You* Think?

1. I agree with/disagree with/am not sure about the conclusions of this chapter because......

2. As far as I'm concerned, a 'saint' is a person who......

3. The fact that there are some hypocrites in the Christian Church bothers me a lot/bothers me some/doesn't bother me at all because......

4. I agree/disagree that the most important question for me is not how consistent other people are, but how I measure up to what God intended me to be because ......

Chapter Eleven

CAN WE LOVE & DO AS WE PLEASE?

"I give you a new commandment: love one another. As I have loved you, so you must love one another. If you have love for one another, then everyone will know that you are my disciples."   John 13: 34-35

Looking Through the Microscope |

Roving Reporter

Good afternoon ladies and gentlemen. This is Sam Spade, your NPR roving reporter with the 'Question of the Day.' I'm standing in Time Square in the Big Apple with crowds milling all around me. Each day, as you know, I interview a number of people and ask them our 'Question of the Day.' The answers I get are often thoughtful, sometimes unexpected and now and then very funny.

"Our 'Question of the Day' on this beautiful sunny Tuesday afternoon is this: 'What is a Christian?' As you know, New York is a cosmopolitan city with people from all over the world living here. Wherever people go, they take their religion with them, and New York is no exception. This city has Hindu temples, Muslim Mosques, Jewish synagogues, Buddhist temples ... well, you name it, and New York's got it.

"Now and then we've asked a question about one of these religions. Today it's Christianity's turn. I suppose there are more Christian churches and schools in New York than there are of any other religion. So it's only natural that a good number of New Yorkers would have some interesting answers to our 'Question of the Day.'"

Sam Spade: "Excuse me, may I ask you our NPR 'Question of the Day'? Before I do, will you please tell me your name and occupation?

Interviewee: "I'm Hayden Williams and I'm a junior at Fordham University."

Sam Spade: "I see. That's a Catholic school, isn't it?"

Hayden: "Yes it is."

Sam Spade: "Well, *you're* certainly qualified to answer our 'Question of the Day', which is: 'What is a Christian?'"

Hayden: "Well ... I'd say that a Christian is a person who goes to church and tries to live a good life."

Sam Spade: "I see. Thank you very much ... And who are you, please?"

Interviewee: "I'm Betty Mack and I'm a homemaker."

Sam Spade: "Do you have any children?"

Betty: (laughing) "Too many! I have eight."

Sam Spade: "My goodness! That must keep you busy. Tell me, Betty, what do you think a Christian is?"

Betty: "Uh ... I'm not one myself, but I have a friend who is. She spends a lot of time praying and reading the

Bible, so I guess I would say that a Christian is somebody who does that."

Sam Spade: "Thank you Betty ... Hello there! My but you have a bright sweater on! What do those initials stand for?"

Interviewee: "Oh, you mean R.O.B.E.? (Laughing) That stands for 'Royal Order of Big Eaters.' It's a club we have at school, and our members love to eat. Our favorite restaurant is Mama Mia's Pizzeria."

Sam Spade: (laughing) "That sounds like a fun club to belong to Tell me your name and how *you* would answer our 'Question of the Day.'"

Interviewee: "I'm Jason Jones and I'm a senior at NYU. From what I can see of them, Christians are people who *don't* ... they   don't smoke; they don't dance; they don't drink; they   don't   work   on   Sunday;   they don't go to 'R' rated movies ... and a whole lot of other don'ts. I don't think I'd ever want to be one. They've got too many strict rules and regulations."

Sam Spade: (laughing) "I'll bet they *do* eat though! ... Hello there. I'm Sam Spade of NPR. Will you tell us your name please and what you do?

Interviewee: "Yeah, sure. I'm Bill Pringle and I drive a bus."

Sam Spade: "Bill, how would you answer our 'Question of the Day'- 'What is a Christian?'"

Bill: "I don't think I could answer it very well because I don't have much time for religion, what with driving a bus 12 hours a day. I don't know much about Christians. I did go to the Baptist Hospital in Brooklyn once when I got hurt though. Those Christians run a pretty good hospital ... so I suppose you could say that they really do good deeds for society."

Sam Spade: "Thank you Bill ... Excuse me young lady. You heard what Bill said. Is that the way you would   answer our 'Question of the Day'?"

Interviewee: "I think what Bill said is okay as far as it goes, but there's a lot more to it than that. You see, I'm a Christian, and I'd say that a Christian is a person who believes in the ideas of Jesus Christ and tries to live out his lifestyle in society. *Part* of being a Christian is doing good works, like Bill said, but being able to do those good works only really comes about if a person has faith in Christ and is really serious about following him.

Sam Spade: "I see. I'm sorry. I forget to ask your name and what you do."

Interviewee: "You won't believe this, but my name is Nancy Bruner, and I'm a nurse at the Baptist Hospital in Brooklyn!"

Sam Spade: "You're kidding! Why what a coincidence. I don't suppose you took care of Bill, did you?"

Nancy: (laughing) "No, I don't believe I did."

Sam Spade: "We have time to ask one more person our 'Question of the Day'... Hello sweetie. What's your name and how old are you?"

Interviewee: "Oh ... my name is Elizabeth and I'm eight years old."

Sam Spade: "And you're very pretty too! ... How would *you*

answer our 'Question of the Day'? What do you think a Christian is?"

Elizabeth: "Ummm … somebody who loves God and everybody else."

Sam Spade: "Well, we couldn't get a much better answer than that, could we? … Thank you very much for listening in to 'Roving Reporter' today. Be sure to tune in again tomorrow when I'll be in Central Park asking another 'Question of the Day.'... Meanwhile, this is your roving reporter, Sam Spade, wishing you a happy day."

What Do *You* Think?

1. Who do you think answered Sam Spade's 'Question of the Day' best and why?

2. Who do you think gave the least satisfactory answer and why?

3. What do you think of the four other answers?

4. Suppose Sam Spade were to ask *you* this question? How would you answer it?

5. Most interviewees put their emphasis on what Christians do or don't do rather than on what they are or believe. Do you agree with that? Explain.

Bringing Things Into Focus |

Love is …

Here are eleven statements from the Bible describing what love is.

- "If someone says he loves God, but hates his brother, he is a liar.

For he cannot love God whom he has not seen, if he does not love his brother, whom he has seen." 1 John 4:20

- "Love is patient and kind; it is not envious or boastful or proud; love is not rude or selfish or angry; love does not keep a record of wrongs; love is not happy with evil but is happy with the truth. Love never gives up; and its protection, trust and hope never fail." 1 Corinthians 13: 4-8

- "Knowledge puffs a person up with pride; but love builds up." 1 Corinthians 8:1

- "Serve one another in love." Galatians 5:13

- "Be always humble, and gentle. Show your love by being patient with one another." Ephesians 4:2

- "By speaking the truth in a spirit of love, we must grow up in every way to Christ, who is the head." Ephesians 4:15

- "Above everything, love one another earnestly, because love covers many sins." 1 Peter 4: 8

- "My children, our love should not be just words and talk; it must be true action which shows itself in love." 1 John 3:18

- "Love your enemies and pray for those who persecute you...Why should God love you if you love only the people who love you?" Matthew 5:44, 46

- "The greatest love a person can have for his friends is to give his life for them." 1 John 15:13

- "Do not ill treat aliens who are living in your land. Treat them as you would a fellow Israelite, and love them as you love yourselves." Leviticus 19:33-34

What Do *You* Think?

1. What would you say is the one theme these statements all have in common?

2. In your opinion, which statement best sums up what Christians believe love is? Why?

3. Do you think it's possible to actually practice 1 John 15:13 in our world today? Why or why not?

4. Describe a real life event that in your opinion demonstrated Leviticus 19:33-34.

Gaining a Perspective |

Tom, Dick and Gerry

The following are samples of what our friends Tom, Dick and Gerry have to say about 'love.'

Gerry is sitting near her friend Peter who is busy playing his cello with a newspaper in her hand. She says, "Look Pete, they printed my letter in the paper." She reads her letter to him while he pays no attention to her. "Dear Sally. I'm in love with a guy who doesn't even know I exist. All he ever thinks of is his dumb cello and that dumb ol' Bach. Can you give me any advice?" Peter straightens up and stops playing. She continues to read: "And here's her answer: 'Dear Gerry. Never fall in love with a musician.'" She says, "Hmmm. I kinda suspected that."

****

Tom and Dick are walking along together when Tom's dog comes racing out, stops, jumps up on Dick with his front legs outstretched and gives him a big hug. Then he jumps up on Tom and gives *him* a big hug as Dick looks on with a quizzical look on his face. Tom then says to Dick, "He loves people."

****

Gerry and Dick are looking out the window. Gerry looks depressed. Dick says, "When you feel like this, you should try to think of what you can give thanks for...in other words, count your many blessings." Gerry angrily replies, "Ha! That's a good one! I could count my blessings on one hand! I've never *had* any blessings, and I never *will* have any blessings!" She continues, "I never seem to get any of the breaks that other people do. Nothing ever seems to go right for me! So you talk about counting blessings? You talk about being thankful? What do *I* have to be thankful for? Dick wistfully replies, "Well, for one thing, you have one little brother who loves you." Gerry turns to look at him. Then she hugs him and cries. Dick remarks to nobody in particular, "Every now and then I say something good."

****

Gerry is skipping rope and comments to Dick, "*You* a dentist? HA! That's quite a laugh!" She stops skipping and continues, "You could never be a dentist! You know why?" She resumes skipping and says, "Because you don't love humanity, that's why!" Dick retorts, "I love humanity. It's individuals I can't stand!!"

What Do *You* Think?

1. What is the point or message of each exchange?

2. What kind of 'love' is being talked about in each of these exchanges?

3. Which exchange most demonstrates the idea that love can get through to the most stony heart, and why?

4. In your opinion, do these exchanges have any relationship to the Christian faith? Explain.

<u>Drawing Conclusions</u> |

If We Love, We *Can* Do as We Please

'Love' is probably the most overworked word in the dictionary. People talk about it, sing about it, wear it on the front of their T-shirts, watch it 'happening' on movie and computer screens, name boats, TV programs and who knows what else with it - and more. 'Love' has become such an overused word that when people do use it, we hardly pay attention to what they're saying; it more or less goes in one ear and out the other.

As a result, 'love' has become a meaningless word. We're tired of hearing so many people say, "What the world needs is love," in a way that makes it seem like some empty, abstract, idealistic theory that nobody really takes seriously 'down on the street.' 'Love' has become a nostalgic sentimentality with which to close a celebrity TV special - empty, sugary words about getting everybody together to be nice to each other - words that are often about as fake as the smiles on the faces of the people who say them. It seems as though the less love is really practiced, the louder and the longer people seem to want to talk about it. We feel uneasy about all this easy use of a word that so few are actually *doing*. We're tempted to sigh rather cynically, and say, "Here comes the love pitch again."

'Love' has also become a fuzzy word. People have used it to describe so many things in so many ways that it's become a word that confuses more than a word that clarifies. A singer blares out, "Love is a many-splendored thing." A teenager declares, "I love MacDonald's hamburgers!" A hiker exclaims, "I love the view from this peak." A child whispers, "I love you Mommy." A pastor at a soldier's funeral says, "He loved his country." A priest tells his people they should, "love your neighbors as yourselves." The city of Philadelphia is called by its citizens "the city of brotherly love." A community chest official praises a wealthy merchant who hands over a check as a man who "loves this community." All these people are using the same word, but they certainly don't mean the same thing!

What Christians Mean When They Use the Word 'Love'

If 'love' is such a problematic word, why have we entitled this chapter, "Can People Really Love and Do as They Please?" One reason is to understand what *Christians* mean when they use the word 'love' since they have some very definite ideas about what that word means. Another reason is to get rid of some false ideas people have about Christianity as being a religion of rules. Some people are so hung up with trying to find 'dos' and 'don'ts' in the Bible that they miss the main idea as to what the Christian life is all about. A third reason is to realize that this rather startling statement "Love, and do as you please" was first made by a 5th century Christian named Augustine whose experiences in life served to underline his words. This idea was not some abstract theological theory thought up in a monastery, but a practical summary of a long life of Christian struggle. (You'll want to read an account of the life of this influential Christian when you have time.)

Much of the confusion over the word 'love' is due to the fact that English-speaking people try to express some six different ideas using this one word! The Greek language, from which all these ideas come, had individual words to express each of these ideas separately. When the Greeks used what we translate as the word 'love,' they knew exactly what they were talking about, while we have to guess by the context whether we're talking about motherly love, brotherly love, patriotism, romantic love, aesthetic love, love of animals, or whatever.

The Bible, of course, talks about all these kinds of love too, but the great majority of the time it talks about self-giving love. To love your brother, wife, children, employees, friends, enemies, strangers with self-giving love means to be as concerned about him/her/their need(s), welfare, happiness, problems or hopes, as you are about your own. It means to be willing to give of your time, energy, money and self in such a way that their welfare is advanced, their happiness is increased, their problems are solved and their hopes are realized. When Jesus said, "Love your neighbor (whoever you come into contact with) as yourself," he was stating the core of what Christians mean when they talk about 'love.' We all know how concerned we are about ourselves and our interests. Self-giving love means that we'll be just as intensely concerned about *others* and *their* interests.

How Does 'Love' Actually Work?

Well, so much for the theory. What about the practice? How does this idea actually work out 'where the rubber hits the road?' Jesus didn't give us some abstract, ethereal, nice sounding but impractical theory. One look at his life and actions is enough to convince us of that! It's true that we're simply told over and over again in the Bible that we're *supposed* to love people. But just *how* are we to go about it? How does Christian love work itself out in the nitty gritty of real life? Does the Bible say anything about that?

Look back over the eleven statements in 'Bringing Things into Focus' above. Would you say they're more abstract or more concrete, more theoretical or more practical? The answer will become clear if you condense those statements into one long statement - something like this:

> Self-giving love means people will not be afraid of me or be hated by me. It means I'll be patient with them, kind to them, glad when they succeed and sad when they fail. It means I'll look for the good in them and forgive the bad in them. It means I'll be courteous to them, generous to them and consider them as being just as important, or capable, or whatever, as I am. It means I'll be honest with them, believe in them even when they're weak and never give up on them. It means I'll encourage them, be gentle with them and give them the right to disagree with me. It means I'll be friendly to strangers, seek reconciliation rather than revenge with my enemies and be willing to risk my life for my friends. Above all, it means I'll concentrate on actually loving rather than on merely talking about it.

Certainly nobody could be hazy or fuzzy about what it means to love after reading that! Love is a state of mind, an attitude, a way of life that expresses itself in concrete action. How we're to love is very clear. To go ahead and *do* so is perhaps another story. But that too is possible, and we'll discuss more about how it becomes possible in another chapter.

Love and Commandments

That love is the key to the whole of what being a Christian is all about is made even clearer when it comes to talking about commandments. Becoming a Christian has nothing to do with making an agreement to follow a set of laws or rules, but of being set free to love. A Christian doesn't look at God's commands like an army private looks at military regulations. No, a Christian looks at those commandments as concrete descriptions of love in action. A Christian doesn't see the commandments as something to fear, or feel trapped by, or as 'fun spoilers,' but as things s/he enjoys doing in giving herself or himself for others.

It's the person who has trouble loving who puts great emphasis on keeping commandments, following rules and observing rituals. That's why Jesus had such trouble with the Pharisees. He had come to set people free from the law as a *burden*. He had come to enable people to love, and to joyfully fulfill the law in the process. The Pharisees were frightened of this freedom and hung onto all their rules and regulations - and their burden! Only un-loving people see commandments as regulations and keep them as a burdensome duty.

A Christian who truly loves can forget about commandments altogether and do what s/he pleases, since a loving person doing what s/he pleases will never be contradicted by any commandments of a loving God. That's why Jesus and his followers stressed again and again that those who love can throw out the rule book as it were. Love does all that's right, good, selfless and true. It fulfills the whole law - and more! The law only talks about what I should keep from doing to harm my neighbors, but love knows that I need to do more than simply not doing my neighbors in or leaving them alone to deal with their problems - I must reach out to them and help them meet their needs as persons. And in so doing, I will find meaning for my own life as a person. "He who loses his life for my sake," said Jesus, "will find it." Matthew 16:25

Here are two statements from the Bible that will make this idea very clear.

> Jesus said, "Love the Lord your God with all your heart, with all your soul and with all your mind … Love your neighbor as you love yourself. The whole law of Moses and the teachings of the prophets depend on these two commandments." Matthew 22:37-40

> Paul wrote, "The only obligation you have is to love one another. Whoever does this has obeyed the law…If you love someone, you will never do him wrong; to love, then, is to obey the whole law." Romans 1:8, 10

Loving God and Loving Self

We've been talking about loving *others* without feeling that it's our duty to do so or that we're forced by regulations to do so. But what about the other two people mentioned in Jesus' statement above - God and you!? As far as loving *God* is concerned, we'll simply say here what John makes so plain in his first letter - that it's impossible to separate love for neighbor from love for God, and that the source of our love for neighbor is God himself. "We love because God first loved us." (See 1 John 4:7-21). And we'll also say with Paul that "God is ready to pour out his love into our hearts by means of the Holy Spirit." Romans 5:5 (We'll save the rest of this subject for another chapter).

But what about loving *you*? You'll notice that Jesus said, "Love your neighbor *as you love yourself*." God doesn't want us to be *more* concerned about ourselves than we are about others (that's selfishness), but he does want us to be concerned about ourselves - to love ourselves. Here's where some people who don't know much about Christian love get themselves into difficulty. In their desire to know *how* to love themselves, they make the same mistake the Pharisees made and start looking at loving as a duty prescribed by regulations. They begin to make all kinds of rules for themselves (and often for others!) about doing this and not doing that, and the joyful, free adventure of life as a follower of Christ becomes a rather dull and laborious thing.

A careful search of the New Testament will reveal that there are plenty of practical clues as to how a healthy love for self works itself out in real life. But the emphasis is always on freedom, not imprisonment, and on principles, not on rules. For example, Paul puts it this way: "Fill your minds with those things that are good and that deserve praise: things that are true, noble, right, pure, lovely and honorable." Philippians 4:8 That's the kind of 'love yourself' statement that will mean nothing but joy, fulfillment, satisfaction and growth for anybody who puts it into practice. Notice that it doesn't give any instructions about smoking, drinking, dancing, movies and the like. In fact, there isn't *any* place in the Bible where you can find specifics about these types of things. Christians who've gotten all hung up making rules and regulations about such things haven't gotten them from the Bible! And the reason they've made such rules at all is because they haven't yet discovered what it means to be *set free* by Christ - to love themselves. (See also Colossians 2:16-3:4)

Truly loving myself will mean that I'll joyfully do all that will help me become the kind of person God intended me to be, and avoid whatever won't. For some people under certain circumstances that might mean one thing. For others under different circumstances that might mean something else. For example, a film that might be helpful to a very mature person might be harmful to an immature person. Paul writes, "Everything that God has created is good; nothing is to be rejected, but everything is to be received with a prayer of thanks." 1 Timothy 4:4 What he means is, there is nothing evil about grapes, films, cards, tobacco leaves, our bodily rhythms, computers and the like *in themselves*. It's what we *do* with them that can make the difference between loving ourselves and harming ourselves. For example, it doesn't make sense to condemn *all* films because *some* are harmful. But neither does it make sense to watch the ones that are harmful.

Loving ourselves as God intended us to will mean that we'll continually need to make our own individual judgments on specifics, basing those judgments on whether something will help us *towards* the true, noble, right, pure, lovely, honorable, or *away* from them.

People who approach life in this way can throw the rule book out. They can love and do what they please, because what will please them will also please God.

Love is what makes Christianity go 'round,' not rules. In the end, it's this word more than any other that explains what a Christian is.

What Do *You* Think?

1. I agree/disagree with/am not sure about the conclusions of this chapter because ......

2. I think it's possible/impossible to love others in the Christian sense of the word because ......

3. I agree/disagree/am not sure that becoming a Christian has nothing to do with agreeing to follow a set of laws or rules because ......

4. I agree/disagree/am not sure that a follower of Jesus can love and do as s/he pleases because ......

Chapter Twelve

WHAT KEEPS CHRISITANS GROWING?

> "Be like new-born babies, always thirsting for the pure spiritual milk, so that by drinking it you may grow up and be saved."   1 Peter 2:2

Looking Through the Microscope |

Facebook Pals

February 30

Hi again Miguel:

"I was glad to get your message the other day. It's neat the way our friendship has grown over the past six months. Even though we've never met, I feel that I know you quite well. I would say that you're now one of my best friends. Hopefully we'll get to meet someday, but Spain is a loooong way away and costs an awful lot of money to get to. Maybe you could come visit me in the States! Wouldn't that be exciting?

"Thanks for the photos. You sure live in a nice looking house. It's got such a biiiig yard around it! Your sister is really cute too! Too bad she's too old for me! (Don't tell her I said that!) Is that your college jacket you're wearing? I suppose that's your dog 'Dasher' that you keep referring to.

"Thanks for the stamps you mailed me too! My Spanish collection has really grown since I met you on Facebook. I hope you'll like the US stamps I sent you. I might eventually be able to get some Canadian stamps for you as well since one of my teachers is from Canada. She's okay, but she's pretty much 'no nonsense' when it comes to learning Spanish!

"One thing in your letter kind of puzzled me. I didn't know you were religious. You mention going to church, reading the Bible, praying and all that. Yes, I know about that because I go to a school that's run by a church and I've got some friends who are Christians. No, I'm not one myself. I guess I don't really pay much attention to religion, although I've got one class in it where we're studying a book called 'Christianity under the Microscope.' It's sort of interesting, but sometimes it's a little boring too.

"Frankly, one of the reasons why I'm not a Christian is because of all the things you have to do. You have to go to church, read the Bible every day, pray a lot of times, go to Youth Fellowship, go to the school's Christian Fellowship, and all that. People are always expecting you to take time to do service projects, to join study groups and to try to get other people to become Christians. I know that you might think all this is cool, and I don't want to hurt your feelings, but I wonder when you have any fun in life, get your homework done and go out with girls and all that. I find that I am plenty busy already without adding religion to my life.

"It all sounds so serious and, well, rather boring. I mean, like in church (I went with a friend once!) most of what you do is sit there and listen to a long lecture. And I would find 'talking' to somebody I couldn't even see and who never answered back pretty hard. Some parts of the Bible I've read are sort of interesting, but there are other parts that are boring and repetitive and there are lots of things that are hard to understand. I hope *you* understand and don't take any of this personally. Religion does a lot of good for people, and I'm sure it must do that for you. Maybe you can write more about how you feel about it in your next post.

"Our big game is tomorrow, and so is my big Spanish exam! I hope old 'Miss Canada' has a little mercy on us. If we win this game, we'll have won the championship! I'll write you again and tell you how it turns out - the *game* I mean! Seriously, I've *got* to pass that exam!

"So I'd better sign off for now. Have a great Easter holiday, and write again soon.

Best,   George"

****

April 15

"Hi back George:

"I'm sorry it's taken me so long to answer your message. I've been meaning to get to it, but the time has just slipped by.

"Thanks a whole lot for the stamps which I received yesterday. I really liked the ones with the national parks on them. You're lucky. In the States, you have fantastic scenery and lots of neat fish and birds and snakes that we only get to see in books or on TV - or that cost a lot of money to buy in the pet shop. And in America you're *surrounded* by 'em! I really would like to come and visit you, but right now the only way I could get there would be to paddle my canoe over 'the pond.' Maybe someday we can swing it when we both become world famous doctors and earn a lot of money!

"I'm eager to hear how your big game turned out - *and* how your Spanish exam turned out. Hopefully you won the championship and did well in the exam too! From what you've written, I know how important a good grade in Spanish is for your future, especially as you hit the home stretch in gearing up for grad school. I'll be praying for you during the months ahead as you take your exams and explore different grad programs.

"Speaking of praying, thanks for being so honest about where you stand as far as 'religion' is concerned. I know exactly what you mean, because I was just like you once - standing on the outside looking in. Without sounding like I'm trying to convince you, let me tell you that it's very different when you're on the inside looking out.

"I became a Christian two years ago through an organization called 'Christian Athletes.' The guys who belonged to this group were very different from what I'd ever experienced going to church with my parents when I was a kid. Following Christ wasn't a matter of going through boring rituals and attending a bunch of meetings just because they were expected to. They were the first people I'd ever met who actually *enjoyed* reading the Bible and talking about what it meant. Prayer to them was something that really put them in touch with somebody.

They were guys you could always count on to help you out with some problem or to be pulling on the right side of things. They didn't see their religion as something extra that got in the way of life or fun or anything, but that was a part of everything. Church to them wasn't a lecture, but a fellowship of 'alive' people who they enjoyed being with and who worshipped God in a way that made his presence real. They were very enthusiastic, all-around guys, and I was greatly attracted to them and to their organization.

"To make a long story short, through them I became convinced that Jesus' ideas were right and that his lifestyle was for me. At first, like you, I wondered whether I would ever enjoy reading the Bible, worshipping God and all that. I also wondered whether those things would interfere with other things I wanted to do. But once I became convinced that it was crucial for me not only to stay spiritually alive, but to 'grow up' as a Christian, I began to get enthused about it. And the kinds of discussions and worship and community spirit Christians had in their churches helped me a lot too. There *are* a lot of live churches, you know. I'm just sorry that your first experience was with one that seemed rather dead without much involvement or enjoyment by the people. Anyway, I'm not out to convince you, but am just trying to explain to you, seeing as you asked. I can write more about it later if you're interested.

"You're wrong about my sister! Not about her good looks, but about her age! She's a year younger than you, and she lives at the same address I do. Hint! Hint!

"Yep, that was my dog in the picture. I've had him for five years now. He likes to go hiking with me and chase squirrels. He gets very frustrated when they zip up a tree and he can never catch one. It's a dog's life!

"Well, I've got to get to football practice now (you call it soccer). I'll be looking for your next post - and hopefully for some good news on the exam and the game.

"Your Amigo,

Miguel

What Do *You* Think?

1. What do you think of George's opinion of religion in general and Christianity in particular?

2. What do you think of Miguel's experience with Christianity?

3. If you were writing to a friend about your religious beliefs, would it be more like George's letter, or more like Miguel's? Explain.

4. Complete the following:

   a. I often/sometimes/seldom read the Bible because......

   b. I often/sometimes/seldom pray because......

   c. I often/sometimes/seldom attend a church service because......

   d. I often/sometimes/seldom participate in a service project because......

Bringing Things Into Focus |

Vitamins for the Spiritual Life

Perhaps you're not a Christian. In that case, you probably haven't done much of what Christians consider vital for their spiritual life and growth. Even so, you can still play the 'what if' game. That is, you can think about some of these things from the standpoint that if you *were* to do any of them, what might interest you the most? What might you say or think? What might be most helpful to you as a person? If you *are* a Christian, then, of course, you'll be in 'home territory' on these things, so to speak.

Christians believe that *prayer* is vital for their spiritual growth.

- When Christians pray, they praise God for who he is, what he's done in the past, what he's doing in the present and what he's promised to do in the future.

- When Christians pray, they confess what they don't feel very good about in their lives and ask God to forgive and heal them.

- When Christians pray, they thank God for his blessings.

- When Christians pray, they bring other people's needs to God.

- When Christians pray, they ask God to meet their own needs.

Christians believe that *worship* is vital for their spiritual growth.

- When they worship, Christians sing, pray and read the Bible. They also listen to someone explain the ideas in the Bible and how they can be lived out in today's world.

- When they worship, Christians reaffirm their commitment to God by repeating a brief summary of their faith called a 'creed.'

- When they worship, Christians participate in the Christian sacraments of baptism and the Lord's Supper (or the Mass). (These sacraments are outward physical signs and seals that reflect and assure inward spiritual happenings. Baptism is a rite that symbolizes a person's entering into the new life that Christ brings through his Spirit and is the gateway through which a person becomes a member of the Christian church. The Lord's Supper (or the Mass) is a rite that helps Christians remember that Christ died for their salvation, that he is present in their lives through his Spirit and that he will someday come again to welcome his people into his realm).

- When they worship, Christians celebrate festivals like the birth of Christ at Christmas and the resurrection of Christ from the dead at Easter.

- When they worship, Christians offer their money and themselves for God's service.

Christians believe that *Bible study* is vital for their spiritual growth.

- Christians read and study the Bible and spiritually uplifting literature individually through the week but also gather in groups to stimulate each other's understanding and application of the Bible's teachings to their daily lives.

- Christians also memorize key passages from the Bible so that they can call them to mind in whatever circumstances they might find themselves.

- Christians use a number of aids to help them better understand the background and meaning of the contents of the Bible. Here is a list of reference books that you might find useful.

  A **Bible Commentary** is a book that describes and interprets the material in the Bible.

  A **Bible Atlas** is a book that contains maps and geographical information about the Bible.

A **Bible Concordance** is a book that lists all the words and their references in the Bible in alphabetical order.

A **Bible Encyclopedia** is a book that contains extensive articles about every person, place, thing and subject in the Bible in alphabetical order.

A **Bible Harmony** is a book that weaves similar parts of the Bible into one account.

A **Bible Handbook** is a book that contains background information about various subjects in the Bible.

A **Bible Dictionary** is a book that includes definitions and proper names for Biblical words with their references and usually includes the original Greek and Hebrew word with its meaning.

A **Bible Survey** is a book that gives an overview of the books of the Bible along with archaeological, historical and cultural information.

A **Bible Introduction** is a book that introduces a reader to either the Old Testament or the New Testament of the Bible by spelling out information on the background, language, interpretation, and content of a Testament and each book within a Testament.

A **Bible Biography** is a book that introduces one to the life and times of an important Bible character.

Christians believe that *being God's servants and change agents in the world* is vital for their spiritual growth.

- Christians think their Christian theory must be put into practice wherever they are and in whatever they do. Christians become stronger in their faith and life when they not only believe but also *do*.

- Christians believe that "The more you give away, the more you have," not necessarily in physical terms but in terms of the inner quality of life. Giving enhances living.

- Christians think they should strive to contribute to the furthering of peace and justice in the world wherever and whenever they have an opportunity to do so. Being involved in a fight for the right and the oppressed deepens one's faith roots and brings joy and fulfillment to one's life

- Christians feel they should share the Good News of Christ with their families, neighbors, friends, colleagues and others, not just keep such an enriching way of life to themselves.

What Do Y*ou* Think?

1. What might be one thing *you* can think of that you might want to praise God for, confess to God or thank God for?

2. Who's somebody in need that *you* might want to pray for? What need might *you* have that you might like God to do something about?

3. Is there a Christian song that might be a particular favorite of yours? Have you ever heard anyone speak on a topic about Christianity that interested you very much? If so, what was the topic?

4. Christians often recite a creed that expresses what they believe. What kind of a 'creed' would express what *you* believe?

5. Have you ever observed Christians being baptized or been baptized yourself? Have you ever seen Christians celebrating the Lord's Supper (or the Mass) or have you ever done so yourself? If so, what were your impressions?

6. What Christian festival do you most enjoy, and why?

7. Have you given a gift to or offered your services for a charity or a public welfare organization? Do you think it's necessary for the church to collect money? Explain.

8. If you were to read the Bible, would you try to read it through from beginning to end like any other book? What kind(s) of literature in the Bible interest(s) you the most - History, Poetry, Proverbs, Parables (stories), Biography, Psalms (songs), Prophetic teaching, Letters, Essays? How many books of the Bible have you done at least some reading in? Which books have you or might you find most interesting and helpful, and why? If you were to summarize the main message of the Bible in one sentence, what would it be? What person in the Bible most interests you and why?

9. Do *you* know of Christians who have put their 'theory' into practice in society? What impressed you the most about them? Do you think that "The more you give away, the more you have" is a true statement? Why, or why not?

Gaining a Perspective |

Unity in Community

People are constantly being separated and driven apart in our world today. Barriers are continually being built to wall people in or wall them out - barriers of age, sex, race, culture, nationality, education, class, lifestyle, values, ideologies, and the like.

One of the things that Christians find so stimulating and helpful to their life and growth is that they can be a part of a fellowship called the Christian Church whose aim is to bring people of all kinds together for mutual sharing, caring, learning and serving. Christians find their spiritual 'family' to be as vital to their growth and development as whole persons as their physical family is.

Here are some of the ways in which the Bible describes the unity of the Christian community as over against the divisions that separate the human community.

- "So there is no difference between Jews and Gentiles, between slaves and free people, between men and women; you are all one in union with Christ Jesus." Galatians 3:28

- "And because of God's gracious gift to me I say to every one of you: Do not think of yourself more highly than you should. Instead, be modest in your thinking, and judge yourself according to the amount of faith that God has given you. We have many parts in the one body, and all these parts have different functions. In the same way, though we are many, we are one body in union with Christ, and we are all joined to each other as different parts of one body." Romans 12:3-5

- "And so there is no division in the body, but all its different parts have the same concern for one another. If one part of the body suffers, all the other parts suffer with it; if one part is praised, all the other parts share its happiness. All of you are Christ's body, and each one is a part of it." 1 Corinthians 12:25-27

- "But if we live in the light - just as he is in the light - then we have fellowship with one another, and the blood of Jesus, his Son, purifies us from every sin." 1 John 1:7

- "Be always humble, gentle, and patient. Show your love by being tolerant with one another. Do your best to preserve the unity which the Spirit gives by means of the peace that binds you together. There is one body and one Spirit, just as there is one hope to which God has called you. There is one Lord, one faith, one baptism; there is one God and Father of all people, who is Lord of all, works through all, and is in all." Ephesians 4:2-6

- "By speaking the truth in a spirit of love, we must grow up in every way to Christ, who is the head. Under his control all the different parts of the body fit together, and the whole body is held together by every joint with which it is provided. So when each separate part works as it should, the whole body grows and builds itself up through love." Ephesians 4:15-16

- "I appeal to all of you, my friends, to agree in what you say, so that there will be no divisions among you. Be completely united, with only one thought and one purpose." 1 Corinthians 1:10

- "How wonderful it is, how pleasant, for God's people to live together in harmony!" Psalm 133:1

- "Be tolerant with one another and forgive one another whenever any of you has a complaint against someone else. You must forgive one another just as the Lord has forgiven you. And to all these qualities add love, which binds all things together in perfect unity." Colossians 3:13-14

- "You must not be called 'Teacher,' because you are all equal and have only one Teacher." Matthew 23:8

What Do You Think?

1. What's the main theme that runs throughout these statements?

2. What are some of the things mentioned in these statements that drive people apart?

3. In your opinion, which of these statements is the most difficult for Christians to practice?

4. If you were to summarize in your own words what these statements teach about Christian unity, what would you say?

Drawing Conclusions |

What Keeps Christians Growing?

What would happen if you stopped eating for a day? Not too much, except that your stomach would complain pretty loudly. What if you went on a fast for a week? You would begin to feel exhausted and your body would begin to do more than complain. What if you went on a hunger strike for a month? You would begin to starve and your growth would be stunted. In another two to three weeks you would begin to go blind and a lot of other things would go wrong with you. Two months is the longest the human body can go without food before it gives out altogether and death occurs.

A person's spiritual life is the same. If somebody never gets any spiritual 'food' or 'exercise,' s/he shrivels up and eventually dies spiritually. Unfortunately, many people don't realize that. These same people wouldn't *think* of going without *one* physical meal, let alone starving themselves to death! Yet, simply because they can't see some dramatic physical evidence to the contrary (although even *that* sometimes occurs), they'll allow themselves to spiritually starve to death without blinking an eye.

Christians are convinced that to go without spiritual food is to commit spiritual suicide - to let the core of one's person shrivel and die even while one's physical self is still very much alive. They know that, as far as plants, animals and anything else that is alive are concerned, growth demands drinking, eating and exercising. For humans, that not only means physically, but spiritually too. That's why they feel that tending to their spiritual needs is just as important as tending to their physical needs, or social needs, or any other kinds of needs. In fact, they believe that attending to spiritual needs is of central importance because a person's spiritual condition affects all the rest of what makes up his or her personhood as well.

Spiritual Nourishment

What keeps Christians growing? Christians believe the basic answer to this question is that God's Spirit, the source of all life, does. Paul makes clear to the Christians of Galatia that it's God's Spirit that 'directs' their lives, 'produces' beautiful character traits and 'gives' them life. (See Galatians 5:16, 22, 25). Of course God's Spirit doesn't do this in a vacuum, or through magic, or through a mechanical observance of rites and rituals. He does it through experiences, through people, through books, through silence, through music, through art, through meaningful work, through opportunities to serve others and to share the love of God with them, through...well, through lots of ways! To those who are sensitive to his presence and 'tuned in' to his wavelength, as it were, God's Spirit is present in *all* of life - ever calling, ever working, ever encouraging people to grow and develop into all that God originally intended them to be.

There are ways in which it's particularly noticeable that God's Spirit is present and working to nourish and nurture people who want to spiritually 'eat and drink.' There are certain exercises that are particularly helpful in opening one's self up to spiritual development and in the strengthening of one's 'inner person.' Some of these are quite familiar and have already been mentioned in this chapter - personal prayer and Bible study; participating in the worship and fellowship of a sharing-caring community (the church), and serving the needs of others as opportunities arise. Others aren't as familiar to some - like silence and meditation.

There's a group of Christians known as the Quakers. They've emphasized silence as a means of 'getting in touch' with God. Sometimes a person has a *very* deep sense of the presence and power of God if s/he simply sits still, listens and meditates on some statement from the Bible or on some experience s/he once had, or on some encounter with another person through whom God 'spoke' to him or her. This silence may mean being alone in a beautiful natural setting; it may mean listening to a moving choral work like Handel's "Messiah;" it may mean silently contemplating a great painting like Dali's "Crucifixion of Christ;" it may mean sitting silently with a group concentrating on hearing what God is saying through that 'still, small voice.'

There are too many talkers in the world and too few listeners. This is part of the reason why people, particularly those in big cities, are spiritually impoverished. Who can 'hear' God speaking in silence in the midst of millions of people, all jostling for their place, busily selling their wares, almost oblivious to the shattering sounds of air hammers, pile drivers, airplanes and all the rest? Living in crowded neighborhoods is not exactly conducive to quietness and meditation! Yet, there are places and times where this is possible, if somebody is determined and searches hard enough.

Another way to grow spiritually that we mentioned, but that's practiced by too few people, is being aware of the presence of God's Spirit in all of life. People make a mistake when they look at their faith as only one piece in the pie of life. Those who think of their faith in this way tend to emphasize formal rituals and practices. Once you've 'gone to church' on Sunday, or read your 'chapter for the day' in the Bible, or done your 'good deed for the day,' it's off to live the other part of life - with your 'religious slice' of life often left behind.

Following Jesus Christ as a Way of Life

Our Facebook Spanish friend, Miguel, was so enthused about his Christian experience because he'd come to know it as a *way of life*. God wasn't compartmentalized, to be 'taken down off the shelf' at set or convenient times. He was present in *all* of Miguel's life - giving it that joyful, steady quality that he reflects in his message. This didn't make Miguel some 'holy Joe' who never had any fun and was always seriously 'spiritual.' On the contrary, his 'life in the Spirit' was an enthusiastic adventure in which he, together with God, was continually discovering the *fullness* of life that Jesus came to make possible. (See John 10:10) It's people like Miguel, who are sensitive to and open to God's presence in the whole of life, that don't see their faith as some interfering burden, but as a liberating invitation to taste life in the way God meant it to be lived. Christians of this kind grow. Christians who merely 'carry out their religious duties' with a half-reluctant super piety only limp along.

The complaints that George wrote about in his message are all too valid for this same reason. They're often the reason why many people who are interested in Christ's way of life don't want to take the final step of becoming one of his followers. Such people think that to do so would 'saddle' them with what some immature Christians make appear as burdensome, life-interfering religious duties. This misunderstanding needs to be cleared up.

To become a *slave* to Bible reading, for example, is probably as bad as not reading it at all! There's nothing magic about a chapter a day, or even a verse a day. God knows that our schedules are tough. He's an understanding Father, not a hard taskmaster. On some days we might only have a few moments to 'get in touch' and make sure that we're aware of his presence as we start the day, eat a meal, end the day, or whatever. At other times, our schedules might allow us to take an hour or even two to do some serious study, prayer, meditation, service, and the like. A problem only develops when we do have time, but don't want to use it for spiritual growth; or when we clutter up our lives with so many mundane and meaningless activities that we consistently crowd out most of our spiritual feeding times. Then we'd better do something about re-ordering our priorities! But otherwise, we can relax about this and enjoy our times of worship, fellowship, study, quiet, and so on.

Learning How to Pray

Someone might say, "Most of the spiritual growth 'exercises' you mention are probably beneficial for spiritual growth, but I've got a problem with prayer. For one thing, it's hard for me to strike up a conversation with somebody I can't see or who doesn't respond. For another, God hasn't given me all the things I've asked for. Also, why pray if God knows how everything's going to turn out anyway? And who does God answer when he gets two conflicting requests? Let's take these one at a time.

1. If people pray to some abstract 'spiritual blob out there,' they're probably going to have trouble communicating. However, if they remember that God became a real human person in Jesus who, having risen from the dead, is still alive and still listening to his followers, then prayer as interpersonal communication becomes much more of a reality. The Spirit of God can't be pictured in the mind's 'eye,' but Jesus Christ can. And if people remember that God doesn't answer verbally, but that his answers may be conveyed through his Word (the Bible), through other people who are also 'in touch' with him, through dreams, through a person's inner spirit, through the wonders of his creation and

through the circumstances of life, then they will train themselves
to become more sensitive to 'pick up' those answers from those
sources and spend time cultivating them.

2. Do parents give their children all they ask for? Of course not! If
    they did, we would label them as bad parents. Why? Because
    children don't always ask for what's good for them and
    responsible parents will only give them what they know is good
    for them. In the same way, God often has to say "no" to his
    children who, from their limited and finite perspective, ask for
    what's not good for them or for others or for God's world even
    when it appears to them at the time that it is. God *always* answers
    a sincere prayer, but his children must sometimes learn to take
    "no" for an answer.

    Sometimes God answers "wait." Like typical children, his
    children are always impatient to have their requests granted
    'yesterday.' Like a typical parent, God looks at things long range
    and knows that 'haste often makes waste.' Christians are people
    who must develop the patience of maturity when waiting for
    God's answers, and the trust of commitment when entrusting an
    urgent matter into God's hands.

    At other times, God answers "I can't, at least not for now."
    God sees the big picture, while we only "see through a glass
    dimly," as Paul puts it in 1 Corinthians 13:12. As parents
    sometimes can't explain to small children all the reasons why
    they can't do something or allow them to do something at the
    moment, so God can't communicate to us everything involved in
    some of the decisions he makes. When we pray for someone to
    get well, for example, and they don't, people often make the
    mistake of thinking that God didn't answer their prayers. He did,
    but for deeper reasons than we can understand, he answered, "I
    can't."

    Of course God often answers prayers with a "yes." The
    problem is that people sometimes don't take that "yes" and do
    anything with it. For example, a student who prays, "Please help
    me to do my best in next month's exams," and then goes off to
    play sports or computer games, or to watch TV or to dally on

Facebook by the hour throughout the next month has simply thrown God's "yes" away. Prayer isn't manipulation, and God's answers don't work like magic. He expects his children to follow his will and his ways in order to have his "yes" translated into reality in their lives. In this case, following his will and his ways would mean using a good amount of time utilizing one's God-given talents to master what would be covered by those exams! Someone has well said, "Pray as though God can do everything; work as though God can do nothing."

3. Remember that we said in other chapters that God isn't simply a divine computer who's cranking out a pre-programmed history of the universe; that God didn't create robots but took the risk of creating unpredictable human beings who have the capacity to freely love Him or reject Him; and that God takes time and history seriously? Now we're saying that he also takes human prayers seriously. He's asked us to ask him, and the whole of the experience of the people of the Bible and of Christian history teaches us that when his people do ask him, those requests do carry weight and make a difference in the outcome of things. This doesn't mean, as we said above, that people's prayers can bind God to a course of action that he feels is foolish or wrong. After all, it's he who rules and overrules, not us. We don't pray to change God. We pray because prayer changes us. We're to pray according to *his* will, and as we do, we become partners with him in working that will out in life. God will work his purpose out, but he has made it clear that our prayers are an important element of that 'working out,' and that they do make a difference.

Of course God knows what we need before we ask him. We don't pray to inform God, but to involve God in our daily lives and in our decisions. God has made it clear that he wants us to do so. He wants to hear from us, and get involved with us, but he won't intrude. Instead, he waits for our invitation. Prayer is an opportunity to invite God to become involved our lives. When we pray to God, we should be ready to let him show us the areas in our lives that need to be changed. As we learn what it means to truly pray, and start to pray this way, it will be impossible for us to not change. Just think what the church would be like today if Christians prayed for God to change them according to his will; it they consistently prayed the prayer that never fails, "Your will be done." We don't pray to get *our* will done in Heaven, but to get *God's* will done on earth. Whose will do we want to be accomplished? We really only have two choices - our will, or God's will. Many times we think we know better, or know more than God, and want our will to be done. But God is sovereign, which means that he is God and we're not. *His* will is important and *his* will is in our best interest. The best thing that we can do is to get our will in line with God's will which is made quite plain in the scriptures.

We don't pray because God needs us, but because we need *God*. God made us to serve *him*, not for God to serve *us*. God is complete in himself. If there were no other creatures in the universe, God would still be complete because he needs no one else. God created the human race not because he needs us, but rather for his pleasure. We, however, desperately need God. As St. Augustine once said, "Our hearts are restless until they rest in you." God isn't made complete in us, but we're made complete in him. We pray, not to inform God, not to change him to our way of thinking, not to get our will done, not because he needs us, but because we need him, love him, and long to have a relationship with him.

4. Suppose a devout, drought-stricken farmer prays for rain and an equally devout, needy fisherman in the same area prays for sun. Who is God going to answer? Is it first come, first served, or what? For one thing, God has priorities and answers prayer accordingly. Human beings sometimes have different priorities that make it *appear* as though *whatever* God might do in a given situation, he wouldn't be able to do what was right and good for everybody concerned. However, the Bible makes very clear that if there's one thing about God that can be counted on, it's that he'll always do what's right and good for all of his children.

Sometimes what at first appears to be a dilemma in our eyes isn't a dilemma in God's eyes – or, on second thought, sometimes not even one in our eyes. Take the rain or shine apparent dilemma, for example. A solution for that dilemma might be to provide rain for the farmer during the night and shine for the fisherman during the day! Not all such problems are so easily solved, of course, but God has promised to work out all things for good for those who love him, and those who love him believe he will. (See Romans 8:28) Sometimes it's hard to believe this when things don't turn out the way we think they should. However, as we said before, life is like a tapestry. Sometimes what seems to us to be a tangled mess, when turned over, reveals a beautiful pattern. In the same way, God takes what appears to be a tangled mess in our lives and weaves it into a beautiful pattern – a pattern that's not apparent at the moment, but that eventually appears.

Participating in Joyful Worship

As George writes in his message, nothing is more boring (spiritually deadening) than a dead, formal church service where most of the people involved mostly serve as spectators. Christian worship was not meant to be this way. It was meant to be a joyful participatory celebration! Look at Psalm 150, for example. In the Israelite Temple worship, the Jews had trumpets, harps, lyres, drums, flutes, cymbals, *loud* cymbals, singers and even ... yes! ... dancing! It doesn't sound one bit dull, does it?! The Bible describes the New Testament Church in this way: "Day after day they met as a group in the Temple, and they had their meals together in their homes, eating with glad and humble hearts, praising God, and enjoying the good will of all the people." Acts 2:46-47 There was nothing formal or dull about *that* group either. Somewhere, somehow, some Christians have let the joy fall out their worship. But others certainly still have it - like Miguel's church. If Jack were to look around a bit more, he too could find a church like that and begin to understand Miguel's enthusiasm about Christian worship.

This doesn't mean that worship is all praise and no prayer, or all joy and no confession, or all participation and no instruction, or all sound and no silence, or all comfort and no challenge for the comfortable, or all celebration and no sense of awe in the presence of God, but that a sense of joyful gratitude for God's love and grace is woven into the whole experience.

Someone might say, "Isn't it possible to worship God by yourself? Why is it so necessary to go to church?" Of course it's possible (and enriching) to worship God by yourself, just as it's possible and profitable to do many other things by yourself. Millions of people have been enriched by their personal times of worship down through the centuries. But to stop there is to miss out on a great deal more that happens when Christians gather to worship together. In fact, Christian communal worship might be called just that - a 'happening.' The same is true with other activities like sporting events, auctions, parties, classroom discussions and the like. You can watch them on television, or tap into them on the Internet, but there's nothing like being there in person

For example, a person can decide to celebrate Christmas alone, but that wouldn't be very enjoyable, would it? There's something about such a festival that demands the presence of other people if it's going to be a true celebration. The same is true of Christian communal worship. There's a kind of spiritual 'electricity' in the air when Christians interact with one another and *together* interact with God that's not there when people worship alone.

What Christian would want to be alone all the time in his or her Christian experience and miss out on this? What Christian would want to celebrate Easter alone unless s/he was forced to do so by circumstances beyond his or her control? What Christian would want to miss out on participating in the spiritually strengthening communal sacraments whenever s/he could? What Christian would want to try to sing the great music of the church alone all the time? You only need to ask Christians who've been prevented by illness or old age or persecution from attending public worship for a period of time to understand how much they feel they've been deprived of and how eager they are to physically return to the Christian congregation and participate in its life once again. For example, the Christians in

China who were deprived of an opportunity to gather for public worship during the Maoist era are a living testimony to that very eagerness today.

There's also the reassuring sense that 'I'm not in this thing alone' when gathering with fellow believers. In a truly mature Christian community, people will be able to share their joys, sorrows, hopes and frustrations at a deep level, and even be able to confess their sins to one another, as well as to God. There's something greatly refreshing and renewing in this kind of an experience done on a regular basis. There's great strength to be gained by being a part of such a congregation and such a 'happening' as one heads back into the stresses and strains of everyday reality. It's for this reason that the author of the book of Hebrews says, "Let us be concerned for one another, to help one another to show love and do good. Let us not give up the habit of meeting together ... Instead, let us encourage one another all the more..." Hebrews 10:25

Like we said earlier, Christians know they will either keep growing towards becoming whole people, or begin to wither and die inside. God is always there ready to stimulate such growth in all of life. He wants every person to live life fully, not to 'starve.' And he has made it possible for all people to do so through Jesus Christ. But more about this in the next Chapter,

Being Christ's Heart and Hands in the World

The German theologian Emil Brunner once said, "The Church exists for mission like a fire exists for burning." In other words, Christians see themselves as participating in God's mission as his agents, ambassadors and representatives in the world. God's mission is to bring wholeness to his whole creation. God is at work in his creation through his Spirit to defeat death, disaster, disruption, disease, disharmony and destruction, and to bring about resurrection, re-creation, redemption, renewal, reconciliation and restoration. His vision for wholeness is as broad as his entire creation, with people at the center of his concern.

Christians believe that wherever and whenever individuals or societies, micro-structures or macro-structures, sparrows or ecospheres are not all that God intended them to be, God is there working to bring about wholeness. This means that every aspect of life is included in God's vision for mission. He is committed to bring about spiritual healing and growth in people. He wants to renew systems and restore relationships. He is involved in the redemption of politics and psychology, science and sociology, economics and ecology, education and technology, the arts and theology. As the South African Bishop Desmond Tutu once said, "The only thing that is secular is sin. All the rest belongs to God, and he wants us to join him in redeeming it."

Christians believe that the task of the people of God then is to *participate* in God's mission - to be instruments of restoration and reconciliation in a hurting world and to be channels through which God can advance his Kingdom (the rule of God over all that is being renewed in the totality of reality). A Christian's *vo*cation is to be God's instrument for renewal in the world through his/her *a*vocations - truck driver, teacher, parent, scientist, friend, artist, grandson, farmer, etc. In this way, Christians see themselves as God's agents of redemption and reconciliation sprinkled throughout all spheres of life - light that enlightens, salt that seasons and yeast that penetrates. (See Matthew 5:13, 14-16, 13:33).

Christians believe that the carrying out of God's mission is not limited to 'professional' Christians like pastors, missionaries and other types of church leaders. *All* Christians have gifts to love and serve in the world and are commissioned (sent) and ordained (set apart) by the church. Some may be gifted and ordained for pastoral work; some for parenting; some for cross-cultural ministries; some for medical work; some for artistry; *all* for whatever gifts and skills they exhibit through which they can be an influence for good and for God through their daily involvements.

Christian individuals, families, congregations, denominations and ecumenical bodies and organizations see themselves as called to be communities and communions within which God's healing presence is discernible and growing. Christians aim at being authentic models of the new life in Christ as individuals and in their churches and organizations. People must be able to see a difference in the lives of Christians and their churches in order for Christians to be able to say something to the world around them. The fellowship of the Christian community is a sign that God is, that he is at work, and that he can bring wholeness to individuals, to groups and to the whole world. The more authentic and united the Church is, the more powerful its impact on the world becomes. (See Acts 4:32-35; 5:12-14; John 17:20-23).

These same individuals, families, congregations, denominations and bodies are also called to be instruments and channels through which God's loving presence and healing power can bring wholeness where there is brokenness. Christians authenticate their message by underlining it with their service, sharing, sacrifice and suffering. Christians and their churches aspire to *do* the work of furthering the mission of God in the world. They know that unless they reach out to help people that are hurting and repair systems that are broken in genuine love and humility, they'll not have a right to speak. "Actions speak louder than words." Christian service is also a sign that God is, that he is concerned about his broken people and his broken world, and that he can renew them and redeem it. (The non-verbal 'witness' of the 'Good Samaritan' in Jesus' parable in Luke 10:25-37 is an extraordinary example of the way in which Christians are to act like "God with skin on" to bring about healing and wholeness in the lives of hurting people and in the realm of broken structures).

Christians believe that these same individuals, families, congregations, denominations and bodies are further called to be communicators through whom God's gracious Good News of salvation is shared with the world. The message of the Christian community is the good news that God has translated himself into **THE WORD** (Jesus Christ) who can be encountered through words that bring wholeness and hope to individuals and to the world. (See John 1:1-5; 1 John 1:1-3) Christians believe that the key to effectively carrying out God's mission in the world does not lie in material resources, brilliant strategies, impressive programs or the methods of power, but in an openness to the enabling, sustaining and creative presence of God's Spirit. By obeying Christ's commission, employing the gifts of the Spirit and committing themselves and their resources to carrying out God's mission as the reason for their lives, Christians and their congregations and organizations find that in losing their lives for the sake of God's world, they will find them. (See Matthew 16:25)

What Do *You* Think?

1. Do you agree that people's spiritual 'diets' should be at least as great a concern to them as their physical diets? Explain.

2. Do you feel that being a follower of Jesus is a burdensome, life-interfering religious duty? Explain.

3. Do you feel that you are paying enough attention to meeting your spiritual needs right now? Explain.

4. Do you find one type of spiritual exercise more effective for you at the moment than others? Explain.

Chapter Thirteen

IS IT HARD TO BECOME A CHRISTIAN?

> "I have complete confidence in the gospel; it is God's power to save all who believe."   Romans 1:16
>
> "Everyone has sinned and is far away from God's saving presence. But by the free gift of God's grace all are put right with him through Christ Jesus, who sets them free. God offered him, so that by his death he should become the means by which people's sins are forgiven through their faith in him."   Romans 3:23-26

Looking Through the Microscope |

A Diary of Struggle

December 15

I never expected this to happen! I'm in a quandary over religion! I thought I could simply ignore religion, but here I am in the middle of a struggle over it. I really don't know where this is going to lead, but I know that I must stick to it and see this thing through. I'm tired of so many things hanging at loose ends ... so many questions dangling in the air unanswered. I want to pull my life together. I need to make some kind of decision about things ... have something I believe in ... know where I stand.

"I must confess that I've gotten very interested in the ideas of

Jesus. I never thought I would. I guess I never really *tried* to think about them very seriously before. All the Sunday School stuff I heard as a kid kinda went in one ear and out the other over the years. But this time it's been different. I don't think it's so much the book I just read, or even my new friend who's an earnest Christian, but somehow I'm now at a point in my life where I know I'm not a kid anymore and I've got to grow up and seriously *think* about these ideas ... and be *responsible* for what I decide about them.

"There's something about the way Jesus lived that appeals to me. He was so genuine and unselfish. His friendships were warm and deep ... he encouraged the best out of everybody. And he would never compromise what he believed in to save his own skin. But there are some things about him that I still wonder about. Well ... we'll see.

"I saw Carol today. She's lots of fun to be with. I wonder if she suspects how much I like her. I don't know if I could ever get up the courage to tell her! She's so ..."

December 31

"I think this is the best Christmas I've ever had. The winter weather was perfect ... My Christmas gifts were fabulous ... we had some good family times. The parties this year were great. And the Intervarsity tobogganing event was super. I don't think I've ever enjoyed being with any group more than I did being with that one.

"I'm still kind of tired, but the all-night talks in the dorm (at least it *seemed* like we talked all night!) were really great. We must have covered everything from bananas to religion! How I wish I could be like Charley. He knows so much about Christianity and has such confidence in what he believes. He only became a Christian two years ago, but he sure has learned a lot about it in a short time.

"That's one of my real problems. How can I become a Christian when there are still so many things about the Bible, Christianity, the Church, and all that I don't understand? The Intervarsity group this year has been a big help in throwing more light on a lot of things I was in the dark about before, but I feel there's still so much to learn. I wonder ... how much does somebody *need* to know before they can truly become a Christian? Charley says I know enough already, but I'm not sure."

February 9

"Tonight we talked about miracles in the Intervarsity group. This has always been a tough one for me. I don't find it difficult to believe that the Bible contains truth about God and life and all. And I don't even find it hard anymore to believe that Jesus was God come to be with us in person. I think what the IV study guide we're using had to say about miracles was very interesting - a new approach that I'd never heard before. I'll have to think about that some more. But I still struggle with the apostles raising people from the dead, or Elijah calling down fire from heaven. I *want* to believe everything because I now find myself believing a lot of things that I would've laughed at before ... but I still can't manage it and really be honest with myself. I wonder, do I have to believe *everything* about Christianity before I can become a Christian?

"And sometimes I doubt. Even the things I thought I'd settled - like the existence of God. Some days, if I'm honest with myself, I even waver on that! And yet, I seem to recover. I think I'm gaining on these things, but how can I become a Christian and still have doubts about things? Doesn't making a commitment mean that you have to be *sure* about everything? If only I were a little more naïve ... but I have to be honest. I guess if I've learned anything from Jesus, it would be that pretending to have faith is worse than not having any at all ... This is all such a struggle, but I know it'll be worth sticking to it.

"That chess match today was a struggle too! Hooray! I made it into the semi-finals! I doubt that I've really got a chance to win the tournament - Pete is too good. But who knows? I may be lucky! Dream on, oh fool, dream on!"

March 26

"What a stupid thing to do! I was so embarrassed! I could tell the Dean was pretty disappointed in me. And I can't blame him. As the President of the Student Council, I'm supposed to be an example to the other students, and then I go and do a dumb thing like that! Hanging out with some guys after the big game and getting a bit soused before driving back to campus was high school stuff. And being pulled over by a cop and getting a DUI citation was humiliating. Sometimes you just let yourself do stupid things I guess. The Dean was pretty upset about it. My Dad's not going to be too happy either when I ask him for the money to help pay the ticket.

"This thing got me to thinking about myself. Actually, when you come right down to it, there are some things about me that I'm not too proud of. And there are some things about me that I'm downright ashamed of! I can't understand why I sometimes think the kinds of thoughts I do. I was going to say, good thing nobody knows but me, but I know that God knows. Fortunately, God is so understanding and forgiving. Wait a minute! I've never yet told him that I even believe in him or *asked* for his forgiveness. I'd really like to do that at times, but I guess I'm not quite ready for that.

"Sometimes I'm so selfish. I wish I wasn't. I wish I had more patience with people and could be more tolerant than I am. I wish a lot more things about me could be changed as well. How can I become a Christian when I've still got so much baggage? Isn't that hypocritical? I mean, don't I have to be a *good* person to be eligible to follow Jesus? I wonder if I'll *ever* be good enough."

May 1

"Well, the time for the big crunch is almost here. It's hard to believe that my four years in college are almost over. It seems like only yesterday that I arrived as a green-behind-the ears freshman. Now I'm a senior about to go out into the big wide world and launch a career! I've got one last big hurdle to get over - the finals. In a way, my whole future rests on what I put down on those few pages of exam papers. I think I've been quite faithful through the years in doing my work and preparing, but I must admit that I'm more than a little nervous about it.

"It's great to have friends like Carol and Charlie to brush up on things with, and to be able to encourage each other. I sure have a lot more confidence about things when we're together and can share our worries and hopes. They're really a couple of steady people. Their faith means a great deal to them during anxious times like these. I wish I had a faith like theirs.

"I really would like to become a Christian, but I'm still not sure. It's been a long struggle through this year to get everything into focus. I really appreciate how they've helped me to understand a lot of the things mentioned in the IV study guide and discussed in our group. They make it sound like deciding to follow Christ isn't difficult or complicated. But is it really that easy? I mean, is it really a matter of merely 'sharing your need with God,' explaining that you believe in Jesus and want to become his follower, asking him to send his Spirit into your life and getting 'launched' on a new way of life? I *want* to think it is, but I'm still not sure. But one thing *is* for sure, I want to make up my mind about this ... and soon!"

What Do Y*ou* Think?

1. Do you think a person has to *understand* everything about the Christian faith before s/he can become a Christian? Explain.

2. Do you think a person has to *believe* everything about the Christian faith before s/he can become a Christian? Explain.

3. Do you think a person has to *live a good life* before s/he can become a follower of Jesus?   Explain.

4. Do you think it's hard/fairly hard/not very hard/easy to become a Christian? Explain.

Bringing Things Into Focus |

Questions and Answers

On the next page, match the phrase or question on the left with the correct phrase or answer on the right. Look up the Bible reference clues if you need help.

1. "Sir, what must I do to be saved?" Acts 16:30-31

"For it is by our faith that we are put right with God; it is by our confession that we are saved."

2. "What shall we do brothers?" Acts 2:37-38

"Believe in the Lord Jesus, and you will be saved."

3. "Good Teacher, what must I do to receive eternal life?" Luke 18:18, 22

"For God did not send his Son into the world to be its judge, but to be its savior. Whoever believes in the Son is not judged; but whoever does not believe has already been judged, because he has not believed in God's only Son."

4. "No one can please God without faith …" Hebrews 11:6

"Each one of you must turn away from his sins and be baptized in the name of Jesus Christ, so that your sins will be forgiven; and you will receive God's gift, the Holy Spirit."

5. "If anyone declares publicly that he belongs to me, I will do the same for him before my Father in heaven." Matthew 10:32-33

"Sell all you have and give the money to the poor, and you will have riches in heaven; then come and follow me."

6. "Do not start worrying: 'Where will my food come from? Or my drink? Or my clothes?'" Matthew 6:31, 33-34

"I do have faith, but not enough. Help me to have more!"

7. "What about you? ... Who do you say I am?" Matthew 16:15-16

"... for whoever comes to God must have faith that God exists and rewards those who seek him."

8. "Everything is possible for the person who has faith." Mark 9:23-24

"But if anyone rejects me publicly, I will reject him before my Father in heaven."

9. "For God loved the world so much that He gave his only Son, so that everyone who believes in him may not die, but have eternal life." John 3:16-17

"You may be baptized if you believe with all your heart. 'I do,' he answered; 'I believe that Jesus Christ is the Son of God.'"

10. "What is to keep me from being baptized?" Acts 8:36-37

"You are the Messiah, the Son of the living God."

11. "If you confess that Jesus is Lord and believe that God raised him from death, you will be saved." Romans 10:9-10

"Salvation is to be found through [Jesus] alone; in all the world there is no one else whom God has given who can save us."

12. "Jesus is the one of whom the scripture says, 'The stone that you the builders despised turned out to be the most important of all.' Acts 4:11-12"

"Be concerned above everything else with the Kingdom of God and with what he requires of you, and he will provide you with all these other things. So do not worry about tomorrow."

What Do *You* Think?

Read over the above quotations again and note the seven key words that describe what a person must do in order to become a Christian.

1. What must a person **repent** (turn away) from?

2. What must a person **believe**?

3.   What must a person publically **confess**?

4. Why must a person **be baptized**? (See also Romans 6:4)

5. What will a person **receive**?

6. What must a person *first of all* **be concerned about**?

7. What does it mean to '**follow**' Jesus? (See Matthew 16:24-25)

Gaining a Perspective |

Photo Language

Below are ten photos. Study each one carefully and tell what you think it 'says' about people becoming Christians. Then look up the Bible reference as a clue to one possible way it might be so interpreted.

1. Acts 16:34   2. Matthew 18:3-4

3. Luke 5:3

4. Mark 9:24

5. Mark 10:21

6. Mark 1:15

Repentance
is a change
OF 😊 MIND
and
Heart ♥

7. John 3:3

8. Matthew 13:7, 22

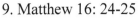 9. Matthew 16: 24-25    10. Romans 12:17-18

What Do *You* Think?

1. In your opinion, which photo best expresses the meaning of the text it illustrates, and why?

2. Which photo least expresses the meaning of the text it illustrates, and why?

3. Do you know anybody who was not a Christian when you first met them, but then became one? Why did they do so and what was their experience like?

4. If you're not a Christian at present, have you ever had anybody try to explain the Christian faith to you? Did you understand what they were saying? Why or why not?

5. If you're a Christian, how would you go about trying to explain the Christian faith to a person who hasn't yet become a follower of Jesus Christ?

Drawing Conclusions |

Crossing the Bridge

Is it hard to become a Christian? In a way, the answer to this question is both yes and no. In one sense it's quite easy to become a Christian. The Bible makes it clear again and again that forgiveness and new life (salvation) are a free gift of God and are available to all for the mere asking. (See Romans 6:23; Galatians 2:16, 20; Ephesians 2:8-10) All people need to do is to:

- Recognize that they need forgiveness and a new life;

- Believe that through what Jesus did and because of who he is, forgiveness and a new life are available;

- Desire to turn away from whatever isn't good in their lives to start life anew in obedience to God;

- Be willing to publicly affirm that they've become followers of Christ through baptism;

- Earnestly desire to put God's concerns at the center of their lives; and

- Simply ask God to come into their lives through his Spirit (as he's promised to do) to begin to change them into new persons who enjoy a close relationship with God, who live a self-giving lifestyle and who enjoy coming together with other Christians to worship him.

What might at first seem simple, however, turns out to be quite a struggle for many people (like it was for our diary writing friend). For one thing, it's *very difficult* for most of us to admit that there's anything wrong with us that needs forgiving or healing or changing. Nobody ever likes to confess that s/he is wrong or has done wrong. We often go to great lengths to avoid that kind of admission - excusing, blaming, lying, covering up, etc, etc.

This problem is complicated by the fact that most of us think of a 'sinner' as somebody who commits some grossly immoral act like robbing a bank, shooting a neighbor, committing adultery, or the like. We're offended when the term is applied to us because we think of ourselves as generally moral people with quite high ethical standards. We may not be perfect but then who is? We may make a mistake now and then, but who doesn't? When Paul writes that Jesus Christ came into the world to save 'sinners' (See I Timothy 1:15), we feel that he can't be talking about us. We're not 'bad' people.

Jesus blew this kind of thinking right out of the water! For one thing, he made it clear that sins of the mind and heart are just as evil as sins of the hand and body (See Matthew chapters 5-7). In fact, they're even worse, because in addition to the 'inner sin,' the person is also committing the sin of hypocrisy - pretending to be righteous on the outside when s/he is unrighteous on the inside. That's why the people Jesus had the most trouble with, and who he roundly condemned, were not the *gross* sinners - the harlots, tax cheaters, adulterers, and the like - but 'private' sinners like the Pharisees - people who lived impeccable public lives, but whose hearts were filled with pride, jealousy, intolerance and hatred.

Another thing Jesus made clear was that sin is a universal spiritual 'disease' that *everybody* is suffering from. Simply because people like the Pharisees refused to admit they had this disease didn't alter the fact that they, like everybody else, were in need of a spiritual 'doctor.' Paul writes: "There is *no one* who is righteous ... they have *all* gone wrong ... *no one* does what is right, *not even one*." (See Romans 3:10-12)

As we honestly review the history of human experience, it confirms this. As we honestly look around us at our situation today, it confirms this. As we honestly look within ourselves, it confirms this. Somewhere after a good beginning, things went very wrong. People decided to do evil. Once evil had made its appearance in the lives of people, it spread to the whole human race like spiritual cancer and polluted the whole creation. (See Romans 5:12; 8:22-23) *Nobody* comes into this spiritually polluted environment without getting 'infected.'

"But," someone says, "things certainly can't be *that* bad. Everybody certainly can't be *that* bad!" Again, that depends on what your definition of 'bad' is. Of course everybody's not as bad as they potentially *could* be. Life in society would be impossible if they (we) were. Fortunately, God keeps his hand on things so that evil doesn't get completely out of control and destroy everything. But suppose we turn the question around. Is everybody as good as they could be or should be or were meant to be when God created them? Any honest person would have to answer this question with a "no." Then why do we object to being labeled 'sinners'? Sinners are simply people who are not completely all that they could be or should be or that God intended them to be.

We've gotten so used to living with moral and spiritual mediocrity that we quickly and complacently settle for the 'nobody's perfect' excuse. Why should we? God originally made human beings able to be perfect and is holding out the possibility of our again becoming so in the future. Why settle for anything but the best? Why be satisfied with being moral and ethical and spiritual 'second class citizens'? Jesus showed us what a 'first class citizen' of the Kingdom of God is like and opens up the way for us to begin moving towards the same ourselves.

Let's not make the mistake of comparing ourselves with criminals or with any of our fellows in an attempt to escape admitting that we are, in fact, 'sinners.' Let's instead compare ourselves with Jesus and honestly confess how far short we've fallen from what God intended us to be. (See Romans 3:23) To make such an admission is very difficult. To acknowledge the need for forgiveness and a new way of life is one of the hardest things you or I or anybody else will ever do. This is what stops many people cold when they think about possibly becoming a Christian. But those who are able to 'swallow their pride' and come to this point already have one foot in the door of the Kingdom of God.

What about the other foot? The other foot is faith - believing that all of God's promises are true; believing that Jesus really was who he said he was and that he really did what he said he had come to do; believing that God is 'there' and that he really will come into our lives through his Spirit and begin to build a new you and a new me; believing that Jesus' ideas and way of life really do bring true meaning and purpose to living even though they often contradict what many people count as success, power, popularity, security... and a lot more.

Again, faith for many people is a struggle. They stand, as it were, on one bank of a deep ravine looking at the other bank (the Kingdom of God). Across the ravine stretches what looks like a very shaky, narrow suspension bridge. They look over at the Kingdom of God and like what they see on the 'other side.' They look at the bridge and begin to calculate whether or not it will hold while they make the journey across. One suspension cable is labeled 'God's promises.' Another is labeled 'miracles.' On some of the planks are engraved things like 'the Bible,' 'testimonies of others,' 'most credible view,' 'relevance to life today,' and the like. In the final analysis, there's no guarantee that the bridge will hold. Everybody has to find that out for himself or herself through personal experience - by taking the risk of walking across! That walk is a little bit scary. What if the bridge should collapse? What if the 'other side' turns out not to be as good as it looks ... or even to be a complete mirage!? What if people on 'this side' should laugh at me for taking such a foolhardy risk? What if ... ?

And so it goes. Some people stand on 'this side' asking the 'what ifs' their whole life long, always calculating, but never daring to cross. Their life is never deeply satisfying, but they just can't get past their skepticism, or fear, or pride to take the risk. Others actually get up the nerve to put their foot on the bridge, and some even get halfway across, but then in panic and disappointment they rush back to 'safety.' What is it that keeps many people from crossing the bridge of faith?

1. One thing that keeps many people from crossing the bridge of faith is that they think they don't yet know enough or understand enough about the Christian faith.

If only they could get all their questions answered and know everything first, *then* they would dare to cross the bridge. It is, of course, necessary for a person to understand the basic ideas of Christianity before s/he can meaningfully become a Christian. However, it may interest you to know that there isn't one Christian alive who has had *all* of his or her questions about the Christian faith answered or who knows everything there is to know about it. If you ever meet Christians who claim otherwise, have nothing to do with them! They're fakes!

It's the most experienced Christians who keep discovering new insights about their faith, who study their Bibles with ever-increasing interest, and who are most open to learning 'new things' from God's Spirit. That's why followers of Jesus are called 'disciples,' meaning 'learners.' Christians don't know all there is to know about their faith when they're baptized. Rather, their baptism is just the beginning of a life-long journey of discovery and learning.

It's interesting to note that even Jesus' disciples (who you think would have known *everything* by then) were still asking him questions that betrayed rather appalling ignorance about some things shortly before he ascended into heaven! (See Acts 1:6-7) All through their three-year training period, Jesus had patiently taught them, corrected them, and enlightened them. However, notice that he called them to become his disciples *before* all of this training, not after it. So it is with anyone who sincerely follows him. Faith means to trust that whatever isn't clear or answered now will eventually become clear or answered in the future - but meanwhile, we're called to follow - to cross the bridge on the basis of what we know. People who've read this book up to this point already know as much as they need to know to take the step of becoming a Christian. Any hesitation based on 'insufficient knowledge' is merely an excuse to avoid the risk of crossing the bridge of faith. Thousands of others have crossed it knowing much less!

2. Another reason that keeps many people from crossing the bridge of faith is that they think they can't yet bring themselves to believe it all.

They're bothered by certain miracle stories, or sometimes struggle with doubts about whether God is even 'there' at all, or wonder whether everything will really end up at the end of time the way the Bible says it will, and so on. How can they become a Christian before they settle these doubts? How can they cross the bridge of faith without being sure about everything?

Again, it may surprise you to know that there isn't a Christian alive who has what might be called 100% faith 100% of the time. If you find 'Christians' who claim that they do, avoid them. Their fakes! Becoming a Christian isn't like crossing a line - yesterday I believed nothing, today I believe everything. The life of faith is not static, but dynamic. That is, it has its ups and downs. Some things, like suffering and death, are the kinds of things some Christians might struggle to 'make sense' out of all their lives - all the while knowing they're in the accepting, loving hand of a God who understands that struggle and will help them through it. God understands that we are "made of dust" as the Psalmist puts it, and he keeps patiently shoring Christians up, forgiving them their lapses of doubt and unbelief, and helping them to make progress towards having more ups than downs.

The story of Jesus' healing of a man's son in Mark 9:14-26 is a beautiful example of this. The man asks Jesus to help "if you possibly can!", thus betraying a wavering faith. Jesus replies: "Everything is possible for the person who has faith." To which the man replies: "I do have faith, but not enough. Help me to have more!" In effect he was saying, "I *want* to believe you can heal my son, but I'm not completely *sure*." Notice that Jesus doesn't give him a lecture on unbelief. He helps him to believe by healing his son! Millions have testified that they've received such help in crossing the bridge of faith, and that they've even received such help after they ran into doubts on the 'other side.'

Jesus' disciples were certainly great doubters. On more than a few occasions, Jesus became upset at their lack of faith. You'll recall that one of them, Thomas, even refused to believe that Jesus had risen from the dead until he had 'certain proof.' Notice that these men were *already* followers of Jesus. They didn't wait, nor did Jesus require them to wait, until they could believe everything and have no more doubts about anything before becoming so. They believed in the integrity, the genuineness and the reliability of Jesus. That was enough for them to cross the bridge when Jesus called them to follow him. They then had a framework of faith *within* which they could stand and *within* which they could work through remaining doubts and unbelief, knowing that Jesus would help them do it. That same help is available to all today who will dare, like the disciples did, to cross the bridge before they can 'believe it all.' By the way, what *looks* like it would be impossible to believe on one side of the ravine often looks quite different from the 'other side' once one's been willing to take the risk of crossing over on the basis of what one now *can* believe.

There's no such thing as crossing the bridge of faith without risk. There's no way that one can prove that the bridge will hold while standing on 'this side.' Those who require such proof in order to believe will never know it when they see it because faith has as much to do with a person's will to believe as it has to do with evidence. They'll be like the Pharisees who saw Jesus cure a man with a withered hand and then made plans to kill him! (See Matthew 12:9-14). Or like the people in Jesus' hometown of Nazareth who knew all about his teaching, his miracles and his ministry, but when the crunch came and he claimed to be the Messiah that Isaiah had foretold, they tried to shove him off a cliff and kill him! (See Luke 4:16-40). Faith involves risk, or it wouldn't be faith at all. The point is, is there enough evidence for the validity of the Christian faith to make the risk worth taking? Millions have decided there is, but in the end, every person must decide for himself or herself.

3. One other thing often keeps people from crossing the bridge of faith (from becoming a Christian) is the idea that they must be qualified to do so.

That is, they must become good people; they must be worthy; they must be it all before they can become a disciple of Christ. How many times have you heard a person say, "But, I'm not *good* enough to become a Christian!" It's easy to see why so many people have this idea. For one thing, as we've seen, it's the basic approach of other religions. In order to win the favor of a 'god' or 'the gods,' I must *be* good, *think* good, and *do* good on the one hand, or 'pay' for my badness with offerings, punishments and the like on the other. *Then*, and only then, will a 'god' consider my case on the basis of my merits. For another thing, it's the last-ditch attempt of proud people to preserve what they conceive of as their self-respect. *They're* not going to be the recipients of spiritual charity! If they need salvation, they'll either buy it or earn it by their own efforts. They'll certainly not humble themselves to receive it as an undeserved gift.

How people could have ever thought that there was any such idea as this in the Christian faith is a great mystery, since the exact opposite is true! As we've seen, the primary condition for becoming a Christian is to admit that we're *un*worthy, that we're sinners who deserve nothing, and who, because of our sinful natures, can't be what God has a right to expect us to be. The sheer joy of the Christian faith is that despite this, God has done something to remedy our needy situation. He's come in Christ to do for us what we can't do for ourselves. He's made it possible to offer us the free gift of forgiveness and new life if we're humble enough to simply receive it and not try to 'save face' by pretending that somehow we deserve it, or can earn it.

Were the people who Jesus asked to follow him asked to do so because they were good people who *deserved* to be asked? Precisely the opposite! Jesus invited bad people to follow him so that he could make them good. One only has to think of people like the tax collector turncoat, Zacchaeus (See Luke 19:1-10), or the woman caught in adultery (See John 8:1-11), or the promiscuous Samaritan woman at the well (See John 4:3-42) to realize that. Even his disciple Peter said, "Go away from me, Lord! I am a sinful man!" Luke 5:8 This is why Jesus kept saying that he had not come to call those who thought they were righteous, but to call sinners to repentance. No Christian should ever claim to be a 'good person' in God's eyes. If you find Christians that do, avoid them. Their fakes! (See Luke 18:9-14)

If people wait to cross the bridge of faith until they're 'good enough,' they'll never do so because they'll *never* be good enough. Becoming a Christian means to be set free from the bondage of fruitlessly trying to be good enough. Paradoxically, the more unworthy people realize themselves to be before God, the more 'worthy' they become as Christians. If you haven't yet crossed the bridge of faith, don't let your 'face,' or your sins, or your ignorance, or even your unbelief stand in your way. Decide to let go of all of that and let God do the rest. Take the first step out on that bridge and don't look back. As Confucius once said, "A journey of a thousand miles begins with the first step." It may take you awhile to get all the way across the bridge, but when you do, you'll be glad that at this moment you had the courage to take that first step and commit your life and your future to God as a follower of Jesus by simply inviting him to come into your life.

<u>What Do *You* Think?</u>

1. I agree with/disagree with/am not sure about the conclusions of this chapter because ...

2. I think/don't think/am not sure that the term 'sinner' applies to me because...

3. I feel that I do/don't know and believe enough about the Christian faith to become a Christian because ...

4. I feel that I'm already eligible/not yet eligible/will never be eligible for God's gift of salvation because ...

Chapter Fourteen

WHAT DOES 'STEWARDSHIP' MEAN?

> "The world and all who are in it belong to the Lord."
>
> Psalm 24:1

The Banker

I've been working at the Bank of Life for 43 years. A lot has happened in the world during that time, and a lot has happened in our Bank as well. If I had the time, I could tell you all sorts of stories about colorful employees, bank robberies, eccentric customers, and all the rest.

"I remember one character who used to be a regular customer of our Bank when I worked as a teller at the time window. This fellow had quite a large deposit with us, and every now and then he used to come in and make a big withdrawal. During my lunch hours, in the evenings and over weekends, I used to see him here and there sitting on a bench in the park glued to his smart phone, hanging around on the street corner with some other characters, going into the casino hoping to strike it rich, or watching TV by the hour. He wasn't a bad fellow, really. In fact, he was quite pleasant to me whenever he came into the Bank, but he just never seemed to be doing anything very worthwhile. He spent his time as though his account would never run out.

"Of course, you can't make deposits in a time account, you can only make withdrawals. You start out with a certain amount in the account, and when it runs out - that's it. I remember warning this fellow once or twice in a friendly way that his account was getting rather low, but he'd just smile nonchalantly, go right on withdrawing and continue to spend his time as if it were water. The day finally came, of course, when it was my sad duty to tell him that his account had been used up - he had no time left ... They held his funeral two days later.

"Then there was the lady who never seemed to withdraw from her goods account, only to deposit. She was a hoarder. This was during the years when I worked at the goods counter. Whenever she'd earn some money or accumulate any goods, she'd buy whatever she wanted for herself, or use only what made her home beautiful and her life comfortable. The rest would all go into her goods account at the Bank.

"Other people, of course, were like her to some degree, but there were some that weren't like her at all. They would give much of what they didn't need for their daily lives to organizations that helped those whose needs were great, but whose incomes were small. They had big hearts and small accounts, but they always seemed to manage. And they appeared to enjoy life a lot more than this woman and others like her. She was always rather demanding and pretentious.

"The woman's account grew and grew. I remember once asking her what would become of her huge goods account when her time account would run out. She fixed me with a cold stare and snapped that it was none of my business. Every penny in that account honestly belonged to her, which gave her the right to jolly well do whatever she pleased with it. I supposed that she might have children she would leave it all to, or that when she got old, she would donate it to some charitable organization that would build a school or a hospital in her name to commemorate her. However, when her time account finally ran out, I was rather surprised to find out that she had no such children or no such plans. Since that was case, the court ruled that her account would become the property of the state. I remember wondering what the point of it all was. Why did she want to hang on so tenaciously to everything when, in the end, it was of no use to her anyway?

"Then there was the Bank's body loan department. I never did much like working in that department, but I spent three years there. The majority of people to whom we loaned bodies took quite good care of them and made them last a long time. But not some people. Oh no! No sooner would they get out of the Bank's door with their body loan than they would start using and abusing it as though it was indestructible and would last forever. They would give it only five or six hours of rest a day. They would forget to exercise it properly so that it would get flabby and turn a pasty color. They would stuff all kinds of junk into it so that its 'pipes' and 'valves' and organs would get all fouled up and eventually stop working. They would even poison it! Smoke, drinks and drugs would be inhaled, swallowed or injected day after day as though these people were oblivious to the fact that they were committing slow suicide.

"At first, of course, they would seemingly get away with it. Our body loans could really take a lot of punishment. But before long, the results of the early years of misuse and abuse would begin to show up. Teeth, organs, skin, bones, hair and muscles would all begin to show signs of wear and tear. Strangely enough, some of these people took the attitude that it was *their* body and they were perfectly well entitled to do with it as they pleased. Somehow, they seemed to have forgotten that in the Bank's eyes, their body was only a loan that would someday have to be accounted for.

"In the end, of course, we would get the loans back. As I said, most of them would've been well taken care of, but it was making the arrangements for the disposition of the others that would make me ill - which is the reason why I got myself transferred out of that department. I often wondered why the Bank Manager took such risks in loaning bodies when he knew that some people would do such harmful things to them. But I guess that's why so many respect him so much. He's willing to give everybody a chance even when he knows that it'll cost him something.

"The place where I most liked working in our Bank was in the talent vault. Here people would store some of the most valuable things they had in life - their abilities. The variety of gifts that people had was amazing. Some had athletic talent in the vault. Others had public speaking, or teaching, or writing skills. Still others stored singing, or playing, or composing in the vault. There were cooking and baking talents in there too, along with carving and sculpting and painting abilities. Some had management, leadership and diplomatic skills in the vault, while others had engineering, medical and law abilities there. The vault was a fascinating place. You could find every human talent, skill and ability imaginable in there.

"People had very different attitudes towards what they kept in the vault. Some would come every day, take all their talents out, use them and then put them back in the vault again for the night. Others would come less often and perhaps take out one or two for awhile, but leave the rest. Still others would hardly ever come at all. They had some very valuable things in their vault deposit boxes, but because they would never take them out to be used, they would begin to wither and crumble. I always felt that that was such a waste.

"Some people were very proud of the talents they had in their boxes. They went about showing them off to others, or bragging that they could do this or that better than some other person, or laughing about the kinds of abilities other people had or didn't have in their deposit boxes. I always thought that was so strange, since nobody had *all* the abilities there were to be had in their box, and since all of their abilities had been gifts from the Bank Manager in the first place. (You can see by now that our Bank Manager is a *very* generous person). How can people brag about things they originally received as gifts? Oh well, you can never figure some people out.

"The job I now have is to manage the Bank's Environmental Co-op Loan Fund. This is an interesting, but tough job. The Bank Manager decided to give me this position because of my many years of experience in dealing with people. The capital for the fund was made available by the Bank Manager. The idea is that people will draw out of this fund as they have need, and put back into the fund what they can as they're able. If everybody cooperates, the scheme should work like a charm. But that's a big 'IF,' as I've already discovered to my dismay. The basic problem is greed. People draw trees and streams and land and air and all the rest of nature's vast resources out of the fund, not just to meet their needs, but to take far more than their fair share and to make huge profits. And to add insult to injury, they couldn't care less about putting any trees, flowers, air filters, water purifiers, alternative energy resources, and the like, back into the fund even though the Bank Manager has specifically asked them to do so. And because they refuse to do so, the assets of the fund are ever more rapidly being depleted.

"These people don't know what the word 'Co-op' means. They act as though everything they draw out of the Bank Manager's fund belongs to *them*! If things keep going the way they are, the majority of the members of the Co-op are going to continue to be robbed of their right to enjoy the assets of the fund, and the whole Co-op scheme is going to be ruined altogether. The Bank Manager is getting pretty upset about all of this, and so am I! But I'm not going to give up. This Environmental Co-op Loan Fund is the last challenge I'll have before my retirement rolls around - and I'm going to make it work. I'm glad to say that the number of people who're getting fed up with this situation and who're anxious to help me do something about it is growing.

What Do *You* Think?

1. I feel that I'm/am not using my time well because ......

2. I think that I'm basically a selfish/generous person because ......

3. I think I'm/am not taking good care of my body because ......

4. I think I am/am not using my talents to the best of my ability because ......

5. I think I'm helping to ruin/restore the environment because ......

<u>Bringing Things Into Focus</u> |

Gifts from God

Some people assume that what they have and enjoy is theirs by right and that they're therefore free to use or abuse what they have without needing to give an account to anyone. The Christian perspective is quite different. Christians believe all that people have and enjoy are gifts from God that are to be used gratefully and carefully.

Here's a list of 20 gifts that Christians believe come from God.

1. The food and drink that keep us alive. (See Matthew 6:25)

2. The clothes we wear. (See Matthew 6:28)

3. The ability to play instruments and to sing. (See Psalm 92:1-3)

4. The Scriptures that give us a roadmap for our faith and life.
                                        (See 2 Timothy 3:16)

5. A strong and healthy body. (See 1 Corinthians 6:19-20)

6. The ability to love. (See 1 John 4:7)

7. Life in all its fullness. (See John 10:10)

8. The sunshine and rain that make things grow. (See Matthew 5:45)

9. Our possessions. (See Luke 12:15)

10. Fellowship with the Christian community. (See Ephesians 1:22)

11. Our ability to dance. (See Psalm 150:4)

12. Domestic and wild animals. (See Genesis 2:18-20)

13. Trees, flowers, grass and crops. (See Genesis 1:11-12)

14. Life. (See Isaiah 42:5)

15. Eternal life. (See John 3:16)

16. The healing of our ailments. (See Matthew 4:23)

17. Our abilities (or talents). (See Matthew 25:14-30)

18. Wisdom, knowledge and understanding. (See Proverbs 2:60)

19. Rest. (See Matthew 11:28)

20. Children. (See Psalm 127:3-5)

What Do *You* Think?

1. Can you add any more gifts you can think of to this list?

2. Which gift in the list is the most important to you, and why?

3. Which gift in the list is the least important to you, and why?

4. Do you agree that all these gifts come from God? Why or why not?

Gaining a Perspective |

Multiple Choice

In your opinion, what answer under each of the following statements most accurately completes that statement?

1. Christians primarily see a 'steward' as a person who ...
   a. serves wine at a banquet,
   b. takes care of the horses at a race track,
   c. is entrusted with the responsibility for another person's property,
   d. serves meals on an airplane.

2. Christians believe that since all things belong to God ...
    a. they can't use what they've been given as though it simply belongs to them,
    b. they've been entrusted with time, talents, goods, etc. that are to be used wisely and carefully,
    c. they'll need to give an accounting to God for the way in which they've used what has been entrusted to them,
    d. all of these.

3. Christians think that people who waste time ...
    a. have a right to do so because it belongs to them,
    b. are poor stewards of one of God's most valuable gifts,
    c. will be more relaxed and enjoy life,
    d. none of these.

4. Christians believe that people who take the wise stewardship of the goods God gives to them seriously will ...
    a. willingly share what they have with those who are in need,
    b. make wise investments and protect every penny to ensure their own security,
    c. tell others how their goods are an indication of how smart, hard-working and competent they are,
    d. feel that the stronger, the quicker and the smarter they are, the more they deserve to have a bigger share of the world's goods than those who are weak, slow and stupid.

5. Christians think that those who take the stewardship of the body God has given them seriously will ...
    a. get plenty of rest,
    b. get plenty of exercise,
    c. eat a nourishing, balanced diet,
    d. all of these.

6. Christians think that an individual who's talented, but who, for one reason or another, doesn't make good use of his or her abilities ...
    a. will eventually lose those abilities,
    b. will only be accountable to him or herself,

c. will probably become wealthy so that in the long run it won't matter anyway,

d. will probably be a more relaxed person who can enjoy life.

7. Christians believe that a person who takes the stewardship of the environment seriously will think ...

a. it's the Government's responsibility to ensure the preservation of the environment,

b. it's his or her personal responsibility to do what s/he can to ensure the preservation of the environment,

c. it's primarily the Conservancy Associations' responsibility to ensure the preservation of the environment,

d. the balance of nature will ensure the preservation of the environment no matter what people may do to it.

8. Christians think that as far as the subject of stewardship is concerned, the Bible ...

a. has little to say about it,

b. has a moderate amount to say about it,

e. has nothing to say about it,

f. has a great deal to say about it.

9. Christians believe that all that exists belongs to God because ...

a. he made it,

b. he redeemed it,

c. he preserves it,

d. all of these

10.Christians think that Jesus' teaching that a good steward will not make goods the center of his or her life, but will hold on to them lightly is best illustrated by his ...

a. parable of the Ten Girls (See Matthew 25:1-13)

b. parable of the Soils (See Matthew 13:1-9, 18-23)

c. parable of the Rich Fool (See Luke 12:13-21)

d. parable of the Pharisee and the Tax Collector (See Luke 18:9-14)

<u>What Do *You* Think?</u>

1. Which of these ten statements do you agree with, and why?

2. Which of these ten statements do you disagree with, and why?

3. Which of these ten statements do you have the most difficulty practicing? Why?

4. Do you think 'global warming' is a serious problem? Why or why not?

<u>Drawing Conclusions |</u>

The Principles of Stewardship

Take another look at the statement at the beginning of this chapter: "The world and all that is in it belong to the Lord." Judging by the way many people conduct their affairs, few people really believe this. Some *say* they believe it, but then go off and live as though they don't. Most people act as though their property, their possessions, their time, and all the rest, belong solely to them and to nobody else. Most nations, companies and individuals stake their claims to buildings and land, stocks and bonds, diamonds and gold, cash and credit cards and spend most of their time figuring out how they can increase their holdings and hang on to every cent or square inch they can get their hands on.

The Definition of Stewardship

Look up at the moon on a clear night. Who owns it? "Nobody ... yet!" someone answers. Then why should anybody own the earth? Doesn't it belong to the same one who 'owns' the moon and all the rest? And isn't it his purpose that every person he's made should enjoy a fair share of what he's made available? The Chinese leader, Sun Yat-sen, once said, "All of the earth belongs to all of the people." Christians would agree with that principle. From their point of view,

God has placed what he's made into people's hands to be used for the mutual benefit of all. He looks at people as *stewards* of what he's entrusted to them - not owners. How could people have wandered so far away from viewing themselves and their 'possessions' in this way and instead get caught up in the 'dog eat dog' economic systems of our day that are designed to generate huge profits for the few and bare existence for the many? As one wag has described it, "The rain, it falleth on both the just and the unjust, but mostly on the just, for the unjust fella has the just's umbrella." This phenomenon can only be explained as the 'fall-out' from humanity's 'fall' into sin.

When people make the false assumption that what they have belongs to them, they're tempted to make an even greater mistake - to think that since what they have 'belongs' to them, they can jolly well do with it as they please and that it's nobody else's business as to what they do with their time, money, talents and goods. These things belong to *them*, and as long as they've come by them honestly, they can do with them as they please. This leaves no room for God in the picture. Christians believe this is a big mistake, because God is very much *in* the picture, whether people recognize that or not. *He's* the owner of all things. He's happy to entrust us with *some* of what he owns, but he has some very definite ideas as to how these things should be used. If people ignore those ideas, they may *think* that they're independent and can do as they please with what they have, but sooner or later this idea will boomerang on them.

Take, for example, Jesus' parable of 'The Rich Fool' in Luke 12. From all outward appearances, this man had made great gains in life. All his friends would have labeled him a 'success.' He had made a pile of money; he had everything anybody could want, and more and his future looked rosy. However, he had one fatal flaw - he'd made his goods his god! He'd become obsessed with his own comfort and security. And in the process, he'd become more and more greedy and had drifted farther and farther away from the true purpose and meaning of life. He'd come to firmly believe that what he had belonged solely to him, and that it could be used by him in whatever way he wished. He'd deluded himself into thinking that even his *time* was subject to his will alone. He'd take his ease, eat, drink and be merry on and on into the dim and distant future. But he was in for a rude shock. *That very night* his time would be up and death would come! All that he had amassed would be left behind! The life of secure ease he'd so carefully planned and slaved for would not last two days! But above all, he'd have to *give an account* to the Owner for misusing what he'd been given in life. No wonder Jesus used such strong language and called this man a "fool!"

What *should* he have done with his goods and with his life? What *should* he have done to earn Jesus' praise rather than his condemnation? The answer is clear from what follows. Jesus addresses himself to the poor crowds and tells them not to worry about where their basic daily needs will come from - their food, clothing and shelter. God will provide for those who trust in him; those who share the concerns of his Kingdom and who live life as disciples of Jesus. But *how* will God provide for them? By raining down these things from the sky like magic while they sit there with their arms crossed? No, but by providing work and emergency provisions *through* the rich 'fools' who see the error of their ways, stop their greedy hoarding, and start generously sharing the resources that have been entrusted to them by God to meet their needs *and* the needs of others. And in so sharing and in so employing, they become wise and discover the real purpose, joy and meaning of life as God intended it to be lived.

Christians believe the following statements reflect the principles that the Owner of all things has laid down for their use:

- People are to recognize that they own nothing, but are merely stewards of what has been entrusted to them. (See Deuteronomy 8:17-18)

- To waste or misuse any of the resources with which they've been entrusted is foolish on their part and an insult to the Owner. (See John 6:12-13)

- People are entrusted with these resources in order to meet their needs and to help meet the needs of others - particularly those who've been robbed of their resources by greedy fools like the one in Jesus' story. (See 2 Corinthians 8:13-14)

What do Christians believe are the implications of these principles for the basic things that God has entrusted people with?

The Use of Our Time

Time is probably the most precious thing God entrusts into the care of human beings and the most wasted thing. Most people use time as though they were going to live for a thousand years. Particularly when someone is young, the issue of time seems unimportant and almost irrelevant. Often when people get older, they realize how much time they've simply frittered away on meaningless things in their younger days and wish they could somehow get that time back again. But then, of course, it's too late. Sometimes a young person's life, very unexpectedly and very tragically, is suddenly cut off. At the time, it *appeared* as though that person had a whole lifetime ahead of him or her, but then, suddenly, his or her time came to an abrupt end.

Christians believe that God considers time precious and wants people to do so as well. He wants them to make the best possible use of the time they have in this life, no matter how short or how long that life might be. (See Ephesians 5:15-17) This doesn't mean, of course, that they need to constantly live with death on their minds as though every moment might be their last. (However, it might be an interesting exercise to write down sometime what changes you might make in your lifestyle if you knew you only had six months to live.) Neither does it mean they're to be involved in a constant frenzy of activity trying to achieve more than they were meant to achieve. Sometimes the best use of time involves resting, relaxing, contemplating, playing and the like. This is why, for example, God designated one day out of seven as rest and refreshment day, a principle that people ignore only at their own peril. (See Exodus 20:8-11) Christians believe that what God does *not* want people to do is to simply throw their time away by spending it in prolonged idleness on the one hand, or in the kind of activity that's not constructive or creative or helpful on the other.

The Use of Our Goods

It seems that the main problem with some people and their possessions is that instead of them possessing their possessions, their possessions possess *them*. If one were to conduct a poll in America and ask people what their main goal in life was, how many people do you think might answer, "To make as much money as I can!"? The percentage would probably be quite high.

Christians don't, of course, believe that there's anything wrong with money and goods in themselves. God graciously supplies us with what we need to live. He is not *anti*-money. The Bible doesn't say that *money* is the root of all evil, but that the *love* of money is the root of all evil. (See 1Timothy 6:10) Neither does Jesus condemn things as such, but rather the greed for *more and more* things - well beyond what's really needed to adequately sustain life. (See Luke 12:15) He never teaches that people should not have any money, but that they should not allow themselves to become the *slaves* of money. (See Matthew 6 24) Money was made for humans, not humans for money. He also teaches that we're not to waste the precious resources that our Heavenly Father gives us in meaningless and extravagant living. (See Luke 15:13) The purpose of having money and goods is to have our needs provided for and to share with those whose needs have not yet been met.

When it comes to possessions, many people get wants and needs mixed up. People who strive to get what they *want* never make their goal since people's 'wants' are endless and insatiable. Meanwhile, such people burn up their lives trying to get more … and more … and more. In the process, at the most, they gain *some* of their wants at the expense of other people's unfulfilled needs. At the least, they make the fulfilling of their wants their consuming passion in life and shut out what actually makes life worth living. (It's interesting to note in this regard that in a rich country like the United States, there's a high incidence of boredom, loneliness, aimlessness and inner emptiness amongst a population that has more material wealth by far than any other people have had in the history of the world). Mahatma Gandhi has well said: "There are enough goods in the world to meet every man's need, but not enough to satisfy every man's greed." If, however, people concentrate on getting their basic needs met and then sharing the rest with those who are still in need, they'll have learned the meaning of what Jesus' idea of being a good steward of God's resources is all about.

The Care of Our Body

People don't often think of their bodies as gifts or as resources. Bodies are simply things that are there to be used automatically, not to be thought about. But those who don't stop to think about their bodies with awe as being some of the most fantastic things in all of creation tend to take them for granted and use them carelessly until they're ready to be discarded like old rusty and worn out washing machines. Bodies aren't like used cars - you can't trade the old one in for a new model. Once a person has abused his or her body over a long period of time, despite its miraculous recovery powers, s/he will suffer the effects for the rest of his or her life.

This is particularly difficult for young people to realize. A young person's body is fresh and strong and can take a lot of punishment. Because this is so, young people sometimes develop abusive habits they think they're getting away with at the time, but which inevitably catch up with them in the long run - and sometimes even in the short run!

- Some overwork themselves and don't get enough rest.

- Some ignore the need for proper and regular exercise.

- Some skip meals and eat an unbalanced diet.

- Some stuff their bodies with garbage (junk food) and poisons (smoke, drugs, alcohol).

- Some ignore the danger signals of minor sicknesses and risk having them develop into major illnesses.

- Some go to see the dentist only when a tooth hurts.

- And more.

Christians believe that God has given everybody the priceless gift of a physical body. He's counting on each person to take care of it and 'get as much mileage out of it' as possible. If people are careful stewards of their bodies, they'll have a much better chance of leading wholesome, satisfying lives. People can be ardent followers of Jesus, but if they neglect caring for their bodies properly, they're proving themselves to be unfaithful stewards of the gift they've been given.

The Use of Our Abilities

Jesus once told a story (recorded in Matthew 25:14-30) that says it all as far as his thinking about people's talents is concerned. In that story, a master entrusts various amounts of money to his three servants before going off on a trip and tells them to invest it wisely so that they'll have made him a profit with it by the time he returns. Two of the servants energetically go about doubling their master's money by wisely investing what he's given them, but the third, lazy and fearful, buries his money in the ground for safety's sake until the master returns. When he does return, he rewards the first two, but punishes the third.

It's not hard to see that in this story the master represents God, the servants represent people, and the money represents the talents God has given to them. It's also not hard to see the principles that Jesus meant people to learn about their abilities from this story:

- Every person has been given *some* abilities by God (even though some people don't seem to think they have any) while nobody has been given *every* ability (even though by the way some people carry on, you'd think they had).

- Those who are willing to work and risk using their abilities will find fulfillment in life and will discover and develop even more abilities.

- Those who are too lazy and afraid to use their abilities will be unfulfilled in life and will lose even the abilities they have.

- God doesn't get upset with people who try, but fail (He's famous for his forgiving love and mercy as shown in the story of the lost son in Luke 15:11-31, for example), but he gets very upset with those who are too lazy and fearful to try and use what he's entrusted to them at all.

The Care of Our Environment

Many Christians feel that the sphere where it's most evident that human beings are failing to be good stewards of the resources that God has entrusted to us is in the way we're mistreating our environment. God commissioned people in the beginning to discover and develop the earth. Rather than seeing the earth as a priceless heritage to be nurtured and preserved, people have more and more come to look at it as 'their' private preserve that they can destroy at will (sometimes even in the name of 'development'!).

This process, which went on at a fairly slow pace throughout most of human history has suddenly mushroomed and accelerated in our day to a point where sober experts are beginning to wonder whether in a hundred years there will *be* any earth left to talk about. What was once God's beautiful garden is rapidly becoming humanity's polluted, stripped and clamorous cesspool.

Faithful stewards are those who try to leave their Master's property in as good as or in even better shape than when it was entrusted to them. This not only pleases the Master, but makes life more pleasant and fulfilling for the stewards as well. What's the basic reason why our beautiful earth is being destroyed? The answer is greed - insatiable greed that wants to live for today and not count the cost for tomorrow. Greed that thinks we can have unlimited growth on a finite planet. But Christians believe that an even more basic reason is spiritual bankruptcy. People who are close to the 'Gardener' don't rush around in his garden felling trees, tearing up the earth, poisoning the air and the water, killing and selling the animals and filling the air with ear-shattering noise. Instead, they respect him and his wishes. They know the garden belongs to him and that he's entrusted it to them to keep it and use it and preserve it for the enjoyment of all for generations to come.

Therefore, a Christian litterbug is a contradiction in terms. A Christian polluter for profit discredits the name 'Christian.' There's no such person as a godly wearer of the furs and feathers of endangered species. Developers who pack people into concrete cubicles like sardines can't possibly be in tune with the Gardener's wishes. These people are all part of the pollution *problem* rather than part of the pollution *solution*. Christians believe the tide will only be turned when we human beings overcome our greed by once again getting in touch with the Gardener. Only a spiritual renewal will lead to a renewal of the earth … a renewal that must take place soon before it's forever too late.

Christians believe Christian stewardship is an old-fashioned idea that needs to make a modern comeback. God has entrusted a great deal *to* each member of the human race and he's expecting a great deal *from* each member of the human race. Followers of Christ can learn a lot about stewardship from him. They can also find, in their relationship with him, the daily strength, wisdom and prudence to put into practice what they learn.

What Do *You* Think?

1. I agree with/disagree with/am not sure about the statement that, "The world and all that is in it belong to the Lord," because ……

2. I agree with/disagree with/am not sure about the statement that, "He who has a surplus possesses the goods of another," because ……

3. I agree with/disagree with/am not sure about the statement that, "There's enough goods in the world to meet every man's need, but not enough to satisfy every man's greed," because ……

4. I agree with/disagree with/am not sure about the statement that, "All of the earth belongs to all of the people," because ……

5. I agree with/disagree with/am not sure about the statement that, "The rain, it falleth on both the just and the unjust, but mostly on the just, for the unjust fella has the just's umbrella," because ……

Chapter Fifteen

CAN CHRIST TRANSFORM RELATIONSHIPS?

> "Do everything possible on your part to live at peace with everybody."　　　　　　　　　Romans 12:18
>
> "Respect everyone, love your fellow-believers, fear God and respect the Emperor."　　　　　　1 Peter 2:17
>
> "It is love, then, that you should strive for."
> 　　　　　　　　　　　　　　　　　1 Corinthians 14:1

Looking Through the Microscope |

The Assignment

Pastor Johnson's voice suddenly interrupted Paul's day-dreaming. He sat up in his seat with a jerk. "Please turn to page 105 in your book. There you'll find six blank boxes. Today in our adult class we're going to explore our feelings about some of the most important people in our lives. In the first box, if you're married, draw something that expresses the way you feel or felt about your spouse. In the second box draw something about how you feel about your parent(s). In the third box, do the same for your brother(s) and/or sister(s). In the fourth box, draw something that expresses the way you feel about your friends. In the fifth box, do the same concerning your feelings about the opposite sex. In the last box, draw something that expresses your feelings about the United States Government.

"Please try to be totally honest. You'll not be asked to explain anything about your drawings that you don't want to. This exercise has nothing to do with your drawing ability. The idea isn't to draw something artistically pleasing to the eye, but to make any kind of marks, symbols, forms, faces, or whatever that express your true feelings. You should think carefully about your relationship(s) to the person(s) represented by a particular square before you draw anything so that what you do draw will be something that truly speaks of your real feelings and your real situation.

"It may help you if you have specific people in mind as you draw. For example, in your 'parents box,' you may want to devote part of the box to your feelings about your mother and part to your feelings about your father. In the box on the opposite sex, you may want to express your feelings about a particular member of that sex."

Everybody laughed. Paul looked at the blank boxes in front of him. Drawing was not exactly his 'thing,' but ...

He began to think about how he felt about his wife. They'd met in college and had fallen madly in love. (He drew two stick figures hugging each other in the middle of the box). They'd now been married ten years and had two kids. (He drew two happy faces, one in each of the upper corners). They'd had their spats, but overall their love for each other had grown deeper over the years. (He drew a tree with deep roots at the bottom of the box). They both were ardent followers of Jesus and active members of their church. (He drew a small church with a steeple in a bottom corner). She was pretty sensitive about some things, while he tended to be like a bull in a China shop, so there was some tension at times, especially when they had to discipline the kids or make some major decision. (He drew two people pulling on opposite ends of a rope in the remaining corner of the box).

On to the next box. How did he feel about his mother? He and his Mom were on pretty good terms. He had some warm feelings about her. (He drew a large smiling face in the left half of the box). She'd done a lot of things for him when he was a kid that he'd sometimes grumbled about, but which he'd grown to really appreciate. (He drew tiny squares, triangles, circles and diamonds around the face). Some things about her did annoy him though, and they had argued sometimes. (He drew some exclamation marks around the face). She usually was still quite interested in what he was doing and what his concerns were, and liked to sit around the table and chat when she had time. (He drew some interlocking circles around the face to illustrate their good communication).

What about his father? His father hadn't been around as much, and when he had, he had seemed rather tired and preoccupied. Paul didn't feel badly about their relationship, but then he didn't feel too good about it either. His father seemed aloof and sort of distant. (He drew a small, somber face in the right half of the box). He'd like to be able to talk with his father more freely and honestly, but it was difficult. It was hard to know what his father was thinking most of the time because he mostly kept his feelings to himself. (He drew a big question mark above the somber face). And his father was so demanding. He'd never had much of a chance to be educated when he was a boy, so when Paul went to school, his father was determined that he was going to be at the top of his class all the way through college. (He drew a big hand pressing down on the head of a small boy).

On to box #3. Paul had one brother and two sisters - all now grown. Paul was the eldest of the lot. Their house had been small, crowded and noisy, with some kid or other always seeming to be arguing and fighting with some other kid about something. (He drew the face of an older boy in the middle of the box with his eyes closed, his fingers in his ears and a look of pain on his face). Because he was the oldest, he usually got the blame if anything was broken or went wrong when his parents were away. "Paul you should've told them not to do that!" (He drew a big scolding finger).

And yet, what would he do without his brother and sisters!? Sometimes as kids they'd been fun to play with. (He drew two kids kicking a ball back and forth). Sometimes they'd been very cute and had given him hugs. They'd depended on him to defend them against bullies in the neighborhood or to help them with some homework problem. (He drew three smiling faces with angel's wings behind them). Now that they'd all grown up, he knew deep down in his heart that he loved them very much, even though they'd been pests at times. (He drew a big heart around the whole box).

Paul had *some* close friends, but he wished he had more. (He drew five smiling faces in the 'friends box' and his own face in the corner of the box with his hand over his eyebrows as though looking for more). Jim was his very best friend. (He drew a circle around one of the faces). The two of them shared things that they would never dream of telling anybody else. (He drew an ear and a hand and a mouth whispering something into the ear). He thought of the things he and his friends liked to do together - play golf and chess, go camping, sing and play guitars, go swimming, participate in the Rotary Club. (He drew little stick pictures of these things around the faces). What would happen if some of them might be transferred and move elsewhere? He'd really miss them. (He drew a big tear drop in the square).

He went on to the next box. Now he had to answer the question about women. He'd been nervous and uncomfortable around girls in high school and college - especially if for some reason he'd been alone with one. (He drew a sweating face in the box). He just hadn't known what to say, and had usually said something stupid. (He put a dunce cap on the head of the face). He'd often day-dreamed about meeting a girl whom he'd feel comfortable being with - and who would be cute to boot! (He drew the figure of the 'girl of his dreams' in one corner of the box, but erased it in haste and re-drew it because the first drawing had been a little too sexy). There was one girl in his college class whom he'd gotten to know better and with whom he'd felt very comfortable. (He drew a design in another corner of the box with her initials in it). She was now his wife and she'd helped him to be more at ease talking to other women and trying to understand their concerns and their needs. (He drew his wife's face in the middle of the box).

He hurried on to the last box. How did he feel about the United States Government? He felt angry that the Government was so dysfunctional these days. It seemed like most people in Congress were more interested in grinding their ideological axe than in solving the problems of the country. (He drew some opposing arrows in the box). He was also upset about so much money being spent on elections - elections that seemed to go on forever. Too many government officials seemed to invest more time and energy into fund raising than into public service. (He drew a big $ sign in the box). And much of that money went into financing attack ads that were more aimed at tearing down another candidate than in promoting policy. (He drew a TV screen with a fist on it in the box).

He was proud of the fact that an African American had finally been elected President. Even though there was still a long way to go in race relations in the country, his election had been an encouraging sign that things were changing. (He drew a smiling black face in the middle of the box). He was also glad that the US had a more cooperative relationship with other countries when it came to foreign policy. (He drew a UN flag in a corner of the box). He approved of steps being taken to boost the use of alternative fuels and to deal with global warming to preserve the environment. (He drew a lump of coal with an X through it in another corner of the box). And he was thankful that, messy as it was, he lived in a country that had a democratic system of government. (He drew a small flag in another corner of the box),

He finished just in time, since Pastor Johnson was now giving instructions as to how they'd share and process their drawings. He looked at his boxes. The drawings were rather funny, but the exercise had been quite interesting.

What Do *You* Think?

1. Name the one feeling or opinion that Paul expressed in the above exercise that you most identify with and why.

2. Name the one feeling or opinion that you least identify with, and why.

3. Which one of the six relationships mentioned is proving to be the most satisfying to you right now, and why?

4. Which one of these relationships is proving to be least satisfying to you right now, and why?

Bringing Things Into Focus |

True or False?

Following are some statements about the five relationships mentioned above. Decide whether or not each statement is true or false in terms of reflecting a Christian perspective on a given relationship.

- Christian citizens are to unquestioningly obey their government as a Christian duty.

- Christian friends are to remain loyal even when things go wrong.

- Christians believe that neglecting the needs of one's brothers and sisters is to deny one's faith.

- Christian parents are not to make their children angry.

- Christian wives are to unquestioningly obey whatever their husbands say or decide.

- It's against a Christian's conscience to pay taxes to a civil government.

- If a Christian is swindled by a Christian friend, s/he is free to take him or her to court and sue.

- Christians believe that Cain's question "Am I my brother's keeper?" should be answered, "Yes."

- Christian teaching does not emphasize a child's filial responsibilities towards its parents.

- Christians believe that a husband should consider his wife's wishes as strongly as he does his own before making decisions.

<u>**What Do *You* Think?**</u>

1. How do you think husband and wife should go about making decisions?

2. What do you think it means to be "my brother's keeper?"

3. Do you think patriotism means that one should follow the dictum: "My country, right or wrong?"

4. What do you think is the best way for a parent to discipline a child?

<u>Gaining a Perspective</u> |

Picture Talk

Now it's *your* turn to express your feelings about your relationships in the way our friend Paul did. Take a few sheets of paper and draw six boxes on them, labeling the first box "My Spouse," the second "My Parents," the third "My Siblings," the fourth "My Friends," the fifth "Members of the Opposite Sex" and the sixth "My Government." (If you're not married or have no siblings, substitute "My Relatives" and "My Neighbors" for those two categories). When you finish your drawings, follow the instructions given below.

- Give one reason why you feel the way you do about each relationship.

- Name one problem that perplexes you about each relationship.

- Suggest one possible practical thing you could do to try and solve the problem you have named for each relationship.

- Which relationship do you find the most satisfying, and why?

- Which relationship do you find the least satisfying, and why?

Drawing Conclusions |

Love: The Key Ingredient

The Christian perspective on relationships goes further and deeper than the teaching of other faiths. For example, Confucius stressed *duty* as the linchpin of human relationships, whereas the Christian emphasis is on self-giving *love* as the key ingredient. True, Confucius does say in one place that we are to "love all men" (Analects, Book 12:22:1), but this is a minor note in his otherwise dominant emphasis on social propriety as a duty. Faithful duty can carry relationships a long way, but not nearly as far as self-g1ving love can. The emphasis in the former is on a predetermined 'ought,' but in the latter on a spontaneous joyful abandon. Duty also leaves more room to think about reciprocity or reward than love does. An ideal relationship built on self-giving love is a relationship in which two people, neither thinking of themselves, meet in the middle while concentrating on each other's needs. This fulfills the needs of *both* without it having been planned that way.

The most important difference, however, is the very minor emphasis most other faiths give to a person's relationship with God. In Islam, God is not knowable in a personal way as one's Heavenly Father. In Buddhism and Hinduism, there's no personal God to relate to at all. In those faiths, therefore, there's no connection whatsoever between one's relationship with God and his or her relationships with others. From the Christian perspective, however, one's relationship with God is of *central* importance and has everything to do with whether a person's human relationships will be successful and satisfying or not.

For example, Confucius taught that people *in and of themselves* have the wherewithal to carry out meaningful relationships, while Christ taught that the self-giving love that makes such relationships possible is only generated through one's relationship with the God of love. It's God who pours out his self-giving love *through* us to others. (See Romans 5:5; 1 John 4:7-8, 19-21)

The Relationship between Husband and Wife

The Bible teaches that wives are to 'submit' themselves to their husbands, and that husbands are to have 'authority' over their wives. (See Ephesians 5:22-23; Colossians 3:18; 1 Peter 3:1) At first glance, this doesn't seem to give women anything more than Confucius offers them, or anything more than Islam offers them. The husband gives the orders and the wife unquestioningly obeys. But wait a minute! There's more to it than that. When introducing this idea of 'submission,' for example, Paul prefaces it with a statement directed to *all* Christians, men included. "Submit yourselves *to one another* because of your reverence to Christ." (See Ephesians 5:21) This includes *everybody*, not just women. Then, to make doubly sure that nobody gets the picture of husband as tyrant and wife as slave, Paul instructs husbands: "Love your wives just as Christ loved the Church ... Men ought to love their wives just as they love their own bodies. A man who loves his wife loves himself ... 'For this reason a man will leave his father and mother and unite with his wife, and the two will become one.'" (See Ephesians 5:25-31)

Now we have the full picture. In any society, *somebody* has to be given the authority to make decisions. In the family it's no different. The husband has been given the authority (and the responsibility!) of doing that. But how does he go about doing that - simply by arbitrarily forcing his wishes on his wife and everybody else? No! Rather, we have two people who are intensely concerned with fulfilling each other's needs meeting in the middle; two people who love each other giving of themselves for each other, not manipulating each other to gratify selfish desires. The oneness of these two people means that they won't make decisions on the basis of power but on the basis of sensitivity to one another's feelings, needs and opinions. When two people are in love *this* way, most decisions will be worked out to the satisfaction of both, even if the one sacrifices this or that on behalf of the other, and vice versa, simply because it's the loving thing to do.

When honest disagreement does occur, however, *somebody* has to make a decision in order to enable things to move forward. That 'somebody,' according to the Bible, is the husband. But he makes the decision within the framework of the overall loving relationship he has with his wife - with sincere regret that on this particular item they haven't broken through to a mutual decision, and with a desire to keep working at it with her until they eventually do come to a decision they are both happy with.

On her part, a wife can accept a decision she may not be entirely happy with because she has the security of knowing that her husband deeply cares for her and has tried his best to understand her and meet her needs. She's not threatened by his decision because she knows he loves her. On his part, the husband may sometimes decide to do what his wife wishes, even though it may not be what he wishes. He's willing to sacrifice his wishes because he wants to meet the needs of his wife insofar as he can without making what he feels is a bad decision that could potentially harm their mutual best interests.

Notice that this submission-authority business has nothing to do with *value*, but only with *function*. That is, simply because the husband has been given the role of ultimate decision maker in the marriage relationship doesn't mean he's any better, or more powerful, or more privileged than his wife. Any ideas like that on his part contradict what self-giving love is all about. It simply means that being ultimately responsible for his wife's and his family's welfare is one of the functions and responsibilities he's been given in life.

The Bible teaches that self-giving love extends to the sexual relationship between husband and wife as well. The attitude isn't, what can I get *out* of this experience, but, what can I put *into* this experience? Jesus words that "There is more happiness in giving than in receiving" Acts 20:35 hold true in this area of the love relationship as well. Having one's sexual needs met is deeply satisfying, but being able to meet the sexual needs of one's spouse in the secure bond of committed love is ultimately satisfying. Men and women who use each other as objects to 'have sex' in order to satisfy themselves miss what making love is all about. Making love has to do with two people who are once and for all committed to each other coming together as subjects to give themselves away to each other, and in so doing, finding the deepest oneness that can be experienced in human relationships. This is why Christians see love making between husband and wife as a deeply meaningful and beautiful experience. Anything less is merely cheap, hollow and unsatisfying 'sex.'

The Relationship between Parents and Children

Paul goes on to say that children are asked to "obey" and to "respect" their parents. (See Ephesians 6:1-2) But again, this isn't the obedience and respect of fear paid to tyrants who have absolute power over their charges. Rather it's an obedience and respect that are generated by self-giving love for Mom and Dad. Mom and Dad, on their part, aren't to treat their children as sub-humans whom they can shout at, hit and order around like dogs. Rather, they're to approach their children with the kind of self-giving love that treats them like people - people who aren't coerced by power, but instructed and disciplined with love. (See Ephesians 6:4)

Like husband and wife, parents and children are to be concerned with meeting each others' needs, with listening to each other and with understanding each other. As such, they won't engage in a power struggle with each other to, for example, prove that Dad is the authority, or that Junior has the power to revolt - a power struggle that finds everybody selfishly guarding his or her own corner. Instead, they'll meet in the middle while on their way to trying to meet each other's needs. When disagreements do occur, despite all efforts to work things out to everyone's satisfaction, they'll trust and love each other enough to enable children to accept Mom and Dad's decision on the one hand, or to enable parents to sometimes sacrifice their own wishes to meet the deeply felt needs of their children on the other.

Like husband and wife, the difference between parents and children has nothing to do with *value*, but everything to do with *function*. *All* people - parents *and* children - are equally valuable in God's sight. Parents have simply been given the function of being ultimately responsible for their children's welfare. From the standpoint of self-giving love, this doesn't automatically make them one whit better, more privileged, or more powerful than their children. Neither does it give children the right to be selfish, demanding, disobedient, or disrespectful. As Christians see it, all these things are foreign to the whole idea of a relationship built on self-giving love.

The Relationship between Siblings

We might demonstrate the idea by contrasting what too often goes on between brothers and sisters with what *would* go on if self-giving love were given a chance.

- "Hey! You can't play with that! That's mine!"
  OR
  "Well, I don't mind if you have a turn, but please be careful with it."

- "I'm older than you, and you'll do as I say - or I'll bop you one!"
  OR
  "When Mom and Dad are gone and you won't cooperate, it makes me feel upset because they're counting on me to be responsible for you when they aren't here."

- "If you do that again, I'm gonna tell Dad on you, and *then* you'll be sorry!"
  OR
  "Look, you're really irritating me. I know I can't stop you by myself, but I don't want to say anything to Dad. We should be able to work this thing out by ourselves."

- "You make life miserable for me! I'm always stuck with taking care of you."
  OR
  "Well, I'd really like to be out playing football, but I know you need somebody to take care of you. I don't really mind all that much ... we'll have fun, just the two of us, won't we."

- "Well, I wasn't the only one that did that Mom, *she* did it too!"
  OR
  "Yes, I did do that Mom ... and I'm sorry."

- "Hey! That's *my* chair you're sitting in! I *always* sit there when we eat. Mom, make her get out of my chair!"
  OR

"Oh, I see that you're sitting where I usually sit. You want to sit on this side for a while? I guess that's okay with me. The food will taste just as good on the other side, and we can switch again later."

- "It's not *my* turn to wash the dishes! I did them two nights ago and once a week before then. It's *your* turn!"
          OR
"Well, I don't really remember it that way. I'll tell you what; suppose I do them tonight, but after this we'll make a schedule sheet and tick off when we do them so we won't have to keep fighting about it. Deal?

It's all summed up in 1 Timothy 5:8 and 1 Peter 4:8. "If anyone does not take care of ... the members of his own family, he has denied the faith." "Above everything, love one another earnestly, because love covers over many sins."

The Relationship between Friends

You can help answer this question by looking deeply within yourself and at your relationships with your friends. Are you concerned to try and meet the needs of your friends, or do you mainly have friends because they can do something for you? People sometimes make 'friends' for very selfish reasons - they want to be popular; they can't stand to be lonely; their 'friends' can lend them money, introduce them to the right people, help them with their homework; they want a girlfriend or a boyfriend to boast about, or to have sex with; and the like. When seen in this light, many of the relationships that people wrongly call 'friendships' are really nothing more than acquaintanceships.

Christians want to have friendships that are built on self-giving love; friendships in which two people meet in the middle in their mutual concern to meet each other's needs. David and Jonathan were friends like that. (See 1 Samuel 18:1-4) They were willing to sacrifice their own interests for one another and even risk their lives for each other. Jonathan knew that David would one day sit on the throne of

Israel in his stead, yet he didn't let that ruin their friendship because he knew it was just.

The love that cements people together like this perseveres through fair weather or foul (See Proverbs 17:17; 18:24; Luke 22:28) and never gives up on the other person (See 1 Corinthians 13:7). When a problem in a relationship with a friend does arise, a Christian friend will patiently persist at seeing it through without resorting to bribes or threats or withdrawal. (For example, Paul strongly urges Christians not to bring their problems to law courts. See 1 Corinthians 6:7-8) When somebody has *this* kind of a relationship with another person, s/he has truly made a *friend*.

The Relationship between Men and Women

The Christian message is unique in the emphasis it places on the dignity and equality of women, who are as fully valued as God's children as men are. Hinduism and Islam, for example, assign a second class status to women. The Christian perspective is very different. As far as the value of human beings is concerned, Jesus bucked the tide in his day and treated *both* women and men with equal respect and love. Paul put it succinctly when he wrote, "There is no difference between men and women; you are all one in union with Christ Jesus." Galatians 3:28 Christians believe that the sexes differ biologically and have different functions in society, but as far as their intrinsic worth, status and dignity are concerned, they're equal. This kind of perspective makes a huge difference in the way men treat women and vice versa.

The Relationship between Government and People

Christians are called upon to be loyal and obedient to those who have been placed in authority over them.

- Civil rulers have been appointed by God for the purpose of serving the people on his behalf - upholding the right and punishing the wrong. (See Romans 13:1-5, 11-17)

- Taxes should be cheerfully paid to support the governing authorities and their programs. (See Romans 13:6-7)

- Christians are to do more than the legal minimum in helping government and society to function. (See Matthew 6:41)

- Christians are to be law-abiding citizens who aim at doing what's good and right and who therefore don't need to fear the authorities. (See 1 Peter 2:13-17)

If all goes as it's supposed to, government servants will be concerned with the welfare of the people, and the people will be concerned with the welfare of the government and its socially beneficial policies and programs. However, we all know from sad experience that things often *don't* go as they're supposed to. Government officials sometimes oppress rather than serve; *do* evil against people rather than suppress it; grow rich through corruption and exploitation; punish the good in the name of the 'good'; lie to their people to prevent them from knowing the truth, and the like. And people are often less than self-giving when it comes to tax evasion, desertion from duty, rebellion, the bribery of officials, destructive criticism, apathy, and all the rest.

So what happens when things go wrong? Do Christians simply go on unquestioningly obeying the authorities simply because they're authorities? From what Paul says about what authorities who are to be obeyed are *supposed* to be and be doing, and from what Peter says to the Jewish authorities who *weren't* being or doing what they were supposed to be being and doing, we can infer that the answer to this question is "No."

Christians are to hold officials responsible for the performance of their duties as God intended, with a concern that grows out of their respect for them and for the society they govern. Peter bluntly tells the Jewish Sanhedrin: "We must obey God, not men." Acts 5:29 In other words, when a government comes into conflict with God's law and his purpose for people, Christians have a duty to speak and to act in a way that makes this clear and seeks to change the situation. How should they do this?

Christians have differed on this question. Some have advocated non-violent means like letters to the press, peaceful protest demonstrations, symbolic acts, boycotts, strikes, passive resistance, and the like. Others have called for violent resistance or revolution when rulers become so evil that their actions and policies bring great harm to large numbers of people. The New Testament writers lean towards the nonviolent way.

Ideally, Christians are to actively engage in opposing oppression and exploitation and in struggling for justice and freedom, but are to do so non-violently - and let the chips fall where they may. "All who take the sword," said Jesus, "will die by the sword." Violence only begets violence, and the second evil becomes worse than the first. "Letting the chips fall where they may" will often lead to suffering and sometimes even to martyrdom, but truth, love and justice will win out in the end. (See 1 Peter 3:13-17) The eventual fall of every tyrant in the history of the world demonstrates that this approach is not just blind, naive idealism.

However, history also demonstrates that there are differences in the types of tyrants and societies one is dealing with and the scale of evil that they're perpetrating. Mahatma Gandhi's campaign of non-violent resistance to British imperialism in India and Martin Luther King's similar campaign against racial discrimination in the United States, for example, were conducted against governments and societies that were for the most part benign, with large segments of those officials and societies already conscience-stricken about the injustices, oppression and exploitation that were being perpetrated against the citizens of those countries.

But the situation in Nazi Germany, for example, was quite different. Some German Christians, like the famous theologian, Dietrich Bonheoffer, were convinced that the evils that Adolph Hitler and his Nazi regime were perpetrating against the peoples of Europe in the 20th century were so great that they were justified in joining a group that tried to assassinate Hitler and other officials. Evil as that act might be, to let Hitler and his regime continue to carry out the mass murder of the Jews and to terrorize the peoples under their control would be a much greater evil.

In other words, when it comes to civil disobedience, Christians are sometimes faced with a tragic moral choice wherein they must choose between a lesser evil and a greater evil. Bonheoffer believed, and some Christians agree, that if a government is doing the opposite of what God intends it to do (See Romans 13:1-5, 11-17), it must be opposed and stopped from perpetrating evil, even if it at times means adopting the use of violent methods. They believe that in so doing, they're expressing self-giving love for those who are being crushed by evil forces.

It's self-giving love, then, that for Christians is the key to making these six relationships work. This love is available to all who wish to have it through a seventh, and primary, relationship - a relationship with the God of love made possible through his Son, Jesus Christ. God in Christ can truly transform a person's relationships as that person opens his or her heart to allow him to do so.

Christians believe that without the power of Christ's self-giving love pouring into a person's life, all that we've been talking about will merely remain hopelessly unattainable ideals, especially if that person's relationships involve other people who don't operate on the basis of that kind of love.

However, when people commit themselves to Jesus Christ and his way of living and relating, he, through his indwelling Spirit, will keep his promise to help them begin the process of working out their relationships on a new basis. Paul's words have proved to be true in many lives and relationships: "Now that we have been put right with God through faith, we have peace with God through our Lord Jesus Christ ... God has poured out his love into our hearts by means of the Holy Spirit who is God's gift to us." Romans 5:1, 5

<u>What Do *You* Think?</u>

1. Do you agree that the Christian perspective on the six relationships discussed in this chapter goes much further and deeper than that expressed by other faiths? Why or why not?

2. Do you agree with the perspectives on family relationships as expressed in this chapter? Why or why not?

3. Do you agree with the perspective on friendship as expressed in this chapter? Why or why not?

4. Do you agree with the perspective on citizenship as expressed in this chapter? Why or why not?

5. Do you agree that people can only truly love others with a self-giving love if they've opened their hearts and lives to the love of God? Why or why not?

Chapter Sixteen

HOW DO CHRISTIANS DEAL WITH OTHERS?

> "Why should God reward you if you love only the people who love you?" Matthew 5:46
>
> "Let us not become tired of doing good ... as often as we have the chance, we should do good to everyone, and especially to those who belong to our family in the faith." Galatians 6:9-10

Looking Through the Microscope |

More Boxes

Rachel was looking forward to the adult class at church today. She had looked ahead in her book and seen that they were going to be doing more of those box drawing exercises. The last ones had been fun to do - and helpful too.

Pastor Johnson arrived and began the class. "I think you all did very well in sharing your feelings about your relationships using the box drawing exercises. Today we're going to be working on four more boxes representing four additional relationships that we all have now or will have in some way or another in the future - our relationship with the elderly, with our employer or employees, with strangers and with our enemies. Since you've now had some experience at how to do this kind of exercise, I won't need to repeat the instructions. Just make sure you give each relationship some serious thought before you draw anything. If you don't have some kind of a job at present, put down your ideas about one that you've had in the past for the employer/employee box. Remember, it helps to keep a particular person in mind if possible for the exercises to be most effective. Any questions? If not, let's get to work."

Rachel opened her book and turned to the page with the first box - relationships with the elderly. She counted up how many elderly people she really knew quite well. There was her maternal grandmother Weber, her paternal grandparents, the Vanderbergs, an elderly man named Rich who lived in the apartment across the hall and old Joe who sold newspapers on the corner. (She wrote a "5" in one corner of the box). Of those five, who was her favorite? She guessed it must be her Grandma Vanderberg. (She drew her Grandmas' smiling face in the middle of the box). She and Grandpa Vanderberg had once lived with Rachel's family when she'd been a little girl. They'd taken care of her while her parents had gone out to work. She recalled the happy times she and Grandma had had together going to the store and the playground, and eventually up and back to primary school every day. (She drew a few small scenes around Grandma Vanderberg's face).

Of course Grandpa Vanderberg was high on her list too. (She drew a serious face in one corner of the box). He was quiet and didn't say much, but he'd given her some kind of candy treat when she'd come home from school every day for as long as she could remember. (She drew candy pieces around the face in the corner). She laughed to herself thinking how funny it was when she was a high school girl and still getting daily treats from her Grandpa, but she knew he would have been hurt if she had told him she didn't really need them anymore. Besides, she still did like candy!

(She drew neighbor Rich's face in another corner, Grandma Weber's in another corner and Joe's craggy face in the last corner). Old Joe had been selling papers on the street, rain or shine, for some 50 years, and his face showed it. He always had a cheery hello and a few comments or questions for her when she picked up the family's daily paper. She liked old Joe a lot. (She drew lines connecting the five faces to a heart that she drew at the top of the box). This was her 'old people's world,' and she knew that her life would've been a lot poorer without them.

Rachel hurried on to the next box – relating to her employer. She figured that she'd worked nine hours a day five days a week for 15 years. That was a lot of work! (She wrote "15x52x5x9=35,100 hours" in the box). No wonder she felt tired sometimes! (She drew a tired face in one corner of the box). Besides her job, of course, she had to meet the family's needs during the evenings and on weekends. Everybody helped out, but she didn't get a whole lot of time to relax. (She drew a clock face with seven hours penciled in for sleep and the rest left white for work or home activities).

She worked in a textile factory on a spinning machine. (She drew a machine). The lighting wasn't too good, it was noisy, and the pay wasn't too good either – the minimum wage. (She wrote down $395 per week). She got some holidays, but only a month's maternity leave. Whenever one of her three children had been born, it had been a real financial strain on the family and a physical strain on her. (She drew three baby faces in the box). How did she feel about her employer whom she'd seldom seen, but whom she knew made big profits? (She drew in a face with both smile and frown lines). She was grateful to have a job, but she knew she should be getting paid more and working under better conditions.

How did she relate to strangers? That was a 'strange' box to think about, she thought. She'd had lots of friends at work and at church, but how could she draw her feelings about strangers? (She drew in lots of dots representing the crowds of strangers that she rubbed elbows with in the subway and on the sidewalks every day). She was rather shy and didn't like to introduce herself to people she didn't know. (She drew a stick figure of herself in one corner - away from most of the dots). In fact, she was rather suspicious of strangers. (She drew a '?' in the box). When she was a girl, her mother had told her never to open the apartment door unless she first recognized the person's voice, and then to keep the chain on until she was sure. (She drew a chain). She knew it was important to be friendly, but strangers were people best kept at a distance. There *had* been that new woman at work whom she'd finally gotten to know, however. (She drew her face large among the dots. She felt good that she'd been the one who'd made the effort to reach out to her and to help her get used to the factory. (She drew a hand reaching out to the face from her stick figure in the corner).

The last box was even harder. She was tempted to leave it blank. "I don't have any enemies that I know of," she thought. But when she thought harder, she knew that she felt very strongly about the gang members she'd seen hanging around the school down the street trying to coerce or coax some of the boys into becoming gang members. She didn't like gang members or any toughs or criminals that made life more difficult for people in Chicago. (She wrote a big 'G' in the box and put an 'X' through it). She didn't like people who paid bribes to corrupt cops either. (She drew a police badge in the box). There was one woman in the factory that she could almost say she hated - a woman who constantly taunted her in front of the other women because she was a conscientious worker and wasn't one of the most beautiful women in the factory. Sometimes, she even felt like sticking out her tongue at her or slapping her in the face! (She drew a face with a tongue sticking out at another very ugly face in the box). Yes, she had enemies all right. Her box wasn't blank after all.

Rachel waited quietly for the other members of the class to finish their boxes. Then they'd get on with the fun part of trying to 'read' each others' drawings ... and minds!

What Do _You_ Think?

1. Name one of Rachel's feelings or opinions that you most identify with, and explain why.

2. Name one of Rachel's feelings or opinions that you least identify with, and explain why.

3. Which one of the four relationships mentioned (the elderly, employer/employee, strangers and enemies) is proving to be the most satisfying to you right now, and why?

4. Which of these four relationships is proving to be least satisfying to you right now, and why?

Bringing Things Into Focus |

True or False?

The following are statements about the four relationships mentioned above. In your opinion, when it comes to the Christian perspective, which statements are true and which are false, and why?

- Unlike the Chinese Confucian tradition, for example, Christian teaching doesn't say much about respecting and caring for the elderly.

- The New Testament talks about the relationship between master and slave, but the same principles are relevant today when applied to the relationship between employer and employee.

- Christian teaching says a lot about loving one's neighbor as oneself, but very little about one's obligation to strangers.

- Islam puts a much greater emphasis on the forgiveness of one's enemies than the Christian faith does.

- With its emphasis on youth, the Christian faith doesn't leave much room for the elderly to make much of a contribution to life and work in society and in the church.

- Christian teaching infers that both employer and employee are ultimately working for God, and that they therefore should do their respective jobs well and treat each other fairly and with respect.

- The Bible teaches that a person's obligation to a stranger is fulfilled if s/he simply refrains from doing him or her harm.

- Christians feel that although loving one's enemies is a beautiful ideal, in real life, it's a practical impossibility.

- Christ taught that in showing loving concern to a stranger, one was at the same time expressing love and devotion to God.

- Christians who are filled with the Spirit of Christ look at enemies as potential friends.

What Do *You* Think?

1. How much contact do you have with elderly people? What can you learn from them?

2. Who was the best boss (or worker) you ever had? Why?

3. Have you ever invited people down the street or in your building that you didn't know very well to your home? Why or why not?

4. What enemies do *you* have? What are some things you could do to try to turn them into friends?

Gaining a Perspective |

Picture Talk

Now it's *your* turn to express your feelings about your relationships in the way our friend Rachel did. Take a few sheets of paper and draw four boxes on them, labeling the first box 'The Elderly,' the second box 'Employer/Employees,' the third box 'Strangers' and the fourth box 'Enemies.' Next, describe how you feel about each relationship by drawing your feelings in the appropriate box. When you finish your drawings, follow the instructions given below.

1. Give one reason why you feel the way you do about each relationship.

2. Name one problem that perplexes you about each relationship.

3. Suggest one possible practical thing you could do to try and solve the problem you've named for each relationship.

4. What difference would being a Christian make in relating to these types of people?

Drawing Conclusions |

The Oil That Lubricates Relationships

As we mentioned in the last chapter, for Christians, the self-giving love that comes into a person's life through his or her relationship with God through Christ is the key to making all human relationships work successfully. The old attitude of, "What can I get *out* of this relationship?" is replaced with a new attitude of, "What can I put *into* this relationship that will really make it work and meet the needs of the person I'm relating to?" As Jesus pointed out, those who enter into relationships in this way end up getting a whole lot more that's truly valuable out of them as a God-given 'surprise bonus' as it were. He said, "Whoever tries to save his own life will lose it; whoever loses his life will save it." Luke 17:33 Or paraphrasing it in the case of relationships: "Whoever relates to people for his or her own benefit will have disappointing results, but whoever relates to people with a concern for their benefit will have rich and satisfying results." Relationships that are rooted in self-giving love prove the truth of this strange paradox - the more you give away, the more you have.

Relating to the Elderly

As far as the elderly are concerned, they can use a lot of this kind of giving and a lot of this kind of loving. They've been giving for a whole lifetime themselves, and now they need others to give to them. In some areas (like wisdom, perspective, love, etc), they still have a lot to give, but in others (like strength, speed, stamina, sight, etc) they must learn more and more how to be gracious receivers of the help, care and love of those who are younger. This transition isn't easy. (Read "An Old Man's Prayer" in Psalm 71 where the anxiety of this aging process clearly comes through between the lines.)

In many societies today, older people are increasingly being 'put on the shelf,' pushed out of the way, ignored in family and social decision making processes and the like. Do you think this is right? Do you think this is loving? Think about your own relationships with older people. Do you really value them? Are you interested in getting to know more of them? Or are they more or less a nuisance in your life?

Christians are people who will oppose any "getting the old people out of the way" mentality. They'll value and treasure the wisdom and friendship of older people. They'll understand the difficulties they face physically and in other ways. They'll be long on patience and short on demands. They'll gladly take care of their needs, especially the needs of those in their own family. (See 1 Timothy 5:4, 8) They'll help them end their days in comfort and dignity, and will assist them in calmly preparing for their final departure from this life.

Relating to Employers/Employees

The Christian viewpoint on work is quite clear. God gave the first humans a number of tasks to do (like cultivating and guarding the garden, bringing the earth under control, managing and naming the animals) which made it clear that work was meant to be a creative and enriching part of life. (See Genesis 1:28; 2:15, 19) (To look at some of our factories today, you'd never know it!) Christians believe that not to work either in the home or in the community is to be lazy, to be a drain on the community, and to live a boring life. (See 2 Thessalonians 3:6-12)

Work brings people into contact with one another. There are fellow-employees to cooperate with and build relationships with (See 1 Corinthians 12:14-27), and there is an employer (or employees) whom one has to learn to relate to with an attitude of self- giving love as well. (Yes, Christians believe that love can even invade a factory and transform competition into cooperation; grudging grinds into cheerful tasks; and exploitation into concern.) If you read Ephesians

6:5-9 and Colossians 3:22-25 and substitute the word 'employee' for 'slave' and 'employer' for 'master,' you'll get the Christian perspective on harmonious labor relations.

Employees are to do an honest, day's work (not just when the boss is watching!) with a cheerful spirit and a willingness to follow instructions. Employers are to motivate their employees with kindness and not threats; are to treat them fairly and justly and are to do an honest day's work with a cheerful spirit themselves. Both employees and employers are to remember that they're working for their mutual Employer in heaven who'll reward them according to their attitudes, honesty and faithfulness. Their work produces part of what society needs in order to function, and as such, can be seen as service to Christ as well as a means of income.

Just think what would happen in our factories, banks, shopping malls, restaurants and all the rest if people ran their businesses on that kind of a basis! There would be no need for labor unions, strikes, and the like, and businesspeople would be concerned first of all with people's needs rather than with the bottom line. In the real world, of course, things seldom work out that way. But they can increasingly become more that way if more and more Christians develop this kind of attitude towards their work and act as yeast in the lump of labor relations.

Relating to Strangers

Probably the most famous story in the Bible is Jesus' story about 'the Good Samaritan' as recorded in Luke 10: 25-37. We've already seen in other chapters how self-giving love is the key to the whole of the Christian gospel. The phrase that spells this out most clearly as far as our relationships with people are concerned is: "Love your neighbor as you love yourself." This statement is repeated nine times in the Bible, which gives us some idea as to its central importance in the life of a Christian. The crucial question that immediately comes to mind was conveniently asked by the lawyer to whom Jesus told this story: "And who is my neighbor?" It's a good thing he asked that question, or we might have been able to maneuver this idea of loving our 'neighbor' around to the point where it would suit us much better and be a lot easier to practice. We can all, after all, find a few literal neighbors in our neighborhood who aren't hard to love at all!

But Jesus makes it clear that my 'neighbor' isn't just that nice lady who lives across the street, but *anybody* who I meet, particularly anybody who's in need. If I see a person faint on the sidewalk, it's *my* responsibility (and privilege) to stop and assist him or her. If I see somebody punching somebody else on the street, it's *my* responsibility (and privilege) to try and stop the fight if I can, or to go get somebody like a policeman to stop it if I can't. Jesus' point is that if I'm a Christian, I'm related to everybody! Every stranger, and particularly one in need, is a potential recipient of my self-giving love and concern to the point that I'm able to offer it. I don't go around trying to avoid involvement with people, passing them on the sidewalk with a blank face or cold stare. I'm the kind of a person whose eyes smile at strangers and invite a return smile, however fleeting it may be. As far as a Christian is concerned, there's *nobody* who's a complete stranger, for *all* people are God's children, whether they acknowledge it or not, and are therefore related to me and I to them.

Relating to Enemies

Now we come to the hardest group in the lot - the people who are the most difficult of all for us to relate to - our enemies. Most people find it difficult to even *talk* about relating to enemies. As far as they're concerned, you don't *relate* to enemies, you *hate* your enemies! You want nothing to do with them. You even sometimes wish they were dead. And in a war, you'll try to make *sure* that they're dead! A relationship with an enemy? Not likely!

The real shocker comes, however, when Jesus calls his followers to go way beyond that - to actually *love* their enemies! (See Matthew 5:43-48) To prove this wasn't just some mental lapse on Jesus' part, or a slip of the tongue, the apostle Paul not only restates the idea, but puts it even more strongly. "If someone has done you wrong, do not repay him with a wrong ... If your enemy is hungry, feed him; if he is thirsty, give him a drink ..." Romans 12:17-20 There's no such word as 'revenge' in the Christian's dictionary. Rather, a Christian is asked to take the first step, reach out to make things right and renew a relationship with a person who has rudely broken, wounded or smashed it to begin with.

Does this mean that Christians will stand there with their hand out and a smile on their face watching an enemy soldier point his rifle at them and pull the trigger, for example? Hardly. But it does mean that it pains Christians to be at war at all; that they'll try to keep from hating the other 'side;' that they'll do all in their power to restore peace; that they'll treat with forgiving kindness a wounded or captured enemy prisoner. (We'll talk more about this particular problem of war in a later chapter.)

When we think of the word 'enemy,' most of us immediately think of a war situation, or a situation in which somebody commits a gross, unforgiveable act against somebody else - like murdering their child. But the word 'enemy' comes much closer to home and daily experience than that. An enemy is anybody whom I find it difficult to forgive and whom I'm tempted to take revenge against in one way or another *at the moment.* This might range from hitting somebody back, to road rage, to spreading gossip about a person you feel has been nasty to you and so on. Fortunately, most relationships with *at the moment* enemies are healable and restorable before they deteriorate to the point of a deep-seated, long-lasting hatred between 'him or her and me.' This is why it's so important to quickly take the first step towards mending any tear, healing any wound and reconciling any differences when a relationship first experiences stress. Waiting means the tear gets bigger, the wound festers and the differences widen.

Forgiveness and reconciliation is a two-way street. Christians are called on to reach out in love to those who have wronged them, or who for some reason unjustly hate them and to keep on reaching out, no matter what kind of a response they might get. (See 1 Peter 3:9, 16-17) In fact, Christians are challenged not to look at *anybody* as an enemy at all, no matter what they've done, but to always see everyone as a potential brother or sister. As far as they're concerned, only the *other* person gives *himself* or *herself* the label 'enemy' when a problem occurs.

But what if the other person refuses the outstretched hand? What if s/he refuses to accept my willingness to forgive and my offer of reconciliation? In that case, the relationship remains ruptured and unhealed. A Christian can't *force* an 'enemy' to accept forgiveness or reconciliation, but that changes nothing, since s/he is called on to continue to *offer* such as long as the problem between them remains unresolved. (See Matthew 6:14-15)

Some people treat this whole business of loving one's enemies as a hopelessly idealistic idea. Part of the reason why they do so is because they confuse the words 'love' and 'like.' Jesus calls on his followers to *love* everybody, even their enemies, but nowhere does he say they have to *like* everybody. For example, I like certain people very much and call them my friends. We somehow seem to click together. I don't click that way with other people whom I neither like nor dislike, but whose names I wouldn't put down on my list of friends.

There are some people that I definitely dislike. This doesn't mean they're my enemies, but they certainly aren't my friends either. There's something about them that simply turns me off, and there's probably something about me which does the same for them. Or perhaps they've done something nasty to me that makes it impossible for me to like them. But does this mean that I can't love them? Of course not. Simply because I don't especially *like* some people and even *dislike* others doesn't mean that I'll try to harm them, or that I'm not concerned about their well-being, or that I wouldn't even help them in a time of need - no matter who they were or what they'd done. Self-giving love isn't a sentimental feeling towards someone (although it may include that). Rather, it's a willingness on my part to act on behalf of someone who's in need even if I don't particularly like him or her. The Good Samaritan probably intensely disliked the wounded Jew lying at the side of the road (for the Jews despised the Samaritans), but he stopped and did the loving thing towards him anyway.

Loving older people and even employers and employees isn't so tough. But when it comes to loving strangers and enemies, we know from experience that this doesn't come naturally. To love in this way, we must have first experienced the wonder of the incredible love that God had (has) for us, *his* 'enemies,' in sacrificing his Son on our behalf. (See Romans 5:10-11) Knowing that kind of self-giving love from personal experience, and becoming open to being channels of it to others, Christians begin to see that Jesus is not talking about some totally unworkable naive idealism, but about something that can really happen in real life. Is it really possible? The testimony of Stephen (See Acts 7:60) and of many other Christians down through history says that it is.

What Do *You* Think?

1. I agree with/disagree with/am not sure about the conclusions of this chapter because ...

2. I agree/disagree/am not sure that the Christian attitude of concern and care for the elderly is more pronounced than in other faiths because ...

3. I think/don't think/am not sure that Christian ideas on labor relations will work in the modern era of 'globalization' and 'dog eat dog' capitalism because ...

4. I think the Christian approach to strangers is fairly workable/workable/unworkable in our postmodern world because ...

5. I think the Christian approach to enemies is fairly workable/workable/unworkable in our postmodern world because ...

Chapter Seventeen

DO CHRISTIANS AVOID REALITY?

> "Build up your strength in union with the Lord and by means of his mighty power. Put on all the armor that God gives you, so that you will be able to stand up against the Devil's evil tricks…Then when the evil day comes, you will be able to resist the enemy's attacks; and after fighting to the end, you will still hold your ground. So, stand ready with truth … righteousness ... readiness to announce the Good News of peace ... faith ... salvation ... the Word of God ... and prayer."
>
> Ephesians 6:10-18

<u>Looking Through the Microscope |</u>

Prisoner #019

The time was April 9, 1945. The place was the little town of Schonberg deep in the Bavarian forest of southern Germany. The SS Black Guards, acting on the direct orders of Heinrich Himmler, the chief of the SS (Schutzstaffel, or Security Services), marched the bespectacled German Lutheran pastor into a small unused schoolhouse, tied a rope around a rafter in the ceiling and ordered him to stand on a chair. With calm dignity the pastor complied. A noose at the end of the rope was put around his neck. Suddenly, the chair was jerked from beneath his feet. His body swung in the air and finally went limp. Prisoner #019 was dead! Two weeks later, allied troops liberated the area.

The life that ended so suddenly and so tragically on that April day had begun 39 years earlier on February 4, 1906 in Breslau, Germany where Dietrich Bonheoffer was born. His parents were clear-sighted, cultured people who were uncompromising in everything that matters in life. His father was a university professor and leading authority on psychiatry and neurology. Many of Dietrich's forebears had been theologians, professors, lawyers and artists.

After his sixth birthday, Dietrich and his three brothers, his twin sister and three other sisters were brought up in Berlin. His family were deeply committed Christians and raised their children in a Christian, humanitarian and liberal tradition that greatly influenced young Dietrich's life from the beginning. Young Bonheoffer was as open as any boy could have been to all the things that make life meaningful - love of family and friends; love of nature; love of music, art and literature and love of Christ. Even as a boy, he was already a person who was characterized by kindness unselfishness, courage and a passion for truth and justice. His friends recalled him as a young man who knew how to listen and who was prepared to help others to the point of self-sacrifice. He also wanted to follow the family tradition of being deeply interested in Christian theology, which explains why at the young age of fourteen, he'd already made up his mind to study theology in university.

Dietrich entered Tubingen University at age seventeen. A year later, he attended theology courses at the famous Berlin University. After serving in a church for a year, he went to the United States where he spent a year at Union Theological Seminary in New York. He was regarded by his professors as a brilliant young man who already had a profound understanding of Christian teaching. He returned to Germany in 1930 and became a lecturer in Christian Theology in Berlin University at the age of twenty four. He began to publish books on Christian ideas that were read and appreciated by theologians around the world. It seemed as though a splendid career in theological scholarship lay open before him.

Then Adolph Hitler and National Socialism emerged on the German scene. During Hitler's rise to power, the German Church became divided. Many believed that some of what Hitler stood for was good for Germany. Others felt that if the Church was not to suffer, it must learn how to compromise. Bonheoffer and others clearly saw that there could be no compromise. What Hitler stood for was evil through and through and, if left unchecked, would eventually result in the destruction of the Church and of Germany. A struggle developed within the Church over which course to take. Bonheoffer increasingly spoke out against Hitler who, as 'the Fuhrer,' was being turned into an idol. He also opposed National Socialism as a political system that was being used to grossly corrupt and mislead the German nation. As late as 1933, he dared to state these views publically over the radio.

After six months of struggle within the Church over these issues, Bonheoffer went to England in late 1933 for two reasons: to protest against the majority in the Church who were for compromise, and to alert the worldwide Church as to what was really happening inside Nazi Germany. In so doing, he gave up his promising academic career since he ended up staying in London for two years as the pastor of two German-speaking congregations. He also helped to form and became the leader of the 'Confessing Church' - a group of German Christians who refused to cooperate with Hitler's regime for the sake of safety, comfort or narrow nationalism. They were prepared to follow the ideas and example of Christ as a witness for the truth in Germany, no matter where it led them or what it cost them.

In 1935, the Confessing Church invited Dietrich Bonheoffer back to Germany to direct a new Training College for young Christian workers and pastors. This College would concentrate on producing a highly committed community of Christian disciples that would live out the Christian life wholeheartedly in relation to the increasingly pagan realities of twentieth century German National Socialist society. Since the goals of this school were contrary to the educational aims of the German Nazi state, it couldn't be registered, and was therefore technically illegal. It was located in Finkewalde in an isolated area. it was there that Bonheoffer wrote two moving books that grew out of his experience in developing this kind of committed Christian community: one entitled *Life Together*, and the other called *The Cost of Discipleship* (both of which are still in print in English and are well worth reading today, some seventy years later).

Up until this point, Bonheoffer had taken the traditional attitude of his Church - that religion and politics don't mix. He also was a pacifist, believing strongly that a Christian should refuse to participate in a war of any kind or to have anything to do with violence. The more he understood the evils of Nazi rule and where it was steering Germany, however, the more he felt that these positions were a 'head in the sand' escape from the reality of fighting this great evil. Through his brother-in-law, Hans von Dohnanyi, who had high connections in political and military circles, he became aware of the development of a secret resistance movement taking shape among alarmed political and military leaders. Slowly, he became more and more interested in this movement as a means to stop Hitler.

By now Bonheoffer was already feeling the heat of the Gestapo. They'd succeeded in getting him sacked from the Berlin University faculty in 1936. Christian colleagues overseas had become increasingly worried over his safety. When war seemed inevitable, these friends wanted him to leave Germany to save his life, for they knew that he would refuse to serve in the German Army in the cause of an aggressive war, and that his continued opposition to Hitler's policies would result in his being labeled a traitor.

In 1939, some American theologians succeeded in getting permission for him to go to the United States on a lecture tour. Wherever he went, his friends put heavy pressure on him to stay in America until things could change for the better in Germany. But the longer he stayed, the more he knew in his heart that he had to return. How could he have anything meaningful or legitimate to say to suffering German Christians and to his countrymen after what he knew would be a disastrous war if he himself had not gone through that suffering with them? He answered his own question by taking one of the last ships to sail from America to Germany before the outbreak of World War II.

Friends in Germany made it possible for him to avoid being drafted into the Army. However, in 1940, the Gestapo closed down the Training College at Finkenwalde. Bonheoffer was forbidden to lecture, to publish books or articles, to make speeches of any kind, or to live in Berlin. He spent the next three years quietly working on behalf of the Confessing Church, writing a book in private on Christian Ethics and supporting the growing underground Resistance Movement. With his international esteem and his many church connections, he was able to make invaluable contacts both inside and outside of Germany for the Resistance. The most important of these was a visit to Stockholm, Sweden in 1942 to meet the English Bishop of Chichester, George Bell. He described the details of the German Resistance movement to him and asked for British Government support. This was not easy to do. He knew what he was doing would contribute to the defeat of his country in the war. Yet, he also knew that his commitment to God compelled him to oppose and help bring down the evil Nazi regime that had seized the reins of his country and was plunging it and the world into ruin.

On April 5, 1943, Dietrich Bonheoffer's sister and brother-in-law were suddenly arrested. Documents found in their home implicated Bonheoffer as also having acted on behalf of the Resistance Movement. Within hours, he too had been arrested and taken to the military section of Tegel Prison in Berlin where he would spend the next year and a half of his life.

Life in Tegel was hard, but not impossible. After some argument, he was given permission to write regularly to his parents. After six months, his Christian warmth and integrity had made such an impact on his warders and medical orderlies that they gladly enabled him to carry on an extensive, uncensored correspondence with family and friends. Codes were worked out so that they could inform him as to the situation of the Confessing Church, friends in sensitive positions and the progress of the Resistance Movement.

On July 20, 1944, the Movement made an attempt to assassinate Hitler that narrowly failed. This, plus the discovery by the Gestapo of the Zossen papers in September spelling out the extent of the involvement of his brother-in-law and others in the Resistance, ended all of this. The failure of the plot against Hitler was a severe blow to Bonheoffer, but an equally severe blow was his removal by the Gestapo on October 5 to close confinement in their maximum security prison on Prinz Albert Strasse in Berlin. All communication with the outside world was cut off, except for one or two last pieces of poetry

Christianity Under the Microscope

composed for special occasions like New Year's Day, 1945.

In February, 1945, the Gestapo prison in Berlin was destroyed by an air raid. Bonheoffer survived and was taken to the infamous concentration camp at Buchenwald, and from there to other places until that fateful day in April when, at the young age of 39, his life was taken from him in Schonberg.

Dietrich Bonheoffer's life and death showed that what he'd written in *The Cost of Discipleship* had not been theoretical. He'd refused to bury his head in the sand and take the easy way out. He'd instead decided to live as a twentieth century disciple of Christ in an alien and dangerous atmosphere, and to let the chips fall where they might. In so doing, he provided an example of hope and courage for the German people as they dug out of the ashes of physical and spiritual destruction to start life anew ... and for all of us.

What was Bonheoffer's attitude while in prison? Was he bitter, despondent, wishing he could have done things differently, filled with self pity, unable to think or create? Quite the contrary. He was a pastor and a rock of strength to his fellow prisoners, particularly to those who were to be executed or who would panic during heavy bombings. He sang hymns, wrote theology, composed poems and conducted worship for fellow prisoners when he could. Many of his letters and poems describing his thoughts, feelings and activities survived the war and have been published in a book called *Letters and Papers from Prison* (still in print and a moving book to read). In a letter to a friend dated August 23rd, 1944, he wrote: "You must never doubt that I am travelling my appointed road with gratitude and cheerfulness. My past life is replete with God's goodness ... l am thankful for all those who have crossed my path, and all I wish is never to cause them sorrow, and that they, like me, will always be thankful for the forgiveness and mercy of God and sure of it." (*Letters and Papers from Prison*, p. 131)

Dietrich Bonheoffer was a Christian who believed deeply, acted courageously and died calmly. He wasn't the first, nor will he be the last Christian to do so. But in doing so, he gave us a modern day example of a person who believed that his faith drove him *into* society, rather than away from it, and *into* action, rather than avoiding it

<u>What Do **Y***ou* Think?</u>

1. Do you think Dietrich Bonheoffer was wise or foolish to do what he did? Explain.

2. What was he was willing to sacrifice in order to live out his faith during the Nazi era?

3. Why did he feel that, as a Christian, he could not ignore what was going on around him and simply continue to teach, preach and write about the Christian faith?

4. Do you think there are some things going on in American society today that Christians should be more concerned about and do more about, but that are being ignored because doing something about them would be too costly? Explain.

<u>Bringing Things Into Focus</u> |

Heroes of Faith

Following is a list of people of God from Bible to modern times who didn't ignore what was going on around them, but did something about it, even at great risk to themselves. Google their names and explain how they got involved, why they got involved and what their involvement cost them.

****

1. Moses   2. Elijah   3. Amos   4. Jeremiah

5. Esther   6. Stephen   7.Jan Hus

8. Martin Luther   9. M. L. King, Jr.   10. Nelson Mandela

****

Gaining a Perspective |

Hymns of Courage

Google the lyrics for each of the following well-known Christian hymns. Carefully read through each one, thinking about the meaning of the words. Then summarize the over-all message of the hymn in one or two sentences. It will help if you keep Dietrich Bonheoffer's situation in mind and think about what each hymn would have said to him, particularly during his two-year imprisonment.

- "Soldiers of Christ Arise"

- "Fight the Good Fight With all Your Might"

- "Rise Up, O Men of God!"

- "Who is On the Lord's Side?"

- "Onward! Christian Soldiers"

- Stand Up, Stand Up for Jesus, You Soldiers of the Cross"

- "A Safe Stronghold Our God Is Still"

- "The Son of Man Goes Forth to War, a Kingly Crown to Gain"

- "If You But Suffer God to Guide You"

- "Christian, Do You See Them!?"

What Do *You* Think?

1. Which hymn do you think best expresses the idea that Christians don't put their heads in the sand and ignore what's going on around them, but play an active part in fighting for justice, truth and righteousness? Explain.

2. In your opinion, which hymn least expressed this idea. Why?

3.   Which hymn do you think Dietrich Bonheoffer might have chosen as his favorite? Why?

4.   Which hymn most speaks to you? Why?

Drawing Conclusions |

Isolationalists or Activists?

Too many people have the idea that Christians are people who turn inward and isolate themselves from the world and from real life. They think Christians withdraw into their own little Church 'club' or Christian Fellowship and invest so much of themselves and their time in it that they have little left for other people or other involvements. In their opinion, Christians enjoy and feel comfortable with their own kind and have very few non-Christian friends (unless it's for the purpose of getting them to join their "Christian Club"). They see Christian Churches as being fortresses that wall out the world and provide a 'safe,' unreal haven for those who are weak and find the world a tough place in which to live. They consider Christian monasteries to be institutions filled with people who are trying to escape from the realities and responsibilities of life in society. They feel that Christians are people who have their heads buried in the sand, concentrating on their prayer books and Bibles in safety, while the rest of the world goes by.

This view is reinforced by what they hear some Christians say. Such Christians seem to look at the world and at life as so much evil and suffering and as something that must be temporarily endured while on the way to real life and happiness in a heavenly life in the future. "This world is not my home, I'm just a passin' through." To them 'the world' is something sinful that God is against and that he's eventually going to destroy. So 'the world' is something to keep away from. People who hear Christians talk like this think Christians are so heavenly minded that they're no earthly good.

It's true that some Christians have been and are this way. And at first glance, it would seem that their being this way is all bad. But surprisingly enough, when we look at the Bible, we find some statements that seem to back up this kind of isolationalist view of Christianity. For example, John warns: "Do not love the world or anything that belongs to the world … The world and everything in it that people desire is passing away." 1 John 2:15, 17 James says: "Pure and genuine religion is this: … to keep oneself from being corrupted by the world." James 1:27 Paul writes: "You have died with Christ and are set free … Why, then, do you live as though you belonged to this world?" Colossians 2:20 Even Jesus tells his disciples: "If you belonged to the world, then the world would love you as its own. But I chose you from this world, and you do not belong to it." John 15:19 Furthermore, Jesus asks people to concentrate on building up treasure in Heaven, not on amassing wealth on earth (See Matthew 6:19-20); and Paul asks them to set their hearts on the things that are in heaven and not on things here on earth. (See Colossians 3: 1-2) There are also many statements in the Bible that have a 'hold on' ring to them. You won't have to endure much longer and the life to come will have been worth it all. (See James 5:7-11; 1 Peter 1:3-7, etc) Are Christians, then, *supposed* to be isolationalists; looking at the present as merely a temporary phase on the way to the real thing?

The answer to this question is both "yes" and "no." It's "yes" in the sense that this world isn't all there is to human existence and we shouldn't live as though it was. Christians believe that in a sense, they *are* merely pilgrims 'passing through' to what will be a more complete and fulfilling life than it's possible to experience now. It's also true that sometimes the going here *does* get pretty rough. Dietrich Bonhoeffer certainly experienced that, and millions of other people have experienced (and are experiencing) that as well. Especially in New Testament times, Christians were continually 'under the gun' as it were - hounded by the Romans on the one hand and persecuted by the Jews on the other. When things like that happen to people, it's only natural that they should put additional emphasis on the "hold on, things will be better in the future" strain in the Christian message.

The answer is also "yes" in the sense that Christians and evil don't mix. All in the world or in life that represents evil, or is produced by evil, or that lures people into evil, is what Christians, through Christ's grace and saving power, are trying to leave behind and overcome. Then why should they continue to flirt with it, or associate with it? To do so is only to risk playing with fire all over again, so to speak. People who think they can continually expose themselves to an evil environment without getting polluted by it are only fooling themselves.

However, there's also a "no" answer to the question of whether Christians should be islolationalists that are separated from the world. The answer is "no" if a person mistakes what the Bible is referring to as the 'world of evil' for the world in general. The Bible writers aren't asking Christians to isolate themselves from the world in general, but only from that which has gone *wrong* with that world - that which is evil. God created the world (including people) good! And there's a great deal of good still left in it (and in us) to be enjoyed, participated in and appreciated. In this sense, Christians are to be world-affirming people, not world-denying people. (See Psalm 8; 24:1 & 1 Corinthians 5:10, for example). Unlike some other religions, they're to see the present world and the people in it as being valuable and well-worth celebrating and enjoying.

The answer is also "no" if a person thinks that the blessings or judgment of the future make life in the present meaningless. Jesus came to give us eternal life. However, his emphasis was not on the future, but on the *now*. Eternal life is to know God through him and to begin to experience the fullness of life that God originally intended us all to have. (See John 17:3 and 10:10) This life begins *now* and goes on forever. Although it will continue to become fuller and deeper as time goes on, the very fact that it's begun now gives Christians a whole new perspective on the meaning and purpose of life *today*. And because they have such a perspective, they have a zest for life, no matter what their circumstances might be, that impels them to use every minute of it to the fullest, with thanksgiving. The 'frosting on the cake,' so to speak, is that the future will give that life still further opportunity to expand, to deepen and to be enriched, rather than merely ending things, period. But the 'frosting' of the future should not keep a Christian from enjoying the 'cake' of the present.

The answer is still "no" if a person thinks that isolation from the evil of the world means merely escaping from it and doing nothing about it. Jesus Christ never retreated into permanent isolation. Instead, he plunged into the world as it was and fought evil with all his might! He declared war on evil, fought the main battle against it, and won! He declared that the future Kingdom of God, which people had been longing for and dreaming about for centuries - the Kingdom of peace and light, of truth and justice and righteousness - had invaded the present. "The Kingdom of God is near", declared Jesus over and over again, and it was (and is)! Mark 1:15

Although Jesus won the decisive battle through his death and resurrection, and although the signs of the Kingdom appeared, thus signaling the defeat of the powers of evil and the manifestation of the reign of God over a creation that is now in the process of being renewed, the war against evil is far from over. As we've noted before, there's still a lot of fighting and suffering and even dying to be done. And it's to this battle and to this risk (and perhaps even ultimate sacrifice) that Jesus calls his followers. Dietrich Bonheoffer fought one of the more spectacular battles in this 'mop-up' war. Other Christians may have contributed in less spectacular ways, but all are called on to contribute in *some* way. Nobody's to hide his or her head in the sand, retreat into a Church fortress, escape into isolation, while there's still one person to rescue from the clutches of evil, one issue of injustice to be fought, one oppressor to struggle against, one greedy company to rebuke.

Like Dietrich Bonheoffer, Christians who understand this clearly don't easily become discouraged in this struggle even when the temporary situation looks bleak, or when they are called on to suffer. They know who's going to win the war! They know that they're not giving up their lives in a school-house in Schonberg, or wherever, for a lost cause or an idealistic mirage. They know that the Hussein's, the Gaddafis, the bin Ladens and the ISIS extremists will fall. They know that the injustices of economic colonialism, the exploitation of multi-national corporations, the terror of the arms race and the threat of global warming can be stopped. They know that hunger and crime and drug addiction can be overcome - maybe not tomorrow, but for sure some day.

It's true that there are some Christians who've not understood all of this very well and have withdrawn from the world into their own Christian cocoons. These Christians have felt that their main task was to rescue other people *from* that world rather than to join God in his struggle to rescue the world itself. But there are many Christians who *have* rightly understood it. Christian history is full of the names of thousands of men and women who have steadfastly joined the battle against the forces of evil, many of them, like Bonheoffer, giving their lives in the struggle. Not a moral or ethical issue can be found on which Christians at some time or in some place have not spoken out on and acted on. Christians have been at the forefront in most of the battles against major human evils. They should have and could have done more, but the record is there nevertheless.

Christians, by and large, have been and continue to be activists, not retreatists. This explains why in many countries, particularly in Asia, Christians, although comprising only a tiny fraction of the population, have an influence in society far beyond what their small numbers would indicate.

A word about monasteries, retreats and the like. All activism and no meditation is as imbalanced and unwise an approach for a Christian as all meditation and no activism. We've been a little hard on church fortresses, monasteries, retreats, isolation, and the like. Actually, any Christian activist who's worth his or her salt will tell you that personal and corporate spiritual nurture are *essential* to meaningful Christian action. Christians who are always 'at the front' and who never take time to re-charge their spiritual batteries will soon wear out and be useless to the Christian mission. Worse yet, they'll most likely advocate a misguided course of action and utilize improper means to achieve an end. They'll too often find themselves out in *front* of God in the battle, rather than following him.

To act wisely and to have the necessary stamina to see the battle through, a Christian needs to soak in God's Word, listen for his Spirit's voice, be strengthened by the witness and fellowship of fellow believers and 'get away from it all' on occasion in order to be revived and renewed. Even Jesus felt the need for that. We read that on a number of occasions he took his disciples to deserted places so they could rest for awhile and be refreshed before plunging back into the fray of daily ministry and conflict. Jesus sometimes went off all by himself and spent whole nights in prayer in a lonely place. And before he began his public ministry, he went on a 40 day retreat into the desert where he prepared himself for what was to come. Here's where we can learn something from Christian cell groups, from those who set up monasteries, from Christians who insist that activism must not diminish worship, prayer, Christian fellowship and the like. Nobody realized this more than Dietrich Bonheoffer. His writings reveal how absolutely essential he considered his times of personal meditation and corporate worship and fellowship to be in carrying on his struggle against the Nazis. Being deprived of all but a minimum of corporate Christian life while in prison proved to be one of his greatest trials.

The point, again, is balance. Christians need to retreat to churches and monasteries and small groups of like-minded people, but they must not *stay* there! Once having been fortified, refreshed and renewed, they're called to go back out into the world to serve the wounded, rescue the captives ... and fight the enemies of right, truth, justice and peace.

Not all Christians will be 'front-line troops,' of course. Some will be supportive, as in any army, but equally essential. It would be hard to say, for example, who suffered more or contributed more to the anti-Nazi cause - Bonheoffer, or his parents. They prayed, wrote letters, sent parcels, suffered separation and grieved over his death and the deaths of several of their other children. And, perhaps most important of all, it had been they who had, through their clear Christian witness, prepared their children early in life to be the kind of disciples of Christ who would not falter when the acid tests came. They too were activists, but playing a different role.

All Christians are called on to join the struggle in some way. No Christian can keep his or her head buried in the sand of Church duties, or whatever, and ignore the battle going on around him or her. To do so is to practice diluted Christianity or no Christianity at all! For as Jesus said: "Whoever wants to save his own life will lose it; but whoever loses his life for my sake will find it." Matthew 16:25) Herein lies the challenge and the reward of Christian living. Every follower of Jesus has to ask himself, "Is my head buried in the sand, or am I involved in the struggle?"

What Do *You* Think?

1. Do you think the battle against evil in the world can ultimately be won? Explain.

2. Do you think that, generally speaking, Christians have tended to be more active or less active in the struggle against evil in society than most other people?

3. Do you agree that activism and meditation are equally important for Christians in their struggle against evil? Explain.

4. Do you think that America's Christians are making a significant impact for good on our society as a whole? On the world? Explain.

Chapter Eighteen

WHAT ABOUT SOCIAL ISSUES?

> "So be careful how you live. Don't live like ignorant people. Make good use of every opportunity you have because these are evil days. Don't be fools, then, but try to find out what the Lord wants you to do."
>
> Ephesians 5:15-17

Looking Through the Microscope |

The City Council

The Mayor took his place, and a hush fell over the Council Chamber. He called the meeting to order and explained the agenda for the day. This session would be devoted to questions and commentary, both by City Counselors and representatives of the public, concerning the budget for the coming year as presented by the Treasurer at the previous session. He nodded his permission to the first speaker who wished to have the floor.

"Mr. Mayor and fellow Councilors, I rise today to challenge the Treasurer on the wholly inadequate budget that he has proposed for the Police Department this year. I have in my hand a recent copy of the Evening Post where it's reported that crime and corruption in our fair city is estimated to actually have *increased* over the last year. I also have a clipping quoting a former gang member who is wanted on corruption charges, but who is living in another state, as saying that he would be willing to return and face the charges against him if and when the District Attorney would go after the "big fish." I have another clipping in my hand that describes the prosecution of several of our policemen for accepting bribes while at the same time spelling out how our police are woefully underpaid and therefore tempted to look elsewhere to supplement their meager income. I have still another clipping bemoaning the lack of moral education in our schools, and the general attitude prevailing among young people that corruption is simply an inevitable part of a way of life in our city.

"With information like this staring us in the face, how can we afford to maintain the Police Department's budget at the level it was last year without allowing for inflation, let alone the need for expansion and for raising the salaries of our underpaid policemen. What a demoralizing blow to those who are dedicated to stamping out crime and corruption in our society! It's obvious from reports such as these that the number of staff, the anti-corruption program of the Department and the salaries of our officers need to be *in*creased, not *de*creased! Other budget areas are needy as well, but if we don't effectively deal with this moral cancer in our midst, it will slowly eat out the innards of our society, leaving a facade of external prosperity, but a reality of internal bankruptcy. I urge you to think again about this matter, and to raise the Police Department's budget by at least 25%. Thank you."

The mayor recognized the next speaker, the principal of a large high school.

"Mr. Mayor, and ladies and gentlemen, I left my school early this morning in order to do a little shopping before attending this session. I began by visiting the shops and news stands near my school and made quite a few purchases. I visited more such shops and stands within a few blocks of this chamber and made a few more purchases. Here are the results of my shopping spree."

With this, the principal walked over to a table at the front of the chamber with a shopping bag in each hand and proceeded to dump some thirty magazines onto the table. There was an audible gasp in the chamber, and the mayor's face turned noticeably red. Every one of the magazines had a half-naked woman on the cover, and the Councilors knew that what was on the insides would be even more explicit.

The Principal continued. "I'm convinced that, whatever statute to the contrary, any student from my school who had the money could go on exactly the same shopping spree I did today ... or that any boy or girl from any other school could do so as well. News vendors are simply not going to act like policemen when the money for expensive magazines like these is waved in their faces by anybody of any age. I personally believe that the reading of such so-called 'literature' by *anybody*, no matter how old or mature they might be, is injurious to their person. But I don't want to get into that. What I do want to get into is the sale of such pornography to school children, or even its display where they can't help but notice it and have their curiosity aroused by it. I think all of us here would agree that this needs to be stopped and that the best way to stop it is to crack down on the publishers and importers of such soul-destroying smut. I realize that young people also have access to pornography on the Internet, but that is something their parents need to monitor and that we have no control over. We *can*, however, do something about smut being peddled on the street.

"Further, I could also 'entertain' the Council this morning with a rather embarrassing power point presentation of the movie marquees that have advertised similar smut being shown with increasing frequency in our theaters in plain view of the eyes of everyone from kindergarten to the old folks home. Our movie theaters have become places that are *rarely* 'suitable for children.' Why have we allowed them to become so? What a marvelous media for entertainment and education good films are! And yet, 90 percent of the time, we allow this media to be used to warp and corrupt people's hearts and minds - many of them being young people and even children who, despite statutes to the contrary, can gain entrance to such films merely by waving the money in front of the ticket seller's face. Again, the ticket sellers can't be expected to be policemen. What needs to be done is to halt the import or production of films unsuitable for children, or at the least, to set up a few truly 'adult' theaters to which these films are limited, and utilize the majority of the theaters for the showing of films suitable for general audiences. However, I notice in the Treasurer's budget, that no funds whatsoever have been allocated for the purpose of combating pornography in our city, I urge him to insert such an item so as to enable the City Council to set up a commission for this purpose. Thank you."

As the Principal put the magazines back into her shopping bags, the Mayor nodded to the next speaker.

"Mr. Mayor and fellow citizens, I'm afraid that I don't have any visual aids to buttress my case like those of the previous speaker." (Prolonged laughter) "However, I could well have brought some along - racing forms, casino ads, lottery tickets, the financial report of the State Lottery Commission and the like. A number of years ago, we were told that the way to solve the illegal gambling problem in our city was to establish legal wager venues which would put the bookies out of business. I don't think there's a person in this room who would deny that this has not proved to be the case. In addition, what used to be the vice of a minority has now become some kind of madness for the majority. Lottery ticket shops now outnumber barber shops in our city.

"On the nights when lottery winners are announced, it seems like the whole city momentarily almost stops breathing. The 'take' from lottery ticket sales and casino operations keeps climbing to ever more staggering heights. Meanwhile, the gambling lobby bulldozes over the toughest opposition. For example, last year, people on the north side vociferously opposed the building of a casino in their neighborhood - but it got built there nevertheless. And all of this is done under the facade of providing tax funds for charitable causes, or for the improvement of educational facilities, or for the funding of social welfare programs and other good causes.

"However, one look at the *complete* financial figures belies that conclusion. And one look at studies made around the world reveals that it's the *poor* who buy the majority of the lottery tickets in a given community in a desperate gamble to strike it rich and escape their poverty in one stroke. Therefore, and ironically, it's the poor that end up providing the majority of the funds to help *themselves*!

"What are the younger members of our society learning from all of this? They're beginning to believe the myth that there *is* such a thing as a free lunch. They're beginning to believe that being a gambler is a respectable past-time, or even a fulltime 'occupation' - if you're smart enough and lucky enough. They're beginning to believe that gambling is just like any other game or entertainment - you can quit or go home whenever you want to. They're beginning to believe that fate, not skill determines things in life - and a lot more.

"In light of this, I think we need to launch a serious, hard-headed study on the growth and effects of gambling in our community before things deteriorate any further. And I want to see the Treasurer include funds for such a study in next year's budget. Thank you."

The Mayor recognized a fourth speaker.

"Mr. Mayor, colleagues and friends, I will be brief and to the point. The Treasurer's allocation of funds for drug prevention and rehabilitation are woefully inadequate. Our community has made some progress in this area in recent years, but we're still considered as one of the prime drug centers in the county. This means that we still have a long way to go in order to even come close to winning this fight. We need to beef up the Narcotics Division of the Police Force. We need to increase anti-drugs education, particularly among young people, four-fold. We need to double the number of Methadone clinics that we are operating at present. We need to hire and train a great number more drug rehabilitation social workers than is planned at present. We also need more long-term drug rehabilitation centers than are now envisioned. And most importantly of all, we need to provide more of the kinds of educational opportunities, recreational facilities and social programs that will make drugs, and the lifestyle that goes with them, increasingly unattractive to our young people.

"In short, we've done fairly well in this area, but we need to do much better. Therefore, I request the Treasurer to at least double the allocation for drug control over the figure listed in his proposed budget. We *cannot* get along on half a loaf in this vital area in the life of our community. Thank you."

The Mayor recognized a fifth speaker.

"Mr. Mayor, colleagues and neighbors, I rise today to address another serious need in our community – the need to have more clinics and counseling for women wishing to have abortions, particularly young women. There are many women in the poorer neighborhoods in this city that at present don't have access to medical personnel or facilities to have a safe abortion because they can't afford it. Every woman has a right to make decisions concerning her own body and our community needs to make sure that every woman has the wherewithal to exercise that right. I know that there are those in our community, and indeed on this Council, who oppose abortion of any kind for any reason. They have a right to their opinion, but they do not have a right to intimidate women who want to have an abortion or to block our city from making abortion clinics and personnel available to those who need them. I also recognize that the needs raised by other councilors are legitimate needs and that there are only so many tax dollars in the pot. However, I believe this is an urgent need that we have failed to address so far and that should be addressed. Therefore, I am asking the Treasurer to allocate funds to meet this need. Thank you."

The Mayor looked at his watch. There was time for one more speaker before the Treasurer would be asked to reply. He nodded to a Councilor in the back row.

"Mr. Mayor and fellow Councilors, I'm sure the Treasurer is scratching his head right now wondering where he's going to come up with all the funds that are being requested. My guess is that he'll resist trying to stretch the budget even further than he has recommended and risk incurring a deficit. But before he succumbs to the temptation to politely dismiss the requests that have been made, I should like to make yet one more plea for an increase in funds to be allocated, a plea based on the alarming facts concerning the increase in the spread and use of guns in our city.

"We all know about the increasing use of hand guns in the committing of robberies, muggings and murders. We also know about the alarming increase in accidental deaths and deaths caused by the use of guns in domestic disputes. And we all have become particularly alarmed at the increase in criminal activity among young people.

"How can we put a stop to all of this? No city has yet come up with a simple answer to that tough question. And indeed, there *is* no simple answer. Rather, the answer is complex and involves many factors. One factor has to do with the basic social conditions that breed crime and produce criminals. For example, why are we surprised that there's been such an upsurge in the acquisition and use of firearms by young people when we've practically eliminated any kind of moral education from our school system, or when we've done very little to create a positive program to wean gang members away from gangs and towards a productive lifestyle?

"As long as we tolerate easy access to, and the proliferation of firearms, violence in our city will remain as prevalent as it is at present. We need to pass an ordinance that will require all gun sales to be registered, with those who have criminal records or a history of mental problems being denied ownership. It should also make it a criminal offense to carry a concealed weapon, to use 'cop killer' bullets, to use large ammunition clips or to own a semi-automatic weapon.

"Another factor has to do with our prisons. In my opinion, our prisons would be much more effective in the long run if they would put much more emphasis on the rehabilitation of people placed in their charge. Our record as far as second and third time offenders is concerned needs to be improved. We're not doing enough in the area of training and providing an adequate number of social workers to run a successful parole system, for example.

"I could go on. But let me say in conclusion that I think the funds allocated in this year's budget fall far short of what is needed to bring about much of an improvement in the reduction of violence and crime in our community. Thank you."

What Do *You* Think?

1. If you were the City Treasurer, how would you rank the six issues raised by these speakers as far as meriting an increase in budget funds was concerned? Explain.

2. Which two speakers do you most agree with, and why?

3. Are there any speakers you strongly disagree with? Explain.

4. What additional social issue that concerns you would you want to add to the list? Explain.

Bringing Things Into Focus |

Brainstorming

Think up one or two practical, workable ideas for each issue raised by the above speakers that could be carried out in your community to help it make better progress towards the solution of each of these problems.

❖ The problem of corruption.

❖ The problem of pornography.

❖ The problem of gambling.

❖ The problem of drug abuse.

❖ The problem of abortion.

❖ The problem of violence.

Gaining a Perspective |

What Does the Bible Say?

Here are eleven statements from the Bible having to do with the way Christians should deal with social issues.

• "In conclusion, my brothers, fill your minds with those things that are good and that deserve praise: things that are true, noble, right, pure, lovely, and honorable." Philippians 4:8

• "There was once a man who had two sons. The younger one said to him, 'Father, give me my share of the property now.' So the man divided his property between his two sons. After a few days the younger son sold his part of the property and left home with the money ... he wasted his money in reckless living ... he was left without a thing ... At last he came to his senses ... So he got up and started back to his father. He was still a long way from home when his father saw him; his heart was filled with pity ... the son said, 'I have sinned against God and against you. I am no longer fit to be called your son.' But the father called his servants ... 'Bring the best robe and put it on him ... Then go and get the prize calf and kill it, and let us celebrate with a feast! For this son of mine was dead, but now he is alive; he was lost, but now he has been found ...'" Luke 15:11-24

- "Don't you know that your body is the temple of the Holy Spirit, who lives in you and who was given to you by God? You do not belong to yourselves but to God; He bought you for a price. So use your bodies for God's glory." 1 Corinthians 6:19-20

- "Where do all the fights and quarrels among you come from? They come from your desires for pleasure ... You want things, but you cannot have them, so you are ready to kill ... so you quarrel and fight. You do not have what you want because you do not ask God for it ... you do not receive it, because your motives are bad ... Whoever wants to be the world's friend makes himself God's enemy ... The spirit that God placed in us is filled with fierce desires. But the grace that God gives is even stronger ... God resists the proud, but gives grace to the humble. So then, submit to God. Resist the Devil, and he will run away from you. Come near to God, and he will come near to you ... Wash your hands, you sinners! ... Humble yourselves before the Lord, and he will lift you up." James 4:1-10

- "So get rid of your old self, which made you live as you used to - the old self that was being destroyed by its deceitful desires. Your hearts and minds must be made completely new, and you must put on the new self, which is created in God's likeness and reveals itself in the true life that is upright and holy ... The man who used to rob must stop robbing and start working, in order to earn an honest living for himself and to be able to help the poor." Ephesians 4:22-24, 28

- "Whoever loves money never has money enough; whoever loves wealth is never satisfied with his income." Ecclesiastes 5:10

- "Since you are God's people, it is not right that any matters of sexual immorality or indecency or greed should even be mentioned among you. Nor is it fitting for you to use language which is obscene, profane, or vulgar ... no one who is immoral, indecent, or greedy (for greed is a form of idolatry) will ever receive a share in the Kingdom of Christ and of God. Do not let anyone deceive you with foolish words; it is because of these very things that God's anger will come upon those who do not obey Him. So have nothing at all to do with such people. You yourselves used to be in the darkness, but since you have become the Lord's people, you are in the light ... Try to learn what pleases the Lord. Have nothing to do with the worthless things that people do, things that belong to the darkness. Instead, bring them out to the light." Ephesians 5: 3-11

- "Religion does make a person very rich, if he is satisfied with what he has. What did we bring into the world? Nothing! What can we take out of the world? Nothing! So then, if we have food and clothes, that should be enough for us. But those who want to get rich fall into temptation and are caught in the trap of many foolish and harmful desires, which pull them down to ruin and destruction. For the love of money is a source of all kinds of evil. Some have been so eager to have it that they have wandered away from the faith and have broken their hearts with many sorrows. But you, man of God, avoid all these things. Strive for righteousness, godliness, faith, love, endurance, and gentleness. Run your best in the race of faith, and with eternal life for yourself; for it was to this life that God called you when you firmly professed your faith before many witnesses." 1 Timothy 6:6-12

- "Do not deceive yourselves; no one makes a fool of God. A person will reap exactly what he sows. If he sows in the field of his natural desires, from it he will gather the harvest of death; if he sows in the field of the Spirit, from the Spirit he will gather the harvest of eternal life. So let us not become tired of doing good; for if we do not give up, the time will come when we will reap the harvest. So then, as often as we have the chance, we should do good to everyone, and especially to those who belong to our family in the faith." Galatians 6:7-10

- "Do not accept a bribe, for a bribe blinds those who see and twists the words of the righteous." Exodus 23:8

- "You created every part of me; you put me together in my mother's womb. I praise you because you are to be feared; all you do is strange and wonderful. I know it with all my heart. When my bones were being formed, carefully put together in my mother's womb, when I was growing there in secret, you knew that I was there - you saw me before I was born." Psalm 139:13-15.

What Do *You* Think?

1. Can you identify which statement(s) refer to which of the six social issues mentioned above?

2. What do you think each of these statements contributes to the solution of the particular issue(s) addressed? Explain.

3. Which statement do you think is the most helpful in formulating a Christian position on a given social issue, and why?

4. Which statement do you think is the least helpful in formulating a Christian position on a given social issue, and why?

Drawing Conclusions |

Problems or Solutions?

If Christians are called upon to be actively involved in working for the common good, it will come as no surprise that they'll be very involved in working for solutions to social problems as well. How would Christians view the social problems mentioned by the speakers at the City Council meeting, and how would they go about trying to help to solve them?

Corruption

Christians view corruption as a base form of dishonesty. Thievery is bad enough, but at least it's fairly straightforward. Corruption, however, is often practiced by seemingly 'respectable' people who, although they're stealing, try to make it appear as though they're not. A 'gentlemen's agreement' is made in which a 'responsible' official looks the other way, for example, while a contractor puts only 75% of the cement in the mix demanded by the building specifications, thus ensuring the construction of a building that will eventually endanger the lives of those living and working in it. The official and the contractor are supposedly 'respected businesspeople,' but in reality, they are the worst kind of thieves who are betraying the community in which they live.

Corruption is a serious problem in many communities. "Everybody does it, so why shouldn't I?" seems to be the attitude of too many people. Yet it's evident that 'everybody' does *not* practice corruption. There are, in fact, a great majority of people in our communities who are very honest and who have a real desire to see corruption stamped out among the minority of the people who practice it. Christians feel that the problem of corruption will not be solved by simply trying to catch people after they've offered or received bribes. They think the problem must be attacked at the root in terms of teaching children and young people about subtle temptations to take a shortcut to 'success' or to get out of difficulty by means of corruption, and introducing them to the moral and spiritual resources available to resist.

People often unthinkingly create an environment in which corruption can be spawned and spread. Children who are bribed by their parents to do this or to refrain from doing that are being subtly trained to accept bribery as a way of life. Teachers who offer prizes and incentives to students to do what they should be doing as a matter of course are doing the same. For example, the practice of trying to influence a school official to admit a relative or an acquaintance as a student, or an employer to hire an employee on the basis of "*who* you know, not *what* you know" is a further example of this. People who've been reared in this kind of environment won't find it too difficult to take the step from this subtle corruption to the gross corruption of attempting to pay a police officer to avoid a ticket, paying a building inspector to overlook structural defects, and the like.

Christians believe that corruption in a community is like a cancer that continues to grow until the community is destroyed by it. It must be vigorously combated at every level, or a fatal moral rot will set in that will eventually lead to ruin. The way to combat corruption is not only for every citizen to disavow corruption in any form or shape at any level, but to be willing to work with others to make it more and more difficult for anyone in the community to practice it.

Being against corruption is not a uniquely Christian virtue, but it can be said that conscientious Christians will be in the forefront in the fight against it. The Bible is very clear about the soul-destroying and community-destroying effects of corruption (See Proverbs 15:34). It also clearly calls on the followers of Christ to be totally honest in their dealings with others and to be a light of honesty in their community (See Philippians 2:14-15). Jesus promises strength to his followers to resist taking the moral 'short-cut' of corruption (See Luke 19:8).

Pornography

Christians believe that another moral cancer that strikes at the 'vital organs' of a community is pornography. As with every other beautiful thing that God has made, Christians are confident that there's nothing wrong in itself with the sexual drive in human beings. Love making between husband and wife is a deeply meaningful and beautiful experience. However, there are those who would take this beautiful act and drag it down into the dirt of lust and debauchery. It would be bad enough if this attitude and behavior went on in private between individuals behind closed doors. But the warped sexual obsessions, fantasies and acts of those who pervert sex have now become a public wave of moral pollution that has swept over our communities and affected us all. It has almost become impossible to walk down our streets, read our newspapers and magazines, watch programs on our television sets and films in our theaters, or work on our computers without being confronted by lewd women, weird sexual acts, sex for sale, obscene T-shirts, dirty jokes, 'sexy' ads and all the rest.

Pornography is something that everyone has had to learn to live with because of the perverted desires of a minority. Like the body adjusting to polluted air, people have had to adjust their minds and lives in order to cope with this moral poison. This 'adjustment' can be deadly. What was shocking before tends to become less shocking now and ends up being accepted as part of the norm in the future, unless one is very careful and very strong. To develop an effective resistance to this moral rot is not easy, particularly for young people who are trying to work out what their sexuality means. When the moral standards of a community decline, it's difficult to swim against the tide.

Christians are called on by God to keep their minds and their lives pure and clean. They're asked to look at their own sexuality and the sexuality of others as gifts to be treasured, not exploited. They're asked to share their sexual selves with another person only within the self-giving commitment of a marriage relationship between a man and a woman. By so doing, they show that they've understood the reason why God gave them their sexual drive and that they value and treasure it as highly as he does. Further, they're asked to shun the misuse, exploitation and perversion of sex by others and not to be contaminated by it. This isn't easy to do in our day and age. However, it wasn't easy to do in the day and age in which the Bible was written either. Sexual immorality is not a 20th century invention. It's been present in gross forms in the societies in which the people of God have had to live and work throughout history. If Christians were able to resist and overcome their morally polluted environment then,

Christians can do so now. If we were to ask a Christian pastor for some ideas on how to deal with pornography in 20th century America, s/he might say something like this.

- "Concentrate on filling your mind, heart and life with that which is good, true, noble and pure. People who lead an active, full life in pursuit of these goals are much more likely to resist pornographic pollution than those who are bored, uninvolved and lethargic.

- "Open your life to receive the strength that Christ can give to resist moral pollution and to develop your sexuality in a healthy, meaningful way. This is essentially a spiritual battle. Those who think they can win it through their own strength alone place themselves in a dangerous position to begin with.

- "Stay away from situations that will make resistance all the more difficult. People who play with matches get their fingers burned. You can't avoid *some* contact with pornographic pollution no matter where you live, but you can resist buying warped literature, viewing obscene material on the Internet, on television or at the theater, getting yourself into compromising sexual situations, and the like.

- "Don't look twice! You can't avoid being exposed to sexual rot at some time or another. That's natural. The danger comes when you allow yourself to stop and examine magazines on a stand that you could have passed by after one glance; or when you see an alluring ad on the Net and Google a site that leads you into a pornographic cul-de-sac, or when you allow yourself to go into a theater to see a film that one glance at the billings in the lobby clearly shows is aimed at arousing people's lust. (See James 1:14-15).

- "Obtain your information about dating, love, marriage, sex, the birth process, changes in your body, same sex attraction, etc from well-informed, trustworthy, honorable people. It's natural and good to be curious and concerned about sex. Problems develop, however, when people are afraid or embarrassed to ask those who can offer real help, understanding and accurate information from a Christian perspective, and instead turn to warped sources of information and become influenced by them.

- "Join the public fight to reduce pornographic pollution in your community. Why should we allow our society to be corrupted when other communities and societies have resisted it? A lot more can be done to reverse this growing menace than people think if like-minded, dedicated people join together and apply pressure in the right places."

Gambling

There's a poster that shows a line of fish in the water with the one in front being the smallest and the one at the back of the line being the biggest. The second fish in line is so intent on swallowing the first fish that it's not aware of the fact that it's about to be swallowed by the bigger fish behind it! The same is true of the third and the fourth fish and so on down the line. The caption on the poster reads: "THERE'S NO SUCH THING AS A FREE LUNCH!"

It's surprising how many people don't believe that. Thousands buy Lottery tickets hoping to get rich quick in one big lucky stroke. Never mind that the odds of successfully winning the jackpot are more than one in 175.2 million, or that the majority of the people buying the tickets can't really afford to do so. The belief that there *is* a free lunch is so strong that it overcomes all logic and common sense. Studies that show that the majority of people who are 'lucky' enough to hit the jackpot end up with their lives being ruined are ignored.

Then there are the thousands of punters who pin their hopes on the horses by either going to a racetrack in person or by placing their bets through a bookie. Some people win some of the time, but the huge profits and cold facts of the odds testify to the fact that most people lose most of the time.

Millions also frequent the now practically ubiquitous gambling casinos. Lured there by low cost food, free transportation and other incentives, people risk their hard-earned cash to strike it lucky. Most of them most of the time simply strike out. They sit in front of slot machines by the hour, pulling levers and looking bored out of their minds, thinking that *this* time they'll hit the big one – or at least win enough to get back what they've already lost.

Even more people play Poker or other gambling games on the Internet. They do so from the comfort and privacy of their own homes. What's the harm of having a little entertainment for the evening? None, except that most people who play on-line Poker end up losing their shirts.

The rationale for the endemic spread of legal gambling in our society is that it will reduce illegal gambling and crime syndicates and raise tax money for educational, charitable and other community services. The facts are that illegal gambling continues to exist and that the monies raised for public causes simply mean a reduction in the amount that would otherwise be raised through taxation. In addition, the social costs of the disasters incurred by people who gamble, but can't really afford to do so, are reflected in the rising social welfare costs for them, and particularly for their families.

The most unsettling fact is, however, that in a comparatively short period of time, gambling has become 'respectable' in our society and has become an all-consuming pastime for an increasing number of people.

Christians believe that gambling not only produces more losers than winners, but that it also eats away at the moral fiber of one's personality. There truly *is* no such thing as a free lunch. Even most of the 'winners' sooner or later become losers in one way or another. For some, the past-time turns into a habit that turns into a passion that becomes an addiction. Eventually even the family's security is risked for the 'big win' that never comes. Or even if it does come, the proceeds merely feed the gambling passion further. For others, it doesn't come to such a serious point, but the fact remains that most of the people who gamble can't afford to do so. They and their families suffer to some extent from such a drain on their income.

Jesus made it very clear that a person who combines faith and work will have his needs met by God without throwing his future into the hands of fate (See Matthew 6). He also made it clear that his followers are to be good stewards of the resources that God makes available to them. They're not to waste them or throw them away in reckless living. The emphasis for his followers is on positive, life-building activities, not negative ones like gambling which have the potential of leading people to ruin.

Drug Abuse

Christians celebrate the fact that modern medical research has produced a vast array of drugs and medicines that have great potential to aid healing. However, as with any good thing, the wrong drugs in the hands of the wrong people become habit-forming, life-destroying tools. The hard facts of logic and experience demonstrate that drug abuse at *any* level is harmful to the body and destructive in terms of one's inner being. Yet a growing number of young people in particular continue to defy such logic and experience, and experiment with drugs. Even over the counter drugs are now being abused by an increasing number of people to the point where our society is facing an opiate epidemic. Add to this the increasing legalization of marijuana for recreational use that has exploded into a major industry despite being marketed at four times the strength than it used to be, that is proven to have detrimental effects (especially in people under 30 years of age) and that lacks sufficient research to determine just how severe its detrimental effects are on people in general.

Why do people do drugs?

- **To conform to the pressure of their peers.** People with problems such as low self-esteem find it very difficult to have the kind of confidence that enables them to be their own person. It's hard for them to stand up to the crowd when the chips are down and the pressure is on, even when they know that what they're being asked to do is against their own best interests.

- **To experience a 'high.'** People hear rumors of how 'good' people feel after taking drugs. They become curious and experiment to see if the rumors are really true. Curiosity often leads to the development of a habit which can lead to addiction. They ignore warnings that the 'highs' impair their ability to function normally and that the 'highs' are invariably followed by 'lows.'

• **To experience the excitement of doing something that's risky and mysterious.** Young people in particular are susceptible to the game of 'brinkmanship' – seeing how close you can get to the edge of disaster without falling over the cliff. The problem is that, in the case of drugs, too many of those who take them for the "thrill" *do* end up falling off the cliff of addiction.

• **To escape from loneliness, boredom or other personal problems and difficult situations.** The impression is often given that it's the 'swingers' (the people who seem to have the world by the tail) who take drugs. Drug abusers often put on a brave, bold front to the outside world. However, a deeper look beneath the surface almost invariably reveals a person who is lonely, fearful, bored, unhappy, unable to successfully relate to well-adjusted people, and the like. Drugs are often a smokescreen to cover up a person's inability to cope with his or her inner problems.

• **To avoid the pain of change.** Once started down the road of drug abuse (like smoking abuse and alcohol abuse), it's difficult to turn back. The more one uses drugs, the more one needs them. It's a vicious cycle. Physical drug withdrawal is difficult enough, but digging into the reasons *why* one is taking drugs and trying to sort out and overcome one's internal problems is emotionally draining and painful.

Jesus Christ not only asks his followers to leave such life-destroying things as drugs completely alone (See 1 Corinthians 6:19-20), but also offers them the strength to resist the temptation of drug abuse. (See 1 Corinthians 10:13). This is good news for those who find themselves hooked on this draining habit. Jesus demonstrated during his ministry that if a person is open to his help, he can enable him or her to break out of the most severe soul-destroying habits or conditions (See Mark 5:2-5, 15). The Christian word 'conversion' is not simply some fancy theological theory; it's a reality that can happen, and *does* happen, in the lives of some of the most hardened drug addicts.

Abortion

There are three basic views on the subject of abortion in the United States:

1. Abortion should be totally outlawed as the murder of innocent human beings,

2. Abortion should only be allowed if the mother's life is in danger, if the fetus has an irreparable physical defect or condition or if the pregnancy was the consequence of rape.

3. Abortion should be available on demand with a woman having the 'right' to control what happens to her own body.

Christians can be found in each of these three camps since there's no direct teaching regarding this issue in the Bible. However, although there is no direct prohibition of the practice in Scripture, many Christians believe that a case can be made against abortion by inference, at least to the point where an abortion, if allowed at all, should only be performed in a case of extreme necessity.

The United States has some of the most liberal abortion laws in the world. The 1973 *Roe v Wade* decision by the Supreme Court was a landmark decision that legalized abortion. The decision declared that a woman has a 'fundamental right' to have unrestricted access to an abortion in the early weeks of pregnancy and the restricted ability to abort in later weeks. However, some Supreme Court Justices have subsequently stated that the 1973 Supreme Court went beyond its authority because the Constitution contains no guarantees as to privacy, and abortion is therefore an issue for legislators, not judges.

A number of States were uncomfortable with the *Roe v Wade* decision and passed laws to require women seeking an abortion to pass through several steps. This can include having a pre-termination ultrasound or attending a counseling session.

The 14th Amendment of the US Constitution states that no one should be 'deprived of life' without recourse to the due process of the law. Contrary to the *Roe v* Wade declaration that a fetus does not become a person until the moment of birth, many Christians believe that a new life comes into being at conception - a being with a unique genetic code and the unlimited potential to live a full and productive life. Aborting a fetus that is unable to defend itself deprives it of life and the ability to enjoy its future liberty and the pursuit of happiness. The *Roe v Wade* decision can lead to bizarre situations where doctors in one operating room of a hospital are attempting to save the life of a premature baby while doctors in an adjoining operating room are performing an abortion on a healthy fetus of the same age.

Unborn babies are protected from murder and violence by Federal Act #38 entitled 'Unborn Victims of Violence.' The act paradoxically considers an unborn baby to be a human being and imposes penalties on those who inflict harm on a fetus - except in the case of an abortion! Thirty eight states also have separate fetal homicide laws, 23 of which protect the fetus from the very earliest stages of pregnancy, regardless of viability outside the womb. These laws make it clear that most people find the killing of a fetus to be repugnant and its life worthy of protection. These same laws, however, permit a mother, who should be protecting the fetus and putting its interests above anyone else's, to have an abortion. The father of an unborn baby is considered a victim when a fetus is killed by a third party, but has no rights at all to prevent or argue against the mother of his child having an abortion.

At present, some 21% of all viable pregnancies end in abortion and half of all the women arranging an abortion have had at least one abortion in the past. In 2010 over 8 percent of all women having an abortion had had three or more in the past. A full range of contraceptives are available to both men and women together with training to ensure that they are used effectively. Of course, they fail when used incorrectly. Consequently, the statistics for multiple abortions suggest that even though half of all US pregnancies are accidental, some women prefer to take the risk of pregnancy as over against using birth control effectively, many probably because they can't afford to buy contraceptives. For the year following the *Roe v Wade* decision, the number of conceptions was shown to have risen by approximately 30 percent, but the number of live births fell by 6 percent demonstrating that abortion was being used by some as an insurance policy.

Just a century ago, a eugenics movement legitimized the condemnation of mixed race marriages and called on society to 'weed out' those who were less than perfect. Several schools of thought suggested that undesirable traits (such as a tendency towards criminality) could be bred out of the human race. The poor were seen as particular targets for eugenics and 'undesirables' were sterilized by force. Now, of course, discrimination on the grounds of race and sex is illegal and full rights and protections are also afforded to those with disabilities. Legislation prevents any person, from the moment of birth, from being discriminated against, but these protections don't extend to unborn children. (The specter of eugenics is again raising its head in the form of a movement to promote 'designer babies' by genetic engineering that would determine a fetus' characteristics by altering its genetic structure while in its mother's womb. It must be asked, if permitted, might this kind of human interference eventually lead to another attempt at the creation of a Nazi-like 'master race?')

The practice of eugenics may be condemned, but one has to ask if this practice is not being enabled through the back door when we allow selective termination to take place. Pregnant women are now given access to a range of screening tests designed to monitor their health and the health of their babies. These tests can identify the baby's sex which, in some cases, prompts a woman to terminate a pregnancy.

We live in a 'throw away anything (and by implication anyone) that is an inconvenience' society. This mindset has spilled over into disposing of the unborn simply because they might be an inconvenience or added expense to a single mother, a working mother, a young couple who want to remain 'unfettered' or an unwed mother. Abortion has become such a big business in America (one in four pregnancies in the US is terminated) that abortion providers do all they can to limit restrictions on access or any pre-abortion counseling and ultrasounds. Providers are often instructed to do all they can to persuade women who have visited a clinic to abort even if they have doubts. Fetuses that survive the abortion process are thrown out with clinical waste and left to die even though they should have all the protections already described.

Studies show that women who have an abortion have to live with this knowledge (which may come back to haunt them strongly on the anniversaries of the abortion and the expected birth date) and therefore suffer an increased risk of depression. This effect can last at least five years after the abortion takes place. Women who have had an abortion are also at greater risk of suicide in the years following the event (154 percent more likely than women who give birth to their babies). However, it's not just women who experience psychological problems following an abortion; the termination can have a negative effect on their spouse or partner as well. Abortions can also result in physical damage. Research shows that women who have had abortions have an increased likelihood of miscarriage and placenta previa in any subsequent pregnancies. Abortions are also shown to increase the risk of breast cancer.

Many families today struggle with the trauma and misery of infertility. They would do almost anything to have a baby and would love to be able to adopt an unwanted baby. As of 2002, there were approximately 2.6 million women (or 14 percent of American women) waiting to adopt children, while just over one percent managed to complete one. Prior to 1973, 9 percent of all babies born in the US were put up for adoption and given to happy and supportive homes. After the decision in *Roe v Wade,* this number dropped dramatically to one percent. These statistics demonstrate that there would be many homes available for babies carried to term, giving them an opportunity to enjoy life, liberty and the pursuit of happiness.

When one looks at the new 4d scans of very young fetuses, one can observe that at 12 weeks they are, if small, fully formed human beings with eyes, fingers, toes, heart and a nervous system. By eight weeks, a fetus can flex its spine, an indication that enough of a nervous system exists to enable it to feel pain. While the majority of abortions that take place are either medical (induced through drugs) or simple vacuum extractions, abortions at a later stage of pregnancy, called 'partial birth abortions,' are more difficult. In this procedure, physicians deliver the body of a fetus up to its head, then kill it by piercing its head inside the womb and then finally extract the entire fetus. (If the baby's head is delivered and the procedure subsequently carried out, it would be considered a murder). This procedure was banned by Congress in 2003 and the constitutionality of the ban was upheld by the Supreme Court in 2007. As a result, many providers now stop the baby's heart with a lethal injection prior to dismembering the fetus in utero. This does not, however, detract from the fact that the fetus is alive and capable of life just seconds before the injection takes effect.

Of course there are certain circumstances where difficult and heartbreaking decisions have to be made (such as a diagnosis of Edward's Syndrome), about subjecting a fetus, if left to term, with a post-birth existence of suffering and pain. Many parents who receive the news that their babies are already suffering from such conditions make the difficult decision to terminate their pregnancy, and they should certainly not be criticized for the hard decision they have had to make. However, care has to be taken with these tests. They are not always accurate and if used by untrained or unregulated personnel can give false results which result in a distraught parent arranging for an abortion of a healthy fetus. One of the conditions regularly screened for is Down Syndrome. While this chromosomal disability can exhibit a wide range of symptoms and effects, many babies born with Down Syndrome are able, with support, to go on and lead a happy and productive life with their families, with some of them even able to attend a main stream school, hold down a job and live independently.

Another difficult decision has to be made about babies being born prematurely. Doctors continue to develop techniques for delivering 'premies' who are in difficulty earlier and earlier, but too often the results of these early induced deliveries result in babies that in the end are not viable. Some 'premies' eventually prove to be viable, but too many don't. A baby might live for a month or even a few years, but the surgeries and treatments (and resultant suffering) that the infant must undergo call this kind of intervention into question. These babies are at high risk for one or more medical complications. Most babies born after about 26 weeks' gestation do survive to one year (about 80 percent of those born at 26 weeks and about 90 percent of those born at 27 weeks), although they may face an extended stay in the neonatal intensive care unit (NICU). Unfortunately, about 25 percent of these very premature babies develop serious lasting disabilities, and up to half may have milder problems, such as learning and behavioral problems. Again, faced with this kind of situation, parents must make agonizing decisions as to whether to attempt to induce a risky premature birth or to undergo an abortion.

Victims of rape also have to make a gut wrenching decision about whether or not to give birth to a child they did not willingly conceive. Again, in such cases, women should not be made to feel guilty for deciding to terminate a tragic pregnancy. The same is true for mothers whose physical or psychological health would be put at risk if a pregnancy were to continue, particularly if she is responsible for the care of other children. At such times, when faced with what we might call a 'tragic moral choice,' we can be sure, as the Psalmist puts it, that "As a father is kind to his children, so the LORD is kind to those who honor him. He knows what we are made of; he remembers that we are dust." Psalm 103:13

Taking into account these tragic circumstances, in a society where we have easy access to contraceptives which if used properly, or in combination, would prevent an unwanted pregnancy, there is simply no excuse for 'abortion on demand,' particularly not of one in four viable pregnancies. However, we live in a society where the 'right' of a woman to 'choose' is seen as being more important than those of the baby she is carrying, the wishes of the baby's father and the wishes of potential parents and grandparents who could love and nurture it. Doctors who perform an abortion take a living human being, capable of breathing, capable of crying and nursing and cut its life short before it has the opportunity to realize its potential. The mother who is supposed to love it more than anyone else in the world and who is supposed to protect it is complicit in its pain, suffering and death. For these reasons, many Christians believe that the policy of 'abortion on demand' should be discarded and all other abortions made illegal except in the extreme circumstances already cited. The sanctity of all lives is a cardinal principle that runs throughout the scriptures. *All* human beings, including those in miniature, are made "in the image of God" and are never to be simply snuffed out, let alone discarded.

Euthanasia

End of life decisions are often as difficult, or even more difficult, than beginning of life decisions. Christians strongly believe in the sanctity of life. All human beings are created in the image of God, and no person should end her or his life, or have her or his life ended, prematurely. But in today's world of medical wonders, end of life matters are not so simple. On the one hand, people can be medically terminated or allowed to die (a process that's known as 'euthanasia'), while on the other hand, people can be prevented from dying a normal death through aggressive medical intervention. The subject gets even more complicated when we consider that there are three types of euthanasia.

- **Voluntary euthanasia** - euthanasia conducted with the consent of the patient. Voluntary euthanasia is legal in Belgium, Luxembourg and the Netherlands. (When the patient brings about his or her own death with the assistance of a physician, the term 'assisted suicide' is often used instead. Assisted suicide is legal in Switzerland and in the states of California, Oregon, Washington, Montana and Vermont.)

- **Non-voluntary euthanasia** - euthanasia conducted when the consent of the patient is unattainable. Examples include patients that are comatose or those that have no medical directive. This form of euthanasia is illegal in all countries

- **Involuntary euthanasia** - euthanasia conducted against the will of the patient (as practiced in Nazi Germany, for example). This form of euthanasia is also illegal in all countries.

These three categories of euthanasia can be divided into two approaches:

- **Passive euthanasia** - the withholding of common treatments, such as antibiotics or food and water that are necessary for the continuance of life. Passive euthanasia is legal throughout the U.S.

- **Active euthanasia** - taking deliberate steps to end a patient's life by the use of lethal substances or forces (such as administering a lethal injection) to kill a patient. Active euthanasia is illegal throughout the U.S.

Christians oppose non-voluntary, involuntary and active euthanasia, but differ about voluntary and passive euthanasia. Some Christians feel that to 'interfere with God' and bring about death or refrain from doing everything to keep a person alive as long as possible amounts to murder. No matter if a person is pronounced terminally ill or how much the person is suffering and has lost the will to live, the person needs to die a 'natural' death at the time that God has determined it. On the one hand, only drugs that will keep a person comfortable without the possibility that they might hasten death should be administered. On the other hand, aggressive measures should be undertaken, feeding tubes inserted and respirators attached to keep people alive as long as possible.

Most Christians support some form of voluntary and passive euthanasia (although they might be uncomfortable using that term because of the other illegal approaches that are under that same umbrella). They support the efforts of hospice ministries that have sprung up across the country whose goal is to alleviate pain and suffering through palliative care and to help people die with dignity. These Christians see a big difference between doing everything possible to help keep a viable person alive and restore him or her to health and keeping a terminally ill person from dying by using what amounts to artificial means. They regard such 'intervention' as being much more of an interference with 'God's will' than extending a person's pain and suffering by the use of aggressive measures. This is especially true in the case of the elderly. Unfortunately, the advances made in modern medicine to heal are too often, towards the end of life, used to prolong life and prevent death.

Studies show that one out of every four Medicare dollars (more than $125 billion) is spent on services for the five percent of beneficiaries in their last year of life. Yet even with Medicare or private insurance, out-of-pocket expenses for Medicare recipients during the five years before their death average about $39,000 for individuals, $51,000 for couples and up to $66,000 for people with long-term illnesses like Alzheimer's. In a recent survey, to their dismay, more than 40 percent of the households affected found that their bills exceeded their *entire* assets.

If spending that much money would help to ensure that the elderly get the best care at the end of life, many Christians would probably think the price was worth it. Yet that's often not the case. With the process frequently driven by the medical system's focus on performing aggressive interventions at any cost (and, incidentally reaping large profits in the process), and the reluctance of families to talk about death, many people who are dying don't get the kind of care they want. Worse, they often suffer through unnecessary, even harmful treatments. When patients have a terminal illness, at some point more treatment doesn't equal better care.

For example, ending up in the hospital often means aggressive, high-cost treatment at the expense of quality of life. A study of elderly cancer patients nearing death found that nine percent had a breathing tube or other life-prolonging procedure in the last month, and at most academic medical centers, more than 40 percent of the patients saw ten or more doctors in the last six months of their lives! If hospitals have the resources, they're always used. Also, lacking a clear understanding of the medical prognosis, families may be overly optimistic about the likely success of aggressive, often costly interventions.

Another recent study found that nearly 70 percent of patients with advanced lung cancer and 81 percent of those with late-stage colon cancer didn't understand that chemotherapy was unlikely to cure them. The same is true for many common supposedly lifesaving treatments. Only 17 percent of patients who receive cardiac pulmonary resuscitation (CPR) recover enough to leave the hospital, and that number drops to only 6 percent of cancer patients. CPR can also cause blunt-force trauma, especially for elderly patients. Feeding tubes can lead to infections while doing little to prolong life in the elderly. And a breathing tube may extend life but detract from its quality. Many patients must be restrained or sedated to avoid pulling out these supports.

Most Christians feel that the compassion that Jesus showed for the sick and suffering is best expressed through enabling people to die with a minimal amount of suffering and a maximal amount of dignity. Life should not be degraded by preventing people from dying through the use of aggressive, artificial and expensive means that bring more heartache than help to both individuals and their families.

Crime and Violence

Most people say that crime doesn't pay, yet many people keep committing crimes. Nobody wants anybody to steal anything from *them*, yet some still keep stealing things from *others* either physically or electronically. Everybody would like to be treated decently, yet some still commit violence against others. Nobody would want somebody to sell drugs to their child, yet some still try to sell them to the children of others. Why do some people keep committing crimes against other people?

• **Because they're desperate.** If they don't steal, they'll starve. If they don't murder, they'll be found out. If they don't sell drugs, they'll be beaten up by a gang and maybe even killed.

• **Because they've never had a fair opportunity in life to develop as a person.** For one reason or another, they've been cheated out of the chance to live a decent life with dignity, and so they turn to crime as an alternate lifestyle.

• **Because the society in which some people live has oppressed and exploited them.** They feel trapped by social systems, political power, economic forces, and the like that are all aimed at keeping them down for the benefit of those at the top. So they rebel. They counter this kind of violence with a violence of their own. They feel, for example, that if society 'steals' from them through sophisticated systems, they're justified in stealing from others too.

• **Because every one of us is a potential criminal.** "*All* have sinned," says Paul, and fallen short of what God made us capable of becoming. (See Romans 3:23). Those who aren't concerned about this potential for evil end up doing evil things, sometimes for reasons they themselves can't explain. Others recognize their need for repentance, forgiveness, renewal and a new way of life and by God's grace overcome this tendency to only love themselves and harm their neighbors.

- **Because some people overlook the basic principle that small things lead to big things.** For example, the first time a child steals money from its mother's purse its conscience will loudly complain. If it ignores it, the next time it steals it'll be that much 'easier.' Unless it checks itself in time, the frequency of its thefts will increase, as well as the amounts it steals. The lies to cover up the thefts will grow bigger, and so on. Before it knows it, the child will have become a teenager stealing at school and shoplifting from stores. Then it will be on to 'bigger things.'

- **Because a massive amount of guns have become easily available to those intending to harm others and to those who think they need a gun to protect themselves from others.** Under the guise of an ill-conceived redefinition of the 2nd Amendment by the US Supreme Court in 2008, a flood of firearms have been sold to the American public for good or for ill. Organizations like the National Rifle Association (NRA) have spread myths and distorted statistics to resist an adequate gun registration system, to promote the use of semi-automatic weapons, 'cop killer' bullets and large ammunition clips and to sanction gun shows where people can buy a variety of deadly weapons with no background check whatsoever. Most Christians would support the opposite.

Retribution or Rehabilitation?

A difficult question facing any community is what to do with or to those who bring harm to others and to the community. Some favor retribution. People who do wrong should be made to pay for what they've done. The range of paybacks runs from fining to imprisonment to execution.

Other people favor a rehabilitative approach. Their emphasis is on providing counseling, developing skills, promoting spiritual renewal and encouraging restitution (as far as is possible) - often in the context of a prison environment that's conducive to such aims. The effectiveness of this approach, of course, depends a great deal on the attitude of the prisoner and on a clear distinction in law between what can be called personal sins for which a person is accountable to God on the one hand, and social crimes for which a person is accountable to both God and the community on the other.

Jesus and the writers of the New Testament consistently encourage Christians to make an effort to rehabilitate offenders in mercy and love - the same kind of mercy and love that God shows to us when we offend him. (See Galatians 6:1) The word 'revenge' doesn't belong in a Christian's 'dictionary.' (See Romans 12:17-20). However, they also make it clear that the words 'revenge' and 'retribution' do not mean the same thing. The former has to do with paying somebody back, while the latter has to do with just punishment. Jesus and the New Testament writers don't simply exonerate those who harm society, even if they are repentant for doing so. While the goal is rehabilitation, at the same time just punishments that fit the crime are to be meted out to offenders.

There are always consequences for wrong doing which must be borne by those who commit crimes. For example, in his letter to the Romans, Paul writes, "Would you like to be unafraid of those in authority? Then do what is good, and they will praise you, because they are God's servants working for your own good. But if you do evil, then be afraid of them, because their power to punish is real. They are God's servants and carry out God's punishment on those who do evil. For this reason you must obey the authorities - not just because of God's punishment, but also as a matter of conscience." Romans 13:3b-5 The *New Revised Standard Version* more graphically translates verse 4b to read, "But if you do what is wrong, you should be afraid, for the authority does not bear the sword in vain! It is the servant of God to execute wrath on the wrongdoer." In other words, Paul is saying that the governing authorities even have the power and the responsibility to administer a death sentence to those it justly deems to have committed a crime worthy of that sentence.

Capital Punishment

In our post-modern society, an increasing number of people (including a good number of Christians) are rejecting the concept of punishment altogether (even when disciplining children). Unfortunately, they've re-framed the retribution/rehabilitation discussion into an either/or proposition when, in fact, it should be seen as a both/and proposition. However, many Christians believe that to abandon the criteria of righteous, proportionate, and just punishment is to abandon all criteria for *any* form of punishment. There's no justice apart from just persons, and there's no justice where a society believes that people can't be held morally responsible for their actions. This belief most noticeably manifests itself in the increasing opposition to capital punishment in our society. Nine reasons are usually given for this opposition.

1. A supposed immunity granted by the eighth amendment to the Constitution. However, in 1791, when the Eighth Amendment was enacted, the death penalty was not considered 'cruel' or 'unusual,' so it can't be cited today as a basis for the abolition of capital punishment.

2. The mistaken view that revenge, rather than retribution, underlies executions. The prohibition against murder is consistently stated in both the Old and New Testaments. (See Exodus 20:13; Deuteronomy 5:17; Matthew 5:21, 19:18; Mark 10:19; Luke 18:20; Romans 13:9; 1 Timothy 1:9; James 2:11-12) Likewise, capital punishment for murder is consistently advocated in both Testaments. (See Genesis 9:6; Exodus 21:12; Leviticus 24:17; Numbers 35:16-21, 30; Deuteronomy 17:16, 19:11-13; Matthew 5:21-22; Revelation 21:8, 22:15). Rather than revenge, the primary reason given for this ultimate retribution is the sanctity of human life - the murdered person having been created in the image of God. "Human beings were made like God, so whoever murders one of them will be killed by someone else." Genesis 9:6 It's precisely *because* we humans are made in the image of God as moral agents that we must hold fellow human beings accountable in proportionate and just ways. To not do so is to fail to recognize the image of God in one another. A justly convicted murderer's execution affirms his or her humanity in that it demonstrates that s/he is a rational and morally responsible being. Capital punishment is not carried out in *spite* of human dignity, but *because* of it. Murdering a fellow human being created in the image of God is the equivalent of effacing God himself, and therefore demands the forfeiture of a person's physical life.

3.   The possibility of executing an innocent person. That mistakes will be made in our attempts to enact justice is inevitable, since working for justice is a human (and therefore imperfect) endeavor. It depends on fallible people striving for just results. Yet we don't give up on justice just because our efforts are imperfect or because of the possibility of error. Instead, many Christians believe we must re-double our efforts to get as close as possible to the ideal. On the one hand, even one tragic mistake is one too many. On the other hand, there is a gross exaggeration of the number of innocent people that have been wrongly executed. The death penalty should never be applied unless the evidence is overwhelming - a convergence of confessions, multiple witnesses, physical evidence [especially DNA] - or unless the crime is heinous - serial killers, mass murderers, those who molest and murder women and children and those who commit crimes against humanity. We also need to take into account the fact that innocent deaths resulting from released on parole criminals are far more frequent and tragic than the rare instance of an innocent person being executed.

4.   The inhumane way in which executions have been carried out. It's true that in our fallible penal justice system run by fallible human beings there have been cases of botched executions where the condemned have gone through needless suffering. However, in general, with the use of lethal injections and gas, the means used today are much more humane than the hangings and electrocutions of the past. One must also ask whether 'life imprisonment' in cases where there is no pardon or release may in the end be more inhumane than execution, let alone what it costs society to maintain those imprisoned for life.

5.   A lack of statistical evidence for the death penalty being a deterrent to serious crime. Deterrence, in the end, is immeasurable. Who can say how many people thought twice about committing a crime because of the risk of being caught and punished? Simply citing the fact that some states that don't have capital punishment have fewer murders than those that do does not solve the problem. Every state, every county and every community are complex entities where people

380 | Page   Christianity Under the Microscope

live in very different contexts. Further, the whole penal justice system operates on the underlying assumption that the more severe the punishment, the less likely it is that criminal acts will be committed. The execution of heinous murderers makes a communal declaration that, despite the moral laxity of our age, premeditated murder embodies evil so terrible, so intolerable, that it utterly defiles the community, and that the community cannot tolerate such defilement. An execution teaches the offender that the community will not tolerate his or her evil behavior. It also demonstrates to *potential* offenders that the community will not tolerate such evil behavior.

6.   The arbitrary way in which people are selected for execution. Our whole justice system rests on arbitrary decisions by both jury and judge. There are built-in guidelines and case precedents, but in the end, attorneys are given great latitude in the jury selection process and judges are given great latitude in determining what sentence will be applied for what crime and what will determine whether parole will be granted or not granted. For example, 'life' sentences are often reduced based on 'good behavior.' Is this not in itself very arbitrary? Many murderers are set free after ten, twenty or thirty years. On what sort of moral math is *this* based?

7.   Racial prejudice when sentencing people to death. There've been racially prejudiced juries and judges in the past that have unjustly sentenced African Americans to death. However, great strides have been made to ensure equal justice for all in our time. Simply looking at comparative statistics for whites and blacks on death row does not take into account other very disturbing but very important facts. There are logical reasons why there are a disproportionate number of African Americans on death row. Despite making up just 13 percent of the population, African Americans commit around half of all homicides in the United States. From 2011-2013, 38.5 per cent of people arrested for murder, manslaughter, rape, robbery, and aggravated assault were black. This figure is three times higher than the 13 percent black population figure. Also, the National Crime Victimization Survey shows that the number of African Americans arrested generally correlates with the number of offenders identified as black by victims.

8. The notion that Jesus abrogated the Old Testament concept of retribution. On the contrary, many Christians believe that Jesus taught the exact opposite.

> "Do not think that I have come to do away with the Law of Moses and the teachings of the prophets. I have not come to do away with them, but to make their teachings come true. Remember that as long as heaven and earth last, not the least point nor the smallest detail of the Law will be done away with - not until the end of all things. So then, whoever disobeys even the least important of the commandments and teaches others to do the same, will be least in the Kingdom of heaven. On the other hand, whoever obeys the Law and teaches others to do the same, will be great in the Kingdom of heaven. I tell you, then, that you will be able to enter the Kingdom of heaven only if you are more faithful than the teachers of the Law and the Pharisees in doing what God requires." Matthew 5:17-20

Jesus not only re-enforced the Law, but required an even more comprehensive obedience to it as spelled out in Matthew 5: 21-22, 27-48.

- "You have heard that people were told in the past, 'Do not commit murder; anyone who does will be brought to trial.' But now I tell you: if you are angry with your brother you will be brought to trial, if you call your brother 'You good-for-nothing!' you will be brought before the Council, and if you call your brother a worthless fool you will be in danger of going to the fire of hell..."

- "You have heard that it was said, 'Do not commit adultery.' But now I tell you: anyone who looks at a woman and wants to possess her is guilty of committing adultery with her in his heart. So if your right eye causes you to sin, take it out and throw it away! It is much better for you to lose a part of your body than to have your whole body thrown into hell. If your right hand causes you to sin, cut it off and throw it away! It is much better for you to lose one of your limbs than to have your whole body go off to hell."

- "It was also said, 'Anyone who divorces his wife must give her a written notice of divorce.' But now I tell you: if a man divorces his wife for any cause other than her unfaithfulness, then he is guilty of making her commit adultery if she marries again; and the man who marries her commits adultery also."

- "You have also heard that people were told in the past, 'Do not break your promise, but do what you have vowed to the Lord to do.' But now I tell you: do not use any vow when you make a promise. Do not swear by heaven, for it is God's throne; nor by earth, for it is the resting place for his feet; nor by Jerusalem, for it is the city of the great King. Do not even swear by your head, because you cannot make a single hair white or black. Just say 'Yes' or 'No' - anything else you say comes from the Evil One."

- "You have heard that it was said, 'An eye for an eye, and a tooth for a tooth.' But now I tell you: do not take revenge on someone who wrongs you. If anyone slaps you on the right cheek, let him slap your left cheek too. And if someone takes you to court to sue you for your shirt, let him have your coat as well. And if one of the occupation troops forces you to carry his pack one mile, carry it two miles. When someone asks you for something, give it to him; when someone wants to borrow something, lend it to him." (Notice that the attitude Jesus is condemning here is *revenge*, not retribution.)

- "You have heard that it was said, 'Love your friends, hate your enemies.' But now I tell you: love your enemies and pray for those who persecute you, so that you may become the children of your Father in heaven. For he makes his sun to shine on bad and good people alike, and gives rain to those who do good and to those who do evil. Why should God reward you if you love only the people who love you? Even the tax collectors do that! And if you speak only to your friends, have you done anything out of the ordinary? Even the pagans do that! You must be perfect - just as your Father in heaven is perfect." (Notice that the attitude Jesus is condemning here is *hatred*. He's not undermining the quest for justice, but asking those who've been victimized by others to be willing to offer them the love of forgiveness and to treat criminals with love while administering justice.)

9.   The Biblical commandments are no longer relevant for our day. One of the characteristics of the postmodern age is, like the children of the Enlightenment, to cut the umbilical cord that has tied our society to the Judeo-Christian spiritual foundation of natural (or revealed) law for over two centuries. The Biblical teaching concerning crime and punishment is no longer considered relevant for our time. The law is now what we make it to be, which means we have entered a subjective no-man's-land when it comes to moral or immoral behavior and to the administration of justice. Arbitrary is now the definitive term that can be used to describe how we approach the whole subject of retribution and reformation concerning those who break what, at least for the moment, are the laws of the land. This is particularly true when it comes to the question of capital punishment for those who commit heinous crimes. In the end, the only conclusion one can come to is that in its rush towards the abolition of the death penalty for those who murder in cold blood, our society is deserting its responsibility to uphold the unique value of human life

Christians believe that Jesus Christ stands ready to enable hisfollowers not only to resist the temptation to *harm* their neighbors, but to bring about the kind of internal change in people's lives that will generate a desire within them to *help* their neighbors. Christians are people who Jesus calls to be builders of society rather than parasites living off society. They're asked to work diligently, not only for their own good, but for the good of all. (See Ephesians 4:28) They're to be people who learn to be satisfied with having their basic needs met rather than always being greedy for more. (See Philippians 4:11-13) They're to be people who uphold the sanctity of life, particularly the life of those who are defenseless. (See Matthew 18:10) They're to be people who try to further their aims peacefully, not violently, even when someone has wronged them. (See Romans 12:17-21) They're to be people who try to change unjust social structures that oppress, exploit and create conditions ripe for the development of criminals.

(See Luke 4:18-19) They're to be people who work for the rehabilitation of those who commit crimes against society, but who also have the courage to insist that people must be held accountable for the consequences of their deeds. (See Romans 13:1-3a)

Overcoming social problems and evils is a long, slow and on-going process. Unless people are deeply motivated by self-giving love and filled with a spiritual strength greater than their own, they'll soon become discouraged and give up. However, Christians are confident that social evils will not ultimately prevail. They believe that God's Kingdom will someday completely overcome them. Therefore, Jesus' followers are motivated to keep pushing on when others have given up. As Paul writes, "So let us not become tired of doing good; for if we do not give up, the time will come when we will reap the harvest." Galatians 6:9

What Do *You* Think?

1. Do you agree with the conclusions drawn about corruption and pornography in this chapter? Explain.

2. Do you agree with the conclusions drawn about gambling and drug abuse in this chapter? Explain.

3. Do you agree with the conclusions drawn about abortion and euthanasia in this chapter? Explain.

4. Do you agree with the conclusions drawn about crime and violence in this chapter? Explain.

5. In your opinion, how should gun violence be dealt with?

6. In your opinion, how should society deal with criminals? Do you favor the death penalty and/or life imprisonment, for example? Explain.

Chapter Nineteen

WHAT ABOUT LGBTQ ISSUES?

> "You must put to death then, the earthly desires at work in you, such as sexual immorality, indecency, lust, evil passions, and greed...for you have put off the old self with its habits and have put on the new self. This is the new being which God, its Creator, is constantly renewing in his own image, in order to bring you to a full knowledge of himself."   Colossians 3:8-10

Looking Through the Microscope |

Reflections on 25 Years of Healing
by Alan Medinger

P erverse and foolish oft I strayed, but yet in love He sought me; and on His shoulder gently laid, and home rejoicing brought me.

These words from an old hymn based on Psalm 23 express perfectly what happened to me twenty-five years ago when I encountered the Lord and he brought me out of homosexuality. My journey fit into the pattern that we see over and over again. I was an unplanned child, born to parents who would have preferred a girl. My older brother was more athletic and generally fit the 'all boy' model far better than I, and somehow, he became Dad's and I became Mom's.

"My parents were good, kind and conscientious people who would do all they could to raise their sons to become successful, well-adjusted men, but one problem in the family tended to shape all of our destinies. My father was subject to severe depression. So severe that he was under psychiatric care for many years, and on a few occasions had to be hospitalized. He could barely cope with life, much less be the husband and father that we needed him to be. In his bad times, he drank heavily and he and my mother fought verbally quite often.

"My mother's life was difficult and to a limited extent I became her comfort and confidant. I certainly identified with her more than with my father. If you are familiar with the most common roots of male homosexuality, you can see that, except for sexual abuse, they were all there for me.

"No parent makes a child homosexual. We have learned that a child's early home environment may provide 'the set-up,' but significant other factors always come to play in steering someone into homosexuality. For me, a couple of those factors were decisions that I made quite early in life. I have a vivid memory of one night, as a young boy, lying in bed listening to my parents fight, and saying to myself quite smugly, 'They can never hurt me; no one will ever hurt me.' I believe that I made a decision that night to never be emotionally vulnerable. As a consequence of that decision, until my conversion years later, I would never be free to truly love anyone again.

"I also retreated into a world of fantasy. Fantasy, sexual and otherwise, became my secure retreat from the pain of life. A typical script for my fantasy would have me a boy hero leading other men into battle, and then when the fighting was over, the men would use me sexually. I both longed for my own manhood and for the manhood of other men. At first my longings weren't sexual; they were simply a craving for a man's attention and interest in me. But, of course, eventually, they did turn sexual. Although my fears of being found out limited my activity, I was homosexually active with other boys from about age 13 through high school.

"I was blessed to grow up in a time and culture in which there was no gay alternative lifestyle out there calling me into it. I knew that were a couple of homosexual bars in Baltimore, and I would visit pornographic book stores to glance at the magazines in the 'male' section, but it never really occurred to me to bail out of the only world I knew and let homosexuality determine the course of my life. Like so many homosexually oriented men of that time, I would get a job, marry, have children and cope the best I could.

"That's exactly what happened. Willa Benson had been my friend from elementary school days. We dated through high school, off and on during college, and two years after college we were married. I told Willa nothing of my homosexual desires. The first years of marriage went well. We had two daughters and I started to move up in the business world. We were active in our little neighborhood Episcopal Church, and we led an active social life. But gradually, the pressures of career and family started to build up on me. My response was to retreat into my old means of finding comfort; homosexual fantasy and pornography, and five years into the marriage, sex with other men.

"At first I drove forty-five miles to Washington, DC to go to a gay bar to find a contact, but as time passed I became more and more reckless until I was openly going to gay bars and gay cruising places in Baltimore. A major part of my homosexuality was masochistic and I started answering ads for sadomasochistic sex. For ten years I led the classic double life - successful in business, vice-president and treasurer of a prestigious Baltimore company, a pillar of my local church, church treasurer, board member and Sunday school teacher. The front was masterfully retained. In reality, my life was out of control and my marriage had become a sham. I was drinking heavily, and turned much of my guilt on Willa. We fought frequently. For the last two years of my homosexual activity, I was unable to function sexually in the marriage. I never justified what I was doing, but I felt powerless to stop it. I saw my life on a downward spiral that eventually would cost me my family, my career, maybe even my life.

"Then, two things happened. Willa, searching for help, got herself into a prayer group. Unbeknownst to her she had stumbled upon a group of older women who were mighty prayer warriors. They started praying for me and for our marriage. Not long after this, a friend at work had a profound religious experience, and surrendered his life to

388 | Page   Christianity Under the Microscope

Christ. As this friend tried to explain to me what had happened, I became certain that he had had a true encounter with the Lord. Somehow I knew that I could too, but this was the most frightening thing I could think of. I knew that such an encounter would involve my homosexuality. As much as I hated it, I didn't think I could live without it. It had been my way of coping with life for as long as I could remember.

"But things were desperate enough that after six or seven weeks of agonizing, on Tuesday, November 26, 1974, I went to the meeting with Jim. He didn't know my problem, nor did anyone there. At some point during the evening, as the two hundred or so people were praising God out loud, I said quietly, 'God, I give up. My life is a total mess. I can't handle it any more. You take over.' And He did. Within a few days, I knew that some profound changes had taken place in me. First of all, I fell head over heels in love with Willa and I desired her physically. My homosexual fantasies that had almost never left me were gone. And most important of all, I knew that Jesus was real, that He loved me, and I was starting to love Him.

"A few weeks later, I told Willa the whole truth about my life. Her years of denial came crashing down and in the months ahead she would encounter the wounds that my years of rejection, deception, anger and blame-casting had caused. Her healing was just beginning and would take a number of years. Being able to trust me and receive my love came very slowly.

"It was about four years before I heard of anyone else who had been set free from homosexuality, and then I read of Love In Action, a ministry for healing homosexuality then in San Rafael, CA. I started to correspond with Frank Worthen and Bob Davies. It would be another year before I actually met another 'ex-gay' at my first Exodus Conference in Seattle, Washington. Exodus leaders were wary of my testimony at first. They had encountered others who claimed to have received sudden miraculous healings from homosexuality, only to find out in a year or two that these healings had been far from complete. In some ways their caution was justifiable, but not because I had not been set free from compulsive behavior and sexual attractions to men. But rather, because homosexuality is more than just sexual attractions and behavior, and I had barely begun to experience healing in other areas.

"The sexual healing was indeed what it seemed to be in 1974 and in the years to follow God touched the emotional neediness. These past couple of years I have gained another insight into how God changed me, one that goes back to the original sexual healing. I always saw that healing as a miracle. I don't any more. I now see it as three miracles. Homosexuality is not an affliction like mental retardation or cancer; it is a group of problems, which together produce homosexual attractions and behavior. Each of these problems must be dealt with individually. Here are the three problems that God dealt with at the time of my initial healing, my three miracles.

"*First, He broke down my wall of self-protection, and I was suddenly able to love.* And who would have been a more logical object of my love than Willa, the person who had loved me and stayed by me all of those terrible years? I fell in love with her, and as happens with many men who come out of homosexuality, out of that love came sexual desire for her.

"*The second miracle is that God 'desexualized' my unmet needs.* For a time, I still longed for a man's love and attention, but that longing was no longer sexual. I still longed to be a man, but this longing was no longer expressed in a desire to possess another man's manhood.

"*Third the sexual addiction was broken.* This is, perhaps, the hardest miracle to understand, but it is the one we encounter most often. Every successful twelve-stepper will tell you how his surrender to God is what broke the power of his sexual addiction.

"I believe these were miracles. But what causes us to call something a miracle is often a matter of timing. God does in a moment what usually takes months or years to occur. Although not too many people experience change the way I did, everything that happened to me: being set free to love, desexualizing my unmet emotional needs, breaking the power of my addiction, having the deep needs of my heart met by Jesus, and growing into manhood (or womanhood) can happen to any man or woman working towards overcoming homosexuality. I know this because I have seen it happen hundreds of times in many lives."

What Do *You* Think?

1. Do you agree with Alan that LGBTQ people are not "born that way," but that they become that way through their childhood relationships and experiences? Why or why not?

2. Do you agree with Alan that LGBTQ people can change their lifestyle and even their orientation, or should their lifestyle and orientation be accepted, affirmed and even celebrated? Explain.

3. Have you ever met or heard about people like Alan who have been practicing gays or lesbians, but who have left that lifestyle behind and gone on to engage in successful heterosexual relationships? Should such change be promoted or discouraged? Why or why not?

4. Do you think that sexual activity outside of the marriage of a man and a woman should be considered a 'sin' that needs to be repented of or, in the case of same sex 'marriage,' should it be accepted as normal behavior? Explain.

5. Can those who believe that LGBTQ lifestyles (whether in short-term or long-term relationships) are not the way God intended people to live relate to LGBTQ people with compassion without compromising their convictions? Why or why not?

Bringing Things Into Focus |

Gender and Sexuality Alphabet Soup

Since the advent of the sexual revolution, a mind boggling array of terms has arisen to describe it. Many people are bewildered and confused when it comes to knowing and understanding what's happening in our society. Here's a glossary of contemporary terms describing various aspects of, and facts about, human gender, sexuality and sexual practice that you might find helpful as you wend your way through the current controversies regarding these subjects.

Aromantic or **Asexual**: a person who experiences little or no romantic attraction to others and/or a lack of interest in forming romantic relationships.

Agender or **Gender-neutral:** a person without gender. This person can be any physical sex, but their body does not necessarily correspond with their lack of gender identity. Often, these people are not concerned with their physical sex, but some may seek to look androgynous.

AIDS: Acquired Immunodeficiency Syndrome (AIDS). The symptoms include one or more unusual infections or cancers, severe loss of weight, and intellectual deterioration (called dementia). (In a Canadian study, 76 percent of all AIDS cases since statistics were first kept occurred in gay and bisexual men and the infection rate was up to 26 times higher than among the population as a whole).

Artificial Insemination: the injection of semen into the vagina or uterus other than by sexual intercourse. (In the case of lesbians, this raises difficulties when it comes to legally determining who the actual parents of the resultant child(ren) are.)

Adultery: having a sexual relationship with another person while married to one's spouse. (Although some long-term faithful relationships do exist within the LGBTQ community, both gays and lesbians have a much higher rate of break-ups or 'divorces' than heterosexuals do).

Androgyny/ous: a gender expression that has elements of both masculinity and femininity. **Intersex:** a person whose sexual anatomy or chromosomes do not fit within the normal female and male gender categories. (For example: people born with both female and male anatomy). **Neutrois**: a term used to describe persons with a null or neutral gender (neither male nor female), and in some cases, a person who tries to reduce signs of their physical sex.

Bisexual: a person who is attracted both to people of their own gender and another gender.

Bigender: a person who fluctuates between traditionally 'woman' and 'man' gender-based behavior and identities, identifying with both genders (and sometimes a third androgynous 'gender').

Biological Sex: a medical term used to refer to the chromosomal, hormonal and anatomical characteristics that are used to classify an individual as female, male or intersex.

Celibate: a person who voluntarily refrains from any kind of sexual relationship outside of heterosexual marriage.

Cisgender: a gender identity where an individual's experience of their own gender matches the sex they were at birth.

Cisnormativity: the assumption, in individuals or in institutions, that everyone is cisgender, and that cisgender identities are superior to 'trans' identities or people.

Coming Out: the process of acknowledging one's LGBTQ sexual orientation and/or gender identity to other people. **In the Closet**: a person who keeps his or her LGBTQ sexual orientation or gender identity a secret from some or all people. **Outing**: an involuntary or unwanted disclosure of another person's sexual orientation, gender identity, or intersex status.

Cystoisospora Belli: (previously known as Isospora belli, a parasite that causes an intestinal disease known as cystoisosporiasis. This protozoan parasite is opportunistic in immune suppressed human hosts. It primarily exists in the epithelial cells of the small intestine, and develops in the cell cytoplasm. Immunocompromised people are more severely affected by *Cystoisospora belli* and can experience extreme diarrhea that can lead to weakness, anorexia, and weight loss. Other symptoms include abdominal pain, cramps, loss of appetite, nausea, vomiting, and fever that can last from weeks to months. (Cystoisospora Belli is found with extraordinary frequency among practicing male homosexuals practitioners as a result of anal intercourse).

Demisexual: an individual who does not experience sexual attraction unless s/he has formed a strong emotional connection with another individual, often within a romantic relationship.

Depression: a psychological condition that results in fatigue, sleep problems, irritability, inability to concentrate, anxiety, alcoholism/drug use, erectile dysfunction, suicidal thoughts, stress and difficulty in making decisions. (It's well established that there are high rates of psychiatric illnesses, including depression, drug abuse, and suicide attempts, among gays, lesbians and transgender people. This is true even in the Netherlands, where gay, lesbian and bisexual relationships are far more socially acceptable than in the U.S. Depression and drug abuse are strongly associated with risky sexual practices that lead to serious medical problems).

Dyke: a term referring to a masculine presenting lesbian. While often used derogatorily, it is adopted affirmatively by many lesbians as a positive self-identity term.

Drug Abuse: being addicted to harmful drugs. (Practicing LGBTQ people are much more prone to drug addiction than the general population).

Drag King or **Drag Queen**: a woman who performs masculinity theatrically or a man who performs femininity theatrically. **Transvestite**: a person who consistently dresses as the opposite gender ('cross-dresses') for relaxation, fun, and sexual gratification.

Fisting: the tearing or ripping of the anal wall when the hand and possibly arm is inserted into the rectum. This also commonly occurs when 'toys' are employed (homosexual lingo for objects which are inserted into the rectum like bottles, carrots and other sex aids).

Fag(got): a derogatory term referring to a gay person, or someone perceived as queer. Occasionally used as a self-identifying affirming term by some gay men, at times in the shortened form 'fag.'

Feminine of Center or **Feminine Presenting** and **Masculine Presenting** or **Masculine of Center**: phrases that indicate a range of terms of gender identity and gender presentation for people who present, understand themselves, relate to others in a more feminine or masculine way. Feminine of center individuals may also identify as **Femme, Submissive, Transfeminine**, etc.; masculine of center individuals may also often identity as **Butch, Stud, Aggressive, Boi,** and **Transmasculine**.

Femme: someone who identifies him or herself as feminine, whether it be physically, mentally or emotionally. Often used to refer to a feminine-presenting queer woman.

Fluid(ity): usually used with another term attached, like **Gender-fluid** or **Fluid-sexuality**. Describes an identity that may change or shift over time between or within the mix of the options available (e.g., man and woman, bi and straight). **Gender Fluid**: a gender identity best described as a dynamic mix of male and female. A person who is gender fluid may always feel like a mix of the two traditional genders, but may feel more man some days, and more woman other days.

Gay: a male who is attracted primarily to someone of the male sex. Can also be used as an umbrella term to refer to the queer community as a whole, or as an individual identity label for anyone who doesn't identify as a heterosexual.

Gender Binary: the idea that there are only two genders - male/female or man/woman and that a person must be strictly gendered as either/or. **Gender Identity**: the sense of 'being' **Male, Female, Genderqueer, Agender**, etc. For some people, gender identity is in accord with physical anatomy. For transgender people, gender identity may differ from physical anatomy or expected social roles.

Gender Expression or Presentation: the external display of one's gender, through a combination of dress, demeanor, social behavior, and other factors, generally measured on scales of masculinity and femininity.

Gender Non-Conforming (GNC) or **Gender Variant**: someone whose gender does not align in a predicted fashion with society's gender-based expectations.

Gender Normative or **Gender Straight**: someone whose gender aligns with society's gender-based expectations.

Genderqueer: a gender identity label often used by people who do not identify as a man or a woman. Can also be an umbrella term for many gender non-conforming identities. Genderqueer people may think of themselves as one or more of the following: may combine aspects of man and woman and other identities (**Bigender, Pangender**); not having a gender or identifying with a gender (**Genderless, Gender**); moving between genders (**Genderfluid**); having a third gender or other-gendered. **Third Gender**: a term describing a person who does not identify with either male or female, but who identifies with another 'gender.'

Gonorrhoea: a sexually transmitted infection caused by the bacterium *Neisseria gonorrhoeae*. The usual symptoms in men are a burning with urination and discharge from the penis. Women have no symptoms about half the time or have vaginal discharge and pelvic pain. In both men and women, if gonorrhea is left untreated, it may spread locally, causing inflammation of the epididymis in men or pelvic inflammatory disease in women. (Gonorrhea can also spread throughout the body and affect joints and heart valves and is much more prevalent among practicing Gays and Lesbians than among the general population).

Golden Shower: slang for the practice of urinating on another person for sexual pleasure - (a more common, disease producing practice among LGBTQ people).

Gay Gene: the claim that homosexual behaviour is caused by nature and not by nurture; that it is inborn and not learned; that there is a 'gay gene.' (After substantial research, no such gene has been discovered. Some believed this gene would be found among the chromosomes analyzed in the Human Genome Project, but the opposite conclusion was reached. Neither the map for the X nor the Y chromosome contains any such gene).

Gynesexual or **Gynephilic**: a person who is primarily attracted to women, females, and/or femininity.

Homosexual: a person who is primarily emotionally, physically, and/or sexually attracted to members of the same sex or gender.

HIV (Human immunodeficiency virus): a virus that causes the usually fatal infectious disease Acquired Immune Deficiency Syndrome (AIDS). (More than 70% of HIV infections are transmitted through sexual contact. In the United States, the majority of HIV cases have been found in homosexual or bisexual men).

Hate Speech: illegal speech that, as originally defined, prohibited speech that offends, threatens, or insults groups, based on race, color, religion, national origin, disability, or other traits. In recent years, it has been expanded to include sexual orientation.

Hookup: a casual sexual encounter, including one-night stands and other related activity, which focuses on physical pleasure without necessarily including emotional bonding or long-term commitment. (Hookups are a common and risky practice among practicing LGBTQ people).

Heterosexual: a person who is only attracted to members of the opposite sex. Also '**Straight.**'

Heteronormativity: the assumption, by individuals or in institutions, that everyone should be heterosexual, that heterosexuality is superior to all other sexualities, that individuals should identify as men and women and be masculine men and feminine women, and that men and women are meant to be a complimentary pair. **Heterosexism**: behavior that grants preferential treatment to heterosexual people, reinforces the idea that heterosexuality is somehow better or more 'right' than queerness, or makes other sexualities invisible

Homophopia, Tansphobia and Biphobia: an aversion toward homosexuality and homosexual people, transgender identification and transgender people, bisexuality and bisexual people as social groups or as individuals.

Human Papilloma Virus (HPV): Over 170 types of HPV have been identified, more than 40 of which are typically transmitted through sexual contact and infect the anogenital region. HPV types 6 and 11 are the etiological cause of genital warts. Persistent infection with 'high-risk' HPV types - different from the ones that cause skin warts - may progress to precancerous lesions and invasive cancer. High-risk HPV infection is a cause of nearly all cases of cervical cancer. (HIV-positive gay or bisexual men have higher levels of both HPV infection and HPV-related disease than heterosexual men. An estimated 61 percent of HIV-negative and 93 percent of HIV-positive gay and bisexual men have anal HPV infections, compared to 50 percent or less of heterosexual men. Men who have sex with men are also at increased risk for anal cancer compared to the general population.)

Lesbian: a woman who is primarily attracted romantically, erotically, and/or emotionally to other women.

Lipstick Lesbian: a lesbian with a feminine gender expression. Is sometimes also used to refer to a lesbian who is assumed to be (or passes for) straight.

Life Expectancy: (Epidemiological studies on the life span of gay men conclude that gay and bisexual men lose up to 20 years of life expectancy. In a recent Norwegian study, married heterosexual men were found to have died at an average age of 77, while 'married' gay men died at an average age of 52. Women married to men in Norway died at an average age of 81 while the average life expectancy for 'married' lesbians was 56. In a similar U.S. study, the median age of death for homosexuals was virtually the same nationwide. Overall, about two percent survived to old age. If AIDS was the listed cause of death, the median age was 39. For the 829 gays who were listed as dying of something other than AIDS, the median age of death was 42 and nine percent died old. The 163 lesbians had a median age of death of 44 and 20 percent died old.)

Long Term Committed Relationship or **Monogamy**: being married to and sexually active exclusively with one partner. (Studies have shown that long-term sexual fidelity is rare in GLBTQ relationships, particularly among gay men. A 2003 study on homosexual relationships found they last one to one-and-a-half years on average. Among heterosexuals, by contrast, 67 percent of first marriages in the United States last at least 10 years, and researchers report that more than three-quarters of married people say they have been faithful to their vows. One study reported that 66 percent of gay couples engaged in sex outside the relationship within the first year, and nearly 90 percent if the relationship lasted five years.

In *The Male Couple,* published in 1984, authors David P. McWhirter and Andrew M. Mattison report that in a study of 156 males in homosexual relationships lasting anywhere from one to 37 years, all couples with relationships more than five years had incorporated some provision for outside sexual activity. They wrote, "Fidelity is not defined in terms of sexual behavior but rather by their emotional commitment to each other. Ninety-five percent of the couples have an arrangement whereby the partners may have sexual activity with others.")

Mental Disorders: A state of mind that is atypical or abnormal. (It's well established that there are high rates of psychiatric illnesses, including depression, drug abuse, and suicide attempts, among gays and lesbians. This is true even in the Netherlands, where gay, lesbian and bisexual relationships are far more socially acceptable than in the U.S. Depression and drug abuse are strongly associated with risky sexual practices that lead to serious medical problems.)

Metrosexual: a man with a strong aesthetic sense who spends more time, energy, or money on his appearance and grooming than is considered gender normative.

MSM or **WSW**: acronyms for "men who have sex with men" and "women who have sex with women," to distinguish sexual behaviors from sexual identities. (E.g., because a man is 'straight,' it doesn't necessarily mean he's not having sex with men).

Mx. a title (e.g. Mr., Ms., etc.) that is gender neutral.

Promiscuity: sexual relationships with one or more partners outside of marriage between a man and a woman. (Prior to the AIDS epidemic, a 1978 study found that 75 percent of white, gay males claimed to have had more than 100 lifetime male sex partners: 15 percent claimed 100-249 sex partners; 17 percent claimed 250-499; 15 percent claimed 500-999; and 28 percent claimed more than 1,000 lifetime male sex partners. Levels of promiscuity subsequently declined, but some observers are concerned that promiscuity is again approaching the levels of the 1970s. A recent Australian study found that 93 percent of lesbians reported also having had sex with men, and lesbians were 4.5 times more likely than heterosexual women to have had more than 50 lifetime male sex partners.)

Polygamy: being 'married' to more than one spouse. **Serial Polygamy**: being married to or co-habiting with a number of 'spouses' through repeated break ups, divorces and re-marriages (practices that are more prevalent in the gay community).

Pansexual: a person who experiences sexual, romantic, physical, and/or spiritual attraction for members of all gender identities/expressions.

Polyamory or **Polyamorous**: the practice of having, desiring to have, or orientation towards having consensually non-monogamous relationships (i.e. relationships that may include multiple partners). This may include open relationships, **polyfidelity** (which involves more than two people being in romantic and/or sexual relationships which aren't open to additional partners), amongst many other set ups. Some poly(amorous) people have a 'primary' relationship or relationship(s) and then 'secondary' relationship(s) which may indicate different allocations of resources, time, or priority. **Constellation**: the arrangement or structure of a polyamorous relationship involving three or more people.

Physical Injuries: Damage to one's physical body. (Sexual relationships between members of the same sex expose gays, lesbians and bisexuals to extreme risks of rectal and vaginal physical injuries compared to heterosexuals whether they are in temporary or long-term relationships).

Penile-anal Sexual Contact: the insertion of a male penis into the anus of another male. (Surveys indicate that about 90 percent of gays have engaged in rectal intercourse, and about two-thirds do it regularly, whether with multiple partners or within a longer term 'marriage.' Rectal sex is *dangerous*. During rectal intercourse, the rectum becomes a mixing bowl for saliva and its germs and/or an artificial lubricant, the recipient's own feces, whatever germs, infections or substances the penis has on it and the seminal fluid of the inserter. The end result is that the fragility of the anus and rectum, along with the immunosuppressive effect of ejaculate, make anal-genital intercourse a most efficient manner of transmitting HIV and other infections. The list of diseases found with extraordinary frequency among practicing male homosexuals, whether in short-term or long-term relationships, as a result of rectal sex is alarming.)

Passing: a term for transgender people being accepted as, or able to 'pass for,' a member of their self-identified gender/sex identity regardless of birth sex *or* an LGBTQ individual who can, or is perceived to be, straight.

Queer: individuals who challenge both gender and sexuality norms and see gender identity and sexual orientation as overlapping and interconnected. Also an umbrella term sometimes used by LGBTQ people to refer to the entire LGBTQ community.

Questioning: the process of exploring and discovering a person's sexual orientation, gender identity, or gender expression.

Rainbow: a symbol chosen by the LGBTQ community to demonstrate social inclusiveness for people of all non-heterosexual identities. (Th rainbow has for millennia been a symbol of God's gracious covenant with humankind. This symbol has now been hijacked by the LGBTQ community to represent what many Christians consider to be destructive and degrading lifestyles).

Sexual orientation: the type of sexual, romantic, emotional/spiritual attraction one feels for others based on the gender relationship between the person and the people they are attracted to.

Syphilis: a disease typically acquired by direct sexual contact with the infectious lesions of another person. Secondary syphilis produces a reddish-pink, non-itchy rash on the trunk and extremities, including the palms and soles Other symptoms may include fever, sore throat, malaise, weight loss, hair loss, and headache Tertiary syphilis is characterized by the formation of chronic gummas, which are soft, tumor-like balls of inflammation that typically affect the skin, bone, and liver, but can occur anywhere. Neurosyphilis refers to an infection involving the central nervous system that is associated with poor balance and lightning pains in the lower extremities. Cardiovascular syphilis may result in aneurysm formation. (Syphilis is much more prevalent among practicing Gays and Lesbians than among the general population. In 2006, for example, 64 percent of the reported cases in the United States were among men who had sex with men).

Suicide: the taking of one's own life. (In a recent Canadian study, suicide rates among homosexuals were anywhere from double to 13.9 times higher than the general population. By their own estimates, homosexuals comprise 30 percent of all suicides in Canada. A recent US study reports that 41 percent of the transgender population have attempted suicide, which vastly exceeds the 4.6 percent of the overall U.S. population and is also higher than the 10-20 percent of lesbian, gay and bisexual adults who report ever attempting suicide.)

Sperm: the male fertilizing agent. Sperm, which is immunocompromising, readily penetrate the rectal lining (which is only one cell thick). Since tearing or bruising of the anal wall is very common during anal/penile sex, multiple foreign substances gain almost direct access to the blood stream. (Unlike heterosexual intercourse - in which sperm cannot penetrate the multilayered vagina and no feces are present - rectal intercourse is probably the most sexually efficient way to spread hepatitis B, HIV, syphilis, and a host of other blood-borne diseases. This is true whether these encounters involve multiple partners or are between two gay men who have a long-term relationship.)

Same Sex "Marriage": a union of two people of the same sex who are committed to a long term relationship. (Although breakup and divorce are common among heterosexuals, the incidence among LGBTQ people is much higher.)

Surrogate Mother: a woman who is impregnated with male semen in order to bear a child on behalf of another. (In the case of gay men, this raises the question as to who the actual parents of the child are, and in the case of lesbians, this raises the question as to who the actual mother is.)

Sodomy: a term derived from the story of Sodom and Gomorrah in chapters 18 and 19 of the Book of Genesis that refers to perverted sexual activity between men. Sodom is mentioned over 20 times in the Bible as being the worst example of the worst immoral behavior imaginable.

Sex Reassignment Surgery (SRS): a group of surgical options that alter a person's biological sex. (In most cases, one or multiple surgeries are required to achieve legal recognition of gender variance. This practice of bodily mutilation to deal with a basically emotional and mental condition is being increasingly called into question by some transgender therapy experts.)

Skoliosexual: a person who is attracted to genderqueer and transsexual people and expressions.

Stud: a term most commonly used to indicate an African-American or Latina masculine lesbian/queer woman. (Also known as **Butch** or **Aggressive**).

Sexually Transmitted Diseases (STDs): diseases like HIV, AIDS, Ghonera, Syphilis, etc. (Sexual relationships between members of the same sex expose gays, lesbians and bisexuals to extreme risks of incurring STDs. Sexual transmission of some of these diseases is so rare in the exclusively heterosexual population as to be virtually unknown. Others, while found among heterosexual and homosexual practitioners, are clearly predominated by those involved in homosexual activity.)

Transgender or **Transsexual**: people who do not identify with their birth gender or with the normal male/female categories and who may undergo medical treatments to change their biological sex (often times to align it with their gender identity) or live their lives as another sex. Also **Dysphoria**: a profound state of unease or dissatisfaction. In a psychiatric context, dysphoria may accompany depression, anxiety or agitation. It can also refer to a state of not being comfortable in one's current body (being **Transgender**), particularly in cases of gender dysphoria. Common reactions to dysphoria include emotional distress or indifference.

Transition(ing): the process a trans* person undergoes when changing his/her bodily appearance either to be more congruent with the gender or sex s/he feels him/herself to be and/or to be in harmony with his/her preferred gender expression.

Transman or **Transwoman**: an identity label sometimes adopted by female-to-male or male-to-female transgender people or transsexuals to signify that they are men or women while still affirming their history as being of the female or male sex at birth.

Viral Hepatitis types B & C: produce an inflammation of the liver that requires treatment in order to prevent progressive liver damage, cirrhosis, liver failure, and liver cancer. (Is prevalent among people with multiple sexual partners, particularly among males who engage in rectal sex.)

Ze or **Hir**: alternate pronouns that are gender neutral and preferred by some trans* people. Pronounced 'zee' and 'here,' they replace 'he' and 'she' and 'his' and 'hers' respectively. Some trans* people use the plural pronoun 'they/their' as a gender neutral singular pronoun.

Zoophilia: a sexual fixation on animals or **Bestiality:** a cross-species sexual activity between humans and animals. (These terms are often used interchangeably).

What Do *You* Think?

1. What are your impressions after reading through this list?

2. What most surprised you when reading through this list?

3. What new information did you gain by reading through this list?

4. Have you changed your opinion about LGBTQ practice in any way after reading through this list? Explain

Gaining a Perspective |

True of False?

1. Therapeutic intervention (reparative therapy) to alter their orientation hasn't worked for LGBTQ people who've attempted it and should therefore be outlawed in all states.

2. The Bible's teaching on LGBTQ issues is either unclear or culturally outdated.

3. Until this century, both Jews (following the O.T.) and Christians (following both Testaments) have consistently interpreted the relevant Scripture passages to mean that all LGBTQ practices (including "loving mutual lifetime relationships") under any circumstances in any place are immoral behaviors that are contradictory to a godly lifestyle.

4. Jesus said nothing about LGBTQ issues, but did say a lot about loving relationships, which would lead one to believe that he wouldn't oppose lifelong same-sex partnerships, gay marriage or bi-sexual or transgender lifestyles.

5. Christians don't follow some of the precepts or practices contained in the Bible now, so those against practicing LGBTQ lifestyles shouldn't be binding either.

6. LGBTQ people don't choose their orientation; they're born that way due to their genetic, God-given makeup. So they have as much right to practice, and indeed celebrate, their way of life as do heterosexuals.

7. A satisfying lifestyle, emotional intimacy and a deep interpersonal commitment are available to LGBTQ people only in the context of a relationship with other LGBTQ people.

8. People that characterize LGBTQ behaviors as illegitimate lifestyles are suffering from an LGBTQ phobia. Once they get to know LGBTQ people personally, they'll discover that they're very nice people whom the church should welcome rather than condemn.

9. LGBTQ people should have the same civil rights as anybody else, including the right to marry someone of the same sex and to 'have' or adopt children.

10. Even if LGBTQ behaviors are sinful, practicing LGBTQ people shouldn't be singled out for special condemnation. We're all sinners who are forgiven, loved and accepted by a gracious God. We should not judge someone whom God accepts.

11. Christians have different points of view on many things. Concerning LGBTQ issues, we should simply "live and let live," come together and get on with the mission of the Church.

12. Long term LGBTQ unions are just as stable as heterosexual ones.

13. Using moral logic, it can be shown that all nine passages in both the Old and New Testaments directly dealing with LGBTQ lifestyles can, in one way or another, be shown to not really mean what they appear to say.

14. The New Testament writers could not possibly have known anything about our modern concept of long term, committed same-sex relationships because there's no mention of such in secular literature prior to or during their day.

15. Those Christians who practice discrimination against practicing LGBTQ people by citing culturally outdated texts from the Bible are making the same mistake that Christians made in the past who argued for the continuation of slavery on the basis of similar texts in the Bible.

16. If there's no scriptural basis upon which to assert that practicing LGBTQ lifestyles are immoral, then there's no basis for denying people their 'right' to enter into any kind of sexual relationship they wish (such as polygamy, incest, polyamorous arrangements, adultery, pedophilia, etc.) so long as the parties involved consent and enter into long-term loving commitments.

17. Celibacy is not a fair option to suggest to people with LGBTQ orientations since it is only a gift for some and denies LGBTQ

persons the intimacy and sexual fulfillment that is the right of every person.

18. Even if LGBTQ orientations were eventually to be discovered to be genetically based, genetic determinism should never be used as an excuse for immoral behavior.

19. Children growing up in LGBTQ households are just as well-developed as those in heterosexual households.

20. The 'proof text method' should not be used in dealing with LGBTQ issues. "A handful of selected Scripture statements" should not be given undue weight in determining the Church's approach to a major social issue. The Christian approach should be determined by 'the rule of faith' principle that brings into play the broader issues of love, acceptance, unity and personal fulfillment.

21. The word 'homosexual' is not found in the Bible. Translators are in error if they use this term because its use actually obscures the meaning of a text rather than clarifies it.

22. Most LGBTQ advocates hold that in the few places where same-sex sexual *acts* are mentioned in Scripture, the context suggests idolatry, violent rape, lust, exploitation, or promiscuity. The Bible says nothing about *orientation* as understood through modern science, nor is anything said about the loving relationship of two same-sex persons who have covenanted to be life partners.

23. Having transgender people use bathrooms, locker rooms and dorm rooms that don't match their birth gender is no big deal.

24. While mutual enjoyment and the fulfillment of the 'one flesh' union of a couple is part of God's design for marriage, the underlying purpose of sexual intercourse is procreation which is why he created humans as biologically complementary male and female.

25. LGBTQ lifestyles present no greater health risks and costs than heterosexual lifestyles do.

26. People should be prosecuted for discrimination or for hate speech if they refuse to sell to, rent to, hire, provide services for or denounce the lifestyles of practicing LGBTQ people.

27. The fact that other species engage in homosexual activities does not make it right for Homo sapiens to do so.

28. Sex change therapy and surgery has enabled transgender people to successfully change genders and live emotionally fulfilling and happy lives.

29. The Supreme Court's June 26, 2015 Obergefell v. Hodges decision to sanction gay marriage was a great step forward for people living LGBTQ lifestyles.

30. LGBTQ practices are neither destructive nor sinful, but should actually be celebrated if practiced in the right way. God *created* heterosexuals, homosexuals, bisexuals, transsexuals and queers. As with our racial, ethnic and other diversities, sexual diversity should also be celebrated as long as these relationships are practiced on a long-term basis with one partner.

What Do *You* Think?

1. Choose five of the above statements with which you most agree. Explain.

2. Choose five of the above statements with which you most disagree. Explain.

3. Have you ever met an LGBTQ person? How has this influenced your views?

4. Should practicing LGBTQ persons be welcomed to attend church services and events?

5. Should practicing LGBTQ persons be accepted as members and leaders in the church?

Drawing Conclusions |

The Sexual Revolution

The 'sexual revolution' burst upon the American scene between the 1960s and 1980s. It had its roots in a much broader seismic change called 'postmodernism.' Following two disastrous World Wars, postmodernism developed as a radical reaction to 'modernism' - a way of thinking launched by the Enlightenment in the 18th century that emphasized the existence of objective reality and absolute truth and subscribed to the ideas of rationality, humanism and progress. By contrast, postmodernism asserts that knowledge and truth are the products of unique systems of social, historical, and political developments and interpretation, and are therefore contextual and constructed. As a result, postmodern thought holds that there are no such things as universally applicable truths, that morality is relative, that all persons have a right to their own opinions and lifestyles as they see fit and that an individual's feelings and personal fulfillment are the summum bonum of life.

Within this philosophical and social context, social and moral norms based on a Judeo-Christian heritage that had been accepted in American society for centuries began to disintegrate. First, extreme feminists that endorsed these new 'norms' hijacked the positive women's liberation movement and convinced many women that they should be defined by their careers rather than by their role as mothers and homemakers. Then in 1960 came 'the pill' that made it possible to redefine sex as primarily being for pleasure rather than for procreation and that made sexual promiscuity possible without unwanted consequences. Next, in the 1970s, 'no fault divorce' became the law of the land - a development that avoided messy court and custody battles, but that also weakened the marriage commitment by making divorce a cheap commodity (currently offered at $139 a case) and by introducing serial polygamy – the idea that one could acquire and dismiss spouses like one acquires and gets rid of used cars.

This was followed in 1973 by the Supreme Court's Roe v. Wade decision to legalize 'abortion on demand.' If the pill or condoms or moral restraint didn't work, one could now simply dispense with the 'inconvenience' of bearing and raising a child through an abortion. In the 1980's the idea of 'co-habitation' took off. Rather than enter into lifetime marriage commitments, couples decided to 'try it out first' and enjoy the benefits of 'togetherness' without assuming the responsibilities of married life. Rather than reserving sex and children for marriage and family, it became increasingly acceptable for young people to not only live together, but to celebrate the birth of children without having made a marriage commitment. (For example, the Olympic swimming champion Michael Phelps' girlfriend showed up at the 2016 Rio Games with their three-week-old baby. Rather than being the cause for any embarrassment, the media made the little tyke the center piece of attention for an adoring public). Of course, many co-habiting couples did not (and do not) stay together, and of those that did (and do) and eventually get married, 20 percent are more likely to divorce than the average married couple.

During that same decade, most colleges and universities abandoned their 'in loco parentis' role and allowed students much more freedom to determine who they lived with and how they behaved. This eventually led to increased alcoholism, drug abuse, sexual promiscuity, sexual harassment and rape on college and university campuses. In 2016, all branches of the military accepted women for combat roles previously reserved for men despite women candidates failing a two-and-a-half year trial period with the Marines. This resulted in the mixing of men and women (many of whom were mothers of small children) far from home and family in close proximity under stressful conditions. As a result, the number of sexual harassment cases soared and the door to the possibility of women being drafted into such military service in the future was opened.

The cumulative effect of these developments resulted in an explosion of single parent 'families' (the great majority of them headed by women) which, in turn, resulted in the advent of 'latch key kids' and the mushrooming day care industry where kids were (and are) farmed out while their mothers are at work or serving in the military.

The biggest sexual revolution bombshell to hit the country,

however, was dropped in New York in Greenwich Village on June 28, 1969 with the Stonewall Rebellion. There, the first in a series of spontaneous, violent demonstrations by members of the gay community against a police raid on a gay establishment took place in the early morning hours on that date. These demonstrations are widely considered to constitute the single most important event leading to the 'gay liberation movement' and the subsequent campaign for LGBTQ rights in the United States. Within six months, two gay activist organizations were formed in New York, concentrating on confrontational tactics (the blueprint for which was followed to the letter in subsequent decades), and three newspapers were established to promote rights for gays and lesbians. Within a few years, gay rights organizations were founded across the U.S. and in some other countries.

On June 28, 1970, the first Gay Pride parades took place in New York, Los Angeles, San Francisco and Chicago commemorating the anniversary of the riots. Today, these commemorative Gay Pride events are held annually in the US and in some other countries toward the end of June. Utilizing LGBTQ-friendly media, entertainment and political figures, the threat of lawsuits, an aggressive public relations campaign and flawed 'research' (like the subsequently discredited 1948 Kinsey Report), the gay rights movement gained steam in subsequent decades. Eventually, in the 2003 landmark case of Lawrence v. Texas, the Supreme Court ruled that all state laws criminalizing same sex sexual activities were unconstitutional. In 2011, the 1994 'Don't ask, don't tell' policy was abandoned by the military and openly practicing LGBTQ people were allowed to serve in the armed forces. In 2015, in another landmark case (Obergefell v. Hodges), the Supreme Court decided to sanction gay marriage.

Also in 2015, a bill labeled the 'Equality Act' was introduced in the House of Representatives by gay rights advocates that sought to amend the Civil Rights Act of 1964 to include sex, sexual orientation, and gender identity among the prohibited categories of discrimination or segregation in places of public accommodation. It expanded the categories of public accommodations to include places or establishments that provide exhibitions, recreation, exercise, amusement, gatherings, displays, goods, services, programs, or transportation services. Among other provisions, it revised public school desegregation standards to provide for the assignment of students without regard to sexual orientation or gender identity. It prohibited programs or activities receiving federal financial assistance from denying benefits to, or discriminating against, persons based on sex, sexual orientation, or gender identity and prohibited employers with 15 or more employees from discriminating based on sexual orientation or gender identity.

With the Equality Act stalled in Congress, the Federal Departments of Education and Justice issued a 'guidance' letter in 2016 directing public schools to allow transgender students to use bathrooms matching their gender identity and "to ensure that transgender students enjoy a supportive and nondiscriminatory school environment." This guidance for schools went beyond the bathroom issue, touching upon privacy rights, education records and sex-segregated athletics, all but guaranteeing transgender students the right to identify in school as they choose. It imposed a new speech code on school employees and students, opened girl's shower rooms to boys, required schools to allow transgender boys to sleep in girl's rooms on overnight field trips, put transgender boys on girls sport teams and required transgender boys to room with girls even in single-sex dorms. Schools were prohibited from making any inquiry to ensure that the boys using the girls' facilities were, in fact, transgender. They could not ask for medical documentation or treatment information or even identification, but simply had to take a boy at 'her' word. Under the administration's interpretation of Title IX, the federal anti-discrimination law in education, schools receiving federal funds could not discriminate based on a student's sex, including a student's transgender status. The letter did not carry the force of law but the message was clear: fall in line or face loss of federal funding.

In 2017, the Department of Health and Human Services issued a 'Final Rule' that, among other things, significantly added gender identification and sex stereotyping to its anti-discrimination list. The Rule states: "…individuals are protected from discrimination in health care on the basis of race, color, national origin, age, disability and sex, including discrimination based on pregnancy, *gender identification and sex stereotyping*." Under this rule, transgender people must be provided transition-related services and cannot be denied healthcare by providers or professionals who receive federal funding. This basically includes any doctor, hospital, clinic, insurance company, etc. which financially engages in pretty much any way with Medicare, Medicaid, the Veteran's Administration, the Indian Health Service or the Affordable Care Act - in other words, just about every doctor, hospital or clinic and insurance company in the country. It also means that transgender people can demand sex change hormonal treatment and even surgery if incarcerated in federal prisons or serving in the military – at the taxpayer's expense!

In terms of the sexual revolution in general and the LGBTQ movement in particular, one of the most radical moral and ethical shifts in the history of the country has taken place in just seven decades. As this shift has evolved, it has become increasingly clear that the underlying agenda of the sexual revolution is to abolish gender distinctions, redefine 'marriage,' jettison the nuclear family and promote limitless sexual expression. As Alexander Webster puts it in a *Touchstones* May/June 2015 article (page 24):

> America is arguably at the mercy of militant secular 'progressives' hell-bent on subverting the cherished moral virtues of life, family, chastity, work, responsibility, and piety. Reaping an unprecedented harvest of more than 55 million legally aborted babies since 1973, our society is drowning in a sea of idolatrous self-worship, pursuing its own modern version of 'bread and circuses' through increasingly violent and vulgar forms of entertainment and self-expression, a permanent welfare state from cradle to grave, unrestricted sex, artificially constructed sexual identities and...publicly sanctioned 'marriages' between persons of the same sex - an unnatural abomination that even ancient Rome at its worst moments never imagined.

The most public demonstrable icon of this moral implosion is the annual week-long *Burning Man* event in the Nevada desert where over

70,000 devotes gather at considerable expense. Although there are rules regarding safety, ecological matters, artistic expressions and commercial transactions, when it comes to self-expression, there are no limits. Nudity, sex, drugs and alcohol abound within a context of pagan 'spirituality.' The huge man statue is burned on the evening of the summer solstice; a temporary 'temple' structure is erected for participants to engage in New Age types of spirituality; 'total freedom' without restraints is practiced. *Burning Man* groups and events have now sprung up around the country and in some foreign countries.

The sexual revolution has been led by what could be described as 'progressive fundamentalists' - people who at first called for dialogue and debates on these issues, but who now have no room for such dialogue and debates. To them, to concede that people can have reasonable disagreement about the morality of LGBTQ behaviors grants that the traditional or conservative side has legitimate arguments grounded in rationality and plausibility. This is now unacceptable to them because granting that religion offers an alternate perspective on the purpose of human sexuality fails to recognize the so-called harm being done to LGBTQ persons whose very lives are at stake, so such positions must be 'stamped out.' For example, the gay rights movement's Human Rights Campaign creates campaigns that increasingly insinuate that anyone dissenting on sexuality is guilty of criminal behavior.

Where have Christians been during these increasingly decadent decades? Externally, rather than challenging the basic premises of the postmodern era and the resultant sexual revolution, too many Christians and their churches have avoided taking what have become increasingly unpopular stances on the false assumption that by so doing, they will retain their membership levels and their influence in an evolving society. The opposite has, of course, been the case. Most mainline Protestant denominations have been losing members at an alarming rate because they have been sounding an 'uncertain trumpet' and have all but abandoned the prophetic voice that this new age needs to hear. Rather than influencing the culture, too many Christians and their churches have been captured by the culture. Like the frog in the beaker, as the cultural water has slowly heated up, they have adjusted to the temperature, not realizing that they need to jump out of the beaker to avoid being slowing cooked to death.

Internally, at the very time when Christians need the discipline and discipleship that living out the lifestyle of Jesus Christ in this era calls for, too many have instead too often been fed easy to digest cafeteria-style theological and biblical deserts rather than the meat, veggies and potatoes they desperately need to keep their moral compass in this confusing and challenging era. As Chuck Colson once put it, "Today's church is a mile wide and an inch deep." Just when Christians need to know what they believe and why they believe it, a growing number have become biblically and doctrinally illiterate. Too many of their pastors are silent on today's sexual issues or have aided and abetted both post-modern concepts and the sexual revolution by spreading what amounts to false teaching. For this reason, particularly concerning the LBGTQ onslaught, too many Christians don't have an in-depth understanding of the scriptural teaching on these issues. Nor can they separate fact from fantasy concerning the sociological data regarding these issues. As a result, there is a great deal of confusion, controversy and division among Christians over how to deal with the sexual revolution in general and the LBGTQ phenomenon in particular.

So what *should* Christians believe and do when it comes to Lesbians, Gays, Bisexuals, Transgenders and Queers? We will address that question in the next chapter.

What Do *You* Think?

1. The thing I most agree with in this chapter is ……

2. The thing I most disagree with in this chapter is …...

3. The thing that bothers me the most about the Post Modern era is …… because …...

4. The thing that bothers me the most about the Sexual Revolution is …… because …...

5. The thing that bothers me the most about this whole LGBTQ controversy is …... because ……

Chapter Twenty

LGBTQ CLAIMS: FACT OR FICTION?

> "Let us conduct ourselves properly, as people who live in the light of day - no orgies or drunkenness, no immorality or indecency, no fighting or jealousy. But take up the weapons of the Lord Jesus Christ, and stop paying attention to your sinful nature and satisfying its desires."   Romans 13:13-14

Looking Through the Microscope |

God Calls in Love by Janet Boynes

A big factor that drew me into a lesbian lifestyle was the abuse I witnessed and experienced as a child. My parental figures were my single mother and the four men who fathered her seven children. I was the middle child of the seven, and saw my mother repeatedly abused by 'big men.' Determined to avoid that same fate for myself, I became a tomboy. I hung out with guys and became known as a bully. I moved from Philadelphia to St. Paul to attend college, and gave my life to Christ at the Jesus People Church. Although I dated men, I still had a fear of them. Then I became engaged to a great Christian guy and we enrolled in pre-marital counseling at our church.

But I was lonely. My fiancé traveled extensively, so I spent a lot of time with girlfriends. When a girl I'd met at work initiated a sexual relationship one night, I was caught off-guard and went along with it. Immediately I knew how Eve must have felt. Condemned! I sought out my pastor the next day, and he told me that, of course, the wedding had to be cancelled. Devastated and repentant, I told my fiancé everything. 'No, that's not you,' he protested. 'You just made a mistake.' But I had such a strong sense that God had turned his eyes away from me that I walked away from the Lord. It was hopeless, I thought, so I might as well have a 'season of fun.'

Now, years later, I know I was mistaken on all counts. God never left me. He continued to protect me and work in my life. I never found the satisfaction I was looking for in the gay lifestyle. Instead, I went from relationship to relationship and became totally confused. Was being gay OK with God? Should I have a sex change? Was the Christian life I had previously enjoyed over for good? Would I die before I could repent and come back to the Lord? Deep down I knew only the Lord could rescue me. Didn't the Bible say Jesus seeks any of his sheep that get lost? I'd see people on the bus reading their Bibles, and I'd want to run up to them and say, 'Help me! I'm a backslidden Christian and I don't know how to get right with the Lord.'

Fourteen years went by. I had a cleaning business and owned my own home in Maple Grove. Whenever I'd pass the Maple Grove Assembly of God Church near my house, an inner voice would tell me that someday I'd be going to that church. The suggestion was so strong that I even mentioned it to my girlfriend and we laughed about it. Yet the idea stayed with me even though I was doing drugs, cheating on my steady girlfriend, suffering from an eating disorder, and extremely unhappy. I knew the Lord was knocking on the door of my heart (See Revelation 3:20), but I didn't know how or even if I should respond.

One night, I ran to the grocery store and noticed a woman in the parking lot with her groceries at 3 a.m. She said she'd been helping her son move into the dorm at North Central Bible College, so I knew right away she was a Christian. We talked and talked, and then she invited me to come to her church - Maple Grove Assembly of God! I accepted her invitation, and a few days later went to her Bible Study.

I came in late, and there sat nine feminine women. I was dressed like a boy in an old shirt and jeans with a hair band around my cropped hair. I wanted them to like me. I knew I wanted Jesus, but I had no idea how to get back to Him. Those nine women loved me as I was. They answered my questions and helped me every way they could. When I asked them, they gave me pointers on how to dress and apply make-up. They educated me about spiritual warfare, and helped me break the stronghold the devil had erected over my life.

The change in me was so dramatic that I sold my home and moved in with a Christian family for a year. I needed that role-modeling of a healthy family life and being held accountable. I never could have survived as a Christian without it. Gradually, my mess became the message of salvation. It was a real struggle, but I wanted God more than I wanted the lesbian lifestyle.

Six years later, I still stay in the Word of God and pray daily that I won't slip back into that lifestyle. I try to stay transparent, accountable, and control my thoughts. I never could have changed my life by myself, but now I can say, 'Look at what the Lord has done!' I know God wants me to speak out about these things. Hollywood makes the homosexual lifestyle look so glamorous. Gay activists are aggressively pushing for society to condone their agenda. But we need to remember that God is 'in the changing business' and wants to transform lives. The Christian women at Maple Grove Assembly loved me and spent time with me, and that made me want to grow spiritually. Too many gays and lesbians 'hate' Christians and feel condemned. But it's the love of Christ - not condemnation - that draws us toward repentance. After all, everybody wants the same thing: love and acceptance. When God calls us out of darkness and into the light (See 1 Peter 2:9), he calls in love.

After attending Exodus International's conference on homosexuality this past summer, I was greatly encouraged by their ministry and look forward to working with them to reach the African-American community. My message and my heart will continue to be for helping those struggling with homosexuality by bringing the church together across racial lines to minister to the hurting in love. I truly believe that what God has done in my life, he can also do in the lives of everyone who calls on his name. When God calls us out of darkness and into light, he calls in love

What Do *You* Think?

1. Do you agree with Janet's comment that she knew her lesbian lifestyle was in conflict with her faith? Why or why not?

2. Do you agree with Janet that "A big factor that drew me into a lesbian lifestyle was the abuse I witnessed and experienced as a child."? Explain.

3. Do you agree with Janet that LGBTQ people can change their lifestyle and even their orientation, or should their lifestyle and orientation be accepted, affirmed and even celebrated? Explain.

4. What would you say were the key steps that enabled Janet to leave her lesbian lifestyle behind?

Bringing Things Into Focus |

Is LGBTQ Change Possible?

The following statement was the first in the True or False list in the previous chapter. Did you decide it's true or false?

Therapeutic intervention (reparative therapy) to alter their orientation hasn't worked for LGBTQ people who've attempted it and should therefore be outlawed in all states.

Many people, including some Christians, agree with this statement. They refer to the decision of British Courage Trust founder Jeremy Marks and Exodus International's President Jeremy Chambers to stop trying to assist practicing homosexuals to change their orientation and instead to enable them to "reconcile their faith and sexuality." They also cite their opinion that these ministries have had a destructive effect on the lives of many gay people and have had a corrosive effect on their faith in God. However, they fail to inform us about a similarly well-known case, only in the opposite direction.

Joe Dallas, founder of Genesis Counseling, is a prominent author and speaker for the ex-gay movement. He was a former gay rights activist and staff member of a gay Metropolitan Community Church. Here is what he has to say on this subject in his book *The Gay Gospel?* (Harvest House 2007, p. 12)

I remember clearly, and with inexpressible regret, the day I convinced myself it was acceptable for me to be both gay and Christian. Not only did I embrace the pro-gay theology - I promoted it as well...Twelve years have passed since I realized my error, and during those years the pro-gay theology has enjoyed unprecedented exposure and acceptance...An answer is required...the Church must respond...While many mental health authorities believe homosexuality is unchangeable, many others believe it *can* be changed...(For example), the Director of the New York Center for Psychoanalytic Training...remarked on the 'misinformation spread by certain circles that homosexuality is untreatable by their saying it has done incalculable harm to thousands.'

These same people also agree with our true/false statement because they see the LGBTQ therapy glass as half empty rather than half full. They highlight the tragic lapses of former ex-gay Christian leaders like John Paulk and Michael Johnston. They feature quotes by present ex-gay leaders like Jeff Ford and Bob Davies that appear on the surface to cast some doubts on the possibility of homosexual healing and transformation. They cite with empathy the fact that the major American mental health associations, representing nearly half a million professionals, are essentially unanimous in rejecting the assumption of reparative therapy (that homosexuality is a disorder that needs a cure) and in challenging the belief that such therapy can enable gays and lesbians to reverse their sexual desires. They frame the issue of whether the likelihood of sexual reorientation is sufficient to encourage the effort with the negative measurement of the 'failure rate' rather than with the positive measurement of the considerable success rate. And they take the testimonials and track records of ex-homosexuals with a skeptical bag of salt.

However, suppose we take the opposite tack. What do we see if we view the LGBTQ therapy glass as half full? There are eight major ministry networks with hundreds of centers all over the world that offer programs of help and support to gays and lesbians that want to leave their homosexual lifestyles behind. These organizations reliably report that such change is not a theoretical possibility - it is a daily reality for thousands of people like Janet, some of whom left homosexuality decades ago. Today, there are nine major ministry organizations, along with many smaller groups, that are working with thousands of LGBTQ people to help them deal with their sexual orientations either through therapy or through celibacy.

--- **One by One** is a ministry group within the Presbyterian Church of the United States of America (PCUSA) that exists to educate and equip churches to minister to those who desire freedom from unwanted same-sex attraction, sexual attraction, sexual addiction, and the effects of sexual abuse.

--- **Courage** is a Roman Catholic ministry group with about 15 centers in North America that helps LGBTQ people deal with their sexual predispositions by electing to live chaste celibate lives.

--- **Evergreen International Inc.**: is a Mormon treatment center, founded in 1989, with 13 branches in the US, Australia and Canada.

--- **Exodus Global Alliance** has five network offices that link enquirers to hundreds of local sexual transformative ministries around the world and that proclaims that faith in Christ and a transformed life is possible for homosexuals through the power of a relationship with Jesus Christ.

--- **Homosexuals Anonymous (HA)** has 38 chapters in the USA, one in Canada and one in Australia. They have created a 14 step program that is similar to *Alcoholics Anonymous'* 12 step recovery program to help sexually conflicted people to transform their lifestyles.

--- **Love in Action** is a residential program located in Memphis, TN. About 10 men, aged typically 21 to 50, live together in a large farmhouse, attempting to leave their gay lifestyle. Most clients spend 13 to 18 months in the program.

--- **New Direction for Life Ministries of Canada** is a major Canadian transformational ministry that offers Christian support to men and women choosing to leave homosexuality, and equipping the church to minister effectively and compassionately to them.

--- **P-FOX** stands for *Parents and Friends of Ex-Gays* and is a support organization that ministers to gays and their families.

--- **Transforming Congregations** is a ministry sponsored by a large number of United Methodist Churches that support gays and lesbians who want to try to change their orientation through the transformative power of God's Spirit.

Unfortunately, despite its documented success rate, reparative therapy has now been outlawed in a number of states, with more states leaning towards doing the same. How ironic that these same states not only allow, but actually advocate transgender therapy for children as well as adults to accept their transgender condition, including the surgical mutilation of their bodies, in spite of the testimony of some leading transgender psychiatrists that transgender people have deep mental and emotional problems that will never be solved by an impossible attempt to change their gender.

On the one hand, the fact that some ex-gay testimonials turn out to be suspect should not lead to what amounts to a wholesale rejection of the plethora of people who have described and demonstrated impressive sexual transformation over a significant period of time. On the other hand, the judgments concerning homosexual reorientation and recovery therapy of the American Psychiatric Association and other mental health associations should be exposed for what they are. Aren't these the same organizations that opined that Freudian psychological archeology was the only way to go in psychiatric treatment not so many years ago? And, when it comes to the subject of homosexuality, have they not too often tended to confuse dispassionate psychological research with political dogma?

In 2009, respected psychologists Stanton L. Jones and Mark A. Yarhouse published the results of an exhaustive seven-year study in which the authors followed 61 homosexual subjects, recording their failures and successes in their attempt to leave homosexuality. They found significant change in 53 percent of their subjects, with 23 percent reporting a successful conversion to heterosexual attractions. A 1997 NARTH survey of homosexual recovery therapy programs showed that homosexuals have *better* recovery statistics than Alcoholics Anonymous (28.8 percent vs. 25-30 percent). That being the case, one would hope LGBTQ advocates would not also favor shutting down alcoholic and drug treatment programs and promoting alcoholism and drug abuse because their success rates aren't high enough. Other studies show that, particularly in transgender oriented children and young people, significant shifts in gender orientation often occur apart from *any* therapeutic treatment.

The New Testament is replete with assertions and testimonials that Jesus Christ, through his Spirit and through his body the Church (some members of which he has equipped with wonderful gifts for spiritually informed psychotherapeutic ministry), can do the equivalent of changing a leopard's spots. For example, Paul writes:

> Surely you know that the wicked will not possess God's Kingdom. Do not fool yourselves; people who are immoral or who worship idols or are adulterers or homosexual perverts or who steal or are greedy or are drunkards or who slander others or are thieves - none of these will possess God's Kingdom. Some of you were like that. But you have been purified from sin; you have been dedicated to God; you have

been put right with God by the Lord Jesus Christ and by the Spirit of our God. 1 Corinthians 6:9-11

Elsewhere, Paul talks about this change as being 'sanctified.' What he means is that having confessed their sins, repented of those sins and believed the gospel, Christians have been declared to be saved through Christ's saving work. They are then called to become what they've been declared to be - a lifelong process during which growth and healing take place, particularly after lapses. ("Be patient, God isn't through with me yet.") When the Kingdom of God comes in all its fullness, Christians believe they will finally reach the goal that they and God have been striving for together - they will be completely saved, changed, healed, and renewed. That seems impossible to secular skeptics, but those who have opened their lives to such power and to such 'therapy,' know better, practicing LGBTQ people included. This is the great hope that *all of us*, not just our homosexual brothers and sisters, rely upon.

There are many stirring testimonials by people with LGBTQ orientations that have chosen to undergo therapy in order to change their orientation or to live in celibacy. Is it unloving for the Church to work with and encourage other practicing LGBTQ people to do the same? Not to do so is to betray the people who have successfully gone through the painful struggle of leaving their sexual practices behind. And is it unkind to ask people who have not yet succeeded in changing their orientation to refrain from a destructive lifestyle and consider the discipline of celibacy? After all, there are thousands of single Christians who do not have the gift of celibacy and who would like to be married, but who nevertheless, in obedience to the Scripture, live their lives in singleness without engaging in promiscuity.

How sad that some of the very people those practicing LGBTQ lifestyles should depend on to tell them the truth about the destructive nature of homosexual practice, and the even greater truth about the Good News of change, are instead discouraging them from renouncing that practice and seeking that change. What a tragedy that the thousands of practicing homosexuals who *have* embarked on this journey of sanctification and who *have* made significant progress are met with skepticism and even irritation because they contradict someone's anti-reparative theory. Where tolerance has increased for the gay community, it has decreased for the ex-gay community.

What Do *You* Think?

1. Do you think it's possible for practicing LGBTQ people to change their orientation? Why or why not?

2. Have you ever met or heard about an ex-gay person who successfully left his or her gay lifestyle behind? Explain.

3. Do you think 'political correctness,' the spread of misinformation and ideological bias have influenced the discussion about reparative therapy? Explain.

4. Do you believe that opening ourselves to the healing power of Jesus can help us all (including drug addicts, alcoholics, practicing LGBTQ people, etc.) overcome the sins that dominate our lives? Why or why not?

Gaining a Perspective |

What the Bible Says about LGBTQ Lifestyles

- **Genesis 19:4-11**. "Before the guests went to bed, the men of Sodom surrounded the house. All the men of the city, both young and old, were there. They called out to Lot and asked, 'Where are the men who came to stay with you tonight? Bring them out to us!' The men of Sodom wanted to have sex with them. Lot went outside and closed the door behind him. He said to them, 'Friends, I beg you, don't do such a wicked thing!'"

- **Leviticus 18:22**. "No man is to have sexual relations with another man; God hates that."

- **Leviticus 20:13.** "If a man has sexual relations with another man, they have done a disgusting thing, and both shall be put to death. They are responsible for their own death."

- **Judges 19:22-25.** "They were enjoying themselves when all of a sudden some sexual perverts from the town surrounded the house and started beating on the door. They said to the old man, 'Bring out that man that came home with you! We want to have sex with him!' But the old man went outside and said to them, 'No, my friends! Please! Don't do such an evil, immoral thing! This man is my guest.'"

- **Romans 1:25-27.** "They exchange the truth about God for a lie; they worship and serve what God has created instead of the Creator himself, who is to be praised forever! Amen. Because they do this, God has given them over to shameful passions. Even the women pervert the natural use of their sex by unnatural acts. In the same way the men give up natural sexual relations with women and burn with passion for each other. Men do shameful things with each other, and as a result they bring upon themselves the punishment they deserve for their wrongdoing."

- **1 Corinthians 6:9.** "Surely you know that the wicked will not possess God's Kingdom. Do not fool yourselves; people who are immoral or who worship idols or are adulterers or homosexual perverts or who steal or are greedy or are drunkards or who slander others or are thieves - none of these will possess God's Kingdom."

- **1 Timothy 1:9-10.** "It must be remembered, of course, that laws are made, not for good people, but for lawbreakers and criminals, for the godless and sinful, for those who are not religious or spiritual, for those who kill their fathers or mothers, for murderers, for the immoral, for sexual perverts, for kidnappers, for those who lie and give false testimony or who do anything else contrary to sound doctrine."

- **2 Peter 2:6-10.** "God condemned the cities of Sodom and Gomorrah, destroying them with fire, and made them an example of what will happen to the godless. He rescued Lot, a good man, who was distressed by the immoral conduct of lawless people. That good man lived among them, and day after day he suffered agony as he saw and heard their evil actions. And so the Lord knows how to rescue godly people from their trials and how to keep the wicked under punishment for the Day of Judgment, especially those who follow their filthy bodily lusts and despise God's authority."

- **Jude 7.** "Remember Sodom and Gomorrah, and the nearby towns, whose people acted as those angels did and indulged in sexual immorality and perversion: they suffer the punishment of eternal fire as a plain warning to all."

What Do *You* Think?

1. Which Scripture text do you find most compelling in forbidding Christians from practicing LGBTQ lifestyles? Why?

2. Which Scripture text do you find least compelling in forbidding Christians from practicing LGBTQ lifestyles? Why?

3. Do you think Biblical statements like these are culturally relative or are they absolutes that are relevant for all peoples in all cultures at all times? Explain.

4. When it comes to LGBTQ issues, which is more important to you, biblical statements or social research? Why?

5. Do you think these biblical statements apply to all people who identify themselves as LGBTQ or only to those who *practice* LGBTQ lifestyles? Explain.

Drawing Conclusions |

Separating Fact from Fiction

How can we separate LGBTQ fact from fiction? Or, to put it another way, what *should* Christians believe and do when it comes to Lesbians, Gays, Bisexuals, Transgenders and Queers? We can best address that by reviewing the rest of the True or False statements that you were asked to decide on in the previous chapter.

1. The Bible's teaching on LGBTQ issues is either unclear or culturally outdated. FALSE

To begin with, besides multiple injunctions in the Old Testament, there are many statements in the New Testament that warn against sexual immorality of any kind in general. For example, "But among you there must not be even a hint of sexual immorality, or of any kind of impurity...because these are improper for God's holy people." Ephesians 5:3 (See also Matthew 15:19-20; 1 Corinthians 6:18, 20; Ephesians 5:3-4, 12; Colossians 3:5-10; 1 Thessalonians 4:3-8; Titus 2:11-12; Hebrews 12:16; 13:41 and 1 John 2:16-17).

Besides these, the writers of Scripture specifically address the subject of homosexual practice, either directly or indirectly, nine times. (See above). Both the Old and New Testaments consistently, clearly and emphatically teach that it's contrary to God's will to engage in homosexual activity. To say that they teach otherwise is to abandon the normal interpretive tools that are used to understand biblical teaching on any other subject. Likewise, to say that the teaching of these passages may now be abandoned because they're no longer relevant to modern culture is to abandon the normal tools that biblical scholars use to apply biblical teaching to today's world on any other subject.

A number of arguments are brought forward to discredit what's plainly taught in Scripture: there are only a few texts that speak directly to the issue of homosexuality; the Bible condemns only exploitative, pederast forms of homosexuality; the Bible primarily condemns homosexuality because of its threat to male domination; the Bible has no category for 'homosexuals' with an exclusively same-sex orientation; homosexuality has a genetic component that the writers of the Bible didn't know about. However, when an honest in-depth investigation is made of the biblical statements on homosexuality, using generally accepted interpretive rules, none of these arguments can be substantiated.

In addition, in both the Old and New Testaments, the writers of Scripture presuppose and promote sexual practice only within the bounds of a heterosexual marriage relationship between a man and a woman. (See Genesis 2-3 and Matthew 19:3-6, for example). Even the initially tolerated pagan practice of polygamy eventually gave way to the biblical concept that a marriage bond should only be forged between *one* man and *one* woman. It's plain that the writers of Scripture would be astounded by the claims of some modern scholars that their writings can be 'reinterpreted' in such a way as to allow for some other kind of sexual practice and relationship.

Many advocates hold that the clear prohibitions and dire consequences of homosexual practice in the Old Testament, such as those in Leviticus 18:22 and 20:13, like so many other prohibitions and punishments of the Israelite holiness code, are culturally conditioned and therefore not applicable to later times. If such teaching were to only be found in the Old Testament and ignored or contradicted by the New Testament, one could rightly apply the principle of 'progressive revelation' and conclude that such teaching was no longer culturally relevant in our day. However, the opposite is true. Of the texts that directly deal with this subject, four are in the New Testament! The two Testaments not only *agree* on this teaching, but the New Testament passages actually *amplify* and *underline* this teaching. All relevant passages in both testaments consistently teach that the practice of homosexuality is destructive, and therefore unacceptable, sinful behavior.

In rightly interpreting biblical statements on any subject and applying them to ever changing cultural conditions, one would expect normal rules of interpretation to be followed. Those arguing that these statements are now culturally irrelevant (like those prohibiting long hair, veils, the role of women, divorce and re-marriage, etc.) too often treat these rules cavalierly in order to alter scriptural teaching to accommodate shifting cultural norms rather than the other way around. For example, one must ask why, in the case of other types of sinful sexual behavior censured in the Bible, such as adultery, incest, bestiality, prostitution, fornication (and in the New Testament, polygamy), only the censure of the practice of homosexual behavior is singled out as irrelevant for our day.

In his book *The Bible and Homosexual Practice*, Robert Gagnon, noted Biblical scholar of Pittsburg Theological Seminary, lists five convincing reasons why the principle of cultural irrelevancy does not apply in the case of any kind of homosexual practice.

> 1) Homosexual practice is proscribed *by both Testaments* that are in complete agreement. 2) It is proscribed *pervasively within each Testament.* There are no dissenting voices anywhere in either Testament. 3) It is *severely* proscribed behavior. The revulsion expressed in both Testaments is as strong as it could be. 4) It is proscribed *absolutely.* The proscription encompasses every, and any, form of homosexual practice. 5) It is proscribed in a way *that makes sense.* The complementarity of male and female is a clear indication in the natural order of God's will for sexuality. (pp. 449-450)

2. Until this century, both Jews (following the O.T.) and Christians (following both Testaments) have consistently interpreted the relevant Scripture passages to mean that all LGBTQ practices (including 'loving mutual lifetime relationships') under any circumstances in any place are immoral behaviors that are contradictory to a Christian lifestyle. TRUE

For over three thousand years, Jewish teaching, based on the writings of the Old Testament, has consistently and emphatically held that homosexual practice is a serious breach of God's will for human behavior, and that it carries the gravest of penalties. For almost two thousand years, Christian teaching, based on the Old and New Testaments, has held the same. Only within the last few decades has what could be termed a pro-homosexual movement challenged this teaching. To overturn such consistent and venerable teaching, the burden of proof lies with recent 'revisionist' scholars to demonstrate beyond doubt that there are compelling reasons to reject or reinterpret this biblically based teaching in light of modern cultural requirements. They've not done so. Some revisionists are at least honest enough to state that a straightforward interpretation of Paul's teaching on this issue doesn't, in fact, support the revisionist position. They admit, for example, that Paul can't be made to say what he doesn't mean in Romans 1 concerning homosexual practice.

If conclusions about biblical teaching are merely extensions of one's personal beliefs, then we're in a subjective no-man's-land where "every person concludes what is right in his/her own eyes." Until this century, both Jews and Christians have consistently interpreted the relevant biblical passages to mean that *all* homosexual practice (including "loving mutual lifetime relationships") under *any* circumstances in *any* place is immoral behavior that's contradictory to both the Jewish and the Christian lifestyles. There've been no compelling reasons or recent been discoveries to abandon their teaching.

3. Jesus said nothing about LGBTQ issues, but did say a lot about loving relationships, which would lead one to believe that he wouldn't oppose lifelong same-sex partnerships, gay marriage or a bi-sexual or transgender lifestyle. <u>FALSE</u>

This is an argument from silence that, as such, is inconclusive. Jesus said nothing about the sexual sins of incest, bestiality or pedophilia either, but does that mean he would have condoned such practices? Hardly. On the contrary, when taking over a millennium of Jewish teaching clearly rejecting homosexual practice into account, Jesus' silence would indicate that he *agreed* with that teaching. He certainly was quick to point out any teaching that he disagreed with. As we've seen, when he did comment on moral and ethical issues, his stance was usually more, not less demanding than that of the Mosaic Law.

But was Jesus really silent? When speaking of sexual relationships, he made it very clear that he believed in an exclusively heterosexual model of monogamy. (See Mark 10:1-12). Some contend that because Jesus welcomed and extended hospitality to the despised and 'sinners' of his day, we should do the same for our practicing LGBTQ brothers and sisters. However, Jesus' encounters with people who were considered to be sexual sinners show that in extending loving forgiveness, he didn't condone their actions. "Go *and sin no more*," he said. John 8:11 Jesus always held out his forgiving and gracious arms to all, but he made it clear that to enter the Kingdom of God, one must repent of one's sinful behavior, believe in his power to enable one to change that behavior and be willing to live a godly life in gratitude for his grace. Why would we expect him to do anything different were he to meet a practicing LGBTQ person today? Finally, to say that Jesus' silence meant that he approved of LGBTQ practices pre-supposes that the Apostle Paul developed moral teaching on both homosexual practice and forgiveness that contradicted the teaching of Jesus. On the contrary, a close examination of his views shows that his ideas were consistent with, and based upon, that teaching.

4. Christians don't follow some of the precepts or practices contained in the Bible now, so those against practicing LGBTQ lifestyles should not be binding either. FALSE

A long list of biblical prohibitions that are no longer in force are usually cited to buttress this view: slavery is no longer tolerated; women do not wear veils any longer, but they do cut their hair, use makeup, wear jewelry and are ordained; the Church has adopted a kinder, gentler view towards divorce, etc. However, upon closer examination, the principle of 'progressive revelation' teaches us that on these matters, God continued to make his will clearer as time went on. In many instances, the Bible as God's revelation itself brought a corrective lens to bear. For example, Isaiah (56:1-7) corrects outdated legislation regarding the status of eunuchs among the people of God. (See Deuteronomy 23:1; Leviticus 21:18-20). Jesus threw new light on Old Testament misperceptions. (See Matthew 5-7) And so on.

In other instances, practices that were dictated by the cultural norms of the day have rightly been abandoned because the cultural symbols of those norms no longer represent what they used to represent. For example, short hair is no longer considered to be a symbol identifying female prostitutes and a woman speaking in public is no longer considered to be culturally unthinkable. However, when it comes to LGBTQ practice, the New Testament passages dealing with this issue consistently make it clear that such practices remain contrary to God's will and to a Christian lifestyle for all time.

5. **LGBTQ people don't choose their orientation, they're born that way due to their genetic, God-given makeup. So they have as much right to practice, and indeed celebrate, their way of life, as do heterosexuals. FALSE**

An LGBTQ person's *claim* that his/her orientation is a given within their genetic birth character does not make it a scientific fact. To date, there's very little scientific evidence to back up that claim. Most evidence points to functional causes of homosexual orientation rather than organic causes. However, there *is* compelling scientific evidence that some people are more prone to alcoholism than others. In that case, who would argue that we should therefore accept alcoholism as normal behavior and shut down the AA's efforts to help alcoholics to change?

The scriptures teach that God created humans "good." Abnormalities like cancer, heart defects, physical deformities, depression, etc. are the results of a fallen, suffering creation. That these were *not* God's intentions can be seen in that God came in Christ to offer *healing* and wholeness to us who suffer the effects of the fall and to give us the strength to bear the unbearable in this life. This is also true for those who are struggling with LGBTQ issues.

The facts are that evidence from brain studies, gene studies, hormonal studies, childhood socialization studies, cross-cultural studies, environmental studies and sexual behavior studies *all* show that genetic influence on LGBTQ orientations is, if existent at all, relatively weak in comparison with family, societal, and other environmental influences. For example, cultural norms, not some form of genetic determinism, play the dominant role as to how and whether homosexuality will come to be practiced. Identical twins studies, for example, show that twins raised in identical environments can develop different sexual orientations, leading to the conclusion that choice does play at least some part in their development. In addition, it's not true that "once gay, always gay." Some 80% of male adolescents who report same-sex attractions no longer do so as adults.

6. **A satisfying lifestyle, emotional intimacy and a deep interpersonal commitment are available to LGBTQ people only in the context of a relationship with other LGBTQ people. <u>FALSE</u>**

Study results conclusively show that practicing LGBTQ people live personally and socially destructive lifestyles. The personal damage suffered by male homosexuals as a result of their lifestyle, for example, is depressing. They can expect a 25-30 year decrease in life expectancy, chronic liver disease, a high incidence of inevitably fatal immune disease, a high incidence of rectal cancer and multiple bowel and other infectious diseases. Both gays and lesbians contract sexually transmitted diseases at a rate two to three times higher than heterosexuals do. They experience significantly higher rates of alcohol and drug abuse. They suffer major depression because of their inability to procreate with their same-sex partners, their obsessive centering on self-gratification, the ever-present ominous possibility of contracting same-sex diseases and their internal shame and guilt over abnormal and unnatural sexual practices. As a result, they have a much higher than usual incidence of suicide, usually over ruptured partnerships. These conditions do not lend themselves to a satisfying lifestyle, emotional intimacy and deep interpersonal commitment, but in most cases, they do produce unfulfilling and unstable relationships.

7. **People that characterize LGBTQ behaviors as illegitimate lifestyles are suffering from an LGBTQ phobia. Once you get to know LGBTQ people personally, you will discover that they're very nice people whom the church should welcome rather than condemn. <u>FALSE</u>**

Christianity Under the Microscope

The term 'homophobiac' is meant to be derogatory, but it's actually complimentary. Christians *should* be homophobiacs. They should also be adulterophobiacs, prostophobiacs, narcophobiacs, polygophobiacs, incestophobiacs and pedophobiacs. That is, in faithfulness to the Scripture, they should not only be fearful of and opposed to LGBTQ practices, but also the practice of adultery, prostitution, drug addiction, incest, polygamy, pedophilia and the like.

Note that this fear does not have to do with a fear of *individuals*, but of their *actions*. Christians are called to love everyone, including practicing LGBTQ people, but not to condone anyone's actions if they're contrary to what God requires. The Bible doesn't reject *people* as such, but their *actions*, and Christians should do so as well.

Whether people are 'nice' or not is beside the point. Nice people sometimes make grievous mistakes. There are some people who mean well but who don't live well. There are other people who are sincere, but who are sincerely wrong. When you get down to it, the Bible doesn't describe any of us as nice people. We're all sinners in need of grace. The calling and responsibility of the Church is to invite *all* of us 'nice' people to repentance, faith and renewal, including those who are practicing LGBTQ people. This call is based on what the Scripture instructs Christians to do, and is to be offered as good news - good news that holds the promise of healing and wholeness.

Of course Christians should welcome all who wish to meet with them, practicing LGBTQ people included. They should feel loved and welcomed, but like all other Christians, they shouldn't presume leadership or even membership on their own terms. They too must promise to "renounce sin and the power of evil" in their lives, just like all other Christians. After all, it's not the Church that sets the terms, but Christ. They should, along with all Christians, expect to be challenged by the good news that can set them, and all people, free from all that would destroy us.

8. LGBTQ people should have the same civil 'rights' as anybody else, including the right to marry someone of the same sex and 'have' or adopt children. <u>FALSE</u>

This statement would be true if LGBTQ lifestyles were to be recognized as legitimate, and even celebrated, lifestyles. Such recognition has been the goal of the LGBTQ movement, both in society and within some churches. However, for reasons already given, Christians can't grant such recognition and should therefore not support the movement's civil rights agenda. Society and the Church have belatedly come to the correct conclusion that LGBTQ practices should be decriminalized and that people with these orientations should be encouraged to 'come out of the closet.' People have wisely discerned that in some cases, including this one, sin and crime are not synonymous.

However, it must be asked, "Once someone has come out of the closet, then what?" The LGBTQ movement would answer this question by saying, "To be set free to live LGBTQ lifestyles; to 'marry;' to 'have' or adopt children; to live whatever lifestyle brings the most fulfillment; to choose whatever vocation one aspires to (including the Christian ministry); to have the same rights as anybody else, without discrimination." The Christian Church must answer this question by saying, "To frankly share one's private struggle with LGBTQ tendencies or practices; to seek healing through the power of faith and prayer; to pursue a change in orientation; to remain celibate until such time that one can successfully enter into a heterosexual marriage."

Despite what some Christians would like to believe, there's no magic middle road between these two responses. To grant LGBTQ practitioners the "same rights as anybody else" while describing their lifestyles as being destructive is a contradiction. Again, it must be asked, do we really want our whole concept of gender, marriage and family redefined, and if so, on what basis? Do we really want our nation's schools, and even our churches, to be staffed by people who openly espouse the LGBTQ agenda, and if so, why?

If Canada is any example, they will be. Canada adopted a Canadian Charter of Rights and Freedoms in 1982 that in essence enshrines the 'rights' of LGBTQ people as a protected minority. In 2005, the Canadian Legislature, in response to heavy pressure from the LGBTQ movement, passed controversial legislation granting same sex rights, including marriage rights, to homosexuals. The legislation has a provision that clergy are not required to perform same-sex marriages against their will, but one might ask how long this provision will be tolerated by the movement and upheld in the courts.

This has resulted in subsequent Canadian court rulings that public officials, school teachers, business people, and even Christian ministers do not have the right of conscience to refuse to endorse gay rights promotional activities, to publicly describe LGBTQ practice as destructive, to refuse to print gay rights materials, and even to refuse to 'marry' same-sex couples. Fines have been imposed, injunctions have been issued and jail has even been threatened. All this in light of the fact that the Canadian people have overwhelmingly rejected such judicial infringement on free speech and free action on the basis of one's religious beliefs. The United States has now headed down this same road which means that Christians will be called upon to make ever more difficult decisions in the future to not only defend their stance based on their faith, but to seek to halt the moral slide that has engulfed our country.

9. **Even if LGBTQ behaviors are sinful, practicing LGBTQ people should not be singled out for special condemnation. We're all sinners who are forgiven, loved and accepted by a gracious God. We should not judge someone whom God accepts. <u>FALSE</u>**

Those who advocate such a position forget that a key word in Scripture is 'repentance.' We can only experience forgiveness if we repent and turn from our sinful ways. If a practicing homosexual sees the error of his/her ways, sincerely repents and commits to seeking God's (and the Church's) help in leaving such practice behind, then the discussion is over. However, if that is not the case, how can the Church allow its members to freely engage in immoral behavior while refusing to repent, and to follow their own flawed moral compass rather than the Scripture (and the teaching of the Church based upon it), with impunity? Would those who advocate such a position feel the same way about people who engage in other forms of sexual immorality like incest, adultery, polygamy and pedophilia? Why then is the sin of homosexual practice singled out for immunity?

All sins are not equal in terms of destructive potential and consequences, both to the individual involved and to others. Surely shoplifting a pen from a store is demonstrably less harmful than committing adultery. Yes, all people need to repent and are in need of forgiveness and grace, but, as Paul demonstrates on many occasions, this should not lead to a policy of appeasement when it comes to sins that have great destructive potential.

The Bible teaches a great deal about 'judgment.' The church is given the responsibility of making judgments (i.e. exercising church discipline) in matters like these. The Corinthian Church in particular would not have survived without the risks that Paul took in making such judgments. In fact, the church is *called*, difficult as it may be, to make such judgments. Otherwise, it becomes an accomplice to behavior that God finds unacceptable. At the same time, such judgment must be free from hypocrisy and carried out in humility. In other words, while making judgments, Christians must not be judgmental.

Christians are also called to live as an example before, and give guidance to, the community at large. To allow, and even in some cases to endorse, LBGTQ practices within the Church sends a confused message to a society that is wrestling with these issues. Even some secular firms still have the courage to make moral judgments! For example, the CEO of the Boeing Corporation was fired some years ago for giving the company a bad image and setting a bad example for employees by having an extra-marital affair with a colleague. Should the Church be any less courageous in holding up a similar standard when it comes to that sin, or to the sin of homosexual practice, or to any other similarly destructive sin?

The Bible teaches that all sin is sin, but that some sins, and especially sexual sins, are more destructive and result in more serious consequences than others do. In commenting on sexual immorality, Paul writes, "Any other sin a man commits does not affect his body; but the man who is guilty of sexual immorality sins against his own body. Don't you know that your body is the temple of the Holy Spirit, who lives in you and who was given to you by God?" 1 Corinthians 6:18b-19a

Christianity Under the Microscope

10. Christians have different points of view on many things. Concerning LGBTQ issues, we should simply 'live and let live', come together and get on with the mission of the Church. <u>FALSE</u>

Unity is a central theme in the Bible and divisions among Christians are to be avoided if at all possible. However, an even stronger theme is integrity to the gospel. Whenever that's threatened, we're instructed to expel or isolate ourselves from those who would lead the Church astray. It's been demonstrated time and time again throughout the history of the Church that it's possible for people to unite around error which then *undermines* the Church's witness and mission.

A call to unity and mission is a laudable summons, but it must be subservient to adherence to the authority of the Scripture. Authority, not tolerance, must be the foundational concern underlying this whole discussion. "Speaking the *truth* in love" does not mean allowing some to circumvent the clear teaching of Scripture, or to flout carefully agreed upon Standards or positions of the Church, on this or on any other substantive issue, in order to accommodate erroneous cultural pressures. There are also, of course, some cultural issues that the Scripture writers don't address and still others about which their comments don't give precise guidance. On these Christians can agree to disagree and maintain unity. However, on the issue of LGBTQ practice, there is no ambiguity. Christian LGBTQ advocates are simply *creating* ambiguity and calling it another legitimate interpretation of the scriptures.

The Church should always be reforming within a constantly changing cultural context, but reforming *together*. If the issue of authority is dodged now, what will the Church fall back on if, for example, the cultural goal posts were to be moved yet again to the point where *any* extra-marital relationship would be held up as "a basic building block for emotional intimacy and commitment?" What kind of unity would the church have and what kind of a mission would it carry out if people could all do what was "right in their own eyes?"

Unity is a high goal, but not the highest goal. It's futile, and leading people astray, to advocate uniting around error. The goal should be the affirmation of scriptural truth, with unity as a natural by-product.

11. Long term LGBTQ unions are just as stable as heterosexual ones. <u>FALSE</u>

A number of studies show that there's a dearth of lifelong, monogamous relationships among practicing LGBTQ people. The vast majority of males have multiple sexual partners, some of them as many as 100 in their lifetime. The average female has fewer partners (average 10), but their relationships tend to be of even shorter duration. Contrary to what some would have us believe, the facts show that long term, stable relationships among LGBTQ people are rare. *Touchstone Magazine* reports in its January 2005 issue that noted columnist Mike McManus recently wrote that 66 percent of first marriages in America last 10 years, while 50 percent last 20 years or more. By contrast, a 2003-2004 Gay/Lesbian Consumer Online Census found that only 15 percent of homosexual people in "a current relationship" describe it as having lasted 12 years and only 5 percent as having lasted 20 years, and these relationships were rarely monogamous. Another study found that only four-and-a-half percent of homosexual males were faithful to their partner, compared with 85 percent of married males.

12. Using moral logic, it can be shown that all nine passages in both Testaments directly dealing with LGBTQ lifestyles can, in one way or another, be shown to not really mean what they appear to say. <u>FALSE</u>

Some Christian scholars maintain that by using 'moral logic' - a logic that doesn't interpret a text by what it appears to *say*, but by what it *means* - the Bible can be shown to actually endorse long-term same-sex unions. However, in this case, the outcome is neither moral nor logical. It's not moral in that it moralizes what is clearly described as immoral in the texts dealing with sexual immorality in general and homosexual practice in particular, and it's not logical in that it ignores one of the most fundamental interpretive tools available - common sense. Of the nine passages in both testaments directly dealing with this subject in one way or another, we're asked to believe that *all nine* don't really mean what they appear to say. How can this illogical conclusion be termed logical?

Of the texts that directly or indirectly deal with this subject in both testaments of the Bible, *all* teach that homosexual practice is destructive and therefore unacceptable sinful behavior. One would hope that Christian LGBTQ advocates could acknowledge that at least a few of these passages actually teach what they say. However, such an acknowledgment would prove problematical. Therefore, by a leap of the imagination in the name of 'scholarship,' most advocates say that *all* of these texts teach what they don't say. If all subjects covered in the Bible were to be dealt with in this manner, the Bible could be made to say whatever one wanted it to say, and at least some 'scholar' could probably be found to back it up.

13. The New Testament writers couldn't possibly have known anything about our modern concept of long term, committed same-sex relationships because there's no mention of such in secular literature prior to or during their day. <u>FALSE</u>

This assertion cannot be substantiated. For example, long discourses extolling this view of homosexual relations can already be found in Plato's *Symposium* (416 B.C.) and in the Pseudo-Lucianic *Affairs of the Heart* (300 A.D.). Seven of Greek poet Theocritus' (c. 200 B.C.) thirty *Idylls* are homoerotic. It's common knowledge that homosexuality and bisexuality were considered 'normal' in many if not most parts of the Roman Empire during the first century. Pauline contemporaries such as Virgil, who wrote "The love of Corydon and Alexis" in his *Second Eclogue* and Tibillus, who wrote *The Marathus Cycle*, extol what we today call long term, committed same-sex relationships. So did the Roman poet Juvenal and the Spanish poet Martial, writing around the end of the first century. And this list could be added to.

14. Those Christians who practice discrimination against

practicing **LGBTQ** people by citing culturally outdated texts from the Bible are making the same mistake that Christians made in the past who argued for the continuation of slavery on the basis of similar texts in the Bible. <u>FALSE</u>

This assertion is to draw a bad analogy. The Bible nowhere expresses a vested interest in preserving slavery, but it does express a clear countercultural interest in preserving an exclusive male-female dynamic to human sexual relationships. The biblical stance on slavery was fairly liberating in relation to the cultures out of which these texts emerged. The precise opposite is the case with its stance on same-sex intercourse in that it expresses far greater disapproval of such behavior than do the cultures of its day. One can discern a trajectory within the Bible that critiques slavery, but there is no indication in either testament that same-sex intercourse is anything other than an immoral practice to be rejected under all circumstances.

15. If there's no scriptural basis upon which to assert that practicing LGBTQ lifestyles are immoral, then there's no basis for denying people their 'right' to enter into any kind of sexual relationship they wish (such as co-habitation, polygamy, incest, polyamorous arrangements, adulterous relationships, etc.) so long as the parties involved consent and enter into long-term loving commitments. <u>TRUE</u>

This is, in fact, what's now happening in American society. Co-habitation is mushrooming. TV reality shows feature 'loving' polygamist households. For example, Jillian Keenan writes, "While the Supreme Court and the rest of us are all focused on the human right of marriage equality, let's not forget that the fight doesn't end with same-sex marriage. We need to legalize polygamy too, which is the constitutional, feminist, and sex-positive choice that would actually help protect, empower, and strengthen women, children, and families." (April 15, 2013, Slate.com). A casual perusal of the Internet reveals that the advocates for consensual incestual relationships are not far behind.

Since the courts have now scrambled the definition of marriage, increasing numbers of people are embracing relationships that involve more than two persons. Prominent advocates hope to use gay marriage as a wedge to abolish governmental support for traditional marriage altogether. Law Professor Martha Ertman of the University of Utah, for example, wants to render the distinction between traditional marriage and 'polyamory' (group marriage) "morally neutral." She argues that greater openness to gay partnerships will help us establish this moral neutrality (Spring/Summer 2001 Duke Journal of Gender Law & Policy). University of Michigan law professor David Chambers wrote in a widely cited 1996 Michigan Law Review piece that he expects gay marriage will lead government to be "more receptive to marital units of three or more" (1996 Michigan Law Review).

A striking example of what this kind of stance can lead to was reported in the June 12, 2016 issue of the New York Post. A 40-year-old man named Ari Nagel, a CUNY Kingsborough math professor, serves as a sperm donor for dozens of local women, siring 22 children over 12 years with 18 women of various backgrounds. His goal is to help lesbian couples and single women wanting to have a baby without the expense of going through a sperm bank. Sometimes he masturbates and makes his semen available in a cup. At other times, "a lesbian looking to conceive will have her partner in the bed for moral support while I have intercourse with her."

Nagel's name appears on the birth certificate for half of what he considers to be his 'offspring.' He has a Facebook album of photos of 'his kids' (who now live in seven states and Israel), regularly baby-sits and attends birthday parties and graduations and has even been present for a handful of deliveries. He sees some once a week, but has never met others. All 'partners' promise in advance that they won't sue him for child support, but the first five (out of 22) that he has 'serviced' did so saying they weren't aware that he wasn't going to help support and co-parent 'their'child. One woman who conceived two boys through intercourse with Nagel said she had no idea that he had plans to "father an entire baseball team…My kids got left in the dust…You can't co-parent with 20-something kids." As for Nagel, he says that he gets the benefit of having a large brood "without the hassle."

16. **Celibacy isn't a fair option to suggest to people with LGBTQ orientations since it's only a gift for some and denies LGBTQ persons the intimacy and sexual fulfillment that's the right of every person to enjoy. FALSE**

Christian LGBTQ advocates argue that even though not ideal, it's better for LGBTQ people to have a stable relationship within which they can find intimacy and sexual fulfillment than to be driven to engage prostitutes or have one night stands. But what about single heterosexual-oriented persons who wish to get married, but who can't find a mate? How can these Christian singles be asked to accept the teaching of Scripture that asks them to abstain from fulfilling their longings for intimacy and sexual fulfillment outside of marriage while same-sex unions are partially justified on the basis of satisfying those same longings? And since when are moral questions decided on a sliding scale - namely, since people can't achieve the ideal, they're to be allowed some sexual slack in order to keep them from engaging in even more destructive sexual practices? As we've seen, the Scripture clearly teaches that there is to be no sexual activity outside of a one man - one woman marital union under any circumstances.

Advocates argue that celibacy isn't everyone's gift. It can be a burden for some who haven't succeeded in finding an intimate partner to share their life with, and therefore it's not a state of life that can be imposed on a Christian by the law of the Church. One might ask, are not at least *some* homosexuals gifted with celibacy? The facts are that there are thousands of single Christians who don't have the gift of celibacy and who would like to be married, but who nevertheless live their lives in singleness without engaging in promiscuity in obedience to the Scripture. Would these advocates then argue that the Church should not 'impose' this kind of morality on single Christians as well?

17. **Even if LGBTQ orientations were eventually discovered to be genetically based, genetic determinism should never be used as an excuse for immoral behavior. TRUE**

For example, suppose we were to discover that some people have a klepto gene that makes them more prone to stealing than others, or a pyro gene that makes them more prone to setting forest fires. Does that mean we would then excuse them for stealing or for arson? Various studies have shown that a variety of behaviors, such as alcoholism, violent behavior, and even infidelity, may be rooted in genetics or biology. Should it then be said that alcoholism, violence and marital infidelity are now acceptable behaviors because they are in some way inherited? Whether LGBTQ orientations are inborn or acquired, if practiced, they still involve sexual conduct apart from the marriage of one man and one woman that, according to biblical teaching, is immoral.

18. Children growing up in LGBTQ households are just as well-developed as those in heterosexual households. <u>FALSE</u>

In a historic 2012 study of children raised by homosexual parents, sociologist Mark Regnerus of the University of Texas at Austin overturned the conventional academic wisdom that such children suffer no disadvantages when compared to children raised by married mothers and fathers. Published in the journal *Social Science Research*, the most careful, rigorous, and methodologically sound study ever conducted on this issue found numerous and significant differences between children raised by heterosexual parents and those raised by homosexuals.

An important article published in tandem with the Regnerus study (by Loren Marks, Louisiana State University) analyzed the 59 previous studies cited in a 2005 policy brief on homosexual parents by the American Psychological Association (APA). Marks debunked the APA's claim that "not a single study has found children of lesbian or gay parents to be disadvantaged in any significant respect relative to children of heterosexual parents." Marks also pointed out that only four of the 59 studies cited by the APA even met the APA's own standards by "providing evidence of statistical power." As Marks so carefully documents, "Not one of the 59 studies referenced in the 2005 APA Brief compares a large, random, representative sample of lesbian or gay 'parents' and their children with a large, random, representative sample of married heterosexual parents and their children."

By contrast, Regnerus included specific comparisons with children raised by homosexual 'parents' and put together a representative, population-based sample that was large enough to draw scientifically and statistically valid conclusions. For these reasons, his "New Family Structures Study" (NFSS) deserves to be considered the 'gold standard' in this field.

The study looked at 40 different outcomes, but reported data for children with "lesbian mothers" and those with "gay fathers" separately. When compared with outcomes for children raised by an "intact biological family" (with a married, biological mother and father), *the children of homosexuals did worse or* (in the case of their own sexual orientation), *were more likely to deviate from the societal norm on 77 out of 80 outcome measures.*

Compared with children raised by their married biological parents, children of homosexual parents:

- Are *much* more likely to have received welfare
- Have lower educational attainment
- Report less safety and security in their family of origin
- Report more ongoing 'negative impact' from their family of origin
- Are more likely to suffer from depression
- Have been arrested more often
- If they are female, have had more sexual partners - both male *and* female

Children of lesbian mothers:

- Are more likely to be currently cohabiting
- Are almost four times more likely to be currently on public assistance
- Are less likely to be currently employed full-time
- Are more than three times more likely to be unemployed

- Are nearly four times more likely to identify as something *other than* entirely heterosexual
- Are three times as likely to have had an affair while married or cohabiting
- Are ten times more likely to have been "touched sexually by a parent or other adult caregiver."
- Are nearly four times as likely to have been "physically forced" to have sex against their will
- Are more likely to have 'attachment' problems related to the ability to depend on others
- Use marijuana more frequently
- Smoke more frequently
- Watch TV for long periods more frequently
- Have more often pled guilty to a non-minor offense

When comparing children of homosexuals with children of married biological parents, the differences in sexuality (experiences of sexual abuse, number of sexual partners, and homosexual feelings and experiences among the children themselves) were among the most striking. At one time, defenders of homosexual parents not only argued that their children do fine on psychological and developmental measures, but they also said that children of homosexuals "are no more likely to be gay" than children of heterosexuals. That claim is impossible to maintain in light of this study. It found that children of homosexual fathers are nearly three times as likely, and children of lesbian mothers are nearly four times as likely, to identify as something other than entirely heterosexual. Children of lesbian mothers are 75 percent more likely, and children of homosexual fathers are two times more likely, to be currently in a same-sex romantic relationship.

The same holds true with the number of sexual partners. Both males and females who were raised by both lesbian mothers and homosexual fathers have more opposite-sex (heterosexual) partners than children of married biological parents (daughters of homosexual fathers had twice as many). But the differences in homosexual conduct are even greater. The daughters of lesbians have four times as many female (that is, same-sex) sexual partners than the daughters of married biological parents, and the daughters of homosexual fathers have six times as many. Meanwhile, the sons of both lesbian mothers and homosexual fathers have seven times as many male (same-sex) sexual partners as sons of married biological parents.

The most shocking and troubling outcomes, however, are those related to sexual abuse. Twenty-three percent of Children raised by a lesbian mother reported that they had been "touched sexually by a parent or other adult caregiver" versus only two percent for children of married biological parents. (Six percent of those raised by a homosexual father reported the same as compared to two percent of those with married biological parents.) As to the question of whether "you have ever been physically forced to have sex against your will" (not necessarily in childhood), affirmative answers came from eight percent of children of married biological parents, thirty one percent of children of lesbian mothers and twenty five percent of the children of homosexual fathers.

19. **The 'proof text method' shouldn't be used in dealing with LGBTQ issues. "A handful of selected Scripture statements" shouldn't be given undue weight in determining the Church's approach to a major social issue. Our approach should be determined by 'the rule of faith' principle that brings into play the broader issues of love, acceptance, unity and personal fulfillment. FALSE**
The fallacy in this view can be seen in the New Testament itself and in the Standards of the Church. New Testament writers constantly cite key snippets of Old Testament teaching to underpin the points they're trying to make. A casual glance at the footnotes of the *Heidelberg Catechism*, for example, will also reveal the citation of a host of biblical references to support doctrinal teaching. Why should this common theological method be declared out of bounds when it comes to this particular subject?

Furthermore, the number of times something is mentioned in Scripture does not necessarily determine the importance of a subject. For example, bestiality, prostitution and incest (and in the New Testament, polygamy) are not frequently directly condemned in the

Bible, but all recognize that the few negative references made to them are decisive. For example, had the case of a man sleeping with his stepmother not occurred in the Corinthian Church, there wouldn't have been a single text in the New Testament forbidding the practice of incest. Likewise, in the case of homosexuality, the practice was considered to be so abhorrent and so rare in Hebrew culture that frequent reference to its prohibition was unnecessary.

20. The word 'homosexual' isn't found in the Bible. Translators are in error if they use this term because its use actually obscures the meaning of a text rather than clarifies it. <u>FALSE</u>

In his book *The Bible and Homosexual Practice*, Robert Gagnon, points out that,

> The two key Greek words that Paul uses in Romans 1 to describe homosexual practice are *malakoi* (literally meaning 'the soft ones') and *arsenokoitai* (literally meaning 'male-bedders'). When taking into account the meaning given to these words by Paul's contemporary, Philo, and the severity of the penalty for such behavior, it is obvious that both Paul and Philo have the clear prohibitions and penalties of homosexual practice (as expressed in Leviticus 18:22 and 20:13, for example) in mind.

> In this case, and in 1 Timothy 1:10 where *arsenokoitais* is also used, the term *malakoi* is rightly translated as 'effeminate males who play the sexual role of females,' and the term *arsenokoitai* is rightly translated as 'males who take other males to bed.' No terms in modern English more appropriately describe these concepts than those used in the 2003 New English Translation that renders them as 'passive homosexual partners' and 'practicing homosexuals.' A survey of modern translations of 1 Corinthians 6:9-10 bears this out. From the 1961 New English Bible to the 2003 New English Translation, seven use the literal term 'homosexual,' three use the term 'sodomite' (meaning the same thing), two use 'sexual pervert' and only one uses 'male prostitute.'

21. **In the few places where same-sex sexual *acts* are mentioned in Scripture, the context suggests idolatry, violent rape, lust, exploitation, or promiscuity. The Bible says nothing about homosexual *orientation* as understood through modern science.** <u>FALSE</u>

Again quoting Robert Gagnon,

> However, when one examines the scriptural data on these subjects, it is clear that these are viewpoints that are *imposed* on Scripture rather than *taught* by Scripture. Nowhere do the passages dealing with homosexual practice limit their rejection of such practice to exploitative forms.
>
> For example, the prohibitions in Leviticus 18:22; 20:13 apply to *any* sexual interaction between same-sex partners. If they were only dealing with exploitative acts, why would they demand the death penalty for *both* participants - the exploited as well as the exploiter? These prohibitions are as absolute as the prohibitions against incest and adultery.
>
> Similarly, Paul's statement in Romans 1:26-27 rejects both lesbian and male homosexual forms of behavior on grounds other than their exploitative or oppressive character. He does not contrast 'loving' homosexual relationships with exploitative ones, but *all* forms of homosexual practice with heterosexual practice. What he condemns is sexual gratification with someone of the same sex rather than someone of the opposite sex. He states that *both* parties will come under judgment, not just the so-called exploitative active partner. In his view, homosexual 'couples' are engaging in a *mutual* degrading of their bodies by distorting God's intended design for their sexuality by doing what their bodies were not created to do. In 1 Corinthians 6:9 he pronounces judgment both on effeminate males who play the role of females in male homosexual intercourse (*malakoi*) and on active male partners who take the former to bed (*arsenokoitai*). He sees both partners as seeking to gratify their urges with one another and

together reaping the consequences for their mutually degrading conduct.

22. **Having transgender people use bathrooms, locker rooms and dorm rooms that don't match their birth gender is no big deal. FALSE**

Granting transgender people, and especially children and young people, access to facilities that don't match their birth gender encourages the proliferation of transgender behavior which prominent psychiatrists at Johns Hopkins specializing in transgender treatment have diagnosed as a debilitating mental disorder. Dr. Eric Vilain, a pediatric geneticist at the University of California, Los Angeles, probes the brain and genome for what determines whether children feel male or female, and whether they're attracted to the same or opposite sex. Vilain hopes to test whether kids can outgrow gender dysphoria, challenging the recent push among parents to help them transition as early as possible. In fact, he remains skeptical of the very concept of gender identity.

Transgender access to opposite sex facilities or playing on opposite sex sport teams also increases the prospects of sexual titillation and even sexual abuse. It further results in reverse discrimination. A great majority of people feel anxious about having people of a different sex in the same bathroom, let alone in school dorms and locker rooms where undressed young people share communal space and showers.

23. **While mutual enjoyment and the fulfillment of the "one flesh" union of a couple is part of God's design for marriage, the underlying purpose of sexual intercourse is procreation which is why he created humans as biologically complementarily male and female. TRUE**

Some Christian LGBTQ advocates, in making a case against biological gender complementarity being considered as the essential purpose of marriage and in advocating the unitive meaning of marriage, downgrade the former and promote the latter. Why elevate one and demote the other when Scripture considers *both* concepts to be of equal importance? For example, regarding the term "one flesh" in Genesis 2:18-25, they declare that it's important not to overgenitalize or oversexualize this passage. True, but it's equally important not to *under*genitalize or *under*sexualize it.

They also argue by extension that since none of the creeds of the church, nor any of the great confessional documents of the Reformation, mention biological gender complementarity, we more up to date moderns can ignore it. However, if the authors of these documents were alive today, they would be astounded by such a claim. They had no need to mention biological gender complementarity since that concept has been universally held by Judeo-Christians for millennia. Actually, the *Westminster* and *Second Helvetic Confessions* do say something about this subject when they define marriage as being a union "between one man and one woman."

24. LGBTQ lifestyles present no greater health risks and costs than heterosexual lifestyles do. <u>FALSE</u>

AIDS is a very debilitating disease that was first generated among male homosexuals in the 1980s and spread from them to others (e.g., drug abusers, wives, prostitutes, blood recipients, etc.). Today, half (50.3 percent) of the people in the United States living with AIDS are males who have sex with males (MSM). The proportion of HIV infections in MSM keeps rising. Simply adding up the medical costs of one disease - AIDS - leads to the conclusion that the treatment of a typical homosexual costs society somewhere between three and four times the amount of the costs for a typical non-homosexual. And the problem is likely to get worse. Another 20,000 or so MSM get infected with HIV each year. Since fewer than 6,000 homosexuals are dying of AIDS per year, the number for whom society will be paying medical costs is bound to grow.

AIDS research is also expensive, and it has sucked funding from the research funds for other diseases. For example, in 2001, The

National Institutes of Health allocated $2.5 billion in research funds for AIDS (14,175 people died of AIDS in that year), $790 million for diabetes (from which 71,372 died), $640 million for breast cancer (421,809 deaths), $595 million for Alzheimer's disease (53,852 deaths), and $345 million for prostate cancer (30,719 deaths). Translated, these figures amount to about $178,000 per AIDS death, $16,000 per breast cancer death, and $11,000 per death for diabetes, Alzheimer's, and prostate cancer. Privately funded research is similarly biased toward AIDS. Since then, the picture hasn't changed, but only gotten worse.

In FY 2016, federal funding to combat domestic HIV/AIDS was raised to $27.4 billion. Of the funds dedicated, the largest share ($19.7 billion) was for care, $3.0 billion for cash and housing assistance, $2.7 billion for research, and $0.9 billion for prevention. By contrast, in 2016, *for the first time in eight years*, Congress raised the amount of funds for cancer research and treatment, but only by $260.5 million to a total of $4.9 billion. This despite the fact that in 2015 there were an estimated 1,658,370 new cancer cases diagnosed and 589,430 cancer deaths as over against 1.2 million infected with HIV and 13,000 AIDS deaths.

When a person is on disability, Social Security will pay his or her living expenses, such as food, rent, and entertainment. Many male homosexuals with AIDS are on disability Social Security. The total government dollars allocated to homosexuals with AIDS are staggering. And these costs only represent a single disease. As we've seen, those who engage in homosexuality are also much more apt to have other kinds of medical conditions. Some of these diseases are acquired the same way HIV is - through sex. Gays are many times more apt to get anal or rectal cancer. A census of cancer cases in Scotland discovered that HIV-infected MSM were 21 times more apt to get cancer than the general population. Likewise for hepatitis B and C which are transmitted via rectal sex.

Gays are also more apt to get esophageal or stomach cancer, and hepatitis A - apparently from oral sex. And lesbians are much more apt to get breast cancer and other cancers of the reproductive organs. Syphilis is still a growing problem, and ironically, a significant reason for this is the expensive anti-viral treatments that are used to keep homosexuals with AIDS alive. Homosexuals are also fairly certain to disproportionately suffer from the diseases and ailments - in addition to AIDS - that those who use illegal drugs are prone to get. They're also more apt to require drug treatment (In one study, eleven percent of homosexuals versus four percent of non-homosexuals reported having gotten substance abuse treatment).

In light of these facts, one must ask why such a small amount is being allocated by Congress to combat an array of cancer diseases that afflict huge numbers of innocent men, women and children while such a huge amount is being allocated to combat an epidemic that affects a relatively small percentage of the population and that originated with, and is being perpetuated by, people who are living immoral lifestyles.

25. People should be prosecuted for discrimination or for hate speech if they refuse to sell to, rent to, hire, provide services for or denounce the lifestyles of practicing LGBTQ people. <u>FALSE</u>

It's not uncommon to see a sign in a restaurant that reads, "We reserve the right to deny service to anyone." If someone walks into a restaurant and isn't appropriately dressed, most people would agree that the restaurant has the right to refuse service. In a sense, this is a form of discrimination. The question is, how do we protect the private rights of businesses while protecting the public right not to be discriminated against?

In recent cases where LGBTQ persons have sued businesses or public institutions over similar issues, it's not that business owners or schools don't want to 'refuse service' to LGBTQ people simply because they're LGBTQ; it's that some business owners and school administrators - particularly those who work in the wedding industry or are administering schools - don't want to be forced to provide services for, or bathrooms for, people who are living lifestyles that defy their deeply held religious convictions. The LGBTQ movement claims that this kind of 'discrimination' is similar to making LGBTQ people sit in the back of the bus and drink out of separate fountains. However, true discrimination only takes place when an immoral person commits an immoral act towards a moral person.

Forcing a Christian baker or photographer to proffer their serves to facilitate gay weddings or a school principal to admit males into a female locker room is the opposite of discrimination. It's the equivalent of forcing moral people to commit immoral acts for people who are living immoral lifestyles.

The courts shouldn't force private citizens to actively participate in a particular act which they find morally objectionable. In none of these cases did a business owner or institution refuse service to an LGBTQ person out of some kind of disgust or animosity towards LGBTQ people. They simply wished to take no part in their activities. To call this 'discrimination' is to make no distinction between an LGBTQ *person* and the *activity* of that person. Blacks were denied basic services because they were *black* - not because of their activity. LGBT people in these cases are asking Christians or Christian institutions to specifically *participate* in a morally objectionable act. Someone can say that gay weddings, for example, are not morally objectionable, but that isn't up to them to decide. That's simply their opinion.

Christians believe they also have a right to their belief. To tell a Christian or a Christian institution that they must provide services to LGBTQ people because that's what they want, is to say that one must condone the actions of an LGBTQ person in order to affirm the dignity and inherent human worth of that person. No other group is given such privileges. For example, a Jewish deli can't be forced to provide someone with non kosher meat. A Muslim caterer can't be forced to serve pork. A pro-choice business can't be forced to buy ad space on someone's website. However, the LGBTQ movement is, in effect, trying to do the equivalent by denying the free speech and expression of other citizens through their lobbying, legislating, and litigating. This violates the First Amendment of the Constitution: "Congress shall make no law respecting an establishment of religion, *or prohibiting the free exercise thereof*; or abridging the freedom of speech, or of the press; or the right of the people peaceably to assemble, and to petition the Government for a redress of grievances." As much as the LGBTQ community wants to make this an issue about gay rights, this is about religious freedom, not gay rights.

Christians who don't want to sanction gay marriage are being sued, prosecuted and driven out of business for doing nothing more than living up to their Christian beliefs, which are incompatible with condoning gay marriage. Christian schools are being badgered into providing bathroom and locker room access to people who they believe should not have such access. Although clergy are, at present, not being forced to conduct same-sex 'marriages,' if things continue to go the way they've been going, that exemption will also be short-lived.

Supporting gay marriage is incompatible with the Christian faith. Baking a cake for a gay marriage, renting out a building in which to hold it, taking the pictures of it, etc. could fairly be considered sanctioning the marriage. To force a Christian to do this violates the First Amendment and is a misguided attempt to legally force people to accept gay marriage. Shaming, accusing, or ruining the business of a baker for refusing to bake a gay wedding cake, for example, reflects a spirit of pride and control, not one that promotes love, peace, understanding and equality.

Unfortunately, rather than recognizing every person's right to express her or his opinion on this subject, any serious attempt to dialogue with the political, social and judicial engineers of the LGBTQ juggernaut is met with howls of denunciation labeling people who disagree with them as 'hate-filled,' 'bigoted,' and 'homophobic.' A vengeful and vicious campaign of repression, oppression, and the elimination from public life of anyone who dissents from the new sexual orthodoxy is being wrongfully waged. It reminds one of the adage, "If you can't deal with the message, shoot the messenger."

26. The fact that other species engage in homosexual activities doesn't make it right for Homo sapiens to do so. TRUE

Homosexual activity has been detected in a number of other species. However, the great majority of sexual activity in the natural world only occurs between males and females. Since the whole of creation was infected by the moral pollution of the fall, no one should be surprised to find abnormal sexual activity amongst other species as well. As Paul points out in Romans 8:20-23: "...there was the hope that creation itself would one day be set free from its slavery to decay and would share the glorious freedom of the children of God. For we know that up to the present time all of creation groans with pain, like the pain of childbirth. But it is not just creation alone which groans; we who have the Spirit as the first of God's gifts also groan within ourselves as we wait for God to make us his children and set our whole being free."

Not only are homosexual acts among animals and other creatures unnatural, but so are those among Homo sapiens. Paul calls such acts "perverted," "unnatural" and "shameful" acts of "wrongdoing" that will incur punishment. "Even the women pervert the natural use of their sex by unnatural acts. In the same way the men give up natural sexual relations with women and burn with passion for each other. Men do shameful things with each other, and as a result they bring upon themselves the punishment they deserve for their wrongdoing. Because those people refuse to keep in mind the true knowledge about God, he has given them over to corrupted minds, so that they do the things that they should not do." Romans 1:26-28

27. **Sex change therapy and surgery has enabled transgender people to successfully change genders and live emotionally fulfilling and happy lives. FALSE**

The Johns Hopkins Hospital runs one of the nation's oldest and most respected sexual behaviors clinics, with a reputation for outstanding research and clinical expertise. Dr. Paul R. McHugh served as the Henry Phipps professor of psychiatry, director of the Department of Psychiatry and Behavioral Sciences at the Johns Hopkins University School of Medicine, and psychiatrist in chief at the Johns Hopkins Hospital from 1975 to 2001. The Johns Hopkins University School of Medicine named him distinguished service professor in 1998. In a June 2, 2015 interview by CNS News, Dr. McHugh said that transgenderism is a "mental disorder" that merits treatment that sex change is "biologically impossible" and that people who promote sexual reassignment surgery are collaborating with and promoting a mental disorder. Dr. McHugh further noted that studies done by Vanderbilt University and London's Portman Clinic, showed

that among children who had expressed transgender feelings, over time, 70-80 percent "spontaneously lost those feelings. "And so," he said, "at Hopkins we stopped doing sex-reassignment surgery, since producing a 'satisfied' but still troubled patient seemed an inadequate reason for surgically amputating normal organs.
He also said,

There are misguided doctors who, working with very young children who seem to imitate the opposite sex, will administer puberty-delaying hormones to render later sex-change surgeries less onerous - even though the drugs stunt the children's growth and risk causing sterility. Such action comes close to child abuse, given that close to 80 percent of those kids will abandon their confusion and grow naturally into adult life if untreated...'Sex change' is biologically impossible. People who undergo sex-reassignment surgery do not change from men to women or vice versa. Rather, they become feminized men or masculinized women. Claiming that this is a civil-rights matter and encouraging surgical intervention is in reality to collaborate with and promote a mental disorder.
   It is starkly, nakedly false that sex change is possible...The champions of this meme, encouraged by their alliance with the broader LGBT movement, claim that whether you are a man or a woman, a boy or a girl, is more of a disposition or feeling about yourself than a fact of nature. And, much like any other feeling, it can change at any time, and for all sorts of reasons. Therefore, no one could predict who would swap this fact of their makeup, nor could one justifiably criticize such a decision.
   At Johns Hopkins, after pioneering sex-change surgery, we demonstrated that the practice brought no important benefits. As a result, we stopped offering that form of treatment in the 1970s. The most thorough follow-up of sex-reassigned people - extending over thirty years and conducted in Sweden, where the culture is strongly supportive of the transgendered - documents their lifelong mental unrest. Ten to fifteen years after surgical reassignment, the suicide rate of those who had undergone sex-reassignment surgery rose to twenty times that

of comparable peers. Another review of more than 100 international medical studies of post-operative transsexuals found up to 20percent regret transitioning with no conclusive evidence that showed that gender reassignment surgery improves the lives of transsexuals, with many people remaining severely distressed and even suicidal after the operation.

The grim fact is that most of these youngsters do not find therapists willing to assess and guide them in ways that permit them to work out their conflicts and correct their assumptions. Rather, they and their families find only 'gender counselors' who encourage them in their sexual misassumptions. The idea that one's sex is fluid and a matter open to choice runs unquestioned through our culture and is reflected everywhere in the media, the theater, the classroom, and in many medical clinics. It has taken on cult-like features: its own special lingo, internet chat rooms providing slick answers to new recruits, and clubs for easy access to dresses and styles supporting the sex change. It is doing much damage to families, adolescents, and children and should be confronted as an opinion without biological foundation wherever it emerges.

28. The Supreme Court's June 26, 2015 Obergefell v. Hodges decision to sanction gay marriage was a great step forward for people living LGBTQ lifestyles. <u>FALSE</u>

The Supreme Court, through its 2015 decision sanctioning gay 'marriage,' demonstrated that moral and social issues are increasingly being decided by activist judges, too many of whom do not subscribe to moral absolutes, rather than by the democratic will of the people. The majority of people in the United States would still define marriage as the life-long union of a man and a woman. However, it's now clear that the Judeo-Christian tradition that provided a common basis for law and social organization in the USA is now dead. Any appeal to the values of that tradition, or an argument that there was a shared consensus for a moral basis for the law is gone. It has been replaced by a positivistic view of the law - the law is what we make it, and any appeal to the external values of the Judeo-Christian tradition (Nature and Nature's God) is increasingly being dismissed.

The first casualty of the Obergefull v. Hodges decision has been the very definition of marriage itself. For thousands of years and in every Western society, marriage has meant the life-long union of a man and a woman. The concept of marriage necessarily includes the idea of a man and woman committing themselves to each other. Any other arrangement contradicts this basic definition.

By re-defining marriage, the Supreme Court has altered our fundamental understanding of human social relations and institutions. One effect has been the detachment of sexual fidelity from the commitment of marriage. The advocates of gay marriage themselves admit as much. Troy Perry, the former moderator of the Metropolitan Community Church, a largely homosexual denomination, explained to the media: "Monogamy is not a word the gay community uses. We talk about fidelity. That means you live in a loving, caring, honest relationship with your partner. But we have people with widely varying opinions as to what that means. Some would say that committed couples could have multiple sexual partners as long as there's no deception."

As we've already noted, gay marriage is also detrimental to children. Research clearly shows that family structure matters for children, and the family structure that helps the most is a family headed by two biological parents in a low-conflict marriage. Children raised by homosexuals are more dissatisfied with their own gender, suffer a greater rate of molestation within the family, and have homosexual experiences more often. Despite this evidence, gay marriage is leading to more gay couples adopting children, while more lesbian couples are having children through anonymous sperm donations (which means some children are being purposefully created without knowledge of one of their biological parents).

Gay marriage is also encouraging teens that are unsure of their sexuality to embrace a lifestyle that, as we've seen, suffers high rates of suicide, depression, HIV, drug abuse, STDs, and other pathogens. This is particularly alarming because studies show that over 25 percent of young boys feel uncertain about their sexual orientation and lesbianism is becoming more 'chic' in certain elite social sectors. Gay 'marriage' has promoted the notion that marriage is primarily about adult yearnings for intimacy and that it's not essentially connected to raising children. Children will be hurt by those who will too easily bail out of a marriage because it's not 'fulfilling' to them.

29. **LGBTQ practices are neither destructive nor sinful, but should actually be celebrated if practiced in the 'right' way. God *created* heterosexuals, homosexuals, bisexuals, transsexuals and queers. As with our racial, ethnic and other diversities, sexual diversity should also be celebrated as long as these relationships are practiced on a long-term basis with one partner. FALSE**

There's not one specific statement in Scripture that can be cited to support such a view. Rather, in both the Old and New Testaments, the writers of Scripture presuppose and promote sexual practice only within the bounds of a heterosexual marriage relationship between a man and a woman. From the beginning, this ideal is held up in these familiar words: "That is why a man leaves his father and mother and is united with his wife, and they become one." Genesis. 2:24 During the initial post-fall period, this ideal of monogamous marriage was not maintained. However, even the pagan practice of polygamy eventually gave way to this original ideal with the reassertion of the concept that a marriage bond should only be forged between one man and one woman. When asked about this subject, Jesus underlines the Genesis ideal when he cites this very sentence to define his concept of marriage. (See Matthew 19:3-6; Mark. 10:7-8) Later, Paul repeats it *twice more* to emphatically endorse Jesus' teaching. (See 1 Corinthians 6:16; Ephesians 5:31) It's plain that the writers of Scripture would be astounded by the claims of some modern scholars that their writings can be 'reinterpreted' in such a way as to allow for some other kind of sexual practice and relationship.

There's one small word that has loomed large throughout the whole of Scripture and in the life of the people of God down through the ages - the word 'repentance.' It is the responsibility of the Church to invite *all* people to *repentance*, faith and renewal, including those who are practicing LGBTQ people. Christians believe they too, like the rest of us, must promise to "renounce sin and the power of evil" in their lives. To confess Jesus as Lord and commit themselves to following him means to ask for God's grace to repent (change direction), to leave the past behind and to embrace the good news that Christ can set us free from all that would destroy us. How can one embrace the way of Christ, but insist on continuing to go one's own way? And how can the Church maintain the integrity of the Gospel and the grace that God offers if it cheapens and dilutes it in the name of inclusivity?

Unfortunately, an increasing number of our practicing LGBTQ friends do not see their lifestyles as being 'broken' and in need of healing. Rather, they celebrate that lifestyle and, despite not one word in the Scriptures to support it, claim that God created them this way and that he affirms them in their conduct. They see nothing to be ashamed of, to repent of, or to seek to be transformed from. They resent the Church's attempts to minister 'to' them as though they needed to change something. If the authority of the Scripture for Christian faith and practice means anything at all, it means that this perspective cannot be blessed - for this un-repented sin or for any other un-repented sin. The Church's doors should certainly be open to all of us sinners no matter what, but when it comes to membership and leadership, any of us, no matter what the sin, cannot be embraced without confession, repentance and re-commitment to the way of Christ, no matter how difficult that way might prove to be.

In conclusion, it must be said that even though many Christians and churches have made forthright statements concerning our responsibility to minister to people with LGBTQ orientations, Christians have been remiss in their attitudes towards them, in their acceptance of them as *fellow* fallen human beings, in their lack of sensitive ministry to meet their particular needs and in their efforts to help them find a renewed way of life. Christians need to expend a great deal more effort in order to overcome these deficiencies. Nevertheless, shortcomings in one direction should not lead to error in another. In the end, that would be to do yet another *dis*service to one's LGBTQ friends. What Christians need is compassion without compromise. The Roman Catholic position is a good example of this. When asked in 2013 about his attitude towards accepting practicing gays as candidates for the priesthood, Pope Francis remarked, "Who am I to judge?" Meaning that as a sinful human being, he was following Jesus' warning not to be *judgmental* when it comes to casting stones at fellow sinners. This was followed in December 2016 by a document reaffirming the Church's *judgment* that there should be no compromise when it comes to practicing LGBTQ persons.

> "The Church, while profoundly respecting the persons in question, cannot admit to the seminary or to holy orders those who practice homosexuality, present deep-seated homosexual tendencies or support the so-called 'gay culture.' Such persons, in fact, find themselves in a situation that gravely hinders them from relating correctly to men and women. One must in no way overlook the negative consequences that can derive from the ordination of persons with deep-seated homosexual tendencies."

Note that in our discussion of LGBTQ issues, we've been very careful to distinguish between people who are *struggling* with LGBTQ *orientations* and those who are *practicing* LGBTQ *lifestyles*. Christians need to welcome LGBTQ people who have committed themselves to celibacy or to working towards the transformation of their orientation into membership and leadership in their churches. At the same time, they also need to reach out to those who are still practicing LGBTQ lifestyles with love and compassion, offering counseling, friendship, understanding and prayer.

To sum up, the Bible, both in the Old and the New Testaments, clearly, consistently and emphatically teaches that all forms of debilitating sexual relationships under any circumstances and at all times are sinful and destructive behaviors that result in dire consequences. At the same time, the Bible majors in the Good News that God's grace, forgiveness, power (to resist and even to change) and hope are available to all who have "sinned and fallen short of the glory of God" in this respect or in any other respect. This is the good news that Christians must share as they reach out in love to their neighbors and particularly to their practicing LGBTQ neighbors.

What Do *You* Think?

1. The thing that surprised me most in this chapter was......because......

2. The thing that bothered me the most in this chapter was ......because......

3. I accept all/most of/some of the facts presented in the TRUE/FALSE section of this chapter. Explain.

4. Regarding LGBTQ people, I think it is/is not possible to have compassion without compromise because ......

Chapter Twenty One

WHAT ABOUT WORLD PROBLEMS?

"You are like salt for all mankind ... You are light for the whole world." Matthew 5:13, 14

"Do everything without complaining or arguing, so that you may be innocent and pure as God's perfect children who live in a world of corrupt and sinful people. You must shine among them like stars lighting up the sky." Philippians 2:14-15

Looking Through the Microscope |

The United Nations

The President called the meeting to order. At a previous meeting of the current session of the General Assembly of the United Nations, the member states had agreed to an agenda of six pressing world problems to be debated at this meeting. The purpose of the debate was to prioritize them and to decide which problem should be attacked as the major target for the year in terms of the use of the human and financial resources of the world body.

The President of the General Assembly recognized the first speaker - the delegate from India.

"Mr. President and fellow delegates, I rise this morning to put before you the case for giving the highest urgency to the mobilization of our resources this year to launch a renewed effort to eliminate extreme poverty and hunger in the world. There's not a person in this chamber who doesn't know the gravity of the present situation and the dim prospects that await us in the future as a human race if this problem is not urgently and aggressively tackled. If anyone doubts that such a 'war' on poverty should be our first priority, let me invite him or her to tour the villages and slums of my country, and those of the other countries of the third world, and s/he will have no doubt as to the accuracy of my assertion. Even in a rich country like the United States, there are today 45 million people living below what the Americans define as their 'poverty line'! It goes without saying, of course, that America's 'poverty line' is well above the income level of most of the one half of the earth's people who are abysmally poor.

"You may be aware that at the present moment half of the world's people aren't getting sufficient food, and because they're not getting sufficient food, they're prone to illness. Over 700 million of these people will die this year - that's about one every three seconds! That means that while I've been speaking to you, some 32 people have died from lack of proper food! You may also be aware that at the present moment, one percent of the world's people own over half of the world's wealth. This is neither fair nor just. The problem of poverty and hunger is certainly solvable. The earth has enough resources to meet everyone's needs. What we need is a new economic order that will enable a fairer distribution of the world's goods and resources. This can be done, and I urge you to dedicate yourselves to making this our top priority as a General Assembly this year. Thank you."

The President recognized the next speaker - the delegate from the People's Republic of China.

"Distinguished colleagues. As you know, I represent a country that has the largest population in the world. You will therefore not be surprised that I'm asking you to make population control our number one priority for the year. As you know, the People's Republic of China has over 1.3 billion people, a quarter of the earth's inhabitants. Despite our considerable efforts to control population expansion over the years, we continue to face ever-increasing pressure as far as population growth is concerned. This growth simply cannot continue. Our population must be stabilized. If it isn't, all of our strenuous efforts at modernization, the up-grading of agriculture, the improvement of health and educational services, and all the rest will, in the end, be frustrated.

"China's problem is not unique. The last 50 years have seen a rapid increase in the rate of population growth due to medical advances and substantial increases in agricultural productivity, particularly made possible by the Green Revolution in the '60s. Therefore, population growth, I should say population *explosion*, is a dire threat to every developing country. For example, in my distinguished colleague's country, India, the population is projected to increase to 1.7 billion by mid-century, the highest in the world! It is also, I might add, an indirect threat to the developed countries as well. The United Nations Population Division has estimated that the world's population will likely surpass 10 billion in 2055. That's only a few decades from now!

"If the population bomb is not defused soon, the desperation of the masses of the earth's poor and hungry peoples that my colleague speaks about will result in the kind of revolution and chaos that will affect *every* country of the globe. Growth in Africa remains so high that the population there could more than triple in this century, rising from today's one billion to 3.6 billion … a sobering forecast for a continent already struggling to provide food and water for its people. Women and children especially face hardship when it comes to childbirth and family size. In Afghanistan, for instance, a woman is 200 times more likely to die in childbirth than to be killed by a bomb or a bullet.

"I agree with my distinguished Indian colleague that poverty and hunger are extremely important problems to tackle. But if we don't tackle the population problem *first of all*, no matter what kind of new economic order we come up with in the future, it's bound to fail. I also know that the traditions and beliefs of many people at present are prejudiced against the use of contraceptives, abortion, sterilization, and the like as population control measures. But I also ask these people to think of the terrible alternative for the future of our race if we don't employ *every* means presently known to humankind to halt the explosive growth of the world's population. Therefore, on behalf of my own country, and indeed on behalf of the human race, I appeal to you to give population control the highest priority in the setting of our action goals this year. Thank you."

The next speaker to be recognized was the delegate from Sweden.

"Ladies and Gentlemen, I stand before you this morning to plead with you to make the cause of disarmament our top priority for the year. At this very moment, as I speak, the wheels of industry in a number of the great countries of the world are whirring and churning in order to produce weapons of mass destruction. The weapons stockpiles of the world's Super Powers are growing larger and larger. The arms sales contracts to smaller nations are growing fatter and fatter. The proliferation of deadly weapons of war among the nations of the earth continues to spread. The development of newer and ever more terrible implements of destruction continues to accelerate. The incidence of small wars between or within small countries continues to multiply, with each such spark having an ever greater potential to set off a world-wide conflagration of such horrible proportions that it's difficult to imagine how the human race could survive it.

"All of us here this morning know that war in today's world is sheer madness - and yet we keep busily preparing for it! All of us know that nobody would win and everybody would lose - and yet we continue to stall and to block any effective means of freezing armaments at their present levels, let alone work out any effective measures to bring about *dis*armament! All of us know that to continue to probe each other's defenses, or to expand our spheres of influence, or to use smaller countries as surrogates for larger countries' aggressive policies risks pushing the existing tension over the precipice of no return - and yet we continue to push.

"What my esteemed colleagues from India and China have so eloquently spelled out to you in terms of the need to eliminate poverty and hunger and to control population growth is correct. I wholeheartedly agree with them. The problem is, however, that unless we somehow find a solution to the arms race and to the ever present reality of being on the brink of a war that will destroy the world as we know it, there's no sense in talking about the elimination of poverty and the control of population - since such a war will 'solve' both of these problems! If such a war should take place (and it *will* take place unless we take prompt action), there won't *be* any more people to be poor or to overpopulate the earth! I therefore appeal to you today, in the name of the entire human race that lives in terror of this impending holocaust, to make the ending of the arms race, arms trade and arms development our over-riding priority for this year's UN agenda. Thank you."

The President recognized a fourth speaker – the delegate from the Netherlands.

"Mr. President and fellow colleagues, thank you for this opportunity to address you on the subject of the environment. As you well know, the environment on this marvelous, but fragile, planet of ours is rapidly deteriorating. On the one hand, the irreplaceable resources of our earth are being used up at an alarming rate. It is now projected, for example, that the known and expected to be discovered reserves of oil will last us a little more than 40-50 years at the projected rate of consumption. The same situation faces us on every other resource front. The world's nations at present are committed to an unlimited economic growth philosophy. This means that people will produce and consume more and more every year, and that, as our friend from China has so well reminded us, the increasing population of the world will exacerbate and accelerate this process even further. That's good news for business, but bad news for our planet! It is merely a matter of simple logic. How can a finite planet with limited resources continue to produce an ever-growing and unlimited amount of goods for human use and consumption? The answer, of course, is that it can't.
"Some people would 'solve' this problem with scientific miracles and magic. For example, if we run out of oil, we can use natural gas or atomic energy or solar or wind power. If we run out of magnesium, we'll probably be able to eventually find it and mine it on other

planets. But nature is sending us different signals. The miracle 'solutions' of atomic energy, 'miracle rice,' insecticides, fertilizers and all the rest are often producing more problems than they solve. And then there's the looming disaster of global warming that's being exacerbated by our carbon emissions. The current warming trend is of particular significance because too much of it is human-induced and proceeding at a rate that is unprecedented in the past 1,300 years. The evidence for rapid climate change is compelling: sea level rise, global temperature rise, warming oceans, shrinking ice sheets, declining arctic sea ice, glacial retreat, extreme weather events, ocean acidification and decreased snow cover. All these conditions have been exacerbated by human activity. There's a toleration point in nature beyond which science can't go without paying a price. Nobody knows at present, for example, precisely what will happen in the long-term future as a result of burying atomic wastes in the ground.

"On the other hand, our head-long rush into maximum production has made our earth garden unrecognizable from what it was just 50 years ago. What it will be like 50 years from now if drastic measures aren't taken is too horrible to contemplate. Air pollution, water pollution, land pollution and noise pollution are turning our once beautiful world into a giant cesspool. Fish, animals, birds and flora are rapidly disappearing. How long it will be before we humans ourselves are overcome by our own pollution is anybody's guess.

"The other problems that have been mentioned by my friends from India, China and Sweden are serious and need attention. However, I feel that the destruction of the earth's environment is one problem, which, above all others, cannot wait one more day or one more hour. We *must* make the solution of this problem our priority for this year. Thank you."

The fifth delegate to speak was from Nigeria.

"Distinguished delegates, I have listened with great sympathy to the four speakers who've preceded me. There's no doubt in my mind that the problems they have so ably articulated are all urgent and need our attention. Unfortunately, we don't have the wherewithal to attack all of them simultaneously. Therefore we must choose. And it will be a hard choice!

"Before we do choose, however, I would like to introduce a fifth priority for us to consider which, in my mind, is equally screaming for our attention. This priority is not a relatively new problem like the population explosion, atomic war, or global warming and pollution. It's a problem that is as old as humanity - the problem of prejudice. You will recall that people on the other side of the globe in a country called South Africa used to be graded like oranges - this one is pure white; that one is tainted white; a third one is 'colored;' a fourth is coal black and so on. In a diabolical system called 'apartheid,' the color of a person's skin determined the kind of job s/he could get, where s/he could live, who his or her friends could be, whom s/he could marry, where s/he could go to school, what s/he could buy and where s/he could buy it - and a lot more.

"I would like to tell you that this was one isolated case in our world. I would also like to tell you that in recent times man has 'come of age' and put racial prejudice, ethnic bigotry, blind nationalism, and creedal intolerance behind him. But you and I both know that to do so would be to tell a monstrous and hypocritical lie. No, prejudice, bigotry and intolerance (and the exploitation, oppression and domination that are their handmaidens) are, unfortunately, still very much alive and well in our world. One speaker has spoken of the pollution of our lakes, our rivers and our air. I speak to you about a pollution that's far more serious and far more deadly as far as the future of the human race is concerned - a pollution of the soul, the pollution of prejudice! Unless we find some way to 'clean up' this kind of *spiritual* pollution, poverty and hunger will persist, wars will be fought and the environment will continue to be exploited by the rich and the powerful.

"We must create programs that will help to put people in contact with other people across present boundaries in such a way that persistent racial, ethnic and national barriers will fall. We need to adopt sanctions and bring pressure to bear on any nation that continues to engage in blatant discrimination. We need to support and encourage groups of any kind who are working for understanding and brother- hood. Unless we launch such an offensive against prejudice in our world, all of our other plans and programs will come to naught. Therefore, I urge you in the name of the human spirit, to initiate a crusade against prejudice as our priority program for the year. Thank you."

The President introduced the last speaker of the day before the beginning of the debate - the delegate from the Ukraine.

"Mr. President, fellow delegates and friends, I have great sympathy with what was just said by the distinguished delegate from Nigeria. It is closely related, in a way, to the problem that I wish to share with you today - the problem of competing ideologies. You all know that in recent years my country has experienced an evolution in its policy and in its political thinking. At the end of World War II, our position was a fairly doctrinaire and militant communist stance. As such, we found ourselves trapped in a network of communist states that had a black-white view of the world - East and West, Warsaw Pact and NATO, 'them and us.' We eventually realized that a world carved up into two hostile blocks could not last for long. We also wanted to conduct trade, exchange ideas and establish relations with nations that were different from us, but with whom we felt we could agree to disagree, as it were, while still maintaining cordial ties and even friendships.

"As time went on, we were able to break away from this communist bloc of countries and establish our independence as a nation that wanted to reach out to all nations, regardless of ideology, and build bridges of understanding and mutual benefit. We hoped that eventually we could work our way into a position of helping to promote understanding between East and West, or to at least lessen the hostility between them. We also remained staunch supporters of the United Nations, believing that in this institution lay the promise for a future world that would no longer be dominated by ideologies or national self-interest, but one that would see the development of a world community based on international law and mutual respect. Despite recent events that have overtaken us, we've not given up on that belief and we have not lessened our support.

"We hope the nations of the world can move beyond the era of competing 'isms' to one of cooperative unity - the kind of unity wherein everyone is not forced to think like everyone else, but wherein diversity is respected and even treasured as a sign of vitality in the one body of nations. As someone has well said, with our ever increasing interlocking economic, cultural and communication networks through the process of globalization, our planet can no longer afford to view itself as a group of separate nations, each with its own political, economic and social ideology and agenda that it wants to impose on others, or as a group of unrelated states, each pursuing its own narrow self-interest. No, we must instead view ourselves as a 'global village' that's on its way to *inter*national government under *inter*national law. Only then can there be any rational future for our planet, and only then can international progress of any kind - be they programs to combat poverty, over-population, war, pollution, prejudice, or whatever - work!

"Therefore, I urge you to use our resources this year to set up a special commission, call a world-wide conference and promote in every way an end to ideological conflict and a new beginning of international cooperation. Thank you."

What Do *You* Think?

1. If you were a UN delegate, how would you rank the six problems raised by these speakers in their order of importance? Explain the reasons for your choice.

2. What is one additional world problem that you would want to add to this list, and why?

3. Do you have great/some/little confidence in the United Nations? Explain.

4. Do you have great/some/little confidence in the future of the world? Explain.

Bringing Things Into Focus |

Brainstorming

People often think that big problems can only be dealt with by big organizations that come up with big solutions. However, progress in solving big problems can often be made through the insight and dedication of individuals who think up and work out practical measures for solving such problems where they are. For each of the world problems mentioned in the UN meeting, think up one or two practical, workable ideas that could be carried out in your own community to help make further progress towards the solution of these problems.

- ❖ The elimination of poverty and hunger.

- ❖ The slowing of population growth.

- ❖ The realization of disarmament.

- ❖ The conservation and protection of the environment.

- ❖ The elimination of prejudice.

- ❖ The elimination of ideological conflicts.

Gaining a Perspective |

What Does the Bible Say?

Following is a list of 13 statements from the Bible. For each, tell which of the six world problems it speaks to and what course of action it suggests in working out a solution to that particular problem. (You will, in some cases need to deduce principles applicable to world affairs from language in the Bible that applies to the Christian Church or community).

- "You must never treat people in different ways according to their outward appearance. Suppose a rich man wearing a gold ring and fine clothes comes to your meeting, and a poor man in ragged clothes also comes. If you show more respect to the well-dressed man and say to him, 'Have this best seat here,' but say to the poor man, 'Stand over there, or sit here on the floor by my feet,' then you are guilty of creating distinctions among yourselves and of making judgments based on evil motives." James 2:1-4

- "Suppose there are brothers or sisters who need clothes and don't have enough to eat. What good is there in your saying to them, 'God bless you! Keep warm and eat well!' if you don't give them the necessities of life?" James 2:15-16

- "Where do all the fights and quarrels among you come from? They come from your desires for pleasure, which are constantly fighting within you. You want things, but you cannot have them, so you are ready to kill; you strongly desire things, but you cannot get them, so you quarrel and fight. You do not have what you want because you do not ask God for it. And when you ask, you do not receive it, because your motives are bad; you ask for things to use for your own pleasures." James 4:1-3

- "God ... made known to us the secret plan he had already decided to complete by means of Christ. This plan, which God will complete when the time is right, is to bring all creation together, everything in heaven and on earth, with Christ as head ... By speaking the truth in a spirit of love we must grow up in every way to Christ, who is the head. Under his control all the different parts of the body fit together, and the whole body is held together by every joint with which it is provided. So when each separate part works as it should, the whole body grows and builds itself up through love." Ephesians 1:9-10; 4:15-16

- "God created human beings ... and said, ... 'I am putting you in charge of the fish, the birds, and all the wild animals!' ... God looked at everything he had made, and he was very pleased ...

Then God placed the man in the Garden of Eden to cultivate it and guard it. The man named all the birds and all the animals." Genesis 1:27-28, 31; 2:15, 20

- "Be tolerant with one another and forgive one another whenever any of you has a complaint against someone else. You must forgive one another just as the Lord has forgiven you. And to all these qualities add love, which binds all things together in perfect unity. The peace that Christ gives is to guide you in the decisions you make; for it is to this peace that God has called you together in the one body." Colossians 3:13-15

- "Command those who are rich in the things of this life not to be proud, but to place their hope, not in such an uncertain thing as riches, but in God, who generously gives us everything for our enjoyment. Command them to do good, to be rich in good works and to be generous and ready to share with others. In this way they will store up for themselves a treasure which will be a solid foundation for the future. And then they will be able to win the life which is true life." 1 Timothy 6:17-19

- "Put your sword back in its place. All who take the sword will die by the sword." Matthew 26:52

- "The world and all that is in it belong to the Lord; the earth and all who live on it are his." Psalm 24:1

- "I now realize that it is true that God treats everyone on the same basis. Whoever worships him and does what is right is acceptable to him, no matter what race he belongs to." Acts 10:34-35

- "On the first day of the second month in the second year after the people of Israel left Egypt, the LORD spoke to Moses there in the Tent of his presence in the Sinai Desert. He said, 'You and Aaron are to take a census of the people of Israel by clans and families.'" Numbers 1:1-2

- "Children and babies are fainting in the streets of the city. Hungry and thirsty, they cry to their mothers; they fall in the streets as though they were wounded, and slowly die in their mother's arms." Lamentations 3:11-12

- "Everything must be done in a proper and orderly way." 1 Corinthians 14:40

What Do *You* Think?

1. When applied to these world problems, do you think these statements are too idealistic or that they're practical? Explain.

2. Which statement do you find most helpful, and why?

3. Which statement do you find least helpful, and why?

4. Can you think of other statements in the Bible that are applicable to the solution of these problems?

Drawing Conclusions |

Saving the 'Global Village'

To people who lived long ago, the world was a very big place. Travel from one place to another was difficult and slow. Communications between peoples were also slow. Trade was minimal in quantity and scope. Pollution was almost unknown. Wars were fought on a limited scale using limited means. There were relatively few people on earth, and most of them were quite spread out with plenty of room. Nobody, of course, had ever left the earth to journey into space and return to report that the earth, rather than being huge and at the center of everything, was in fact only a tiny speck in the infinity of space. People and nations had their problems, but none of them could qualify as *world* problems as we know them today.

In a comparatively short period of time, everything has changed. People have multiplied. Travel and communications have accelerated at an almost dizzying speed. International trade and commerce have mushroomed and become interdependent. Wars have been fought on a global scale. Pollution has gone from a walk to a gallop. Space travel has put our planet into perspective ... And a lot more. 'Future Shock' has arrived in the present.

The end result of all of this has been a reduction of the size of the world in people's minds. Geographically speaking, of course, it's still the same size it has always been. But psychologically speaking, it's rapidly shrinking to the point where its swelling population is beginning to feel like we're living in a crowded elevator! In such a world, or more appropriately in such a 'global village,' what affects one increasingly affects all. It used to be that peoples and nations dealt with problems in relative isolation from one another. But not anymore. Now *somebody's* problems are *everybody's* problems. And the very phenomena that have rapidly brought the world of people into elbow-rubbing distance of each other have intensified these problems and even created some new ones.

Response to World Problems

So, where's it all headed? Unless enough people do something, and do it fast, our world is headed for a very big 'crunch' within *our* lifetime - a crunch wherein the world's problems will overwhelm the world's wherewithal to deal with them. According to most experts, it's no longer a question of *whether* a crunch will come if we don't act promptly, drastically and sacrificially to deal with the world's problems, but *when* it will come. People respond to this situation in various ways.

- Some hide their heads in the sand, do nothing and hope that somehow the problems will go away.

- Some try to escape to a remote place like some island paradise and hope they can leave the problems behind.

- Some think that no matter how big our problems may become, science will always come up with adequate solutions.

- Some "eat, drink and are merry" in the present and put the future out of their minds.

- Some pray for miracle solutions to be developed by others, but do nothing practical themselves.

- Some pretend that the problems are being exaggerated by the 'prophets of doom' and that they aren't really as bad as they make them out to be.

- Some join others in doing something practical to help make progress in solving such problems.

Go back over this list and choose the option you think a sincere follower of Jesus would choose. It should, of course, be the last one. As we pointed out in Chapter 17, Christians aren't people who have their heads buried in the sand. They're activists. They're people who believe the world is worth saving. They're believers in the inevitability of the triumph of God's Kingdom over any problems that humans might develop. They're people who hear Jesus' call to follow him into the world and who see the world's problems as opportunities for service, not as things to run away from or to throw up their hands in despair about, or to ignore.

For example, committed Christians will be very involved in attacking the six world problems mentioned by the United Nations' speakers at the beginning of this chapter. What direction would their attack take? There's no simple answer to that question. The Bible gives guidelines and spells out principles, but it doesn't present a detailed blueprint for the solution of the modern world's ills. Some modern problems, like over-population, for example, were not even anticipated by the Bible writers, since the world was a comparatively empty place in their day, and the feeling was - the more children, the better. For this reason, sincerely devout Christians may find themselves disagreeing on the *kinds* of actions to be taken in coping with today's problems - but they'll all agree that Christ calls on his people to *act*!

The Problem of Mass Poverty and Hunger

When it comes to the problem of mass poverty and hunger, the Bible is very clear - Christians are to share what they have with those who are in need, not simply giving day to day handouts, but providing the long term wherewithal to help people help themselves. Christians agree with Mahatma Gandhi when he said, "Give a man a fish, and he will eat for a day. Teach a man to fish, and he will eat for a lifetime." To that we might add that a man needs access to the lake if he's going to catch any fish! Like Gandhi, Christians believe the main problem is not a lack of capital or food in the world, but the unequal access to and distribution of it.

The Bible speaks often and speaks bluntly about the difficulties of being rich and being a Christian at the same time. The people of God in the Old Testament were to redress economic imbalances in the community of Israel every seven years, and return all property to its original owners every 50 years (the Year of Jubilee), but greed overcame creed and they never implemented it. The early Christians followed the practice of sharing what they had in common (See Acts 4:32-36), but unfortunately that practice fast faded from view. Jesus made it clear that the question is not about becoming wealthy (as long as that wealth is obtained honestly and not through the exploitation of those who are powerless), but about how one *uses* one's wealth.

True, there are too many Christians today who are part of a profit-making system that tends to get rich at the expense of the poor, but there are also many wealthy Christians who use their wealth for the good of others. And there are Christian organizations like Church World Service, World Vision, Caritas, Christian Aid and Habitat for Humanity that have spearheaded the Christian Churches' response to hunger, poverty and distress around the world on a large scale. However, much more needs to be done. Christians need to press, for example, for a new economic order in the world that will reverse the process whereby the richest third of the world continues to get richer at the expense of the two thirds of the world's peoples who are poor.

The Problem of Over-population

As far as over-population is concerned, all Christians would agree that the population bomb needs to be defused or it will mean disaster for us all. God told mankind to, "...have many children, so that your descendants will live all over the earth and bring it under their control." Genesis 1: 28 That's one commandment of God that people have obeyed with a vengeance! But now we have more than accomplished what God has asked us to do. Our descendants *do* live all over the earth and we don't need to raise the population density anymore. (One day's living in a place like India will convince anybody of that.)

The question is, how? How should we go about bringing a halt to the proliferation of people - through contraceptives, abortion, delayed marriage laws, taxation penalties, sterilization and the like? Here some rather sticky moral and ethical questions enter into the discussion. As we've seen, some Christians believe that it's wrong to use artificial means to prevent the conception of a baby. They also believe that a person 'begins' at conception and not at birth, so that to perform an abortion is to actually murder a person through medical means.

Other Christians believe that preventing conception by simply refraining from sexual intercourse accomplishes the same thing as the use of contraceptives, and that therefore, ethically speaking, there's no difference between the two. They also believe that a fetus doesn't become a 'person' until well after conception, so that an early abortion, carried out for a good reason, is similar to any other medical procedure.

As we said, there are no 'easy' solutions to these problems. However, Christians will always be on the side of having a high regard for human beings created in the image of God. They will not easily be persuaded to either prevent or take human life unless there are overwhelming reasons for doing so.

The Problem of Disarmament

It can be said with certainty that Christians, like their Master, are against war. But they have different opinions when it comes to the

484 | P a g e   C h r i s t i a n i t y U n d e r t h e M i c r o s c o p e

questions of disarmament and participation in a defensive war. Some Christians would identify themselves as 'pacifists' - people who renounce the use of violence altogether under any circumstances. These Christians think passive resistance to evil forces in the name of truth, by an example of love, and with a willingness to suffer if need be, will in the end overcome evil force more effectively, more lastingly and even at times more quickly than resorting to the use of force in the name of justice. They believe that the power of 'weakness' will overcome the weakness of power. They're totally opposed to the development, stockpiling and proliferation of weapons of any kind. They'll go to jail if need be to resist being conscripted into military service. To them, killing of any kind is a violation of the sixth commandment - "You shall not kill." As we've seen in other chapters, there's certainly a strain of thinking in the Bible that supports this viewpoint (See 1 Peter 2:18-25; 3:8-17; 4:12-16).

On the other hand, other Christians point to Paul's teaching in Romans 13:1-5 wherein the state is given the power to execute wrongdoers. They argue that if a nation needs a police force (or domestic army as it were) to stop criminals from committing evil crimes, it also needs a defense force (or international police force as it were) to help police the world in order to stop evil tyrants from using the resources and power of their nations to carry out crimes of aggression and oppression against humanity. They also argue that a careful interpretation of the sixth commandment shows that it only prohibits pre-meditated *murder*, not all killing for whatever reason. They would go to war reluctantly, knowing that any war is not a black and white case of 'good against evil,' and that they would therefore be involved in a nasty, unhappy business involving many tragic moral choices. They would feel that they had been thrust into a situation whereby they would reluctantly participate in a 'lesser evil' in order to oppose a monstrous evil. They would also advocate the necessity of keeping their nation armed to the point where it could adequately defend itself, and hopefully deter other nations with aggressive tendencies from engaging in aggressive actions. They would not be opposed to the development and production of armaments to make such a defense and deterrent possible, and to help other weaker nations to do the same.

The Problem of the Degradation of the Environment

The Christian view on the environment is that God gave us an unspoiled, beautiful earth garden to discover, develop, control, cultivate, guard and enjoy. (See Genesis 1:28; 7; 2:15) As we've seen, nowhere in the Bible does it say that it *belongs* to us! It has merely been *entrusted* to us to use wisely as God's stewards. Yet most people have somehow gotten the idea that things belong to *them* and that because they do, they can do with them as they please. How have we been doing with our trust? How have we been treating God's earth garden? One look at the brownish air above most of our cities, or the brownish color of many of our rivers, or the scarred hillsides left by strip mines, or the concrete jungles in our ghettos will give you the answer. As the UN speaker said, our earth is ever more rapidly being destroyed - by *us,* the very people to whom God entrusted his masterpiece!

Christians, if they read their Bibles, will be active conservationists. For example, they will be in favor of limiting production and consumption to preserve the environment. They will campaign for strict anti-pollution legislation. They will encourage the development of alternative energy resources. They will oppose the fur, feather and animal parts trade and work to save endangered species. They will encourage the mass planting of trees and a respect for nature. They will support efforts to slow the human footprint on global warming. And they will try to make it possible for even city people to keep in touch with the land.

The Problem of Prejudice

We've seen in other chapters how many Christians have been at the forefront in the fight to recognize *all* men and women as equal brothers and sisters with equal rights to all of life's dignity and opportunities. Unfortunately, not all Christians practice what they preach in this regard, but it can still be said that Christians have played a leading part in promoting these ideas throughout the world and in putting them into practice within the worldwide Christian fellowship. For example, Philip Potter, a black from the island of Dominica in the

Caribbean, was elected as the General Secretary of the World Council of Churches in 1972, a position he held until 1984. Dr. Potter later won the Nobel Peace Prize in 1986 for his work of reconciliation in the world.

The Christian sacrament of the Lord's Supper (or the Mass) symbolizes the unity and respect that people of all cultures, races, nationalities, sexes, ages and classes can experience within the Christian fellowship. Here people of all kinds sit down around the Lord's Table to eat a sacred meal together as brothers and sisters in Christ. Christians are determined to continue to work for the recognition of all people as children of God and as equally valuable in his sight (and therefore to be equally valued in each other's sight) through whatever means are available. Prejudice was as foreign to Jesus and his disciples as oil is foreign to water. They constantly emphasized that Christians are not to think of themselves as being one whit better than anybody else, but instead to be humble and to treat others as equals. (See Luke 18:9-14; Matthew 7:1-5; Acts 10: 34; Romans 12:3)

The Problem of Conflicting Ideologies

Contrary to what some people might think, Christians don't have an ideology. The Christian movement cannot be called an 'ism.' Christians don't first of all commit themselves to a set of beliefs or dogmas, but to a *person* - Jesus Christ. Through his teaching and example, and the inward power of his Spirit, Christians have certain pre-suppositions, adhere to certain principles and embrace certain ideas - but these are the kind of fundamental pre-suppositions, principles and ideas that underlie the basics of human existence rather than spell out a specific ideological blueprint for human society.

The Christian faith is trans-cultural, trans-national and trans-ideological. This is why one can find Christians in every culture and every nation adhering to various ideologies in the world. The Christian faith conforms to no one culture or national policy or ideology, but argues at some point or another with them all, and calls upon the Christians in them or adhering to them not to allow themselves to be totally identified with them or defined by them. There's nothing especially Christian about Capitalism, Westernism, or even Democracy. Neither is there anything more or less Christian about Communism, Easternism, or even the Dictatorship of the Proletariat. Jesus could find some things to bless and some things to judge in all of them. This explains why there can be Christians in all countries, living under quite different systems, yet all following the same Christ. In so doing, they're *all* living under tension at whatever point(s) their Christian faith stands over against their culture, national policy or ideological system.

Some Christians would heartily endorse a pluralistic world united under one government based on law - a government that would allow for flexibility in terms of culture, outlook, economic systems, and the like, but that would dismantle the barriers of strident ideology, narrow nationalism and destructively competitive systems that now dominate the world scene. This approach to our 'global village' would move much closer to the ideal that Christians envisage for our world. Perhaps this is an unattainable ideal, but do we have any reasonable alternative in a day when the perpetuation of our present hostile selfish systems and competitive ideologies will lead to nothing but disaster in light of the new conditions under which we are now living?

Actions Speak Louder Than Words

One thing is certain; to do nothing about these growing world problems will guarantee that the future of our world will be bleak indeed. The story is told of two men who were discussing how the problem of poverty could be solved. "Well," said the one man, "if I had two houses, I'd keep one and give the other to the poor." "What if you had two cars?" asked his friend. "I'd keep one and give the other to the poor." "What if you had two TV sets?" "I'd keep one and give the other to the poor." "What if you had two cows?" "I'd keep one and give the other to the poor." "What if you had two chickens?" 'I'd keep 'em both." "Why?" asked the friend. "Because I've *got* two chickens!" he replied.

It's only when a person is willing to part with his or her 'chicken' and get involved in solving the problems of the world where s/he is with what s/he's got, that these problems will have any chance of being solved at all. Jesus makes it clear that he calls on his followers to do precisely that and that he will equip those followers to accomplish precisely that.

What Do *You* Think?

1. I agree with/disagree with/am not sure about the conclusions of this chapter because ......

2. I agree/disagree/am not sure that the world is headed for disaster within my lifetime unless drastic and speedy solutions are found to solve the major problems it now faces because ......

3. I agree/disagree/am not sure that Christians should support a policy of reducing the wealth gap between the rich and the poor because ......

4. I agree/disagree/am not sure that a Christian should support birth control as a legitimate means of curtailing the world's population because......

5. I agree/disagree/am not sure that a Christian should be a pacifist when it comes to trying to solve the problem of violence and war in the world because ......

6. I agree/disagree/am not sure that a Christian should support drastic measures to combat pollution and global warming because ......

7. I agree/disagree/am not sure that a Christian should be an activist in combating racism and discrimination in this country and abroad because ......

8. I agree/disagree/am not sure that we should aim at a pluralistic world united under one government based on law because ......

CONCLUSION

Looking at *Myself* through the Microscope

Throughout this book, we've had our microscope trained on Christians and their faith - warts and all. We've tried to honestly and openly deal with the major questions that people ask again and again in their quest for truth. Now it's time to train the microscope on *YOU* the reader! Go ahead ... take a look! What do you see?

- A person who's had previous doubts and misgivings about the Christian faith reinforced?

- A person who's still floundering around not really sure about much of anything as far as religious beliefs are concerned?

- A person who feels that his or her questions about the Christian faith have been fairly well answered?

- A person who's ready to walk out on the 'bridge of faith' and decide to become a follower of Jesus?

- A person who's crossed over that bridge and has had his or her faith strengthened by his or her journey through this book?

- A person who .... (You fill it in).

Turn back to the Table of Contents and review the list of questions we've dealt with in this book. How many of those questions do you now feel you have satisfactory answers for? Are there questions that you're still struggling with? Which ones? What are you going to do about them - just forget about them and walk away from continuing the struggle for truth and faith? Or are you going to push on to get the answers that will satisfy you by one means or another? If so, what are one or two things you're going to do? Are there further questions you have about the Christian faith that you feel haven't been answered in this book? If so, what are they?

In the beginning, we said that, like a drop of water viewed under a microscope, the Christian faith has a lot more to it than first meets the eye. Hopefully, as you've worked your way through this book, you've discovered a good bit of what that 'more' is all about. We've tried to be honest in dealing with tough and sticky issues, for it's no good building one's faith on the kind of 'easy answer' sand that will quickly wash away when the storms of doubt and testing come along in life. And they will come along! Our aim has been to help you see that it's possible for a 21st century Christian to be *both* intellectually honest and sincerely devout at the same time.

We've also said that *CHRIST*ianity is not first of all following a set of rules, or believing in a certain set of ideas, but following a *person* - Jesus Christ. He's the heart of what it's all about. And he stands today as the living, risen Christ calling to all through his Spirit to come and join him in living out a life of self-giving love and joy as children of God and servants of humanity. He doesn't offer a life of security, comfort and status, but he does offer a life that's meaningful, purposeful and fulfilling - a life that can begin to be lived now the way life was intended to be lived in the beginning.

If you haven't done so already, perhaps you'll want to take this opportunity to respond to Christ's call before you close this book and leave it behind …. and then, move out into your future with new vigor and new hope! God (through Christ) will be out in front of you lighting your way, leading you into his truth and sharing his life of love and joy with you - a life, a love and a joy that are eternal.

Of course, as in any relationship, to know God well enough to commit yourself to living the life he's created you to live, you need to know as much about him (what he came to do and teach and the kind of Movement he launched through Jesus Christ) as you can. Although it's beyond the scope of this book to explore all that in detail, the Appendix has an outline in acrostic form of the ten most important ideas underlying the Christian faith that you might find helpful. Look up the scripture texts given in order to gain a fuller understanding of each idea. Follow that up by discussing these ideas with someone like a pastor or a Christian friend who can help you 'put more meat on the bones.'

> "And now may the LORD bless you and take care of you;
> May the LORD be kind and gracious to you;
> May the LORD look on you with favor and give you peace."
> **Numbers 6:24-26**

APPENDIX

ACROSTIC THEOLOGY

Truth, authority Mt 4:4; Jn 17:17; Is 40:6-8

History (Josh-Esth, Acts), Poetry (Ps, Song of Songs), Wisdom (Prov, Ecces, Job), Prophecy (Is-Mal)

Existence of God assumed, Enlightens Gen 1:1; Rom 1:20; 1 Jn 1:1-4

Hebrew, (O.T.) Aramaic (O.T. & N.T.) & Greek (N.T.)

Old and New Testaments (covenants) Israel → Christ ← Church

Law (Gn-Dt) Letters (Rom-3Jn) Biography (Mt-Jn) Apocalyptic (Dan, Rev)

Yardstick for faith & life Ps 119:1-176; Heb 4:12

Books 37+29 = 66; Chaps 1,150; Verses 31,102

Inspired 2 Tm 3:16a; 2 Pet 1:21, Inerrant (in what it intends to teach) Rev 1:1-2, Interpreted (according to rules) 1 Tim 2:15

Book expressing God's revelation through mighty acts & interpretation of those acts; THE WORD (Jesus) being God's 'main act' Heb 1:1-2

Library written by variety of authors and editors - 1400 B.C. to 100 A.D. O.T. finalized 100 A.D. (Jamnia); N.T. 393 A.D. (Hippo)

Enlightens, equips Ps 119:105; 2 Tm 3:16b-17

****

Good, gracious, great Ps 1454:9; Eph 1:5-8; Ps 47:2

Omniscient Jer 32:19, Omnipotent Jer 32:17-18, Omnipresent Ps 139:1-4

Divine member of the Trinity 2 Cor 13:14

Trustworthy 2 Sam 7:28; James 1:17

Helper Ps 46:1

Eternal Ps 90:4; Rev 1:8

Faithful, forgiving Ps 100:5; Ps 86:5

All loving Ps 103:8-14; Jn 3:16; Rom 5:8

Truthful, just Jn 3:33; Ps 9:7-8

Holy, healer 1 Pet 1:16; Ps 103:3

Earth's creator Gn 1:1; Rom 1:20; Heb 11:3

Righteous, ruler Ps 11:7; 1 Tim 6:15-16

****

The Word, Way (vine, bread of life) Jn 1:1-2; 14:6; 5:1; 6:35

High Priest (prophet, king) Heb 2:17; 4:14-16; Lk 4:24; Acts 7:37; Mt 1:32-33

Eternal life (source of) Jn 3:15-16; 10:10

Lord, Lamb of God, Light of world, Life Rom 10:9-13; Jn 1:29; Jn 8:12; Jn 11:25

Only Savior Mt 1:21; 1 Jn 4:14; Acts 4:12

Resurrection Jn 11:25-26; 1 Cor 15:3-8

Door, Died for us, (buried, rose, ascended) Mt 27:45-50; Lk 23:50-56; Jn 10:7-9; Acts 1:6-9

Judge 2 Cor 5:10

Emmanuel = "God with us" Mt 1:23

Shepherd (provides, guides, protects, heals) Ps 23; Jn 10:11-15

Unique God-Man Lk 1:35; Phil 2:15-11; Rm 1:2-4

Son of Man Jn 9:35-37; Lk 19:10 (Messianic secret) Mt 17:9-13; 9:27-31

Christ = Messiah = 'anointed one' Mt 16:16; Lk 4:16-21

Healer (power over disease, demonic, deformity, domain of nature, death) Mt 4:23

Redeemer Titus 2:14; 1 Pet 1:18

Incarnate (God born as man) Jn 1:14; Gal 4:4

Son of God (member of Trinity) Mt 3:17; 16:16; Jn 1:32-34; 2 Cor 13:14; Col 1:19

Truth, Teacher: Ser on Mt, Parables, Kg of God Mt 5:1-7:29; 13:1-58; Mk 1:14-15; Jn 14:6

****

Tells, Trinity (member of) Jn 16:13-15; 2 Cor 13:14

Hears Rom 8:26-27

Empowers, Equips, Encourages Acts 1:8; Rom 12:6-8; 1 Cor 12:7-11

Helps Mk 13:11; Phil 1:19

Ordains Joel 2:28-30; 1 Sam 16:13; Acts 20:28; 1 Cor 12:4

Lives within Jn 14:16; Rom 8:9

Yields fruit in Christian's life Gal 5:22-23

Sanctifies, Seals (our inheritance) Rom 8:16; 2 Cor 3:3; Eph 1:13-14; Phil 1:6; 1 Pet 1:3-4

Persuades Jn 16:7

Inspires 2 Pet 1:21

Renews, Regenerates Jn 3:5-8; Titus 3:5

Illumines 1 Cor 2:12

Teaches, guides Jn 14:26; 16:13; Rom 8:5-6

****

The fall Gn 3:1-1-24

Head of all things Gn 1:1:28a; 2:15-20

Every person a sinner Rom 3:23; 5:1-12

Human bondage and freedom Eph 2:1-3; Rom 6:17-23

Use resources well Gn 1:28-31; 2:15-20

Male & female, Marriage Gn 1:27a-28; 21-24; Heb 13:4

Alienated from God, Others, Creation, Self Gn 3:8-11,12-13, 17-19; 4:4-7

Need forgiveness, salvation, life Jn 6:37-40; Acts 3:19-20; Tit 2:11-14

Relational, Representative, Responsible Gn 1:27-30   Gn 1:28; 2:19-20   Gn 2:16-17

A physical/spiritual being Gn 2:7; 1:26a

Created in God's image Gn 1:26a

Enjoy God, Emancipated by Christ Gn 1:28-2:24; Rom 5:8-11; Col 2:11-14

****

Saved *from* sin *for* service (past, present, future) Rom 3:24-26; 12:1-2; 2 Cor 5:14-15

Adopted as child of God Eph 1:4

Loved by God Eph 3:17-19; 1Jn 4:9-10

Valued by God Lk 12:24; Jn 3:16-17

Atonement = 'at onement' (substitution, redemption, reconciliation)
    Rom 5:1-2, 8-11; 2 Cor 5:21; Col 1:20; 1 Pet 1:18

Transformed Jn 3:5-7; Eph 4:22-24; Col 3:9

Inheritance (glorified) Rom 8:16-17; 1 Pt 1:3-4

Only by God's grace Rom 3:23-24; Eph 2:4-9

Need to acknowledge, repent, believe Acts 2:37-41; Rom 4:21-31; 10:9-10

****

Tasked with a mission Mic 6:8; Mt 28:19-20; Lk 10:25-37; 1 Pet 3:15-16

Headship of Christ Eph 2:19-22; Col 1:18

Evangelical (believe & proclaim Good News) Acts 1:8; 5:42; Rom 10:14-16; 1 Cor 15:3-5

Catholic = universal Eph 4:4-6; Col 3:11

Holy (set apart *from* evil *to* God) Dt 14:2; Eph 5:3; 1 Pet 2:9-10

United Acts 4:32; Rom 12:4; Phil 2:1-2

Reformed & reforming Tit 2:1-8; James 1:19-27, 2:14-17; Jude 1:3

Communion of Saints Eph 6:18; Rev 8:3-4

Household of God Eph 2:19; 1 Pet 2:4-8

****

Teach God's Word 2 Tim 2:15; James 3:1

Hear and Heed God's Word Ex 20:1-17; Dt 6:4-9; James 1:22-25; Rev 2:7

Evangelize Lk 8:37-39; Acts 8:1, 4

Celebrate sacraments (Baptism & Communion) Mt 28:19; Lk 22:14-20; Acts 2:40-42; 10:45-48

Heal those that hurt Lk 4:18-19; Heb 13:3; James 5:14-16

Read, study & memorize God's Word Ps 1:1-2; 119:11; Acts 17:10-11

Intercede, praise, confess, thank, ask Mt 6:9-13; Jude 20-21

Serve others, Share and care Mt 25:34-40; Mk 10:42-45; James 1:27; 2:14-17

Trust in God's promises Ps 56:3-4; Prov 3:5-6; Mt 6:31-34

Illumine culture, society (light, stars) Mt 5:14-16; Acts 13:46-48; Eph 5:8-10; Phil 2:14-16a

Ambassadors, Agents of change Mt 25:14-30; 2 Cor 5:18-21

Notice other's Needs Lk 10:30-37

Learn from Christ as his disciple Mt 11:28-29; 28:20; Jn 13:12-17

Inspire others by word & example 1 Tim 4:12; 1 Pet 5:1-7

Follow Christ as his disciple Mt 4:18-22; 10:34-39; Acts 4:17-20

Engage in worship Ps 100; Col 3:15-17; Heb 10:25; 13:15

****

Angel of the Lord Nu 22:21-35; 2 Kgs 1

Near us to help us Ps 34:7; 91:9-11; Acts 5:19; 12:5-11; Heb 1:14; 13:2

God's messengers (to Abram Gn 18; Elijah 2 Kgs 1; Daniel Dn 8, 10; Zechariah & Mary Lk 1; Joseph Mt 1; Shepherds Lk 2, Peter Acts 12:6-10)

Ethereal beings (created Ps 148:2, 5), (immaterial Heb 1:7) (personal Rev 22:8), (immortal Lk 20:36) (celibate Mk 12:35)

Legion in number Dn 7:10; Mt 26:53; Heb 12:22; Rev 5:11

Serve & worship God Ps 103:20-21; Col 3:16-17; Heb 12:28

Deceivers, depraved 1 Tim 4:1; Rev 18:2

Evil spirits Mt 8:16; 10:1; 12:43-45

Mobs Mk 5:2-13; Acts 8:7

Opponents of good, grace & God Mt 9:32; 12:22; Mk 1:23-25; Lk 13:11; Eph 6:12

Nasty beings Mk 5:5; 9:17-26; Acts 19:16

Scared of Christ Mt 8:29; Mk 1:34; 3:11

Satan = devil (The FOE = Forces Of Evil), Stand against Satan Jn 17:15; Eph 6:11, 16; 2 Thes 3:3; James 4:7-8; 1 Pet 5:8-9; 1 Jn 5:18

Attacker (roaring lion), Adversary Mt 13:19; 13:38; 1 Pet 5:8

Tempter, Trickster Gen 3:1-13; Mt 4:1-11; 6:13; 1 Thess 3:5; 2 Thess 2:9-12

Author of evil, Apollyon = destroyer Mt 6:13; 1 Jn 3:10   Rev 9:11

Notorious liar (father of lies) Jn 8:44

THREE GARDENS

Eden [creation]

Gethsemane [redemption]

New Jerusalem [culmination]

Door into eternity Mt 7:13-14; Lk 13:24-28; Heb 9:27

Eternal choice Mt 25:46; Jn 3:18; Heb 3:12-19; 2 Pet 2:4-9; 1 Jn 5:12

Awaiting resurrection and judgment Heb 9:27; Rev 20:11-13

The consequence of sin (1st & 2nd Death) Gn 2:15-17; Jn 11:25-26; Rom 6:23a; 5:12-21; 1 Cor 15:21; Rev 21:8

Hell ahead for unbelievers 2 Thess 1:8-9; Rev 20:14-15

AND

Living hope 1 Cor 15:19-20; Titus 1:1-3; 1 Pet 1:3

Imperishable 1 Cor 15:52-53; 1 Pet 1:4

Final victory over death Rom 7:24; 1 Cor 15:54-58; 2 Tim 1:9-10; Rev 2:11; 20:6

Eternal joy in the presence of God Jn 17:3; Jude 24; Rev 22:3-4

****

The second coming of Christ Mal 3:2; Phil 3:20-21; 2 Thess 1:6; Rev 1:4-7

Heaven and Hell Jn 14:1-4; Rev 5:8-13; 7:9, 14; 14:2; 15:1-4; 22:3b-5; 2 Thess 1:8-9; Rev 14:9-11

End of sorrow, suffering, pain, death Is 25:8; Rev 7:16-17; 21:4

Light and Life Is 60:19-20; 22:3-5; Jn 14:3; Col 1:12; Rev 3:12; 19:6-9

Armageddon Rev 16:12-16

Satan and hosts destroyed 2 Thess 2:8; Rev 20:10

The resurrection (1st & 2nd) 1 Cor 15:51-53; 1 Thess 4:17; Rev 20:4-6

The judgment Mt 13:47-50; 25:31-33, 31-46; Rev 11:16; 20:13

Healing of the nations Rev 22:1

Immortality 1 Cor 15:35-50; 2 Cor 5:1-5; Rev 2:7;

New heavens & New earth Is 11:6-9; 35:1-10; 65:17, 20-25; Rom 8:18-22; Heb 12:22; 2 Pet 3:10-12; Rev 3:12; 21:1-2, 5

God's reign extends to totality of reality 1 Cor 15:22-28; Eph 1:8a-12

Salvation completed Eph 1:9-10; Rev 19:6-7; 21:6-7

An Outline of the Book of Romans

Guilt, Grace, Gratitude / Sin, Salvation, Service

Condemnation ---- 1:1-3:20

Justification ---- 3:20-4:25

Reconciliation ---- 5:1-21

Identification---- 6:1-23

Liberation ---- 7:1-25

Sanctification ---- 8:1-30

Election ---- 9:1-11:36

Transformation ---- 12:1-15:13

Son

Spirit

Father

2 Cor 13:14   **The Holy Trinity**   Mat 18:19

1+1+1=1 ONE God Gal 3:20

2 Cor 5:19   **The Father**   Acts 2:17

God in Christ   *God-breathed*

The Son of God   *The Spirit of God*

Mt 16:16   *Christ-breathed   Spirit of Christ*   2 Cor 3:3

Jn 20:22 **The Son**   **The Spirit** Gal 4:6

All involved in
Creation, Redemption, Renewal

Other Books Written by the Author
Available on Amazon.com

The Lifestyle of Jesus, Amazon Createspace, 2016. (215 pp.)

The Church Under the Cross: Mission in Asia in Times of Turmoil, **Volume II**, Eerdmans Publishing Co., Grand Rapids, 2012. (801 pp.)

The Church Under the Cross: Mission in Asia in Times of Turmoil, **Volume I**, Eerdmans Publishing Co., Grand Rapids, 2010. (454 pp.)

People Who Knew God, Chinese Christian Literature Council, Hong Kong, 1996. (305 pp.)

Living Life Fully, Chinese Christian Literature Council, Hong Kong, 1995. (227 pp.) Revised & reprinted, 1998.

Man On a Mission: The Life and Work of Jesus the Christ, Chinese Christian Literature Council, Hong Kong, 1994. (226 pp.). Revised & reprinted, 1998, 2016.

Made in the USA
Middletown, DE
22 July 2017